TABLE OF CONTENTS

ACKNOWLEDGEMENTS

I should like especially to thank Professor Gwynne B. Evans, who, at considerable sacrifice of his time, gave me invaluable criticism and aid during the progress of this work.

Thanks are due also to Eva Faye Benson, Isabelle Grant, and many others on the staff of the University of Illinois Library for their countless endeavors in my behalf. Finally, I wish to thank Janet Wright, Amy Kizer, and Paula Geminder for their generous and painstaking cooperation in typing the final draft of this work.

INTRODUCTION

A. Biographical and Critical

1. The Author

There is no question concerning the authorship of <u>Richardus</u> <u>Tertius</u>.
References in the manuscripts themselves and in contemporary writers all
agree in assigning the play to Thomas Legge.

Thomas Legge[1] was born in Norwich about 1535, matriculated at Corpus
Christi College in November, 1552, "and was afterwards, 1555, a scholar
at Trinity, whence he graduated B.A. in 1556/7, and M.A. in 1560." He
was a fellow of Trinity from 1560-1568, then migrated to Jesus, where he
was a fellow from 1568-1573. Dr. Caius designated him his successor as
Master of Caius College, a position he assumed in 1573. He received an
LL.D. in 1575, was appointed Commissary to the University in 1579, and
held the office of Vice-Chancellor in 1578/9, and during part of 1592/3.
In 1593, he was a Master in Chancery and in 1597 a Justice of the Peace
for the town of Cambridge. He died in residence at Caius on July 12,
1607.

Until Legge went to Jesus College, his continuing interest in the
dramatic activities of Trinity are readily traceable in the college accounts
of Trinity for the years he spent there as a student and a fellow. Except
for one year in the period from 1558/9 through 1566/7, the Junior Bursar's
Accounts or the Steward's Book has at least one entry of payment to Legge

---

[1]The following account of Legge's life is taken from John Venn's Biographical History of Gonville and Caius College 1349-1897 (Cambridge, 1897),
III, 64-69.

for his part in the plays performed at Trinity. More than likely his connection with the plays performed there was as a director or perhaps as the
translator of a number of plays including Medea, Adelphus, Stichus, Asinaria,
and Jepthes. The following entries are pertinent: "It geven to Sr Legg
& Sr West for their players ii^s (1559)"; "It' paid to Mr Legge for ye ex-
penses aboughte the settinge forthe of Medea as appeareth [by a bill]
xxxiii^s vii^d (1560-1561)"; "To Mr Legg for his playe ii^s (1560-1561)"; "It'
to Master Legge & Bingam for the charges of Adelphus iiii^s i^d (1562-1563)";
"Itm to masters legg and foorde for the seconde playe iii^s (1563-1564)";
"Inprimis to Mr Legge & Mr Powel for the charges of Stichus iiii^s xi^d (1564-
1565)"; "It' to Mr Legge and Mr Gibson for Asinaria iii^s viii^d (1565-1566)";
"Itm to Mr Legge in regarde of his playe ii^s (1566-1567)"; and "To Mr Legge
ffor the charges offe Jepthes as appearith by his bille xviii^s i^d (1566-
1567)."[2]

After Legge left Trinity, his name is not associated with the dramatic activities in any college at Cambridge until the performance of his
own play Richardus Tertius in 1579/80 at St. John's College. Apparently
after he migrated to Jesus College his energies were directed to teaching
and the scholary endeavors that won him the recognition of Dr. Caius, one
of the founders of Gonville-Caius College, who chose him to be his successor as Master of Caius College.

Considering that only one of Legge's plays is known to have been performed, his contemporary reputation was indeed great. Meres placed Legge

[2]G. C. Moore Smith, ed., "The Academic Drama at Cambridge: Extracts
from the College Records," Collections (The Malone Society, 1923), Vol.
II, Pt. II, pp. 159, 161-166.

in the company of Marlowe, Peele, Shakespeare, Kyd, Drayton, Chapman, Dekker and Jonson in his list of "our best for Tragedie."[3] Meres added that "Doctor Leg hath penned two famous tragedies. the one of Richard the 3. the other of the destruction of Jerusalem."[4] When Harington defended tragedy as "a most worthy kind of Poesie" so long as it was "well handled," he singled out Richardus Tertius as exemplary: "and for Tragedies, to omit other famous Tragedies: That, that was playd at S. Johns in Cambridge, of Richard the 3. would move (I thinke) Phalaris the tyraunt, and terrifie all tyrannous minded men, from following their foolish ambitious humors..."[5] Less trustworthy, because derivative, testimony of Legge's reputation as a dramatist is Fuller's statement that Legge "made a Tragedy of the Life of King Richard the Third, presented with great applause (Queen Elizabeth, I suppose, being a beholder thereof)[6] in Saint John's Colledge-hall."[7]

Of the non-extant Destruction of Jerusalem little is known of its fate beyond what is contained in Fuller's brief notes: "and [Legge] having

---

[3]Francis Meres, Palladis Tamia (London, 1598), p. 283.

[4]Ibid.

[5]Sir John Harington, An Apologie of Poetrie in Ancient Critical Essays upon English Poets and Poesy, ed. Joseph Haslewood (London, 1815), II, 135. Thomas Heywood, in his Apology for Actors (1612 sig. F4^v), makes a reference to Richardus Tertius similar to that of Harington, but it is unlikely that he saw the play at Cambridge as Harington probably did (see below). More than likely he borrowed the allusion from Harington.

[6]Queen Elizabeth was not present at the St. John's performance, nor at any other performance for which there is any evidence.

[7]Thomas Fuller, The History of the Worthies of England, ed. John Nichols (1811), II, 156.

at last refined it to the <u>purity of the publique Standard</u>, some <u>Plageary</u> filched it from him, just as it was to be acted."[8]

2. Date of the Play

When Legge wrote <u>Richardus Tertius</u> is not known. It was, however, undoubtedly written sometime between 1573 (the earliest date found in any manuscript) and March, 1579/80 (the date of its first recorded performance). The only evidence in support of the 1573 date is the notation in the Caius MS. ("tragoedia trium vesperum habita in collegio Divi Johannis Evangelistae, Comitiis Bacchalaureorum Anno 1573."), which notation E. K. Chambers is not so sure "may not point to an earlier production"[9] than the one at St. John's in March, 1579/80. No other evidence can be found to confirm this date. No one who attempts to date university dramas[10] even mentions 1573 as a possibility, and it is unlikely that a three-part tragedy which required three nights for a complete presentation could have escaped contemporary notice of some kind.

There is, on the other hand, a good deal of evidence for a date around 1579 for the production of the play. First is the testimony that the play was presented at St. John's at the Bachelors' Commencement in

---

[8]<u>Ibid</u>.

[9]<u>The Elizabethan Stage</u> (Oxford, 1923), III, 408.

[10]Alfred Harbage, <u>Annals of English Drama</u> (Philadelphia, 1940); Frederick S. Boas, <u>University Drama in the Tudor Age</u> (Oxford, 1914), p. 388; G. C. Moore Smith, <u>College Plays</u> (Cambridge, 1923), pp. 61-62; and George B. Churchill and Wolfgang Keller, "Die lateinischen Universitäts-Dramen Englands in der Zeit der Königin Elisabeth," <u>Jahrbuch der Deutschen Shakespeare-Gesellschaft</u>, XXXIV (1898), 221-323.

March 1579/80,[11] the date given in the Cambridge University Library MS., in the Caius MS., and in the Clare MS. Second, Harington's reference to Richardus Tertius in his Apologie of Poetrie strongly implies that he actually witnessed the play while at Cambridge. Harington matriculated at King's College in 1576, took his B.A. in 1577/78, his M.A. in 1581, and was admitted at Lincoln's Inn on Nov. 27, 1581. It is quite likely therefore that he saw the performance at St. John's College in 1579/80. Finally, MS.Tanner 306 (MS.G) notes that the play was "acted in St. Johns Hall before the Earle of Essex 17 March 1582." The date entry has been dismissed by both Moore Smith and Chambers as "apparently added later" by a different hand,[12] but my examination reveals that the date entry is in the same hand that wrote the rest of the note that listed the dramatis personae immediately above it. The date, however, is no doubt in error since the Earl of Essex had left Cambridge after taking his M.A. on July 6, 1581. It is more likely that Essex, like Harington, was present at the performance in March 1579/80, for he came to Trinity College in May, 1577. The names in the actors' list appearing in MS. Tanner 306 fairly confirm that the scribe had the St. John's performance in mind when he

---

[11]Of possible relevance in this connection are the following entries appearing in the accounts of St. John's College for the last quarter of 1577/78: "for paper to write out ye bookes for ye tragedy iiis"; "Item for more paper ii^s"; "for paper incke & pinduste xx^d"; "It. for paper incke quilles & pindust wch I allowed to Mr Stringer & lefte out xvi^d." The possibility that Richardus Tertius is the "tragedy" being transcribed into production "bookes" is suggested by the fact that a "Mr Stringer" played the part of the Duke of Buckingham in the St. John's performance. Also, the unusual length of the play lends some significance to the items "for more paper" and "for paper incke quilles & pindust" (Moore Smith, p. 224).

[12]Chambers, p. 408; and G. C. Moore Smith, "Notes on Some English University Plays," MLR, III (1907-1908), 141.

penned his note about the Earl of Essex's presence. With only occasional
uncertainty, all the names on the list can be traced to people teaching
or studying at St. John's in March 1579/80.[13] Some of these names cannot be found in the rolls of St. John's earlier,[14] nor can others be
found later, than this date.

3. The Cade Transcription of Legge's Holograph

The statements of Sir John Harington and Frances Meres about the
play and its author, and the comparatively large number of manuscripts
in which the play is preserved (there were undoubtedly more than the
eleven extant manuscripts) attest to the high contemporary reputation of
both Richardus Tertius and its author Thomas Legge. Perhaps more significant of the contemporary appraisal of both is that Richardus Tertius was
apparently prepared for publication in 1582/3. The title page of the
Clare College MS. notes: "Descripta ex Autoris autographo, A. Cadi manu/
"Impressum U.C. 1582 Januariis Calendis." Though brief, this note is
full of important information. Anthony Cade (his first name is also given
on the title page) copied what is now the Clare College MS. from a holograph copy of Richardus Tertius. Apparently this manuscript was to be
printed at the University of Cambridge, but was not; hence, the cancellation of "Impressum U.C."

---

[13]Boas, pp. 394-397; and Charles H. Cooper, "The Actors in Dr. Legge's
Tragedy of Richardus Tertius, performed at St. John's College, at the
Bachelors' Commencement, 1579-80," Antiquarian Communications (Cambridge,
1859), I, 347-355.

[14]G. C. Moore Smith notes this in showing that Hymeneus was probably
acted at St. John's in March 1578/79 (Hymeneus [Cambridge, 1908], pp. vii-x).

There seems little reason to doubt that Cade had access to Legge's
holograph. Legge knew Cade personally, for "the Master, Thomas Legge"
was his "Surety" when Cade was admitted sizar to Gonville and Caius
College on February 9, 1580/1.[15] Furthermore, Cade's later career as
a scholar, tutor and author[16] shows that Cade had the sort of academic
qualifications which would appeal to Legge. The Legge-Cade relationship
need not be questioned.

What is not so clear is why the play was not printed. Unfortunately,
we can only conjecture on the basis of the few facts available as to what
happened. First of all, from the notation ("Impressum U.C. Januariis
Calendis.") at the bottom of the title page of the Clare MS. someone has
stricken out with a single line the words "Impressum U.C.," indicating
that he either knew that the play would not be printed, or that it had
not been printed. This cancellation may or may not have been by Cade.
At the very end of the play is a note in Cade's hand, giving his name and
the date, January 1583, more than likely the date on which the transcription was completed. If the January, 1583 date is not a mistake for January,
1582, then Cade for some reason did not complete his task until a year after
the date originally assigned for its printing.

But, even had Cade finished transcribing the play in January, 1582,
it would have been impossible for the play to have been printed, at least

---

[15]John Venn, compiler, Biographical History of Gonville and Caius
College, 1349-1897 (Cambridge, 1897), I, 109.

[16]Anthony Cade took his B.A. in 1584/85, his M.A. in 1588, and a B.D.
in 1589. He was incorporated at Oxford in 1607, and for a time was tutor
and chaplain to George Villiers, Duke of Buckingham. He is the author of
St. Paul's Agony, 1618; On Conscience, 1621; and Justification of the Church
of England, 1630. Ibid.

at Cambridge. Printing at Cambridge had been suspended some years before. In fact, it was only shortly after Cade finished his transcription that "the University made an attempt to revive printing."[17] About May, 1583, the University had appointed Thomas Thomas, an M.A. from King's College as University printer.[18] In a letter dated June 14, 1583, from the Vice-Chancellor John Bell and the other college heads (including Thomas Legge), we learn that "the University of Cambridge appeals to Lord Burghley their Chancellor against the seizure by Wardens of the Stationers of their Presse and of their printer, Thomas Thomas."[19] The letter complains that the Stationers in London "have sought to hinder the[e]-erectinge of a print [i.e. a printing press] within the university of Cambrdige," and urges that Lord Burghley might "direct your favorable warrant to the wardeynes of the Stationers yat he [i.e. Thomas Thomas] may have his presse delivered with speed, least...by their delayes he be prevented of ...bookes made within the university, and now redy for ye presse."[20] It seems highly probable that Cade's transcription of Richardus Tertius was one of the books referred to here as "now redy for ye presse."

---

[17]Charles H. Cooper, Annals of Cambridge (Cambridge, 1843), II, 393.

[18]Ibid.

[19]Edward Arber, ed., A Transcript of the Registers of the Company of Stationers of London 1554-1640 A.D. (London, 1875-77), II, 782.

[20]Ibid. The reasons given by Jack London, the warden of the Stationers who seized Thomas and the press, are found in his letter to the Bishop of London, dated June 1, 1583: In this letter, London reports that he has "found sundrie presses and furniture for printinge in secret and Darke cellers" including one press which belonged to Thomas Thomas "a man (as I heare) vtterlie ignoraunte in printinge, and pretendinge that he intendeth to be the printer for the vniversitie of Cambridge [sic]." He appeals to the Bishop not to order him to release the press to Cambridge lest the "printer and his mynisters" who are "suspicious persons" use it to circulate matters "perillous to religion and state" (Ibid., I, 246-7).

When the press and the printer were restored to Cambridge is not known, but no printing could have taken place before March 18, 1583/4, the date on which Lord Burghley ended the controversy between the Stationers and the University of Cambridge. In a letter to the Vice-Chancellor and the Heads of the Colleges he agreed that the University's charter to print was valid and that they could appoint Thomas Thomas to print what they deemed fit on the condition that "the parties that shall be licensed, or authorized to print" should be bound "to stand to the order of the chancellor."[21]

Of course, neither the delay in Cade's finishing his transcription nor the delay caused by the seizure of the press explains why Richardus Tertius was not ultimately printed at Cambridge. We only know that it was not, and that this series of delays may have had something to do with the change in the plans for its publication.

4. Legge's Use of His Historical Sources

Richardus Tertius shows that Legge's composition, with few exceptions, is slavisly dependent upon material about the life of Richard III found in the chronicles of Hall[22] and More.[23]

Except for a few passages which (since no other source for them can be found) are probably due to Legge's invention, almost every scene--and

---

[21]Cooper, Annals, p. 394.

[22]Hall's Chronicle (London, 1809).

[23]Legge apparently used Rastell's edition of More's English History of Richard the Third (1557), in which edition Rastell inserted and marked passages which he took from More's Latin Historia Richardi Regis Tertii (Omnia...Opera Latina [Louvain, 1566]). These passages do not appear in Hall since he used Grafton's edition (1543) of More's History.

to a great extent, every circumstance therein--has a basis in either Hall or More or both. That each of these chronicles was used by Legge is apparent. More could not have been the sole basis since his account breaks off in the middle of Buckingham's speech to the Bishop of Ely.[24] Nor could Hall, for on three occasions More provides an exclusive basis for passages in Legge.[25] Contrary to what these exclusive uses of More might suggest, Legge apparently did not use More to the point where his chronicle breaks off and then switch to Hall for the remainder of his composition. He used both chronicles concurrently, for even before the point at which More ends, Hall provides the sole basis for a name reference,[26] for two passages,[27] and for an entire scene.[28]

Legge's dependence on his sources is everywhere evident. So closely does Legge follow his sources (compare, for example, the chronicle account of the Queen's argument for keeping the young Duke of York with her in

---

[24]See Translation, Footnote 103.

[25]See Translation, Footnotes 41, 48, and 92.

[26]See Translation, Footnote 20.

[27]See Translation, Footnotes 15 and 66. The latter note suggests that the Mirror for Magistrates may also provide a basis for the passage under discussion. Hall is the more probable source, however, since his is a primary source for Legge whereas the Mirror for Magistrates has only one other reference--which may also be attributed to Hall (see Footnote 10)--that may have provided a basis for an allusion in Legge's play.

[28]See Translation, Footnote 101.

sanctuary[29] with the same argument in the play)[30] that the chronicles often provided a valuable guide to my translation. Entire scenes and speeches are borrowed complete from the chronicles. Sometimes, of course, Legge embroiders or lengthens what is recorded in his sources, but he seldom departs from the substance of their accounts. He even follows, in general, the chronological order of his sources, which to a large extent explains the lack of dramatic focus in his play and in it central character.

Legge's failure to make Richard a strong central character, the unifying force that he is in Richard III, and The True Tragedie of Richard the Third is perhaps attributable to his over-dependence on Hall. Richard in Legge's play is a fearful, vacillating, often subordinate character just as he is in the latter part of Hall's account. Observe Richard in the scene[31] in which he is portrayed as fearful of losing his crown upon hearing the rumor of the proposed marriage of Richmond and Princess Elizabeth. Lovel first encourages him to take heart, to drive out his "cowardly fears." Richard's first thought, as always in Legge, is to end his fear with the sword, by slaying Elizabeth; but Lovel admonishes him not to resort to unnecessary evil when he might allay his fears by marrying Elizabeth himself. Then, Catesby, another subordinate, advises Richard that the way to such a marriage may be cleared with Anne's death. Despite Lovel's suggestion of preparing for the murder of Anne by rumoring her death about, Richard is for using his unsubtle sword on her; but in the end characteristically he yields to the advice of his evil counsellors.

---

[29]Hall's Chronicle, p. 357

[30]Part I, IV, iii.

[31]Part III, IV.i.

Though Legge's defects as a dramatist are readily apparent when he follows his sources most closely, conversely his strengths appear in those few scenes that seem to be primarily the product of his own imagination. Such a scene, for which the chronicles afford only the merest hint,[32] is the one in which Dr. Shaw's guilt-ridden conscience expresses genuine remorse for his part in Richard's treachery.[33]

> Heaven has seen [my] wicked crime, and [even] the inconstant earth has been aware of [my]   great shame. The shameful ruin of my mind has made me so unlike my [true] self that I fly nothing more than myself, and I have been made an unhappy deserter of myself [so] that [my] care-worn mind prays for a long-lasting separation from [my] body.... What are worthless men saying about me?

Another scene of real dramatic value, which can be ascribed to Legge's invention, is the one in which Richard woos Princess Elizabeth. The chronicle basis for this scene is slight.[34] From a brief suggestion in the chronicles that Richard made unsuccessful overtures of marriage to Elizabeth, Legge sensed the dramatic possibilities of presenting a scene in which the murderer of the princes not only confronts their hate-filled sister, but confidently asks her to marry him. He created an atmosphere of dramatic tension merely by putting such opposites together on the same stage. And Richard's offer of his sword and his bared breast to Elizabeth as proof of his sorrow, if somewhat melodramatic, is nevertheless a brilliant coup de théâtre--one worthy of Shakespeare.

---

[32] See Translation, Footnote 90.

[33] Part II, IV.i.

[34] See Translation, Footnote 128.

Indeed, Richard's wooing of Anne in Shakespeare's <u>Richard III</u>[35] is
so strikingly reminiscent at times of the wooing scene in Legge's play[36]
that various commentators[37] have considered <u>Richardus Tertius</u> as at
least an indirect influence on Shakespeare's play. First of all, the
chronicles offer no real basis for either scene. The only hint for
Legge's scene is found in Hall:

> The kyng thus (accordyng to his long desire) losed out
> of the bondes of matrimony, beganne to cast a foolyshe
> phantasie to Lady Elizabeth his nece, making much suite
> to haue her ioyned with him in lawfull matrimony. But
> because all men, and the mayden her selfe moost of all,
> detested and abhorred this vnlawfull and in maner
> vnnaturall copulacion, he determined to prolonge and
> deferre the matter till he were in a more quietnes.[38]

On the basis of this passage, Legge composes--in effect, invents--his
scene wherein Richard confronts Elizabeth and abruptly asks her to marry
him. Elizabeth vehemently refuses, accusing him of murdering her brothers.
Richard tries to calm her with: "Come now, maiden, banish your harsh words
lest both [our] persons waste away on account of a single crime," confesses
his crimes, and expresses sorrow for them: "Have your brothers been slain?
I am sorry; the dead grieves [me]. Are they dead? Tears avail nothing.
What do you wish that I do?" Then to evidence the sincerity of his sorrow
he continues: "Perhaps I may repay the twin destruction of [your] brothers
with [my] blood poured forth by this [my]

---

[35]J.D. Wilson, ed. <u>Richard III</u> (Cambridge University Press, 1954).

[36]Part III, IV. v.

[37]See especially George B. Churchill, "Richard the Third up to Shakespeare"
<u>Palaestra</u>, X (Berlin, 1900); and R.J. Lordi, "The Relationship of <u>Richardus
Tertius</u> to the Main Richard III Plays," Boston University <u>Studies in English</u>,
V (1961), 139-153. See also Chambers, <u>Elizabethan Stage</u>, III, 408; and
Irving Ribner, <u>The English History Play in the Age of Shakespeare</u> (London,
1964), p. 67.

[38]<u>Hall's Chronicle</u>, p. 407.

right hand? I will do [it]: I will offer my breast to readied swords,
and if it is more pleasing [to you], I shall die by your arms (i.e. at
your hands]."

The wooing scene in Shakespeare--despite its many obvious differences,
some the inevitable result of the different dramatic purposes of the scenes
in the two plays--is remarkably similar in certain particulars with Legge's
scene. In Shakespeare's play, the same abruptness of Richard's proposal,
followed by the bitter invective and accusations of Anne, recalls a similar
features in Legge's scene. Shakespeare's Richard tries to calm Anne with:

> But gentle Anne,
> To leave this keen encounter of our wits,
> And fall something into a slower method (11. 114-116),

the purpose and tone of which are consonant with the words with which
Legge's Richard tries to Elizabeth.   Immediately thereafter,
Shakespeare has Richard admit his crimes (as Legge's Richard does), but
with the added subtle twist of making Richard's desire for Anne the mo-
tive for his crime. Then, a good deal later than in Legge's scene, comes
Richard's offer of his sword and naked breast to Anne. His purpose is
more to disarm Anne than to prove the sincerity of his sorrow, the purpose of Legge's Richard, but the offer itself is remarkably like that in
Legge:

> Lo, here I lend thee this sharp-pointed sword,
> Which if thou please to hide in this true breast
> And let the soul forth that adoreth thee,
> I lay it naked to the deadly stroke,
> And humbly beg the death upon my knee (11. 174-178).

Although these similarities do not add up to conclusive proof of a
direct connection between Shakespeare's play and Legge's Richardus Tertius
it seems reasonable to accept Churchill's conclusion that "it is difficult
to compare the wooing scenes and not cherish the suspicion" that Legge's

play had at least some indirect influence on Shakespeare's Richard III.[39]
It is entirely possible that Shakespeare knew the play first-hand. The
play was well known, and there certainly were enough copies of it so
that he might well have seen one. His knowledge of Latin has long since
been proved adequate to read the play.[40] However, despite the possibility
of Shakespeare's direct acquaintance, it seems much more likely that, if
he knew the play at all, he knew it indirectly, either through report or
through an anterior lost Richard-play that made use of Legge's play. For,
if he had had first-hand acquaintance with Richard Tertius, and especially
if he had read it, he probably would have made more use of it than he did.
That he could have known of the play by report is evidenced by the fact
that his contemporaries (Sir John Harington, and Frances Meres) made
specific references to it. Although there is no substantial proof that
an anterior Richard-play ever existed, the possibility of such a play is
argued by J. Oscar Campbell to explain elements found in the Dutch Richard
that cannot be accounted for except by positing a lost Richard play,[41]
which version, Campbell maintains, is the basis for van den Bos' translation of the Dutch Richard (published in Amsterdam in 1651).[42]

---

[39]Churchill, p. 395.

[40]T. W. Baldwin, Small Latine & Less Greeke (Urbana, 1944), Vols. I
and II, passim.

[41]Campbell, pp. 56-57. For further statements concerning the exis-
tence of a lost Richard-play, see F. Fleay, Chronicle History of the Life
and Work of William Shakespeare (London, 1968 pp. 278-279 and Wilson,
pp. xxix-xxx.

[42]Campbell, p. 3.

B. Textual

1. Note on the Manuscript Consulted in Preparing This Edition

For convenience in reference throughout this edition, the nine manuscripts of Richardus Tertuis collated in the preparation of this edition have been arbitarily lettered from A through I. A = MS. MM4.40 (University Library at Cambridge); B = Gonville and Caius MS. 125.62 (Caius College Library at Cambridge); C = Clare College MS. KK. 3.12 (Clare College Library at Cambridge); D = Emmanuel College MS. 1.3.19 (Emmanuel College at Cambridge)*; E = MSS. Harley 2412 (British Museum Library); F = MSS. Harley 6926 (British Museum Library); G = Tanner MS. 306 (Bodleian Library at Oxford); H = MS. Lat. Misc. e. 16 (Bodleian Library at Oxford); I = Finch-Hatton MS. 320 (Northamptonshire Record Office).

When my work on the above nine manuscripts was nearly completed, two other manuscripts of Richardus Tertius (Folger MS. 1877.1 and Hungtington MS. 179) were brought to my attention. I collated both these manuscripts, but since inclusion of their variants would have necessitated complete revision of the charts and tables on which the textual study rests and because their variants produced no evidence that seriously affects the Genealogical Tree as presented below (see Footnote 48), I decided not to include them.

2. Comparative Study of the Manuscripts

A comparative study of the manuscripts involves both a distributional study and a genealogical study of the variants in all the manuscripts. A distributional study considers "the arrangement of differences in the

---

*This Ms. was reprinted by Barron Field, the "few blanks" of which he filled from Ms. A (London, 1844). W.C. Hazlitt reprinted Field's edition for Shakespeare Library (London, 1875). Both editions are full of errors and hence unreliable.

surviving texts...without attention to the nature of the differences."[43]
A genealogical study compares "the individual differences [in the surviving
texts] with each other in the hope of discovering the direction of change."[44]
Although each of these studies has a different immediate objective, the
ultimate objective of each of them is the same. Hence, in studying a set
of variants it is often necessary to use both approaches simultaneously.
The object of the present comparative study is to determine--in so far as
possible from the variants in the nine extant manuscripts concerned---the
relationship of manuscripts and, in the absence of any holograph
manuscripts, to determine which of the manuscripts most nearly approxi-
mates the author's original.

A distributional study of all of the variants occurring in the 215 lines
of Act II, Scene i of Part I, indicates that the nine manuscripts here
considered fall into three family groupings: (1) ACEH; (2) DF; and (3)
BGI.[45]

The following analysis of Chart I (see Appendix B) reveals the general
basis for assuming these family groups. With regard to the ACEH grouping,
it will be noted that A agrees with C 50 times (2 of which variants it
shares uniquely with C); A agrees with E 47 times (4 uniquely shared);
and A agrees with H 40 times (no unique agreements). Figures for the

---

[43]Archibald A. Hill, "Some Postulates for Distributional Study of
Texts," Studies in Bibliography, III (1950-1951), 63.

[44]Ibid.

[45]Samples from Parts II and III will be discussed later.

substantive variants[46] are proportionately high: A=C (19); A=E (15); and A=H (12). The pattern of variants of C, E and H with each of the other three manuscripts of the ACEH family is similar to that of A. Only E shows relationships with manuscripts outside this family grouping that cannot be, at first glance, reconciled to the ACEH grouping. However, E is somewhat anomalous; that is, it appears to be the product of collation, a possibility which will be discussed later.

That D and F form a family group is immediately evident from Chart I. F varies fairly uniformly from all manuscripts, except D. Of the times that D appears in a significant group,[47] F agrees with D 84 times with 13 uniquely shared readings. The substantive variants also show a comparatively high total: 44 (8).

That the third group BGI has well-defined outlines is not made clear by Chart I. The relationship between G and I is clear enough since G and I agree with each other 45 times and share uniquely 17 readings. However, though B shows positive relationship to G (39 agreements with 1 uniquely shared reading) and to I (33 agreements with 4 uniquely shared readings), it also shows high correlation with all other manuscripts, except F.

Hence, although the distributional evidence reported in Chart I is of value in clarifying the groupings of some manuscripts, it cannot answer

---

[46]A substantive variant, in this study, is defined as (1) any addition to, or omission from, the control of a word or a line; or (2) any word which differs completely in meaning from that of the control.

[47]A significant group, in this study, is defined as the grouping of two or more manuscripts in agreement on a particular reading against any other manuscript or group(s) of manuscripts.

all the questions arising out of the relationships posited above. Such evidence can suggest the family groupings; in some cases it can be used to assert definite relationships between manuscripts, but only in a few cases can it confirm the suggested family groupings. An analysis of Chart II (see Appendix B) may help to confirm and to clarify the family groupings suggested by the analysis of Chart I.

The list of significant groupings of variants in Chart II is helpful in determining both the family groupings and the direction of change within these groupings. The family groupings ACEH, DF, BGI suggested by the analysis of Chart I are immediately evident in the significant groupings of variants: ABCEH, ABCE, AC, ACE, ACEH, EH, DF, BGI, BI, GI. The frequency of occurrence of these significant groupings fairly well establishes the suggested family groupings. For instance, that DF is a family is beyond doubt. Of 51 significant groups, D and F form a significant group 10 times. D and F are unique in wanting lines 6a, 6b, and 157a. Because common omissions (or additions, when these occur) generally indicate derivation and are seldom attributable to chance, they offer the strongest kind of evidence for positing a definite relatinship between manuscripts. Variants of the kind found in lines 52, 69, and 71 also point clearly to the close relationship of D and F.

The family group ACEH is only slightly less clearly defined than that of DF. Of the 52 significant groups ACEH occurs 6 times; ACE 3 times; EH 4 times; ABCEH twice; ABCE once; AC twice - a total of 18 times in which A, C, E, or H occurs with at least one other member of the family. (The disconcerting presence of B in this family group will be clarified in the discussion of the direction of change). Although the ACEH family has no addition or omission not shared with one of the other families, the variant in line 204 strongly affirms the outline of this family. Agreement on a reading manifestly wrong (i.e. a nonsense reading) is evidence equally as strong for positing relationship as that of addition or omission. Such is the ACEH variant (tace) in line 204. C apparently has tace, for tale, an easy enough mis-reading for its scribe to make. However, if the scribes of A, E and H were not slavisly copying, one or all would have caught the impossible reading and changed it, if not to tale, then to some other word that would make sense in the context. Similar copying no doubt accounts for the variants in lines 53 and 89, both of which add support to the conclusion that ACEH forms a family group.

In the family group, BGI, if B at times is a doubtful member because of its frequent affinity with other manuscripts, there is no doubt that G and I should be grouped together. G and I constitute 21 of the 52 significant groups in Chart II. The nature of these 21 agreements emphasizes their relationship as much as does the number. No fewer than 8 lines (55, 57, 79, 144, 152, 166, 167, 170) are wholly or at least considerably different from those of the other manuscripts, so much different, in fact, that revision somewhere in the family is strongly indicated. The lack in G and I of line 145 and of ut in line 41 corroborates the relationship. B's relationship to G and I is far less clear than the relationship of G to I. In fact, like E, B is somewhat of an anomaly. Nevertheless, that B belongs very definitely with G and I is observable in lines 83 and 101 and in line 59 where regulum and a different word order set B, G and I apart from the other manuscripts. Line 77 hints at the anomalous nature of B. The B-scribe apparently started this line following a reading that would agree with all manuscripts except G and I: half-way through the line, he apparently reversed his field, crossed out three of the four words he had written, and then completed the line so that the end result coincides, except for a misspelling in I, exactly with the line as found in G and I.

A glance at line 83 will summarize the family groupings that have been suggested thus far. In this line, we have three different readings, dividing precisely according to the DF, ACEH, and BGI groupings already noted.

Thus far the family groupings ACEH, DF, and BGI have been based solely on variants taken from Part I. A similar comparative study of samples from Parts II and III is now in order. The distributional evidence of the first 100 lines of ACT III, Part II and of the first 100 lines of Act III, Part III (tabulated in Chart III) confirms and clarifies the position of every manuscript within the family groupings suggested by the analysis of Charts I and II, with the exception of E which appears to have shifted its family loyalty. An analysis of Chart III (see Appendix B) calls for the reassessment only of E's position in the ACEH family. Its anomalous nature, suspected earlier, is now apparent. It seems that its closest relationship is with the DF family and not with ACH. In fact, whereas it is likely that the E-scribe copied from A, C, H or their common ancestor in Part I, there is no doubt that he does not copy from any of these manuscripts when he comes to Parts II and III. For, Chart III shows that whereas E has no substantive variants in common with any of the members of the ACH family group, it does have two in common with D. It shares substantive variants only with D, B and I, showing a strong relationship with D, agreeing with D 56 times as against 23 times each with C and H, the closest rivals of D. Of E's 56 agreements with D, two are uniquely shared, and 29 are substantive. In contrast, E has only two substantive agreements with B and but one with I, weak evidence for

asserting a close relationship. The agreement of E with B, as shown in
Chart IV at line 45, Part III (magis DF; mox BE; item ACH,with an omission in I) is somewhat nullified by E's substantive agreement in the
very same line with DF (dedi DEF; misi BI; addi ACH). This tendency of
E to show significant relationship with two different family groups within the same line illustrates the ambiguity of E noted earlier, and urges
the conclusion that E is a product of collation.

Also noteworthy is E's affinity with D and not with F, since the DF
family apparently remains a unit throughout Parts II and III. F agrees
with D 57 times (with 5 uniquely shared agreements); that is, over twice
as many times as with any other manuscript. Of these 57 agreements, 32
are substantive. F, in fact, has no substantive agreement--except for
one with B and I (O ACDEH; O omitted BFI)--with any other manuscript.
That D and F still belong together is evident, and that E in the last
two Parts belongs with them to form the family DEF is highly probable.

The formerly anomalous position of B is somewhat clarified by Chart
III. The ambiguity displayed in B's frequent presence with the ACEH
group in Part I vanishes in Parts II and III. If the B-scribe was looking at two manuscripts when composing Part I (see Collation, Part I, I.ii.
77), he was looking at only one manuscript when he copied Parts II and
III, and that one bears little direct relationship to the ACH family, and
great relationship to the GI grouping. B shares 58 variants with I, 33
of which are shared only with I; 32 of the 58 are substantive variants,
30 of which are uniquely shared with I. There is a far greater number of
agreements between B and I than between any other two manuscripts. The
absence of G from these tabulations, since G is wanting Parts II and III,

does not prevent the confirmation of the family group BGI, since I's close
association to G has already been confirmed by the analysis of the Part
I variants. Hence, the three family groups now appear to be: ACH, BGI,
and DF, with E leaning towards the DF family.

An analysis of the significant groups of variants from the 200 lines
of Parts II and III as found in Chart IV will support these family
groupings. Of the 32 significant groups of variants appearing in Chart
IV, BI occurs 25 times, ACH 8 times, DEF 5 times, DF 3 times, BE once and
AC twice. If the number of occurrences of the BI group (25 of 32) does
not sufficiently prove that BGI constitutes a family, the most cursory
look at the nature of BI variants will. The many omissions, additions
and completely different lines leave no doubt that BGI is a family. If
B's loyalty was divided in Part I, it is not in Parts II and III. B's
position is no longer ambiguous.

Except for E's apparent vagrancy, the ACH family remains stable,
and is further confirmed both quantitatively and qualitatively by Chart
IV. Of the 32 significant groups, ACH makes up 8. Both on the line-
unit of variant (see 1.80, Pt II; 1. 48, Part III) and on word-unit (1.4:
quilibet BDEFH; quaelibet ACH; 1. 66: sanxerint BDEFH; finxerint ACH),
the ACH family asserts its unity and its qualitative separation from the
other two family groups.

Although Chart IV shows only three DF significant groups, there are
5 DEF groups, for a proportionately high total of 8, if E is included
with DF, and, as was seen above, it probably should be. Nor does a qualitative analysis of these significant groups deny the conclusion that D, E,
and F make up a family. D and F form a significant group only in lines
45, 48, and 52 of Part III. The DEF family grouping is fairly well established by the nature of the variants in line 90 of Part II (o cives probe

DEF; o cives mei BI; optimi viri ACH); in line 96 of Part II (spernas DEF; non vis ACH; renuis B; word omitted I); and in line 45 of Part III (dedi DEF; addi ACH; misi BI). On the line-unit of significant groupings, the DEF grouping is seen in lines 19 and 80 of Part II. These examples are sufficient to posit the DEF family grouping, even in the face of the recalcitrance of E observable in line 48 of Part III.

The last five examples cited not only establish the DEF family, but also re-confirm the ACH and BI(G) groupings which all previous evidence has suggested. Both the distributional and genealogical evidence of Part I point to the family groupings ACEH, BIG and DF, and to the ambiguity of B and E. Similar evidence of Parts II and III clarifies the ambiguity surrounding B, and (although not clarifying E's ambiguity) reassesses E's position, at the same time reaffirming the positions of all other manuscripts--the end result of which is the family groupings ACH, BI(G), and DEF. The distributional sample from the three Parts is sufficiently large to support this conclusion. The examples from our genealogical study, although small in number, are so distinct in nature that they can be attributable only to derivation, and not to chance. Hence, this study will proceed on the assumption that ACH, BI(G), and DF constitute family groups and that E is a product of collation.

a. Direction of Change within the ACH(E) Family

Of the manuscripts in the ACH(E) family, there can be little doubt that C is the most reliable. Evidence, extrinsic to a strictly comparative study, virtually assures us that not only is C the most reliable manuscript in the ACH(E) grouping, but also that C most closely resembles the author's original. The notations on its title page indicate that C is a direct copy of Legge's holograph. However, this does not eliminate the possibility that other manuscripts were not also copied directly from a holograph. Hence, the authority of C, its primacy, can be established only by discovering the direction of derivation in the various manuscripts.

That C is the most reliable manuscript in the ACH(E) group can be proved by a study of certain significant groups and the omissions, additions, inversions and nonsense words that occur in these four manuscripts. It is important to note at the very outset that the ACH(E) family is comprised of the two sub-families, AC and EH. A hint of this family division is seen in the fact that A and C have virtually no marginal stage directions in any of the three Parts (see Appendix C). Also A and C alone agree in omitting two lines (IV.ii.135; V.vii.43) and in adding a word to a line (II.i.146) (see Chart V).

The AC sub-family is confirmed by a look at the substantive variants listed in Charts II and IV. The AC sub-group is found alone once in each list; moreover, every time C appears in a significant group, A appears with it, which suggests that A is derived from C since the number of unique variants in A as compared with the number in C urges the conclusion that A is a terminal manuscript. Chart I shows A to have 43 unique variants, 11 of which are substantive, whereas C has only one unique variant. Chart III presents a similar picture. Further evidence that A is derived from C may be seen in the many word omissions (II.i.157a; III.i.56; IV.ii.195; IV.iii.3; IV.iii.37; IV.iii.44) and line omissions (III.i.20; IV.ii.70; IV.iii.71; V.i.20; V.ii.24; V.vi.18) in A (see Chart V).

All remarks made about the EH sub-family are, of course, subject to the qualification made earlier: that is, E and H are a sub-family only part of the time, since E is ambiguous, often shifting its allegiance (especially after Part II) to the DF family grouping. In Part I, however,

EH is a fairly steady sub-family of the ACH(E) group. Chart II reveals
that E and H form a significant group four times. Only two variants are
of real importance: one is the omission in line 15 and the other the
inversion (always a good indication of relationship) in line 174. An
analysis of Chart V firmly establishes E and H as a sub-family. E and
H, alone, share agreements that make little or no sense (I.i.91; II.ii.
28; II.iii.19); they also uniquely share one inversion (III.i.7). Chief
proof of this sub-family is its unique omission of three lines (III.i.29-
31), the omission of which can be attributed only to the fact that they
are related either by a single line of descent (that is, either E or H
is derived from the other) or by radiation (that is, both E and H have
separate lines of descent joined by a common ancestor). The latter
alternative is more likely inasmuch as both E and H have many variants--
some nonsense readings, omissions and inversions--that are unique to
each. Chart I shows 50 unique variants in E,20 of which are substantive
variants. H has a total of 24 with 7 substantive variants. These
figures suggest that both E and H are terminal, which, in turn, indicates
radiation. H omits several words (I.i.18; I.i.19; I.i.108; II.i.207;
II.ii.43; III.ii.11; III.iii.21; IV.ii.60; IV.ii.157; IV.iii.54; IV.iii.
76; V.vi.25; V.vii.17; V.vii.64) and several lines (I.i.109-111; II.i.67;
III.ii.32; IV.iii.221; V.vi.54; V.vi.123; V.vii.18). These omissions,
all unique to H, prove beyond a doubt that neither E, nor any other manuscript, is derived from H.

But the converse, that H is derived from E, is still a possibility.
Indeed, the evidence to disprove this possibility is not strong. The
fact that E has so many unique variants is an indication that it is terminal
but by no means proves that it is. Nor are the word (III.iii.8) and line

(II.ii.32) omissions sufficient to prove that H is not derived from E.
An omission of a single word and a single line does not make a strong
case. Any number of things might have occurred to make possible the
fact that, although H is derived from E, it has a word or two not found
in E. The only good reason for denying H's possible derivation from E
is that E, as we have seen above, by the end of Part I, and throughout
Parts II and III is showing great affinity for the DF family, a family
quite distinct from the ACH group.

Hence, it is concluded that during a large portion of Part I, E and
H constitute a recognizable sub-family, that neither is derivable directly
from the other, but that they are derivable from a common ancestor, and,
finally, that their relationship to each other is by radiation; that is,
their relationship is collateral.

b. Direction of Change within the DF(E) Family

That D and F form a family group has already been established. The
only question is whether they are related to each other by a direct line
of descent, or by radiation from their common ancestor.

As in the case of E and H, the latter alternative is more acceptable,
but with much more certainty. As Chart V shows, D has several unique
nonsense readings (IV.ii.13; IV.ii.98; IV.ii.101; IV.iii.138; V.vi.32)
and some unique line omissions (II.ii.27a; IV.iii.326a-326d; V.ii.36a-36e;
V.v.74a). Also in IV.iii. D combines lines 204-205 into a single nonsense
line, which F does not include. At the same time, F has its share of
unique omissions, both of the word-unit kind (I.i.102; II.i.88; IV.iii.
39; IV.iii.175; V.vi.74; V.vii.54) and of the line-unit kind (II.i.128;
II.i.193; V.vi.103). These unique differences in D and F are of a nature

and number sufficient to indicate that D and F are related to each other collaterally, or by radiation from a common ancestor.

It is now necessary to clear up some of the ambiguity surrounding E. The possibility of E's being the common ancestor of D and F at once arises. But there is evidence against such a possibility. First, it has already been established that E, for a time at least, is a bona fide member of the ACH(E) family. In other words, E shares many substantive agreements with the ACH group that it does not share with the DF group. Second, E's high total of unique variants indicates that it is a terminal manuscript. Finally, E omits at least one word (III.iii. 8) and one line (II.ii.32) that appear in D and F. The last point is, of course, as was seen above, weak evidence for supposing that E cannot be the common ancestor of D and F, but when the other two points are added to it, a fairly strong case can be made for denying this conclusion. Indeed the only conclusion that seems to fit all the facts, and that will clear up much of the ambiguity surrounding it is that E is a product of collation: that is, E for the first few acts of Part I is derived mainly from the common ancestor of the EH sub-family, and for the rest of the play mainly from the ancestor of the common ancestor of the DF family. (See the Genealogical Tree, below). The two dotted lines converging into the letter E indicates the collation involved in E.)

c. Direction of Change within the BI(G) Family

Since B, like E, is somewhat ambiguous, it is well to clarify the relationship of G and I before trying to pigeonhole B. First of all, as Chart I indicates, G and I show a closer affinity in Part I than any other pair of manuscripts. That they far surpass any other two manuscripts

in the number of uniquely shared variants would seemingly indicate direct
derivation of one from the other. Strangely enough, however, this is not
the case. I is obviously not derived from G because G omits lines 37-79
in Act V, Scene vii, most of which are present in I. But neither is G derived from I. I shares not only more unique variants with G than with
any other manuscript, but also more substantive variants with G than occur
between any two other manuscripts that form groups, that is AC, EH, and DF.
Incompatible, too, with the supposition that G is derived from I are the
numerous word omissions (See Chart V: II.i.80; II.i.92; II.i.140; II.i.
185; III.i.36; III.i.37; III.i.111; IV.ii.121; V.i.83; V.vi.74) and the
line omissions (II.i.67; II.i.102-103; II.i.158; II.ii.46; V.ii.21; V.vii.
37-38) found in I. However, it is still possible that B and I (that is,
when B is being a loyal member of the BI(G) family) are derived from a
common ancestor. On several occasions before G breaks off, B and I are
found together forming significant groups both of the line-unit kind
(V.i.59) and of the word-unit kind (II.i.101; II.i.190; V.i.37; V.ii.2;
V.iii.12; V.v.24; V.vii.5). These variants unique to B and I are of such
a nature that they lead to one of two possible conclusions: (1) that one
of the two is derived from the other; or (2) that they have a common
ancestor. The many omissions already noted in I rule out the possibility
that B is derived from I. And that I can be derived from B is incompatible
with the evidence that made necessary the earlier conclusion that B is not
always a loyal member of the BI(G) family, especially in Part I. Indeed,
in Part I, B agrees more often with the variants of the ACH(E) family than
it does with those of the GI group. Only in Parts II and III does B show
itself a true member of the BI(G) family. Further evidence that B is not
the ancestor of I is seen in the word omissions (II.iii.26; IV.iii.309),

the line omission (IV.iii.85), the inversion (V.i.90) and other unique
variants (III.iii.11; III.iii.13; IV.iii.51; V.ii.2; V.iii.1) that occur
in B but not in I. Hence, it is highly probable that the second alternative, that B and I have a common ancestor, is correct; in other words, B
and I show a collateral relationship during the greater half ot he play.

But this explanation immediately gives rise to two more questions:
First, if B and I are related to a common ancestor, why then does I show
far more agreements with G than with B in Part I? Second, if G does not
share a common ancestor with either B or I, where does G fit into the
BI(G) family?

The answer to the second question is simple and helps to provide an
answer to the first. The immediate ancestor of G must also be the ancestor
common to B and I (see the Genealogical Tree below). G agrees with all
other manuscripts against B and I on a number of occasions (V.i.37; V.i.59;
V.ii.2; V.iii.12; V.v.24; V.vii.5), agreements that indicate G's ancestor
is closer to a holograph than the common ancestor of B and I.

A brief look at Chart I will indicate the reason for the second question. I has 45 agreements with G, 17 of which are uniquely shared, totals
which seemingly disprove the collateral relationship of B and I since I
has 33 agreements with B, only 4 of which are uniquely shared. However,
this paradox is resolved when the ambiguous nature of B is recalled. It
was shown earlier that the B-scribe, for most of Part I, must have been
looking at two manuscripts, and, in fact, favoring a manuscript closely
related to the ACH(E) group. Hence, since the B-scribe took nearly all
his readings for Part I from a manuscript more closely related to the
ACH(E) family than to the GI group, it is clear why G and I are often

in agreement. In Parts II and III the B-scribe, for some unknown reason, abandoned all favoritism for the manuscript related to the ACH(E) group and derived most of his readings from the ancestor common to B and I.

The many unique agreements between G and I observable in Chart I would seem to debar positing a closer relationship between B and I than between G and I. But, nowhere throughout Part I (and in the case of G this represents the entire play) do we find in either Chart I or Chart V a BG significant group, whereas we find BI significant groups on several occasions (II.i.101; II.i.190; II.i.206; IV.ii.127; V.i.37; V.i.59; V.ii. 2; V.ii.94; V.iii.12; V.v.24; V.vii.5). Had B paid more attention in Part I to the ancestor common to B and I instead of to the manuscript related to the ACH(E) family, there would have been a far greater number of BI significant groups. Only through default of B do we find so many agreements between G and I.

Another check of Chart I will substantiate this claim. It will be noticed that whereas G has 45 agreements (17 uniquely shared) with I, G has 39 (one uniquely shared) with B, totals not significantly different from those of its agreements with C and H. In fact, G uniquely shares no substantive agreements with B. On the other hand, I has 33 agreements (4 uniquely shared) with B, totals more significant than those for G. Also, three of I's uniquely shared agreements with B are substantive.

If G were complete, doubtless the relationship among B, I and G would have become clearer. Unfortunately, it is not. From Charts II and IV we have already noted the very close relationship that B and I maintain throughout Parts II and III. All evidence points to the conclusion that if G had been completed, Chart III would have shown a far different picture with regard to B, I and G than does Chart I. More than likely G

would have shown, if it were complete, as close a relationship in Chart
III to B and I as it does in Chart I to I.

d. The Genealogical Tree

From the evidence so far advanced, it is now possible to construct
a Genealogical Tree:

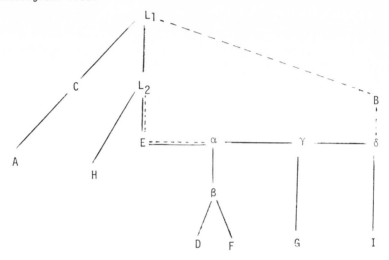

In this diagram, the sigla A, B, C, D, E, F, G, H, and I stand for
the nine manuscripts studied. L_1 stands for Legge's original manuscript,
and L_2 also for a holograph, or the direct copy of it prepared for the
St. John's performance in 1579/80. The Greek letters (α, β, γ, δ)
are used to indicate manuscripts that exist unknown, or that must have
existed at one time.

The Genealogical Tree, as diagrammed, clearly suggests[48] the interrelationships of all the manuscripts already determined by the preceding comparative study. Our study shows that there are three family groups: $\underline{ACH(E)}$, $\underline{DF(E)}$, $\underline{BI(G)}$, the outlines of which are readily observable in the Tree. It showed also that $\underline{C}$ is derived from a holograph ($\underline{L_1}$), and that $\underline{A}$ is derived from $\underline{C}$ to form the $\underline{AC}$ sub-family. $\underline{EH}$ was shown to be a sub-family closely related to the $\underline{AC}$ sub-family, but yet different in significant respects. If $\underline{H}$ and $\underline{E}$ (in Part I) are derived from the production copy of a holograph ($\underline{L_2}$), as is indicated by the Tree, then the similarities and differences in these two sub-families are easily accounted for. The broken lines leading into $\underline{E}$ indicate that it is a product of collation: in Part I taking most of its readings from $\underline{L_2}$, and in Parts II and III favoring the ancestor ($\underline{\alpha}$) of the common ancestor (β) of $\underline{D}$ and $\underline{F}$.

It will be recalled that though their many substantive agreements clearly marked $\underline{D}$ and $\underline{F}$ as a family group, yet their mutually exclusive differences proved that neither of them is derived from the other, but

---

[48]The word "suggests" is used because the Tree is to be considered a suggested outline of the probable interrelationships of the manuscripts here studied, and not the only outline. In this connection, it should be recalled that two known manuscripts of Richardus Tertius (Folger MS. 1877.1; and Huntington MS. 179) have not been included in this study (see Footnote 44). The collection of the Folger MS. proves it to be so closely related to $\underline{G}$ that one is almost certainly a direct copy of the other. The collation of the Huntington MS. definitely places it in the $\underline{AC}$ sub-family, and strongly suggests that $\underline{A}$ is derived from the Huntington MS., which, in turn, is probably derived directly from $\underline{C}$.

instead that each is derived from a common ancestor (β). $\underline{E}$'s close relationship to the $\underline{DF}$ family in Parts II and III is sufficiently explained
by its relationship to the ancestor (α) of the common ancestor (β) of $\underline{DF}$.

The ambiguous nature of $\underline{B}$ in the $\underline{BI(G)}$ family is expressed by the
broken lines leading into it. $\underline{B}$'s affinity for the $\underline{ACH(E)}$ family in Part
I is shown by its derivation from $\underline{L_1}$, and its remarkably high number of
agreements in Parts II and III with $\underline{I}$ is explained by its derivation from
$\underline{\delta}$, the common ancestor of $\underline{B}$ and $\underline{I}$. $\underline{B}$'s dependence on $\underline{L_1}$ in Part I also
explains the large number of agreements between $\underline{G}$ and $\underline{I}$ in Part I. The
differences between $\underline{G}$ and $\underline{I}$, and the fact that $\underline{G}$ does not show as close
an affinity for $\underline{B}$ in Part I as $\underline{I}$ does is indicated by positing an ancestor (γ) for $\underline{G}$, which is also the ancestor of the common ancestor ($\underline{\delta}$) of
$\underline{B}$ and $\underline{I}$.

The Genealogical Tree, as arranged, will explain every significant
grouping of variants in Part I, and in the two hundred lines of Parts II
and III. In fact, the Tree renders comprehensible even such perplexing
variants as the frequent grouping of $\underline{D}$, $\underline{F}$, $\underline{G}$, and $\underline{I}$ (I.i.102; I.i.139;
III.i.6; III.i.51; III.ii.29; IV.ii.2); the line omission in $\underline{DEFGI}$ (IV.
ii.215a); the line omissions in $\underline{AC}$ (IV.ii.135; V.vii.43); the unique
variants in $\underline{B}$ (III.iii.11, 13; IV.iii.51; IV.iii.309; V.iii.1; V.v.17; V.
v.31); and the revision in $\underline{B}$ (I.i.42). Hence, the comparative study of
a portion of the variants in the nine manuscripts has made possible the
construction of a Tree that will adequately explain or account for nearly
all variants not considered by the study.

3. The Stage Directions

A complete list of the stage directions found in the nine manuscripts appears in Appendix C. In general, the stage directions are of little value for showing the direction of change, but of great value for confirming the family groupings arrived at by the comparative study as outlined in the Genealogical Tree.

First of all, an analysis of the stage directions confirms that $\underline{A}$ and $\underline{C}$ form a group. With but minor differences in spelling, $\underline{A}$'s stage directions are the same as $\underline{C}$'s. Both have only three generally brief marginal stage directions (Part III: V.viii.46; V.viii.54; and at the start of the Epilogue), and both agree with all other manuscripts in having all the non-marginal stage directions.

Confirmation that $\underline{E}$ and $\underline{H}$ form a sub-group in the $\underline{ACH(E)}$ family is seen in the many stage directions found in these manuscripts, which do not appear in $\underline{A}$ and $\underline{C}$. In fact, the absence of stage directions in Parts I and II of $\underline{A}$ and $\underline{C}$ supports the argument for a separate line of descent for these two manuscripts, separate not only from $\underline{E}$ and $\underline{H}$ but from all other manuscripts; and for the necessity of deriving all manuscripts, except $\underline{A}$ and $\underline{C}$, from an ancestor ($\underline{L}_2$) that had all the stage directions shared in common by $\underline{BDEF(G)HI}$ (Part I: IV.ii.216; Part II: III.i.27; III.ii.76).

Substantiation of the $\underline{DF}$ group is observed in the frequent coincidence of similar stage directions for these two manuscripts. $\underline{F}$ has no stage direction that does not appear in $\underline{D}$, whereas $\underline{D}$, which has more stage directions than any other manuscript, has only three that do not appear in $\underline{F}$ (Part I: III.ii.6; III.ii.11; III.iii.21).

The problem of pigeonholing E is not resolved by an analysis of the stage directions for E. Most of its marginal stage directions appear in a separate list at the end of the play with instructions for inserting them in the margins where they apply. Two of these are unique to E (Part III: V.v.i; V.vi.1). And, in addition to containing the non-marginal stage directions shared by all manuscripts, E has three marginal stage directions in the text beside the lines to which they apply. One of these three (Part I: III.iii.21) is found also in the list at the end. Nevertheless, despite the inconsistency in its stage directions, E's affinity with the DF group after Part I is readily observable. In Parts II and III, E shares every one of the sixteen stage directions that D and F have in common except for the easily overlooked notation "The battell" (Part III: V.viii.54). Further evidence that DF(E) form a family group in Parts II and III is the two stage directions shared uniquely by D, E, and F (Part III: V.i.14; V.viii.43). Also, D, E and F alone have the last stage direction in the play as a marginal direction.

No less clearly is the BI(G) family established by a study of the stage directions. For some reason, I has only one stage direction in Part I (Part I: IV.ii.216). On the other hand, G has every stage direction listed for Part I. In fact G has one in Latin (Part I: III.i. beside the list of characters) which it duplicates later in English (Part I: III.i.64). Of G's nine different stage directions in Part I, B shares eight (Part I: III.i.16; III.i.20; III.i.64; III.ii.6; III.ii.11; III.iii. 21; IV.ii.216; V.vi.73) with some slight variations in wording. The relationship between the stage directions in B and G is sufficiently close to indicate that they belong to the same family, but also sufficiently different to re-affirm that neither is derived directly from the other.

G lacks Parts II and III. Fortunately the I-scribe pays more attention to stage directions in Parts II and III than he did in Part I
so that the relationship of B and I can be easily determined.   In
Parts II and III, B and I's stage directions are almost exactly the
same. They always occur together except on two occasions. Once I has
a unique stage direction (Part II: II.ii.186), and once I has no
direction at all (Part III: V.iii.12). Twice B and I share unique
stage directions (Part II: III.i.8; V.i. after the line ending Part
II), and once they agree in having no stage direction (Part III: V.viii.
46). These facts further establish the family group BI(G).

4. The Songs and Pageantry

The presence of songs and pageantry (or the mention thereof) in
some manuscripts and their absence in others is to some extent valuable
for affirming manuscript relationships. There is some form of, or at
least mention of, songs or pageants at the end of each Part in seven of
the manuscripts. In all cases, the songs and pageants are intimately
related in meaning to the scene that ends each Part.

At the end of Part I, every manuscript has the notation Processio
Solennis, which the previous dialogue indicates refers to the penitential
procession through the streets of London for Jane Shore. After the brief
notation, every manuscript indicates that a "Chorus" is to sing a song,
and each presents a ten-line song in Latin, the theme of which is adultery
and is obviously intended to be sung as the procession moves across the
stage. E is unique in presenting this song again at the very end of the
manuscript with words and musical notations (see Appendix C for a copy
of the song as it appears in E). Up through the song and the epilogue
which follows the song, all manuscripts agree essentially. After the

epilogue, however, only D, E, F, G, and H actually present a list of
eight marchers (G gives only seven) taking part in "The Shewe of the
Procession."

The last scene in Part II describes the coronation procession of
King Richard. Immediately after the end of Part II, however, B, D, E,
F, H, and I alone mention "The Shewe of the Coronation," and each of
these same manuscripts actually gives a rather long list of the marchers
in the procession. The number of marchers in each list is in some cases
difficult to determine because some manuscripts do not maintain clear
distir ions in their entries. However, there are approximately 30
entries in B's list, 34 in D's, 34 in E's, 36 in F's, 25 in H's, and 28
in I's.

Of the six manuscripts that present the list of marchers in the
coronation procession, only H fails to mention a song. B and I call for
"singers [to] singe being placed on the toppe of some of the houses"
during the coronation ceremonies (see Appendix C,; Part II: V.i. after
the end of Part II). Neither B nor I present the song to be sung. Following the list of marchers in the procession, D, E, and F have the following note: "During solemnity of the coronation let this following
songe be songe with instruments." And, all three give essentially the
same ten-line song in Latin, the theme of which is directly related to
coronation proceedings.

At the end of Part III, the only mention of pageantry is the crowning
of the Earl of Richmond as King Henry. All eight manuscripts mention this
coronation in the final direction of the play (See Appendix C; Part III:
V. beside the Epilogue), but, added to this same direction in only D, E, F,

and $\underline{H}$ is mention of a song. $\underline{D}$, $\underline{E}$, and $\underline{H}$ add: "and the songe sunge which

is in the end of the booke";[49] $\underline{F}$ adds: "and the songe be sounge which is

in the first copye." $\underline{E}$ is alone in having a song at the end of the manu-

script, but that cannot be the song referred to here, since, as already

noted, the song at the end of $\underline{E}$ duplicates the song found at the end of

Part I in all manuscripts. It is highly unlikely that it was intended

that this same song be sung twice, once at the end of Part I and once at

the end of Part III, for, as we have seen, the themes of the songs in the

play have been intimately related to the proceedings on stage. Hence,

the song referred to in $\underline{D}$, $\underline{E}$, $\underline{F}$ and $\underline{H}$ must have appeared in a manuscript

from which these four manuscripts are ultimately derived. The manuscript

that contained the song is the "book" or "copy" referred to. It is likely

that this "book" or "copy" was the original copy (MS. $\underline{L}_2$) used in the pro-

duction of the play at the St. John's Bachelors' Commencement in 1579/80.

5. The Arguments and Epilogues

The arguments and epilogues also provide supporting evidence, how-

ever, slight, for the family groupings already ascertained. All manu-

scripts have an argument for Part I. Manuscripts $\underline{A}$, $\underline{B}$, $\underline{C}$, $\underline{E}$ and $\underline{H}$ pre-

sent the argument for Part I in 36 lines in verse form. $\underline{D}$, $\underline{F}$, $\underline{G}$ and $\underline{I}$

present it in prose, the number of lines varying from 20 to 35.[50]

Every manuscript has essentially the same ten-line verse epilogue at the

end of Part I. In Part II, all arguments except that of $\underline{B}$ are in prose.

---

[49]This reference to the "booke," the word used to describe a production text (see Footnote 11), may very well relate these manuscripts with
that of the original performance.

[50]The number of lines is not itself proof of anything since the simi-
larity or divergence in the number of lines used may be coincidental. However, since identity in the number of lines used may suggest derivation, especially when supported by other evidence, the information is included in
this section.

A, C, D and H have exactly 15 lines; E and F have 17; B has 19; I has 11.
Definite signs of group relationship between D, E and F are seen in their
having an "epilogue" to end Part II; whereas A, B, D, H and I do not have
an epilogue here. The epilogue in D, E and F is the Furor-speech which
serves as the argument of Part III for all other manuscripts.

In Part III, only A, B, C, H, and I have an argument, the same Furor-
speech that D, E and F use as the epilogue of Part II. Undoubtedly the
Furor-speech is properly the argument of Part III inasmuch as it sets the
atmosphere of horror in the opening scenes of Part III, the scenes concerned with the murder of the young princes. At the end of Part III, all
manuscripts (except G which is imperfect) give an epilogue, in every case
35 lines of verse.

6. The Choice of the Clare College MS. (MS. C)

The reasons for choosing MS. C as the basis of this edition are
apparent in all that has been written thus far about this manuscript.
One of the strongest arguments in its favor, of course, is the fact that
its transcription by Anthony Cade was undoubtedly made with approval of the
author, and from a holograph copy. As we have seen, there is no reason
to doubt this fact. Cade was at Cambridge at the time of MS. C's transcription, and knew Thomas Legge intimately.

Strong evidence in favor of the choice of C is provided by the comparative study, which solidly confirms Cade's statement that he transcribed
Legge's holograph. Our study of the variants has aided greatly in
establishing the primacy of C by showing (1) that C is derived from no
other known manuscript, and (2) that every other manuscript studied,
except B, is too deficient in a number of respects to warrant serious

consideration as the copy-text of this edition. The numerous word and
line omissions and the many nonsense readings in A, D, E, F, G, H, and
I, noted in our study, are sufficient to disqualify these manuscripts.
B, on the other hand, cannot be so easily dismissed. The comparative
study established that it, along with C, is directly derivable in Part
I from a Legge holograph. But the comparative study also established
that B is not directly related to a Legge holograph in Parts II and III,
but is, in fact, a member of the BI(G) family, the common ancestor of
which is more than likely a product of considerable revision. The question of preference between B and C is therefore narrowed down to a consideration of Part I only.

The substantive agreement of the variants of B and C in Part I, as
was observed in the comparative study, made necessary the conclusion
that B in Part I was directly derivable from a Legge holograph. Their
substantive disagreements in Part I obviously cannot be accounted for in
the same way. Two explanations for these differences are possible. First,
the scribes of each manuscript undoubtedly mis-copied certain readings in
Legge's manuscript that the other did not (see II.i.204: tace B] tale C).
Second, Legge probably revised his original manuscript more than once,
and if so B and C may have copied it at different stages, or in different
states, of its revision. On seventeen occasions (Part I: II.i.84; II.i.
89; II.iii.3; III.i.6; III.i.51; III.ii.29; III.ii.30; III.ii.32; IV.ii.
121; IV.ii.215a; IV.iii.319; V.i.116; V.v.1; V.vii.26; Part II: III.i.96;
Part III: III.i.45; III.i.48) in the lines studied, C has variant readings in an Italian hand, most of which are in brackets (see Appenix A:
Collation of Manuscripts). An analysis of these variants seems to indicate
(1) that the original copy of Legge's manuscript (L_1) was revised at
least twice (and probably again for production, L_2), and (2)

that Part I of <u>B</u> is derived from the first stage, and <u>C</u> from the final
stage, of the revision. The probability of this theory is illustrated by
the variant readings for line 319 of Act IV, Scene iii, of Part I:
<u>miseram</u>] [<u>MISERAM</u>] <u>C</u>: <u>anhelans</u> <u>DEFGI</u>. <u>Anhelans</u> was most likely the
original reading of the production copy of Legge's play, which reading
Legge, probably for reasons of style or meter, changed in his first
revision to [<u>MISERAM</u>]. The <u>anhelans</u> was likely crossed out and [<u>MISERAM</u>]
inserted above it. Cade, probably for reasons of exaggerated accuracy,
apparently not only copied the correction in an Italian hand but even
left it in brackets. The <u>B</u>-scribe was satisfied with copying the correction in his regular hand. This theory accounts for practically every
case where the Italian hand is observable in <u>C</u>. The stages in Legge's
revision can be seen in the variants in line 89, Act II, Scene i,
of Part I (<u>heu</u>] <u>HEU</u> <u>C</u>; <u>una</u> <u>BDFGI</u>) where <u>una</u>, the original reading,
was left unchanged in the first revision (which explains the presence
of this reading in <u>B</u>), and was finally changed to <u>HEU</u> in the final
revision. Obviously if the theory of revision as presented is correct,
then even in Part I, <u>C</u> should be preferred to <u>B</u> as the basis of our text.

7. <u>Note</u> <u>to</u> <u>the</u> <u>Text</u>

Unless otherwise recorded in the Notes at the bottom of each page
of text, every reading of the text (including punctuation and spelling)
derives from MS. <u>C</u> (Clare College MS.), which is used throughout a copy-
text. Abbreviations in the text of <u>C</u> have been silently expanded.
All words and lines (including the line numbers) not found in <u>C</u> have
been set off in the text in square brackets.

Every emendation to the text is disclosed by a note at the bottom
of the text-page in which it occurs. For example, the emendation in
Part I.i.82 reading "authorem] autorem C; auctorem E" means that the copy-
text (MS. C) read autorem, but was amended to authorem, which reading is
found in all other manuscripts, except E, which has auctorem.

The following procedures were observed whenever an emendation of
the copy-text C was deemed necessary: (1) B was looked to first as a
source of emendation, since B is closest to C in priority of choice of
copy-text; (2) if the B reading was not valid, then a valid reading was
taken from another manuscript, with preference given (in a case where two
or more manuscripts have different valid readings) to the reading that
best fit the context; and (3) if no manuscript provided an acceptable
reading, an editorial emendation was made and duly noted (ed.).

The notes for Parts II and III are slightly different from those of
Part I since only MSS. B and C were completely collated in Parts II and
III. In Part I, the lemma includes all manuscripts not otherwise listed
with readings outside the bracket. In Parts II and III, the lemma reading is always the B reading alone, except when the B reading (along
with the C reading) is rejected. In this case, the other manuscripts
have been consulted for an acceptable reading, and noted thus (Part III,
IV.i.82); meaque] H; meoque BC. When no acceptable reading could be found
in the any manuscript, an editorial emendation has been made and noted
(ed.).

All marginal stage directions found in any of the manuscripts studied
are also given (followed by the manuscript sigla that include them) in
the notes. In every case, a stage direction is reproduced from the first

manuscript listed after it. Other manuscripts noted as having the same
stage direction may have slight variations in spelling and in location.

8. Note to the Translation

In translating, two main objectives were sought, but, because they
were somewhat at cross purposes, could only be imperfectly realized.
One object was to present a translation close enough to the Latin text
to enable a reader with only a slight knowledge of Latin to follow it
readily. The second was to present a translation in a readily understand-
able idiom, and generally free of the awkwardnesses of style that oftentimes mar a literal translation. To approach these opposing objects, a
compromise has been made, which may or may not please the reader, depending on his views of what a translation should strive to accomplish.

Both objectives have to some extent been realized only at the expense of numerous insertions in brackets that too often clutter the page.
To achieve a literal translation, the following insertions were necessary:
(1) words not found in the Latin text but readily understood from the
context or sense of the text; (2) explanatory phrases, generally intro-
duced by i.e.; and (3) brief stage directions when needed to put the
words of a speaker in a proper context. In seeking the second objective,
whenever the literal translation would have been awkward, unidiomatic or
vague, a smoother, more idiomatic, clearer translation has been substituted (insofar as possible without diverging from the text) with the liberal
translation given in brackets headed by lit.

Notes to the translation have been added to supplement both the clarity
and meaning of the translation. Notes are presented in the following in-
stances: (1) whenever quotation from the chronicles on which a passage

or scene is based increases the clarity of the translation; (2) whenever
material in the chronicles is highly pertinent to the composition of a
speech or scene; (3) whenever the understanding of a classical allusion
is necessary for fully understanding the text; and (4) whenever explanatory material is too long to be included in brackets in the text of the
translation.

Thomae Legge legum

Doctoris, Collegii

Caiogoneviliensis,

in Acade-

mia Can-

ta-

brigiensi, magistri

ac rectoris,

Richardus tertius, tragaedia trive-

spera, habita in Coll. Divi

Iohannis Evan-

gelistae

Comitiis Baccholaureorum

Anno. 1579.

Anthonius   Cadus

Descripta ex Autoris autographo, A. Cadi manu

~~Impressum U.C.~~   1582   Ianuariis Calendis.

Richardus tertius

Tragedia in tres actiones divisa

Dramatis personae.

Elizabeth regina.

Cardinalis archiepiscopus Cantuariensis.

Nuncius.

Edwardus rex quindecim annorum.

Dux Glocestrensis, postea Richardus rex

Dux Buckinghamiae.

Riverius

Hastingus

Stanleius

Howardus postea dux Norfolciensis $\left.\right\}$ Barones

Lovellus

Episcopus Eliensis

Ancilla reginae.

Catsbeius juris peritus.

Howardus equestris ordinis.

Servus ducis Gloc.

Servus regis.

Hastingus prosecutor vulgo pursevaunt.

Civis londiensis.

Chorus tumultuantium civium.

Satelles

Archiepiscopus Eboracensis.

Praetor Londiensis

Chorus procerum tumultuantium

Serviens ad arma. vulgo serveaunt ad armes.

Nuncius

Chorus civium Londinensium

Fitzwillium Recordator Lond. vulgo recorder.

Doctor Shawe.

Civis primus.

Civis secundus.

Hospes

Servi duci Buck.

Civis amicus Shai.

Filia major Edw. regis

Brackinburius praefectus arcis.

Tirellus gener.

Ludovicus medicus.

Anna regina

Nuncius 1

Nuncius 2

Nuncius 3

Hungerforde $\left.\right\}$

Burchier $\left.\right\}$ equestris ordinis.

Miles.

Dominus Straunge.

Centurio

Braa servus.

Dighton Carnifex.

Muti

Richardus dux Eboracensis.

Graius heros adolescens.

Vaghannus.

Conjunx Shori.

Hawt equestris ordinis.

Sacerdos

Quinque filiae Elizabethae reginae.

Actio Prima

Argumentum primae actionis

Edwardus quartus rex Anglorum obiit:

His duos reliquis filios, quorum

Edwardus major nata princeps Walliae

annos habebat quindecim:

alter Richardus dux Eboracensis undecimum   [5]

vitae annum egit. Richardus dux

Glocestriae frater Edwardi defuncti

homo nimia ambitione elatus, cum

nepotis teneram adhuc aetatem viderat,

facile ad regnum sibi aditum   [10]

patere putat. Itaque primum Reginae per

amicos persuadet, ut Edwardi iter

nullo milite armaret, dum Londinum

e Wallorum finibus properaret.

Interim ipse clam cum amicis communicat   [15]

quantum inde periculum sibi

crearetur si regis tenelli tutela, solis

reginae propinquis demandaretur.

Oui dum caeteris heroibus inviderent,

facile in eorum perniciem, regis nomine abuti possent.   [20]

Itaque Riverium virum nobilem regis avunculum

et Graium fratrem ejus uterinum a rege ipso avulsum

in vincula conjecit. Qui nec ita multo post

Pontefracti capite plectuntur, regem ipsum tutor

a senatu illustri declaratus, in suam tutelam accipit.   [25]

Porro a Regina quae tum ad asylum metu confugerat

Ducem Eboracensem parvulum per Cardinalem

Archiepiscopum Ebor nihil tum suspicantem abstulit.

ubi regios pueros in arce, tanquam in carcere conclusisset

primum Hastingum nobilem virum, quod nimis eum   [30]

studere nepotibus suspicaretur, injuste damnatum

morte afficit. Cardinalis Episcopus Eliensis, Stanleius

heros in carcerem detruduntur, ne quid inceptis suis

obstarent, quod eorum fidem erga regulos pertimesceret

Postremo Shori conjunx quoniam morte eam damnare   [35]

non poterat, tanquam meretrix infami pena afficitur.

Primae actionis personae.

Elizabetha regina

Cardinalis

Nuncius

Edwardus rex

Dux Gloc

Dux Bucking

Riverius

Hastingus

Stanleius   Barones

Howardus

Lovellus

Episcopus Eliensis

Ancilla reginae

Catsbeius

Howardus equestris ordinis

Servus ducis Glocestrensis

Hastingus prosecutor.

Civis Londinensis.

Chorus tumultuantium civium

Chorus procerum tumultuantium

Archiepiscopus Ebor

Satelles

Serviens ad Arma

Nobilis

Muti

Rich. dux Ebor.

Graius heros

Vahannus

Hawt. equ.

Sacerdos

Quinque filiae Eliz reginae

Actus primus

[I.i] Elizabetha regina, Cardinalis, Nuncius

Regina Quicunque laetis credulus rebus nimis

confidit, et magna potens aula cupit

regnare; blandum quaerit is malum, licet

magnam nihil sperare generosum genus

jubebat, Edwardi tamen regis thoro   [5]

conjuncta sum, postquam tuos thalamos mihi

generose Graie triste fatum sustulit.

dulci venemo gestiebam credula.

et rapuit altis inclytus titulis honos

donec meum apernebat abjectum genus   [10]

cognatus heros regis, et tristem meis

Inimicus affinis parabat exitum

his cura, major filii, quod traditur

et regium curat nepotem avunculus.

Velui meos regi propinquos jungere   [15]

comites, ut animis altius primis amor

hereat: tenera dum surgit aetas grandior.

---

12 Inimicus] inimicis CE; inimicis > inimicus B; inimicis > amicis A

16 animis] annis DFGHI; annis > animis (in margin) C; animis > annis A

17 tenera] tenere ABCEHGI

nec tristis hac contenta peste sors fuit.

prius malum majoris est gradus mali.

Exhalat aegrotum maritus spiritum   [20]

et fata rumpunt regis impia manu

saevae sorores, invident virum mihi.

mortale fatis luditur genus. sibi

spondere quicquam non potest tam stabile,

fortuna quod non versat anceps, sordida   [25]

manet domus tantum beata, dum timet

virtus ruinas magna. postquam duplici

mater sobole ditata sum, regis domum:

petebat haeredem remota Wallia,

nec principe libenter suo gens Cambria   [30]

carebat: hinc iter properat huc filius,

brevis ordo comitatur meorum, ut cingerent

regale diademate caput, matrem licet

gaudere laeta sceptra cogunt filii:

at gaudium sperare promissum sibi   [35]

mens avida non audet, timet adeptum bonum,

metumque parturit semel natus metus,

---

31 properat] properabat CE: properabat > properat B; pro< >p< >rabat
    A

multisque curis pectus urit anxium.

Sin filiis externa vis adhuc nihil

minetur infidum, nec extortum sibi [40]

regnum, domus Lancastriae Edwardo invidet,

nec rapta quondam sceptra victrici manu

pati potest. adhuc tamen domesticus

premit timor magisque formidat nefas

animus malis assuetus: et vario tremor [45]

mentem tumultu, spesque laceram distrahit.

Infaustus o regni favor multis, suam

conversus in poenam ruit, postquam diu

falso viros splendore lusit credulos.

Cardinal Regina praecellens Elizabetha caput [50]

curas cur anxio revolvis pectore

et publicum luctu tuo oneras gaudium?

quin sperne mentis turbidae ludibria,

matrisque tristes laeta deme spiritus:

dum filii caput corona cingitur. [55]

Regina Sacrum caput praestans honore cardinis

Insignis archipresal atque Cantii

nescire quenquam miserias miserum magis.

quod tempus vnquam lachrymis caruit mihi?

Non regis Edwardi gemo diram luem,   [60]

odiumve triste plango demens heroum,

vetus hoc malum: cum Walliam linquens suam

stipatus armato rediret milite,

ut regna patris jure possideat suo,

Edwardus haeres: sermo multoram frequens   [65]

aures fatigat, nec monere desinit,

nullis ut armis sepiat princeps iter,

se subditis committeret nudum suis.

sin clauderet milite suo regis latus,

stipata regem sola Graiorum domus,   [70]

timere cum mali nihil princeps potest:

mox in suam armari necem tot milites

proceres putabunt: nuper extinctae minae

facile fidem dabunt, et vulnera recrudescere

sanata male mox suspicantur: ergo dum   [75]

sese timent objicere inermes hostibus:

ferro simul vitam tuentur illico.

---

67 sepiat]   saeviat (crossed out; forsan sepiat in margin) C
         muniat F

Belli furore totum invndabit solum

Calcante tellus equite terrendum gemet

belli tumultu ardebit insana Anglia   [80]

statimque armoris faedus ictum frangitur.

tum perfidum multabit authorem scelus,

paenasque pendet lapsa Graiorum domus.

primum per artus gelidus excurrit metus.

tandem suis tremebunda monitis animo   [85]

mox literis edico cuncta fratribus.

ut milite nullo filii cingant latus

Pompaque magna regis exonerent iter.

Ubi sola secretos sagax repeto metus,

nova cura mentem concutit formidine,   [90]

ne praeda nudis offeratur hostibus.

Ingens domum nostram invidia premit, furit

ambitio, nullam caeca dum maculam timet.

se medica non tuetur aetas filii.

fratri suo mortem intulit Glocestrius: [95]

quomodo nepoti ambitio parcet patrui?

Cardinal   Cesset timere matris infaelix amor.

---

82 authorem] autorem C; auctorem E

vanosque desine falsa mentiri dolos.

Injustus est rerum aestimator dolor.

Nunquid juvat terrere vano pectora   [100]

tremore? pessimus augur in malis timor

semper sibi falso minatur, et suam

vocat ruinam, quamvis ignotam prius.

proceres sepultis morte regis litibus

longam quietem consecrarunt: nec minas   [105]

veretur extinctas sanata Britannia.

Odia movebit nova rebellis, qui timet

priora.

Nuncius   Medium rex iter sospes tenet.

Regina   Quae filium nunc detinet fessum via?

Nuncius   Bis sera stellifero excidit coelo [dies]   [110]

Northamptonem [cum] fessa membra tangerent.

Regina   Et quanta turba regium claudit latus?

Nuncius   Ubi Walliae mutaret accelerans sedes,

frequens satelles sepiebat principem

illique multos junxit assiduus labor.   [115]

postquam tuas Riverius [heros] litteras

---

110 [dies]] dies omitted (metrical notation for two short syllables
                appear in blank space where dies should be; in margin is
                notation syllaba deest) C; dies omitted A
111 [cum]] cum omitted (apparently notation syllaba deest found in the
                margin between lines 110-111 is meant to refer to this omission
                also, for a blank space is left between Northampton and fessa)
                C; cum omitted A

114 sepiebat] seniebat C; san< >ebat E

116 Riverius [heres] literas] Riveriaras litteras C; Riveriarias literas
                         A; Riverius literas DF; Riverias
                         litteras > Riverius litteras E

13

coepisset,: omni milite corpus principis

Nudavit, vnus commigrat Riverius,

suo junctus Graius heros patruo.

Regina   Dux obviam Glocestrius regi fuit?   [120]

Nuncius   Is literis regi salutem nunciat.

Regno suo praecatur aeternum decus:

multaque prece commune gaudium beat,

honore praestans dux Buckinghamiae.

Affatur officiis iisdem principem,   [125]

Regique promittunt brevi comites fore.

Seribit frequens Riverio Glocestrius,

Invisit et Graium nepotem literis

benigne pollicetur omnia: nunciis

et pars fatigat magna nobilium simul.   [130]

Regina   Postquam favor flatu secundo vexerit

ratem procul: reliquit idem languidus

alto mari, multisque jactat fluctibus.

Res prosperae, si quando laetari jubent,

rursus revolvor in metus, nec desinit   [135]

animus pavere, laeta quamvis cerneret.

Cardinal Facile sinistris credit auguriis timor.

Regina   Nihil sapit, quisquis parum doctus sapit.

Cardinal Hoc facile credunt, quod nimis miseri timent.

Regina   Quisquis cavet futura, torquetur minus. [140]

Cardinal Sperare virtus nunquam magna desinit.

Regina   Quo plura speras falso, turbaris magis.

Cardinal Terrent adhuc sopita nobilium odia?

Regina   Veterata non sanantur illico vulnera.

Cardinal Sancivit icta morte princeps foedera. [145]

Regina   Cum principe mori dubia quaerunt foedera.

Cardinal Privata vincit odia communis salus.

Regina   Privata publicam quietem destruit

ambitio:

Cardinal   Semper esse num miseram juvat?

Regina   Timere didicit quisquis excelsus stetit, [150]

Rebusque magnis alta clauditur quies.

Auro venenum bibitur, ignotum casae

humili malum, ventisque cunctis cognita

superba summo tecta nutant culmine.

---

149 miseram] miserum <u>ABC</u>

Actus secundus

[II.i] Richardus dux Glocestr.:   Henric. dux Buckingham
            Riverius heros, Hastingus heros

Glocestr. Riverianae splendor et decus domus,

Custos pupilli regis, heros nobilis,

qualis cruentae matris eripiens minis

Electra fratrem servat in regnum patris:

Talis nepotem Wallicis tutans agris,   [5]

reddis suae incolumem fidelis patriae,   [6]

en tibi suum gratulatur Anglia principem,   [6a]

et restitutum dulce pignus patriae.   [6b]

populus tuam frequens fidem merito sonat,   [7]

En gratus hic toti labor Brittanniae.

et nos pares persolvimus grates tibi.

castos labores Wallicae norunt sedes,   [10]

curam parem regis fatetur longum iter,

postquam suo Wallia carebat principe,

ac ubi suum mundo diem reparat coma

radiante Titan, et leves umbras fugat:

eras principis jungemur et lateri simul   [15] qua ducitur recta Stonistratfordiam.

Primo die celeri gradu properabimus,

quod nunc locus proceres tot vnus non capit.

River   O Claudiani rector illustris soli,

dux inclyte et generis propago regii: [20]

praestare regi jussit officium meum,

fortuna quicquid nostra praeclaram dedit,

ponenda bello est vita regi debita,

si modo aliter nequeunt minae frangi hostium.

vestrae quia mensae patebant mihi dapes   [25]

hac nocte, vobis jure multum debeo.

jam laxat artus languidos gratus soper,

lectoque fessa membra componi juvat.

placidam quietem noctis opto proximae.

Glocest.   Praeclare dux, et stella Buckinghamiae,   [30]

cui cervus olim nomen haud latens dedit,

et orte claro Hastinge patrum stemmate

en sol vocata nocte fraenos deserens,

sudore fumantes jubas mersit salo

vacuumque caelum Luna perlustrat, viris   [35]

silentium imperans, nitida simul cohors

comitatar, aspergens lumen vagum polo,

porro locus omni liber arbitrio vacat

secretas aures nullus exhibet comes.

Annon vides quam sit miser procerum status? [40]

Diuque spreta ut nobilis virtus jacet?

Regi licet sanguine superbo jungimur,

clarisque lucet inclytum titulis genus,:

aditus tamen mihi nullus ad regem patet,

vetantque cum nepote patruum vivere. [45]

quo tanta matris cedit impudentia?

Iam faeminae succumbit Anglorum decus.

en nostra dubitatur fides, sepultus est

debitus honor, spretusque sanguis nobilis

sordescit, olim matris omnino suae [50]

tutela regis sacra cognatis datur.

Illis honore quando tamen haud cedimus,

et in nepotem aequalis elucet fides.

Parum decebat matris abjectum genus

regni thoros (amor nisi quod impulit) [55]

52cedimus] credimus C; credimus > cedimus AE

claros negare patruos regi suos

minusque nobili comite circumdare

Parum decorum principi aut nobis erit

comes magis potentior tuebitur

quod nos malum manet, si qui male   [60]

nobis precantur, regiumque claudant latus

primosque praeveniant amores principis,

ut illius favore consenescerent.

quocunque mens tenella flectitur statim

atque pueros fucata demulcent leves,   [65]

seris nec animis respuunt, quicquid prius

placet in amores deliciasque pristinas

aetas probat decursa, nec se   corrigit.

Edwardus olim quartus (aetas plenior

quamvis fuit tempusque longum plurima   [70]

serae noverca disciplinae suaserat)

heu multa quondam facta damnavit suae

lapsum priorem nec resarsit tardior

sensus, quod heros sensit (heu) Clarentius

Ille ille novit (heu) nimis, frater meus   [75]

---

58 nobis]   vobis ACE

62 praeveniant]   praeveniunt ACEG;   praeveniempt D;   perveniant F;
                    praevenient H

74 Clarentius]   Clarentus ACG

quam conjugi rex cessit olim credulus.

nimis heu nimis tum nostra suadebant mala

Quod vxor horreat, maritus quem colat.

quam dura nostras sors premebat res diu?

regina quantam mihi creasset tum luem   [80]

perfida, malum mens nisi sagax averterit?

nos ille caelum qui sua torquet manu,

durisque flammis triste vindicat scelus

faelix potenti liberavit dextera.

heu quot brevi frater furore concitus,   [85]

dolis eorum morte damnatos truci

perdidit, inani voce pulsantes Jovem?

nunquam suo parcebat ira sanguini.

stragi suorum (heu) propinquos addidit.

sed vetera plangimus. Novum imminet malum   [90]

nam si tenello solus haeret principi

communis hostis, atque stipabit thronum

infesta nobis una Graiorum domus

mox hostium vires caput nostrum luet,

dum principis sacrato abuti nomine   [95]

audebit ad nostram ruinam atrox domus

---

84 potenti] POTENTI C

89 (heu)] HEU C; una BDFGI

hoc Jupiter tam providus pater vetet.

quod morte sanxit sacra pacis faedera

Edwardus et veteri medetur vulneri

quietis, atque dexteras nos invicem   [100]

coniunximus simulata pacis pignora,

valuit potestas sacra regis tum magis,

quam pace ficta dubia procerum faedera.

pactumque jussu principis percussimus

quemquam ne tantus vexat insanum stupor,   [105]

huic credat ut demens, repente qui novus

ex hoste tam vetusto amicus sumitur?

firmius inhaerebit brevis mensis favor

quam longa multis invidia lustris manens?

nunc ergo mutare consilium decet.   [110]

quo longius serpit malum fieri solet

robustius, viresque semper colligit.

Bucking. O Claudiane rector, atque regia

de stirpe princeps, turbido infaelix quia

visa est tumultu ardere rursus Anglia,   [115] et bella coeperunt fremere civilia:

tuae ut secreto instillet auri murmure

concepta jussi verba servulum meum

tua signa Buckinghamiam sequi ducem.

miscere praesens verba praesenti diu   [120]

quaerebam ut haec tecum possem loqui simul.

Regina nobis insolens abutitur

statim premi scelus decet, majus nefas

parit semel natum malum, et nescit modum.

sanare te regni luem tantam decet.   [125]

Quidvis ferent potius potens procerum cohors,

cruore quam regina nostro luderet,

gnatumque caput armaret in nostrum ferox.

Gloc· Te patriae (dux) ergo vindicem voco,

et scelere materno labantis Angliae,   [130]

te te poli qui jura praecipitis regis,

et vos coruscum testor agmen celitum:

tantum Britonum pristinum quero decus.

Arcis gravi medela confert vulneri.

Regina nunc abest, suis affere opem   [135]

---

120 miscere] misceri AC;   misceri > miscere E

captis nequit, removere jam tuto licet

a rege cunctas patriae labes suas.

quin dormientem comprimere Riverium

intraque tecta claudere hospitem decet.

sin fugerit: tum conscium probat metus. [140]

mox famule illius petas claves domus,

qua nuper hospes se Riverius abdidit.

sin abnuantur, regis imperium urgeas.

nec ullus inde servus erumpat foras

sed sedulo claudantur intus singuli. [145]

nostrisque verbis admone clam servulos

horreret admisse licet non dum die

nox atra, nostrum sepiant corpus tamen

quod luce prima nos nepotem adibimus.

Buck Regis propinquos si coerces vinculis [150]

caecoque captos claudis audax carcere,

illico tumultum plebs ciebit mobilis

Juditia dum non recta sortiris reis

Et criminis parum nocentes arguas.

Gloc Et dignitatem principis laedunt sui [155]

---

137 cunctas] cuntos ACEHI

     labes] labem CEH;   lubem A

146 admone clam] admone iam clam AC;   advove clam D

et nobilem violare sanguinem student,

lacerare querunt Angliam discordiis

sancti senatus quamvis, et jussa patrum   [157a]

longa Britonum classe sulcavit mare

Marchio Graiorum frater in nostram necem

tot milites armare crudelis potest   [160]

profundere atque principum longas opes.

Hasting   At vinculis si patruum premi suum

heros videbit Graius, is rapida manu

stipabit Edwardum, tremens Britannia

parabit arma, seditio miseros trahet.   [165]

ardore belli conflagrabunt omnia

nostraque populus strage purgabit scelus.

Glocestr Aditus viarum munit assiduus vigil

perrumpat hinc ut nemo Northamptoniam

nostrumque prius ad regem iter praeverteret.   [170]

postquam leves discussit umbras Lucifer,

nitidaque jubebit fugam phebea fax,

nos statuimus regem priores visere,

ut grata principi fides sic luceat.

---

161 profundere] perfundere C

Buck   Intende nervos virium, vinci nequit   [175]

generosus ardor mentis et nullus labor

curam fatigat anxiam summi ducis,

nunquam fidem fallam.

Hasting   Polus tristi prius

Jungetur orco, sydera natabunt aquis,   [180]

amicus ignis fluctibus saevis erit,

vincet diem nox: quam meam damnes fidem.

River   Nescio quid animus triste praesagit malum

horrent timore membra, cor pavet metu.

demiror, hi claves quid hospitii petant.   [185]

quae tanta cecidit temporum mutatio?

ultro prioris noctis onerabant dape.

an jam retentum morte mulctant improba?

mihi sunt amici non amat fucos fides.

vacillat animus, haeret, haud placet sibi.   [190]

si fugio: nullus est fugae tutus locus.

si lateo: sceleris conscius demens ero.

en animus ullos innocens negat metus,

manere certum est, quicquid eveniet, feram.

       Duces adibo: causa quae sit audiam.   [195]

Glocest O regis hostis, impium atque audax caput,

       tu nobiles mulctare suppliciis studes,

       et insolentes seminas discordias.

       tu principis nutum ad necem nostram vocas,

       tuisque demens regna misces litibus.   [200]

       praestabis istud credis infandum nefas?

River   Praeclare princeps tale de me nil putes

       hoc absit (ero) crimen a nostra fide.

Glocest Tale scelestum regis exitium tui.

       patiemur ultro sanguinem nostrum peti?   [205]

       perdes Britonum solus excelsum decus?

       at vos atro mulctate raptum carcere

       comitesque nostrum caeteri cingant latus.

River   Quo me trahitis? quam jubet paenam potens

       fortuna? quae nunc me manent miserum mala?   [210]

       si morte mulctent, jure damnent publico.

       num quae salutis spes relinquitur mihi?

---

211 morte]   forte ACE;   forte > morte H

[II.ii] Edwardus rex, Dux Bucking
dux Glocestr. servus regis

Edwardus Amore captus patriae praeceps iter

quamvis facio, dum Wallicas muto sedes:

lubens tamen relinquo Stonistratfordiam

quod huc ferunt properare Glocestrium

quoniam tot unus non capit proceres locus.   [5]

Bucking Cinctus suis Edwardus huc confert gradum.

generosa quos beant avorum stemmata

praeite, plebei sequantur ordines.

Glocest Rex vivat aeternum Britannia inclitus

Edward Gratus mihi conspectus est mi patrue.   [10]

postquam sedes modo barbaras mutavimus

habeoque tantis gratiam votis parem.

Bucking Tibi beatum firmet imperium deus.

Edward Tuam simul laudo fidem dux inclite.

Gloc   Natura me tuis fidelem jussibus   [15]

nescia resisti consecravit, et dolos

genus struere regale me regi vetat.

Cum caeteris commune persuadet fidem

officium. aquas inimicus ignis incolet,

sulcabit astra navis, et saevo mari [20]

ignota quercus surget, oblitum tui

si quando falsa corrumpet fides.

vitam tuis ponam libens bellis, tuis

infestus hostibus mori cupio pie.

Quae te superbe Grai, vel fratrem tuum [25]

ambitio tenet, et Riverium ferum,

dum principem vobis studetis subdere?

atque proceres faedo tumultu scindere,? [27a]

en, pessimis miscetis Anglos litibus.

florensque deridetur ortus sanguinis

Cur usque Dorsetti minatur Marchio [30]

nobis? in arcem irrupit audax Belini

praedatur inde regis opes rapida manu

et classe longum oneravit ingenti salum.

Edwardus   Quid Marchio patravit uterinus mihi

nescio, fides suspecta avunculi mei [35]

Graiique fratris (crede mihi) nunquam fuit.

Gloc   Imo tuas tanti latent aures doli

rex inclite, secretum magis pugnat scelus.

---

33   salum]   solum AC;   satum I

34   uterinus]   ulterius ABC; ulterias > ulterius E;   Dorsettus I

```
              te perduellionis esse aio reum

              sceleste Grai teque sceleris conscium              [40]

              Vaghanne nuncio, proditorem patriae

              perfide voco Hawt, simul squallenti carcere

              abdite statim, patriae graves paenas luant.
Servus regis  Puerum misellum.  lachrymis rigat genas,

              tristia videns ad vincula correptum fratrem        [45]
Glocestrius   Te liberamus serve famulatu tuo,

              nec te volumus haerere lateri principis,

              tu principi fidelis astabis comes?

              regique te perpetuus adjunget labor?


       [II.iii]  Servus regis, servus ducis Glocestrensis

Servus regis  Regni paterni pondus imbellis puer

              non sustinet, suisque victus viribus

              tandem ruit, tuetur hostes impie

              munita nomine sacra majestas suo

              parare dum tristem luem clam cogitat              [5]

              ambitio. regni parva suspecti fides.
```

---

41 Vaghanne] vahame <u>CHI</u>;   vahanne <u>ADE</u>;   vahanme <u>F</u>;   vaghame <u>G</u>

 2 suisque] quisque <u>ACE</u>;   tuisque <u>H</u>

 3 impie] IMPIE <u>C</u>;   intimos <u>DFGI</u>

nec principem sinit anxiam quiescere

secreta soli pugna, qui loco manet

minore tutior, nec amissi premet

sceptri metus, vel dissimilis avorum honor.   [10]

Qui clara torques sydera altitonans pater,

tuisque pingis ignibus caeli globos:

Britanniae potens defende principem.

ut jura verus reddat haeres Angliae.

Quis huc minister advolat celeri pede?   [15]

quo nunc adeo generose praecipitas gradum?

Servus Gloc Misit nepoti nobilis Riverius.

Regis Ser   Ducine tu minister illi carceris?

Gloc ser   Ego Claudiano fidus astabam comes,

Regis Ser   (Quorsum nepoti nuncius patrui venis?)   [20]

Gloc Ser   Ubi mordet impransum fames Glocestrium

ducis onerabant lauta mensam prandia,

oculis pererrat sedulus cunctas dapes,

misitque selectos cibos Riverio.

animoque ferre jussit aequo singula.   [25]

nil rebus illius esse formidabile.

---

15 minister] injuste ACE

18 Ducine] duri ne C;   duci ne DE;   dur< >e > durne H

    illi] ille CE

22 lauta] tanta ACEH;   tanta > lauta G

Regis servus Num respuit benigna demens munera?

Gloc servus   Quem longus usus ferre persuasit malum,

               fortuna quoties dura tristis intonat:

               vitae cupit solamen afflictae minus.   [30]

               ubi gratias pleno refudit pectore,

               Deferre Graio lauta jussit fercula,

               quem fregerat non cognitus prius dolor,

               nec asperos didicit minor casus pati

               ut blanda fractum verba confirment ducis,   [35]

               et turbidam permulceant mentem dupes.

               at jussa me tanti viri decet exequi.

Regis servus An fronte simulatus latet blanda dolus

               ut imperitis alta figat vulnera?

               an forte nos mutata faelici beat   [40]

               fortuna, miseros carceris solvens metu?

               faustus cadet tantis procellis exitus.

---

28 usus] < >osus C

32 lauta]   tanta CEHI

39 imperitis] imperitus CH; imperitus > imperitis E

Actus Tertius

[III.i] Ancilla reginae, Regina, Archiepiscopus Eboracensis*

Ancilla Qui vindices sceleris potens torques manu,

mitisque rebus collocas fessis opem:

miserere jactatae Eboracensis domus,

quis est malorum finis? heu, heu quam diu

regina vitam luctibus diris gravat?   [5]

quae possidet ferox Alecto regiam?

tortos vel angues Megaera crudelis vibrans?

luctumque majorem prior luctus vocat.

et vix malis regina tantis sufficit

quis per me auras turbo raptam devehet   [10]

ne tot misera tristes querelas audiam

mestae domus, luctusque matris lugubres?

Arch Eb Non dum fugata nocte sol reparat diem

nec deserit fratri vices phaebi soror

vel pulsa caelo contrahit lumen vagum.   [15]

nox sera, quorsum noctis umbris parere,

quaeris,? celere solamen immensum malum

desiderat: aeger non patitur animus moras,

---

*In the margin beside the list of characters at the start of this act, G has the following stage direction: deducta scena appareat Regina (velut in Asylo) cum 5 filiabus, et ancillis, sacris et insidentes.

  6 Alecto] [ALECTO] C; (Alecto) AE;   Erinnis DFGI

 15 caelo] caelum AC

 16 s.d.: Let his servants be about him with swordes. BDFG

mentem placare turbidam matris para

sed quis tumultus,? turba quanta regiae [20]

Effare tanti nocte strepitus quid velint?

Ancilla Splendens honore antistes Eboracensium

diros tibi renovare me casus jubes?

postquam soporem Luna fessis suaserat

et caeca nox horreret amisso die: [25]

Increpuit aula, vinculis Riverium

duris praemi, et Graium nepotem, tum locus

quis principem capiat, tenere neminem.

postquam paterent tanta reginae mala,

animus tremore concitus subito stupet [30]

solvuntur heu labante membra spiritu.

postquam trementes misera vires colligit,

en talibus mox astra pulsat vocibus:

O dura fata parcite. heu quid volvitis?

quantum scelus spiratis? an poena placent? [35]

in hoc caput jaculare vindices faces

Irate pater, innocens quid admisit puer?

quid meruit? parvus quid infans perditur?

una ruina concutis totam domum.

---

20 s.d.: Let them be knocking in the palace as removinge BDFG

35 spiratis] spiraris C

non sustinet labante mox cello caput   [40]

largo madescunt imbre perfusae genae,

cor triste magnis aestuat doloribus,.

cultum decorum, regias vestes procul

removet et eximii rubores muricis.,

quieta nunquam constat, huc, illus fugit.   [45]

telli jubet iterumque poni corpora:

et semper impatiens sui status, cito

mutatur, et coelum querelis verberat.

nunc filium gemit, suorum nunc luem.

curamque seram tanta sentiens vulnera,   [50]

dempti satellitis reclamat anxia

mox illa asylo purpuram, servos jubet,

aurumque fulvum capere; suppellectilem

et quas habebat regia excelsas opes.

et ne leves obsint morae vehentibus: [55]

hinc brevior ut pateret ad templum via:

interna jussit perforare moenia,

regis qua asylo clauditur palatium.

Charumque demens filium tenens sinu

et quinque mater filias vocans, fugit   [60]

---

50 sentiens] sensiunt AC; sentiunt DEFGHI

51 reclamat anxia] [RECLAMAT ANXIA] C; (reclamat anxia) AEH; reclamat
                  anxia omitted DFGI

55 vehentibus] vehementibus ACE; vehe< >entibus H

sacras ad ades, interim tremens metu;

qualis leonis faucibus vastis premi

fugiens timet, dum praeda pascitur, fera.

Regina   Eboracensis urbis excellens pater,

ergo deesse quid malis nostris potest?   [65]

aut fata vincere nostra quis potuit miser?

frustra timemus, jam timere, quae horruit,

magnae domus heu reliquiae parvae sumus.

tantumque miseros templa tutantur sacra.

durum parant funus propinqui sanguinis,   [70]

nec quis tenet regem locus, servi sciunt.

an non perimus? ulla spes manet domus?

Arch Ebor   Metus remitte, pone curas anxias.

erroris istud omne, quodcunque est malum.

quicquid gravis animos laevat miseros dolor?   [75]

quin mitius de rebus istis cogita.

mihi nuper ubi suadet soporem caeca nox

me suscitat somno sepultum nuncius,

Hastingus heros misit, hic narrat mihi

traxisse Northamptoniae moras duces,   [80]

---

64   s.d.:   The queene sitting on the ground with fardells about hir BDFG

     s.d.:   A curtaine being drawne let the queene appeare in sanctuary, her
             5 daughters and < > maydes about her sittinge en packs, fardells,
             chests, cofers. DEFG

80   duces]   dulces ACH

	ubi subditis stipatus haeret rex suis.	
	pectus nihil quisquam timore luderet,	
	nam cuncta tandem sorte foelici cadent.	
Regina	Ille, ille, nostri durus hostis sanguinis	
	Hastingus, ille principi exitium parat.	[85]
	En vindices mater deos supplex precor	
	dirum caput flammis nefandis obruant.	
Arch. Eb.	Laxa furentis turgidos animi motus,	
	et siste prudens impetus mentis graves.	
	testor deorum numen astra qui sua	[90]
	torquet manu, si filium praeter tuum	
	quenquam coronant, proximo statim die	
	fratri huic suo decora regni insignia	
	trademus; en magnum sigillum nunc tibi	
	(quod mihi tuus quondam maritus detulit)	[95]
	reddam, tuo quem nunc tueris filio.	
	Archiepiscopus Eboracensis.	
	Rector potens Olimpi, et altitonans pater,	
	ergo placidam sana quietem patriae.	
	ut tractet haeros sceptra puerili manu	

---

87 obruant] obruat ACEH

ne dura regnum poena victori caedat,   [100]

bellique spem fingant novam Lancastriae,

dum caede se litabit hostis impia,

sed quid facis? quae mentis oblivio capit?

cuiquam ne te magnum sigillum tradere?

cui detulisti? foeminae? quin semper fuit   [105]

Invisa, tum fidem duces ludent tuam,

dum magna regni cura temere proditur,

num foeminae credis? facile resistitur,

et in tuum vis saeviat solum caput.

nunc ergo mittam qui sigillum clam petet,   [110]

ut non meum duces levem damnent fidem.

[III. ii] Servus Gloc. Chorus procerum tumultuatium.
          Archiepiscopus Ebor. Hastingus heros.

Servus [Gloc.] Jam quamlibet defendit excubitor viam,

              totamque densae Tamesim sulcant rates,

              ut nemo perrumpat ad Asylum profugus

              nil Claudiane dux sacram metuas fugam

---

101 Lancastriae] Lancastria ACH; Lancastriae > Lancastria E

107 temere] timere CH;   timere E

	quin matris ad templa surripiunt opes.	[5]
	quos hic tumultus concitatis improbi?	
	quo pellit insanos Elizabethae furor?	
Chorus procerum	Urbs, urbs, (cives) ad arma, ad arma,	
	en arma doliis vehuntur abdita,	
	quibus necem ducibus rebelles clam parant.	[10]
	quodnam malum tantus tumultus parturit?	
	Onerata navigiis Tamesis horruit aqua,	
	Regina fugiens arma simul multa vehit	
	quidnam parat regina Crudelis malum?	
	at arma servent, si minentur non vehant	[15]
	dii foeminae tam triste vindicent nefas.	
	At te deus pusille princeps muniat.	
Arch Ebor.	Regni potentis nobilis procerum cohors	
	an rumor audax credulos ludit [metus]	
	Spargens novos: vel crescit in luctus vetus,	[20]
	malum? furensque repetit agnitum prius	
	ambitio thronum, et poscit in praedam sibi?	
	praeceps moras tumultus haud patitur leves,	
	supplex ad aras sternitur mater tremens,	

---

6 s.d.: Certaine come in with harnesse and other cariage like porters.
         BDGH

11 s.d.: Some of these are armed some unarmed or half armed. BDGH

19 [metus] metus omitted ACEH

Regina regnum suspicatur filii [25]

plures atro clauduntur heroes specu,

quorum fides regis tutelam meruit.

imbellis aetas regis admittit nefas

facile, scelusque, concitat quisquis licet

clam rege, at expedere consilium decet [30]

donec quis errat hic dolus patet magis

sed clarus huc Hastingus advolat mihi.

Hastingus   Non vos latebat chara civium cohors?

Rex me quibus complexus est amoribus

arctius, et ejus colere chara pignora [35]

cogunt benigna tanti regis munera.

quorum nisi vitam mea luerem nece

ingrata faedaret magis nulla nota.

laedi, (doleo) rumore, pacem, futili

varioque turbari Britannos murmure. [40]

hospes video tumultuari subditos.

per tota raptores volantes maenia

quorsum metu vexare vana pectora

Juvat, ora quicquid mentiuntur garrula?

---

29   quisquis] [QUISQUIS] C

30   clam rege at] [CLAM REGE AT] C; sanu statim DFGI

32   mihi] [MIHI] C; (mihi) A; mihi omitted DFGI

35   et] ut CEFGHI

38   nulla] nullum CGH; multu > multo E

40   turbari] turbare ACEF

42   raptores] raptori AC; raptari GH; raptare DF; raptori >
       raptores E

perspecta mihi fides Glocestriae satis fuit.   [45]

en ducit alacri regulum pompa modo ut

tenerum corona cingeret fulva caput.

at dura qui premit proceres custodia;

lacerare probris perfidi Glocestrium

querunt ducem, caecoque frigent carcere   [50]

litem sacratus dum senatus poneret,

vnum precor supplex (patros) sententia

no vestra mentem posteram praeverteret.

ne publico lites vigerent funeri,

ad arma ne vos vir rebellis concitet.   [55]

justissima licet bella suaderi queant,

horum feretur causa semper justior

armis suis quicunque claudunt principem,

dum moenibus regalis adventat puer,

urba principi pacata gratuletur suo.   [60]

[III. iii]   Edwardus rex, Praetor Londinensis

Edwar.   Ubi barbaras sedes mutavimus ferae

gentis, revertor sospes ad patrios lares

urbis superbae clarus hic pollet nitor,

---

48 qui] ed.;   quos ABCDEFGHI

50 frigent] figent CEH;   fingunt A

53 posteram] postera ACEH

regnique splendet majus incliti decus.

Urba clara salve: tanta nunquam gaudia   [5]

post tot ruinas Asiae Argivis nunquam

optata patria regna, et Argolicas opes,

cum bella post tam longa, primi viserent,

vix hospiti tot lustra tam laetum tibi

redditum: licet tantis miser naufragiis   ⌊10⌋

ereptus esset dux Cephalerim parant

quam crescit admissa voluptas patriae

hospes diu postquam carebam, et suos

negavit aspectus longum iter mihi.

Praetor Illustre patriae decus rex inclite   [15]

en laeta profudit cohors se civium

ut gratuletur principi multum suo:

sol nostro ut alter luceas faelix polo

haeresque patris jura Brittannis dares.

civis deum pulsabit anxius prece.   [20]

Edwardus en rex noster, o cives mei,

honore fulgens, regio, en potens puer

chari Britanni, principem videte tuum

virtute praestantem fidelis subdite.

---

11 esset] esses ACDEFGHI

12 quam] quia ACEH

13 carebam] carebas ACDEFGHI

21 s.d.: The kinge is now going about the stage with the wordes, BDEGH

23 videte] ed.;   vides ABCDEFGHI

[IV.i] Actus quartus

Hastingus heros

Regina in aedibus squalens sacris sedet,

duris propinqui comprimuntur vinculis

tutorque declaratus Angliae modo

suffragiis Glocestrius nostris fuit.

magnum sigillum praesuli Eboracensi demitur   [5]

hunc voce multum Claudianus vulnerat

quod prodidit levi sigillum foeminae.

foelix beabit cuncta sors hostes jacent

et Pontefracti jam manent tristem necem.

properate fata, mox graves poenas luant,   [10]

sed quid cesso sacrum senatum visere?

---

7   levi] levae AC

[IV.ii] Richardus dux Gloc. Henricus dux
Buck. Episcopus Ebor. Episcopus Eliensis
Stanleius, Hastingus, Howardus
Lovellus, Barones.

Gloc Illustris e procerum cohors quos Anglia

gens nobilis peperit, nihil tandem movet

tam triste reginae scelus? tantam pati

infamiam, generosa mens adhuc potest?

malitia tam diu latebit foeminae?   [5]

en gnatum asylo inimica captivum tenet,

ut querulo rebellis agitet murmure

proceres Britanniae, atque duris vulneret

verbis, tumultu turba concita quasi fides

incerta tutorum sit anxius, quibus   [10]

Senatus Eborum ducis curam dedit

nec parvulum hostis amotus procul

solum tuetur, aut bene notatus cibus,:

trahunt magis moderata puerum ludicra,

aetas suis equata delitiis placet,   [15]

nunquam seni colludit immixtus puer,

fratrique ludo, frater instabit magis.

solere parvis magna saepe crescere

---

9 concita] concite ACDFHI; cancito E

11 Eborum] Eburum CH

quis nescit? ingens regis esset dedecus

nostramque damnet non levis fidem labes,   [20]

dum fama Gallis profuga obgannit, sacras

quod fugit ad aras principis frater metu.

citius nihil volare maledicto potest,

opinio firmata nec statim perit,

ergo viri mittantur assensu sacro,   [25]

quorum dubia nunquam fides regi fuit,

matri minus suspecta, cognita patriae satis:

ut filium sacro solutum carcere

fratri suo restituat at tuam fidem

tantum negotium requirit, cardinis   [30]

honore praestans archipresul inclyte.

praestare si tua non gravetur sanctitas,

hoc regis ingens flagitat solatium,

salusque fratris certa patriae quies.

sin detinet regina gnatum pertinax,   [35]

nec matris infaelix amor morem gerit:

Suprema regis jussa luctantem premant.

malitia constabit, odium protervia.

quae mentis est opinio vestrae? lubens

---

21 profuga] perfuga BCI; p< >fuga AE;   perfida H

28-29 See Collation, Appendix A.

36 gerit] gerat ACEH

audio, (fovente namque spiritum deo)   [40]

nunquam meos urgebo sensus pertinax:

sed facile flectet savior sententia.

Dux Buck   Quem solitudo principis non commovet?

procerumque deflectens honos, aut patriae

salus diu jactata? dum claustris sacris   [45]

gnatum premit vesana mater, dedecus

ingens puer sejunctus affert principi,

nec tutum erit carcere fratre parvulo.

Vulgus probris futile lacerat improbis

quasi nulla regis cura magnates tenet   [50]

non solum prolis mater ortum vendicat

suisque tantum stulta deliciis putet

nasci: vocat regni decus, patrium statim

curare dulcis matris oblitum jubet

quod melius haec suadere sanctus pater   [55]

antistes excellens potest: assentior.

sin pavida amoris mater ignorat modum

vi filium sibi jubebit eripi.

Hasting   Quorsum sacris haereret parvulus?

fratri triumphum regis aut cur invidet?   [60]

---

52   tantum] tantam C;   tantum or tantam E

56   assentior] assentior > assensior C;   assensio F

60   fratri] fratris ACH

        sin filii tremebunda periculum tremit:

        at hic paternum sepiet frequens genus

        hic a sacro jussus senatu tutor est,

        regemque curabunt amantes subditi

        tum mutuum fratrum vocat solatium.   [65]

        proterva mater si recusat mittere

        [Cardineus] illum praesul ereptum avehat.

Arch Ebor Ut fratris aula fratrem oblectet simul

        aut gratus Angliae meus prosit labor:

        meis recuso aequale viribus nihil.   [70]

        gnatum sacra sin mater aede continet,

        solusque fratrem rex suum non impetrat

        promissa templo jura nunquam rumpere

        tamen decet, sanxisse quod divum Petrum

        primum ferunt, mox prisca firmavit fides,   [75]

        Et longus ordo principum pepegit. bonis

        multis sacra pepercisse pacta constitit.

        Nec ullus Isther audet Alanis feris

        prebens fugam violare nec rigens nive

        tellus perimi hircana, vel sparsa Scytha.   [80]

---

61 tremit] tremet ACE;   timet GH

67 [Cardeneus]] Cardineus omitted ACH;   Cardinis DF

77 multis] multos ACE

80 sparsa] ed.; sparsus ADCDEFGH;   spersus I

nemo sacrilegus diis datam rumpit fidem.

at regulo fratrem dabit matris sinus,

nec filii invidet parens solatio.

sin fratris aula, fratre perpetuo vacet,

et filium mater sacro carcere tenet:

nihil mens damnabitur castus labor,

solusque matris impediet [caecus] amor.

Dux Buck Quin matris impediet magis protervia

audebo vitam pignori deponere.

nullam timoris vel sibi causam putet

vel filio: nemo lubens cum faemina

pugnabit: optarem propinquis muliebrem

sexum simul/: perturbet Angliam minus

quibus odium tantum [proprium] peperit scelus

non quod genus suo trahunt de sanguine,

sin chara nec regina nobis, aut sui

essent propinqui: regis at fratrem tamen

edisse, quid juvat? genus cui nobile

Junxit propinquos, at nisi invisus sibi

honor esset, et minetur infamem notam

[85]

[90]

[95]

[100]

---

81 sacrilegus] sacrilega ACEGH

87 [caecus]] caecus omitted ACEH

88 Quin] quum ACEH

92 muliebrem] muliebre CEI

94 [proprium]] proprium omitted AGH; suum DEF

nobis: suum nunquam negaret filium.

suspecta cui nunquam fides procerum fuit,

suum sibi proceres relinquent filium,

sibi si loco mater decoro manserit.

Dux Gloc   Nunc ergo nobis filium si deneget   [105]

quorum fides sibi satis sit cognita:

Immanis haec erit protervia faeminae,

non frigidae mentis pavor: sin adhuc timet

infausta mater, quae timere umbram potest:

tanto magis cavere matris amor jubet   [110]

suspecta ne furtum sacrum, gnatum suum

ad exteros regina mittat. millies

promissa templo jura praestat frangere:

tantum senatus dedecus quam perferat.

alliique nostrum luderent pulchrum caput   [115]

Spectare qui fratrem cadentem principis

possumus: ergo filium matri suum,

templo solutum vi decebit eripi

me jure simus exteris ludibrio.

nec ego fidem lubens asyli laederem,   [120] cui robur aetas longa tribuit plurimum.

nec primus olim privilegium suum

templis dedissem, arisve nunc paciscerer.

si pertinax in debitores creditor

saeviat, et illis vincula minetur horridus,   [125]

adversa quos fortuna damnavit sibi

oppressit aere aut prodigo alienum mare:

ut corpus ereptum ara tueatur: pium

sane. impiis at civibus, vel furibus,

quos nullus unquam continere metus potest   [130]

sicariisque parcere, annon impium?

sin pacta asylo jura tantum protegunt,

iniqua quos fortuna vexat, furibus

cur sacra? cur sicariis? cur civibus

[nequam patent? abundat (heu) malis sacrum]   [135]

nunquid deus patronus impiis erit?

num jura Petrus ista pepegit furibus?

aliena prodigos rapere pius locus

monet, sibique rapta furto credere

onusta spoliis deserit vxor virum   [140]

---

121 tribuit] [TRIBUIT] C; struxit DEFG

135] This line is omitted in AC.

138 prodigos] prodigus AC; prodigas B; prodigas > prodigos G

ludens maritum furta templo condidit.

erumpit hinc cedi frequens sicarius.

tutumque patrato locum sceleri putat

ergo benigna sacra demi furibus

nec jus asyli violat, et gratum deo   [145]

sanctumque erit, quod pontifex mitis nimis

princepsve pactus est misericors nescio

quis, non satis prudens tamen, quod laederent

nunquam superstitione ducti posteri.

sed sua sacris promissa servemus. nihil   [150]

ducem tamen tuentur inclusum sacra.

Injusta damna jus vetat, natura, lex.

nec principem moramur aut Episcopum

contraque vim quisquis locus tutus satis.

Indulta sacra legis impediant minas   [155]

si dura veniam suaserit necessitas.

At quae premit tristis ducem necessitas?

Regi fidelem regium probat genus

persuadet insontem mali aetas nescia

Cur impetret dux innocens sacram fidem?   [160]

---

145 nec] puer AC;   <purum> H

158 regium] regnum C

Alius sacrum infanti lavacrum postulat

at pacta sacris jura quisquis impetrat

imploret ipse mentis impulsa suae

quid innocens poscat puer?   quid meruit?

matura nunquam ferret aetas carcerem   ⌊165⌋

horreret aras illico iratus puer.

aliena si praedatus huc quis advolat?

corpus tuentur sacra, sed cedet bonis

haec pontifex transferre vel princeps nequit.

Episc. Eliensis Ut pacta templo jura creditoribus   [170]

erepta servent debitorum corpora

acerba quos latere forsan sors jubet

divina lex persuasit. indulgent simul

decreta pontificum sacram miseris fugam

aliena cedant aera creditoribus   [175]

tantum: labore rursus ut crescat suo

curaque damnum reparet assidua prius

carcere solutus debitor excussis bonis

in nuda quis saeviret atrox tergora?

Dux Buck   Probatur haec sane mihi sententia   [180]

---

167 si] sit ACH; sin or sui I

169-170 See Collation, Appendix A.

170 jura] iuera ACH; iuera > iura E

172 quos] quas C

173 indulgent] indigent C

178 excussis] excussus CH; excassus A

uxor vivum linquens ad aras si fugit,

non pace Petri, haec eripi templo Petri

potest? puer lascivus exosus scholae

haeret sacris: hunc paedagogus num sinet?

at is tremit virgum: timebat hic nihil.   [185]

indulta novi sacra viris, pueris nihil.

sit ara consciis patrona dum lubet

huic sacra denegantur pacta, debile

quod nescit ingenium petere, nec integra

merere vita patitur, aut tutus malis   [190]

princeps egere potuit, haud laedit sacra

Is quisquis ut prodesse possit, eximet.

Stanleius Quod expedit regi Britannis Angliae
heros
           ut fratris aula frater una luderet

           haerere posthac mens dubia non potest.   [195]

           mulcere mentem matris opto mollius

           Hunc forte sano ducta consilio dabit

           sin filium proterva mater detinet

           sacrisque deneget parere jussibus

           suo ducem fratri satelles liberet   [200]

---

189 ingenium] ignavum CH; ignavit A

197 forte] sorte C

ludoque puerum armata restituat.

Howardus Concessa matri filii incunabula
heros
   aetasque fluxit ludicra deliciis suis

   nunc chara reliquos poscit annos patria

   quaestus graves matris nihil moror   [205]

   si filium negat solutum carcere

   sacro, fratri illum liberabunt milites.

Gloc.   Uno senatus ore matri nuncium

   te poscit antistes: sacrum jussum expedi

   te presuli comitem Dux Buckinghamiae   [210]

   jungas, et Howarde praestans stemmate

   amoris at si mater haud ponit modum

   natumque nobis surripere demens studet

   mox eximent robusti asylo milites.

   frustraque prolem planget ereptum sibi   [215]

   infausta mater filio et petulans nimis.   [215a]

   Nunc te negotium grave Antistes vocat

   responsa matris proximi morabimur.

---

204 poscit] possit C

215a See Collation, Appendix A.
   s.d.: After they be come downe from theyr seate.   BDEFGHI

[IV.iii] Elizabetha regina. Archiepiscopus Ebor.
Howardus heros.

rch. Ebor. Mater potens, illustre Regina caput,

nunc ore quamvis verba dicantur meo

non esse credas nostra, decrevit frequens

procerum senatus, et Glocestrius simul

protector. ut suadente natura licet   [5]

haereret vno matris amplexu puer

aetasque prima cum parente promptius

versetur: haud sinit tamen regni decus.

maculas honorem filii demens tui

denique suis turbata sedibus pax ruit.   [10]

Britanniae falso dum metu pavida sedes

squalens asylo, si tenetur carcere

conclusus unus frater alter principis,

dulci sui fratris carens solatio:

odium fratrum plebs suspicatur illico   [15]

Sacras ad aedes quod fugit metu puer.

ergo tuum reddas solutum carcere

gnatum. tuos e vinculis sic liberas

et principi magnum creas solatium

---

1   Regina] Rigina C; Reginae EGH

12 squalens] squallens ABCEH

13 unus] ed.; una ABCDEFGHI.

19 et] ut ACH

	et gestiet secura nobilium cohors.	[20]
Regina	Summo galeri honore praecellens pater	
	quod fratris in domo simul fratrem decet	
	manere, non repugno: quamvis tutius	
	uterque dulci matris haereret sinu	
	quorum tenera adhuc timere aetas jubet.	[25]
	et cum minus tuetur aetas junior:	
	tum morbus hunc premebat infestus diu	
	curumque matris grande periculum vocat	
	tantum magis minatur egroto tabes	
	recidiva; nec vulnus secundum fortiter	[30]
	natura prius oppressa fert, vel se satis	
	potest tueri, quam frequens operam dabit	
	matrona scio, quae filium curet meum	
	sedulo, mihi tamen meum decet magis	
	gnatum relinqui, cum melius illum scio	[35]
	nutrire, cujus semper ulnis parvulus	
	haesit, nec illum mellius quisquam potest	
	fovere, quam quae ventre mater sustulit.	
Arch. Ebor.	Negare demens nemo regina, (ah) potest,	

quin filius melius tuae relinquitur   [40]

custodiae, nunc matris amplexu puer

ut vivat, heroum inclyta optaret cohors

simul decoro si maneres in loco

utrique. sin matura vitam consecras

sacris tuam, et posthac pie studet preci   [45]

devota mens,: at fratris aula luderet

frater puer, templo solutus nec sacro

carcere pium matris suae furtum haereat

prudenter ulnis matris eripitur puer

nec usque matris garriet petulans sinu   [50]

infans. Ut aleret saeva regem Wallia,

et barbaros luceret inter filius:

nuper fuit contenta majestas tua.

Regina Contenta nunquam. cura non eadem tamen

tenebat utriusque matrem filii: [55]

jussit nihil timere regis tum salus.

huic membra multo lassa morbo desident,

et vix labantes tollunt artus corporis.

quae tanta gnati cura patruum tenet?

---

51 aleret] alat ACDEFGHI

58 tollunt] ed.; tollit BCDEFGHI; tolli A

si filium immatura fata absorbeant,   [60]

et fila chara avidae sorores amputent:

suspecta mors ducem tamen Glocestrium

reum arguet, nec fraudis effugiet notam.

an laedi honorem regis aut, suum putat,

hoc si loco morabitur tutissimo?   [65]

suspecta nulli unquam fuit asyli fides.

hic incolere cum matre filium sinat:

latere templo tuta decrevi magis,

quam cum meis diri timere carceris

poenas: asylo quos latero nunc malim,   [70]

quam vinculis dedisse vestris dextram.

Howardus   Hos aliquid ergo patrasse nosti conscia?

Regina   Patrasse nec quisquam scio nec vincula

quorsum premant. sed non levis timor fuit

ut qui colorem non morantur carceris: [75]

hi mortis omnem [non] negligant causam simul

Arch. Ebor. Movetur ira: [dice] de suis posthac nihil.

parcet tuis agitata causa judici.

nec tibi minatur aliquis heroum metus.

---

76 [non]] ed.; non omitted ABCDEFGHI

77 [dice]] ed.; dice omitted ABCDEFGHI

Regina   Imo timere quid vetat manus pias,   [80]

                cum vita non tuetur innocens meos.

                an hostibus Regina chara sum magis

                tristis malorum causa quae fui meis?

                matrive parcet juncta regi clara stirps?

                [meos propinquum non minus laudat genus]   [85]

                cum frater hic sit regis ille avunculus.

                quin filius mecum morabitur simul,

                meus nisi aliud solertior persuaserit.

                nam suspicor procerum magis tristem fidem,

                quod absque causa filium avide flagitent.   [90]

Arch. Ebor.   Hoc suspicantur matris at sinum magis,

                ne forte gelidus corde perstringens metus

                ad exteros relegare cogat filium

                sin patruo negare filium juvet

                manus tibi violenta posthac exprimet,   [95]

                Seroque justis pulsa viribus dabis

                non hunc asylo pacta jura muniunt,

                quae nec didicit imbellis aetas poscere,

                et vita nil timere jussit integra.

85] This line is omitted in AC.

95 violenta] violentas CDFGI;   violentas > violenta A;   violent < > H

laedi fidem promissam asylo non putant,   [100]

si filium sacris solutum liberent:

sacramque vim minatur invitae tibi

est talis amor erga nepotem patrui

ut principis turpem fugam tremisceret.

Regina   Amore sic teneri nepotis patruus   [105]

ardebat amens, nil ut horreret magis

quam ne suas pusillus evadat manus

nepos, fugum suadere matrem filio,

putat, tabes cui longa discessum negat?

aut quis tueri filium locus magis   [110]

potest Asylo? quod Caucasus nunquam ferox

Immanis aut violavit olim Thracia.

at sacra mereri innocens nescit puer,

Nunc ergo frustra parvulus templum petit.

praeclara tutoris consulit cavum caput.   [115]

furem tuentur sacra, nequaquam pium.

at parvulus non indiget puer sacris,

cujus timere vita prohibet integra,

metaque vacuum jussit esse nescia

aetas mali. faxit deus tandem, precor,   [120]

---

112 Thracia] Thrasia <u>ACEI</u>   Tharsia <u>H</u>

ut corde pellat jure conceptum metum.

haerere templo turpiter gnatum putat

protector, (at protector horum sit, precor,

nec in suos crudelis hostis saeviat.)

an frater una fratris ut ludat domo?   [125]

luscisse morbus jam vetat tristis diu,

pestisque languens: an deesse parvulo

possunt, quibuscum prima gestit ludere

aetas, pares honore nisi dentur modo?

regum superbo juncti atque sanguine?   [130]

quorum minus concors ea esse aetas solet.

falso sibi promittit illustris cohors

fratrum duorum mutuum solatium

ludit sui secura juris aemula

natura, dum fraterna fingeret odia   [135]

pueris lites magis placent domesticae

Suumque volnus sentiunt statim fratrum

turbata pectora, atque se minus pati

possunt. magis lusore quovis gestiet

quam fratre cognato puer, quorum cito   [140]

---

125 ludat] ludet AC; laedet F

126 lucisse] lusisse C

129 dentur] denter C

130 juncti] junctus ABCDEFI; junxit G

140 cognato] ed.; cognatus ABCDEFGHI

     quorum cito] et statim > QUORUM CITO C; et statim DEF

admissa sordescit voluptas, nec diu

domesticae placere deliciae queant.

at sacra non poscebat inscius puer?

quis ista nuncius secreta prodidit?

tu quaere, quaerat Claudianus audiet.   [145]

at non rogasse finge, sive parvulum

non posse sane ardere asylum linquere:

manebit invitus tamen. templum mihi

si posco solum, bona tuebitur simul.

nemo caballum sacrilega sacris eripit   [150]

templo puer securus latere nequit?

quin filium matri pupillum detulit

Britanna lex, possessa si nulli bona

accepta referat, jura sui matri sinum

mandent pupillum: quae suos vis sacris   [155]

inimica tutrici pupillos auferet.

Cum matre victus fugeret hostiles manus

Edwardus inimicis suis linquens miser

extorta manibus sceptra? ad aras mox sacras

fugi gravida, rex ortus in lucem ubi fuit,   [160]

---

153 Britanna] Britinnia ACEH; Britania D; Britanniae FI

160 fugi] fugi > fugit C; fugit A

primosque natales sacros nactus puer

fuit, timor non parvus hostibus patris,

dubiamque fecit pacis incertae fidem

vtrique asylum praebuit tutam sedem.

donec patris gnatum reversi amplexibus   [165]

templum relinquens laeta traderem fides

tam certa regiae sit utinam suae.

quae sit timoris causa nec quisquam roget,

mecum sacris manebit aedibus puer.

quicunque pacta jura asylo rumperet: [170]

precor, sacra fruatur impius fuga

nec invideo duris opem hostibus sacram.

Arch. Ebor. Quid agimus? ira caecam mentem vellicat,

et purgit interdum ferox Glocestrium

nec flectitur prece pectus iratum levi.   [175]

Pugnare verbis non juvat, jussus sacros

summi senatus defero, quibus times

parere frustra. grande suspitionis est

tormentum, arciter errore torquetur suo

decepta. si regina charum patruo [180]

mandas nepotem, et caeteris quos Anglia

proceres suos gens nobilis jactat diu:

charam tibi vitam mihi pro filio

nunquam timebo pignori deponere.

sin filium nobis tuum mater negas: ⌊185⌋

rursus tibi persuasor haud posthac ero,

et filium coacta deferes tamen.

tremescit. anceps cogitat. num vicimus?

Regina Concussit artus nostros horridus timor.

torquetque vinctus frigido sanguis metu. [190]

quid agimus? animum distrahit dubius pavor,

hinc natus urget sortis, illic patruus.

testor deum verum, atque quicquid possident

coeli beatum, conjugis manes mei.

non aliud Edwarde in meo nato mihi [195]

jam quero, quam tua sceptra regali potens

gestaret aula, jura Britannis daret,

regisque laetum vivat aeternum genus.

Quid fluctuaris? ergo prodis filium?

180 patruo] parvulo C; patruo A; avunculo H

182 suos] suo CFI; hoc A

et sponte quaesitum neci mater dabis?   [200]

annon tuorum injusta terrent vincula?

sin cogitet protector Anglorum decus,

en possidet natum priorem principis:

contentus illo sit: suum matri sinat

solatium, non poscit istum patria,   [204a]

is quaerit unum, vtrunque mater postulo.   [205]

vnum dari rogo, duos cui debuit.

at hujus horrescis nihil demens minas?

procerumque vim tantam feres? natum tamen

amittis, et tuo perire vulnere

vides tuos. properare Cardineus pater,   [210]

matris quaevelae nec moras parvas facit.

statim vicinam vim minatur patruus

promissa asylo jura nec prolem tegunt.

nunquam fugae miles viam celeri dabit,

armatus omnes hostis occupat locos   [215]

aut quae capit fidelis amotum sedes?

Obscura Cardinalis haud fides fuit,

semperque sancta autoritas erat patris.

---

203 priorem] prioris ACH; priori > priorem E

218 semperque] semper ACGH
     sancta] sancti ABCDEGI; sacratae H

huic filium manda tuum, quin eripi

sinu videre filium mater potes?   [220]

patrisque funus ultinum regis domus?

horrenda fulminet ferox Glocestrius

potius: feram, patiar. maneat gnatus modo.

erras. utrosque perdis et gnatum simul,

tuosque, ferre nec Glocestrensem potes.   [225]

Arch. Ebor. Dum caeca vires ira colligit in tuam

praceceps ruinam armatur infaelix amor,

cur patruo charam nepotem denegas?

cui cura major Angliae committitur.

immerito nos inertiae damnas simul   [230]

et esse stultos arguis, quando nihil

horum timemus quale tu demens times.

Cum nos tamen Glocestrio iunxit duci

assidua regni cura, nec magis fuit

perspecta cuiquam vita Richardi ducis.   [235]

Regina Tam stulta nunquam, mentis aut inops fui

vex esse stultos ut rear cunctos, fidem

vestramque suspitione laederem mea.

---

226 tuam] tuum AC

acumen ego desidero simul et fidem.

quorum alterum si desit in nostrum caput   [240]

ruet, luemque patriae magnam parit.

nil sacra naturae moratur foedera

regni cupido insana nobilis furit

ambitio fratrum caedem, nec maculam timet.

veterum parum mentita persuasit fides.   [245]

Romana fraterno madebant sanguine

moenia, suo sin regna fratri parcere

verentur, an frustra nepos patruum timet?

si regii diversa fratres incolant,

erit salus utrique, servemus alterum   [250]

utrumque servabis, duos defendere

vnius in vita potes. nec tutum erit

aedibus iisdem vivere ambobus simul.

mercedes non ponit una singulas

Mercator in navi: procella quem frequens   [255]

jubet timere, nec minari turbines

rabidi solent frustra, licet mihi conscia

recti, loco servare sancto filium

---

254 singulas] singulas AC; singules > singulas E
     mercedes] ed.; merces ABCDEFGHI

256 minari] mirari CH; mirare A; marari D; in mari G

258 sancto] sanctum C

me posse sperem, dura quamvis intonet

crudelis, horrendumque patruus fulminet. [260]

en filium vestris tamen manibus. simul

vobis in illo mando fratrem, quos pie

servare vos decebit, a vobis ego

tum mater illum denuo repetam, caro

quando omnis summi ante judicis thronum [265]

posthac simul clangente sistetur tuba

tremebunda. scio quae vestra splendescit fides,

spatiosa quam sit dexterae potentia,

testata tot rebus simul prudentia,

nihil ut meis deesse tutandis queat. [270]

suspecta sin vobis potestas vestra erit:

illum mihi vos per deos relinquite

per regis Edwardi thori castam fidem.

---

272 relinquite] relinquere AC

quantoque me nimis timere dicitis:

tanto timere vos minus, decet parum.   [275]

O dulcis pignus, alterum regni decus,

spes vana matris cui patris laudes ego

demens precabor frustra, avi longos dies.

tibi patronus adsit tot procellis arbiter

mundi deus. tutoque portu collocet   [280]

impulsa vela, maestae matris accipe

infixa labris oscula infoelix tuis

is novit unus rerum habenas qui tenet,

quando dies lucebit altera, tuis denuo

cum nostra labris imprimentur oscula.   [285]

jam quod timebis, id genus dedit tuum

si vulnus haud sentis miser: matris tuae

mutare luctus. sin negat lachrymas tibi

generosus animus: at suos planctus tamen

concede matri, flere novimus prius   [290]

en sume fletus matris, a misero patris

quicquid relictum funere, an quicquid potest

Flebilius esse regis Edwardi nece?

---

286 dedit] dedi CH

292 quicquid (2nd one)] quisquam AC: quicqui <a> E; quicquam GH

at alter Edwardus tamen erat, qui potens

superba regni sceptra gestaret. patris   [295]

hic finxit ora gnatus Edwardi minor.

dicendus at magis meo ex vtero meus.

tum turma sustulit meorum nobilis,

nec morte fatum fregit vna singulos,

nunc dira fratrem carceris custodia   [300]

avulsit, ipsum possidet regem fides

metuenda Richardi, reliquias en patris

solas, in hoc fuit vna spes lapsae domus.

in quo simul nunc auferentur omnia.

quis te manet fili exitus tristis? quibus   [305]

heu fluctibus vita innocens exponitur.

si dura parvum fata quaerant, ultimum

domus tuae funus: petam mater simul

viventis oculos ut mea claudam manu,

et matris in sinu puer pereas, vale.

fili vale, matris vale solatium.   [310]

qualis remota matre crudelis leo

praedem minorem morsibus vastis premens

	raptavit ore: talis e sinu meo	
	crudelis avulsit nepotem patruus.	[315]
Howard	En candidas perfusa lachrymis genas,	
	variis tenellos filii artus implicat	
	amplexibus, suprema spargens oscula	
	nec plura singultus sinit miseram loqui.	
	haesitque medio rapta gutture egredi	[320]
	vox jussa, nec reperit viam, infaelix amor	
	quid matria adeo chara vexas pectora?	
	post terga discedens relinquit filium.	
Arch Ebor	Noli timere nobilis princeps, simul	
	cum fratre colludes tuo, regis domum	[325]
	nil suspicare matris orbatus sinu.	
Gloc	O chara proles regis Edwardi, implico	[326a]
	corpus tuum meis lubens amplexibus	[326b]
	en oscula tuis chara labris imprimo	[326c]
	tibi beatum crescat aeternum decus.	[326d]

---

315 avulsit] evulsit ACEG

319 miseram] [MISERAM] C; anhelans DEFGI

323 relinquit] reliquit ACEFHI

326a proles] See Collation, Appendix A.

Actus quintus

[V.i] Catsbeius Dux Buckingamiae

Catsbeius Plagis teneri laetus imbelles feras

Glocestrius triumphat in manus suas

optata cecidit praeda. tuto fraus loco

versatur. obscuro tenetur carcere

nepos vterq u e, decora regni jam libet   [5]

spondere sibi, soliumque fratris mortui

qualis feras odore longo sentiens

sagax canis, postquam vicinam praedam percipit

cervice celeri pugnat, et presso vias

scrutatur ore: talis omnibus modis   [10]

aptare dextris sceptra fratris dimicat.

regnoque sperato prope Britanniae inhiat.

regni futuri jacta jam sunt semina.

procerum cohors irata reginae nequit

preferre stirpem: poscet ad poenam ferox   [15]

dum lite pugnant, anxii, clam perdere

dux cogitat, quicunque coeptis obstrepant.

duce absque Buckingamiae sed nectere

dolos suos veretur, et fraudes timet.

jussit ducis mentem superbam incendere [20]

et concitare prolis odium regiae

ut sceptra parvis excidant infantibus,

patruique Buckinghamius fraudes juvet

regnumque dux insensus acquirat sibi:

ut suspicentur interim proceres nihil, [25]

hi de creando rege jussi consulunt.

Catsbei quid cessas parare duci thronum?

huc ferre Buckingamium video gradum,

animo tumet superbus, huic noctam dolos.

Flos Angliae praeclara progenies Jovis [30]

et maximum quassae Britanniae decus

quid otium securus alis, immemor

propriae salutis, quale vulnus accipit

collapsus imperii status, si concitus

temere furor juvenilis opprimat inscium, [35]

aetatis haud mulcetur ira fervidae.

Dux Buck At si quis excelsa potens aula, levis

immunis imperio deae suum potest

jactare faelicem statum, haud fragili loco:

---

31 maximum] magnum ACH

38 suum] suam CGH; suae DF; suam > suum E

39 fragili] fragile CH; fragulae > fraguli E

	excelsus id Buckingamus heros potest.	[40]
	quodnam sed omen istud, ambiguus jacis	
	dubio ore? carceris nigri licto specu	
	an hostis in nostrum caput frustra ruit?	
Catsbeius	Locus sed omni liber arbitrio vacet.	
Bucking	Nudate turba servuli vestra latus.	[45]
Catsb	Nihil timet generosa magnanimi indoles	
	se posse vinci magna virtus dum negat.	
	praemia ferunt fastus sui Riverius	
	heros Graiusque: primus hic gradus mali.	
	Rex sceptra puerili manu quassans, furit	[50]
	minatur olim non inultas fore suas	
	Injurias, nec dura fratris vincula	
	nec avunculi tulit sui. mater comam	
	lacerata vindictam petit minor genu	
	quicquid propinquis sit, sibi fieri putat.	[55]
	nunc ergo prudens ista tecum cogita.	
	nam si pepercit hostibus manus tuis	
	et traxerunt matris propinqui spiritum:	
	affine coras rege criminis arguent,	[58a]

---

44 arbitrio] arbitro AC

52 dura] duris AC

  fratris] frater AC

nunquam tuas cessabit in poenas furor

at si timori spiritum evomant tuo, [60]

Iramque justam sanguine extinguant suo,

regem timebis, scelere dum vincet scelus,

domusque cognatae fremat diram luem.

Bucking   Furor brevis pueri statim restinguitur.

Catsb   At ira praeceps est magis pueri levis. [65]

Buck   Minuet dies, vehemens quod est ruet illico.

Catsb.   Nunquam sinet parentis immensus dolor,

mori, incitant matrem suorum vincula;

et filium matris quaerelae.

Buck.   Criminis

pars istius Glocestrius fuit.

Catsbeius   Furor [70]

satiatur ultione: sontem negligit,

punit scelus.

Bucking.   Ducis potest authoritas

ferociam pueri minuere.

Catsb.   Dum puer

est.

---

60 timori] timore CEH; timere A

61 extinguant] extinguat AC

Bucking.   At suum semper timebit patruum.

Catsb.   Quenquam timere nescit imperii decus.

Buck.   Quod nos tueri salubre consilium potest?

Catsb.   Quod principi vestram necem solum vetat.

Bucking.   Pulsabit usque matris ira filium.

Catsb.   Nocere mortuus nihil gnatus potest.

Bucking.   Mali medela sola tollere principem.   [80]

Catsb.   Vinci nisi scelere novo scelus nequit.

quoddam scelus honestum necessitas facit.

plagis tenetur capta dispositis fera:

quasi vinculis vterque servatur nepos.

Levi peribunt Claudii nutu ducis   [85]

periere jamjam, si tibi nunc consulas.

Glocestrium munit satelles clam ducem

mores notat secretus excubitor tuos,

qualem tuorum minime falsum putes,

adversus illum forte si quicquam pares.   [90]

nihil timendum si vides time, tamen

incerta multorum fides: constans nihil

inimica crede cuncta. turbatus solet

simulare multa vultus, et fingit dolos

fratri Thyestes liberos credens suos [95]

mistum suorum sanguinem genitor bibit.

Bucking Quid nunc? cur haeres? quodve consilium

vesane torques? carceri heroas datos

an poenitebit? hoc inertis est viri

huic ira regis terret, an puerum times? [100]

an faeminam? nam fata cognatos premunt

versantur illinc odia splendidi ducis

cujus potestas summa, quem cuncti tremunt.

quaeris salutem? tutus huic eris magis

confide, summis et fidem praesta duci. [105]

Catsb Properata regem fata si vita eximant

parabit haeres sceptra Richardus sibi:

tu sola jactatae columna patriae

ambire regnum ope dux tua Glocestrius

facile potest. vtrique vitam munies. [110]

Bucking Numquam meo ludet cruore regius puer,

cujus minas satiabit ereptum caput.

jactum parva principis, vitam tuam

---

99 inertis] meritis C; meritus A; meritis > inertis H

103 cujus] cuivis CH; qui vis A

tremunt] trement ACEH

112 minas] minis ACH

113 parva] prarva C; parta G

servare si possis. parum pueros decent

decora regni. matris hoc regnum invidae [115]

haud regis esset: cujus impulsu in necem

solum suorum armatur iratus puer.

    [V.ii] Dux Buck. Dux. Gloc. Catsbeius

Bucking [0] Claudiane rector, Ebori domus

spes una, nec non periculi consors mei:

nobis gravem tuus parat necem nepos.

casus suorum maestus Edwardo satus [5]

plangit, minasque fletibus miscet graves

abdenda vinculis opaci carceris

infausta proles regis: aut nostra nece

sua domus litabit ultrices deas.

Gloc Horrere vindicis potentiae faces

cogunt, trucesque regis irati minae. [10]

salubre praecipitare consilium jubet.

quo longius serpit malum robustius

fieri solet, brevisque consiliis mora

---

116 regis] regia ACH

  1 [0]] 0 omitted ACH

  8 sua] ed; suae ABCDEFGHI

datur.

Buck   Medela tristis ingenti malo

paratur, en facile scelus vinci nequit   [15]

semper minatur ira caeca principis

vindicta sceptro armata pugnat acerrime.

testor deum verum, sumumque coelorum decus,

quodcunque consulas sequar vitae ducem.

Gloc   Tremulus per artus horror excurrit vagus.   [20]

juvenile novi regis ingenium, ferox,

Indocile, flecti non potest, frangi potest.

si patimur, exitium nobis parat grave,

redimere vitam vinculis regis licet.

at heu pudet fraterna regna demere   [25]

vndique frequens ridens Lancastrium genus,

lapsamque gaudebit domum aemuli sui.

consulere sed vitae quia propriae decet

nec patriam decet onerare luctibus:

Fraterna posco sceptra jure sanguinis,   [30]

vestraeque fautores salutis vos voce.

coeptis tuam si spondeas nostris fidem

---

19   sequar]   sequor BCEDHI

21   regis]   ragis C; principis H

juro supremos qui tenent coelum deos.

natus meus solamen vnicum, tuam

gnatum maritus vxorem ducet sibi.   [35]

quod vendicas, Hertfordiensis eris comes.

opes, supellex: quicquid ab aula possidet   [36a]

illustre, vobis cuncta succumbent tuis.   [36b]

Buck   Deos eosdem juro: syderibus fretum,   [36c]

et unda flammis, ovibus et lupus rapax,   [36d]

nox atra soli, aeterna jungetur comes   [36e]

aquis carebit Tamesis, aequor piscibus:

partes priusquam perfidus linquam tuas.

Catsb   Nunc ergo coepta vota demens perfice

primumque regulos ad arcem transferas   ⌊40⌋

famulosque substituas novos nepotibus,

dicto tuo quos audientes autumas,

et nulla deinceps ad regem pateat via

populi strepitum ad tuos transfer lares.

et subditorem averte regi lumina,   [45]

[calcentque tua posthac clientes limina.]

Gloc   Quin Angliae proceres latere fraudem convenit

36b succumbent] succumbunt ACE;   subibunt F;   succumbent omitted D

46] This line is omitted in ACFH.

dum rapta nostris sceptra manibus caederent.

Catsb   Adhuc corona regium cingi caput

non posse dimissi monebunt nuncii,   [50]

tuoque jussu confluat procerum cohors,

ut magna celebrentur comitia Britanniae

dum cogitabundi suum capiunt iter

et urbe nudati manebunt viribus,

et arma meditantes priusquam jungerent,   [55]

incerta cum sit invicem fides sibi,

erepta puero sceptra tutus posside.

Bucking At nobilem haud fallet Hastingum dolus.

Stanleius heros urbe quique considet,

Antistes Eliensis astum intelligent.   [60]

si clam coire separatim senserint.

Gloc   De rebus Angliae gravissimis ut consulant

coire proceres singuli jussu meo

ne nostra coepta intentus animus occupet.

Bucking At quis tui simul comes consilii erit,   [65]

res magna paucis expediri non potest.

Gloc   Quem non metu possessa sceptra compriment?

---

50 dimissi] demissi CH

53 suum] sunt ACH;   suum > sunt E

deesse nostro authoritas voto nequit.

Bucking   Pervince multis praemiis vulgus leve

           domisque cumula plurimis, qui partibus   [70]

           ut haereant tuis, facile duci possunt

           vincere pecunia quos nequit, coget metus,

Catsb   Difficile procerum animos statim cognoscere.

Glocest Quasi publicis de rebus anxius nimis

           quos suspicor, sollicitus usque consulam   [75]

           dum multa proponam dubius, et volvimus

           secreta regni: mens patebit abdita.

           Hastingus vnus principi palam studet,

           et debitos defert honores regulis.

           hic gratus Anglis et potens multum, mea   [80]

           juvare sceptra, hunc vel mori prius decet.

Catsb   Is principi favebat Edwardo nimis

           nunquam potest promissa convelli fides.

Gloc   Tentare perversam decet mentem magis

           forsan virum frangas reluctantem metu   [85]

           ego interim rebus Britannis consulam.

Catsb   Quid nunc agis Catsbei, quin tibi consulas

---

74 anxius] anxie ACH

nunc advoca astus animae, nunc fraudes dolos,

totumque Catsbeium thronum, si particeps

fraudis ducis procuret Hastingus: fidem   [90]

tibi derogas, minusque posthac creditur.

si spiritum peremptus inimicum expuat

quasi pertinax amor colat pueros nimis

praeesse solus tu potes Lecestriae

successor Hastingi: duces credent magis.   [95]

bene est. pereat, ut nostra crescat gloria.

infausta dirus rumpat ensis viscera.

studere fingam regulis, durum nimis,

flecti nec ulla pertinax possit prece.

      [V.iii] Stanleius: Hastingus

[Stanl] Pectus stupet, dubioque perculsum metu

agitatur, huc, illuc, rotat, nec potest

se evolvere, ominatur aliquod mens malum.

divulsa quid consilia sibi locis volunt?

dum pars in arce, pars alia praetorio   [5]

---

88 advoca] advotae CH;   ad vota A;   avoca D;   advoca E;   revoca G

94 Lecestriae] Lancastriae ABCH;   Leicestriae FI

```
          deliberat, novit tonans pater ille, quid

          disjunctus heros mente versat callida

          per nos vel imperio inhiare, vel necem

          nobis, vel insidias struere regi queat

          hoc quicquid est metuo nimis.
Hasting                                    Ponas metum          [10]
          illustre Stanlei genus, nec torqueat

          suspitio mentem vana, nihil in nos grave

          patrare possunt, quamdiu meus simul

          Catsbeius adsit (inde qui nunquam solet

          abesse) quod velut ore prolatum suo            [15]

          absens licet non audio.
Stanleius                          Fides et adultera
          non raro tecta fronte blanda absconditur.

          virtutis umbra turpe pugnat vitium.

          falsumque vultum haud exprimunt pauci dies.
Hasting   Cumulata meritis firma constitit fides.        [20]

          jusso meo Lecestrii summe colunt.

          multumque Northamptoniis potens valet,

          rerum mearum summam in illo colloco.
```

---

8 per nos] pueros ACH;   nervos DF

11 Stanlei] Stanleii BCE;   Stanleie I

12 mentem] metum CH;   metu A

Stanleius	Serum est cavendi tempus in mediis malis

Stanleius Serum est cavendi tempus in mediis malis

libido regni caeca nullam via timet.   [25]

Imbellis aetas regis abruitur statim:

in nosque secretum nefas post saeviet

quoscunque particeps timet sceleris sui,

et nuda praeda perfidis sumus hostibus:

repetamus at patrios lares celeri gradu,   [30]

ubi sepiant suis clientes viribus.

incepta forte perfidus metuet furor.

Hasting Frustra timemus prosperam sortem satis,

verbis benignis alloqui blandi duces

solent, mihique plurimum semper student   [35]

et ipsa populi vota, rumores, metus,

communicavi Catsbeio dudum meo

torquebat alios cura magna principis,

quaerunt ducem cives, nepotem negligunt.

quod ista me celavit: haud aeque fero,   [40]

fugere lubet? nos arguet reos fuga,

atque revocatos ira perderet magis.

tutos manentes vita servat innocens.

---

28 sceleris] scelus C;   scelus > sceleris H

40 celavit] caelavit C;   celant C

sin nos malum maneret: alterius velim

scelesta mens, non nostra damnaret fuga.   [45]

fraus ista (crede) nulla quam demens times.

rude prius in coelum chaos mutabitur

prius astra terris haereant, flamine salum:

quam fallat astrictam fidem Catsbeius.

Stanleius   Mox exitus tantis malis fidem dabit.   [50]

[V.iv]   Dux Gloc. Catsbeius. Howardus equestris.

Dux Gloc   Spes concutit mentem, metusque turbidam,

trepidumque gemino pectus eventu labat.

Imago regni semper errat ante oculos mihi,

semperque dubium impellit ambitio gravis,

turbatque pectus, flamma regni concita.   [5]

nescit quiescere, sceptra nunc tantum placent

non desinam dum summum votorum attigi.

multum exagitat incerta nobilium fides

cui nostra certus consilia credam: haud scio,

nec sunt loco tuto sitae fraudes meae.   [10]

---

49   fallat] fallit AC;   fallet H

50   Mox] Moes ACH

    fidem] finem ACH

 6   placent] placet C

 8   fides] sedes ACH

Howard   Quid pectus anxium tumultu verberas?

         nescit timere quisquis audet magna. jam

         regnum petis, fortuna fortes adjuvat.

         ars prima regni posse te cives metu

         retinere,. qui cives timet, rebelles excitat.   [15]

         audebit omnia quisquis imperio regit

         et dura tractat sceptra regali manu.

Gloc   Pectus nihil perturbat ignavus metus.

         excede pietas, mente si nostra lates.

         tuetur ensis quicquid invitum tenes: [20]

         aperire nunc ferre decet fraudi viam.

         mactetur hostis quisquis obstabit mihi.

Howard   Quid Pontefracti vinculis captos tenes

         matris propinquos, nec mori tandem jubes?

         indulta vita caeteris animos dabit,   [25]

         et ultro poenas mite supplicium vocat.

         ferro perempti spiritum infestum expuant.

         firmas amicos, caeteri metu labant.

Gloc   Hostes simul perire presentes volo.

         obstare quos sceptris meis novi sagax   [30]

---

21 aperire] aperive CH;   < >ire G

27 expuant] expiant AC; exprimant D;   expirant FI

```
        ut unus omnes occupet pariter metus,

        quorum dubia studio resistit mens levi

        illos prement mox dura captos vincula.

        quo flectit Hastingus animum?

Catsb                           Tantum in tuum

        Caput.

Gloc          Meis adjutor esse partibus               [35]

        Renuit?

Catsb         Prius profundet artus Ithacum

        fretum, et rapax consistet aqua Siculi maris

        noxque atra terris ante splendorem dabit.

        fraudes abominatur  ferox quassans caput

        se semper Edwardi fidelem filiis               [40]

        fore spondet, hostem regis hostibus gravem.

Gloc    Quid arma possunt regis irati sciet.

        iramque nostram sanguine extinguet suo.

        discant parere principis metu sui.

        at qua via mactabo vesanum caput?             [45]

Catsb   Conjugis amore captus insanit Shori

        flammas libido nec furentes continet.
```

hanc arguas capiti veneficiis tuo

mortem struere: causam suae sin pellicis

amore caecus et furore fervidus   [50]

tuetur infaelix patronus: conscium

sceleris nefandi suspiceris illico,

et proditorem patriae incusa suae.

mox amputet securis infaustum caput.

Gloc   Proceres in arcem confluent jussu meo   [55]

statim, favere quos regi scio.

palam opprimam. reumque criminis arguam.

satelles abscindet bipenni mox caput.

nec sentiet senatus insidias stupens.

Catsbeius Sin abstinet sacris comitiis callidus   [60]

heros; novus quaerendus est fraudi modus.

Gloc   At illico invisa inclytum Howardi caput

blandisque vocibus morantem concita

sacris abesse comitiis noli pati.

Catsb   Solumne poscis dirae Hastingum neci?   [65]

Gloc   Stanleius heros atque Cardineus pater

praesul Eliensis comprimentur vinculis

---

59   sentiet]   sensiet C

61   novus]   novusque ACE

62   invisa] ed: invise ABCDEFGHI

animum ut fidelem carceris domet specus.

sin impotenti animo pertinax abnuat

quisquam, nec Hastingi movet tristis lues: [70]

ferrum secabit triste noxium caput

infida strictus ensis eruet viscera

res est profecto stulta nequitiae modus.

[V.v] Hastingus heros. Howard. Hastingus

miles calligatus

Hastingus Miror quid huc meus jam equus humi turpiter

prosternitur, deus omen avertat malum

sed vana sortis quid movent ludibria?

et dira Stanleius tremebat somnia

visum sibi aprum nunciat somno caput   [5]

lacerare dente, mox fluit humeris cruor.

mihique demens consulit turpem fugam

lasciva nos fortuna gestit ludere,

ridetque turbatos levi casu viros:

quibus tamen nihil minatur invida.   [10]

Howard   Propera nobile Hastinge caput: celera gradum.

---

69 abnuat] abnuet ACEH

70 movet] novit C;   movit A;   monet DI

1 meus jam] [MEUS JAM] C;   eundi BDEFGI

11 Hastinge] Hastingi ACEH

Hast heros	Faelix ades tandem sacrate diis pater,
	secretas aures commoda paululum mihi.
Howard	Omitte tandem: quid sacerdotem diu
	affare? confessore nil adhuc opus. [15]
	nil sui securus infaelix, videt,
	mox quam sibi damnato sacerdote opus erit.
Hasting heros	Hastinge, nunquam excidit menti dies
	olim nefanda, tristis et nimis, istius
	quando sub arcis moenibus totus tremens [20]
	dirae metu necis ultimo te viderim?
Hastingus miles cal	O nominis decus vnicum tui et genus
	illustre: nunquam tam gravis casus mihi
	Aut tristis excidit, tibi nullum tamen
	(diis gratia) malum, tum nec iis lucrum fuit [25]
	aequata sors utrique fuit.
Hast heros	Imo magis
	hoc diceres, secreta mentis nostrae si
	cognosceres, quod singuli posthac scient.
	at nemo adhuc ah Hastinge nunquam quod sciam
	vitae magis dubius fui, quam illo die [30]

---

18 nunquam] nunquid CE;   numquid AGH

nunc temporum mutata series, ad necem

hostes trahuntur Pontefracti isto die

nostram cruore suo quietem sanciunt.

nunquam magis securus ex animo meo

Hastingi vixi, nec metu magis vacat   [35]

jactata nullis fluctibus vita.

Hast. miles   Id deus

faxit.

Hast. heros   Quid haeres.

Hast. miles   Id precor.

Hast. heros   Satis scio.

Howard.   Quin rumpis heros nobilis segnes moras

nam te diu senatus expectat sagax

de rebus ut tot consulat. nobile caput   [40]

discessit. heu nescit miser tristem tibi

luem parari, ah quid nimis pueris faves?

tete fefellit falsa Catsbei fides.

captusque plagis praeda retineris miser.

---

40 consulat] ed.; consulant ABCDEFGHI

42 luem] luem ends l. 41 ACGH

[V. vi.] Dux Gloc. Dux Bucking. Hasting. heros
  Eliensis Episcopus   Satelles.   [Stanleius.]*

Dux Buck. Quam magna regni cura tutorem premit

      ducemque vexat Claudianum, quia, patres,

      ignorat? hunc solum intuetur Anglia

      suisque rebus poscit authorem ducem.

      vestram seorsim selegit prudentiam,   [5]

      quorum fidele consulat canum caput,

      et ut procuret anxius negotia.

      celebrare comitia regis anxius studet

      quo regium diademate caput cingeret.

      ut gratus esse mortuo fratri queat   [10]

      cujus sepulti filium exornat pie.

Gloc.   Veneranda o patrum cohors et maximum

      potentis imperii decus: faustum deus

      indulgeat nunc rebis istis exitium.

      nae somniator ego nimis tardus fui   [15]

      qui tam frequenti serus adsum curiae

      somnus negotiis consultor est gravis meis,

      tantumne mane lectulo elapsus senex

      Eliensis antistes venis? senem quies

---

*[Stanleius] An obvious omission by Legge: see lines 75 and 82 of this
scene.

7 et ut] et tot ACGH; ut tot BE

                 Juvenem labor decet. ferunt hortum tuum   [20]

                 decora fragra plurimum producere

                 mandes precor mihi pauca legi in prandium.   [21a]

Episc. Eliensis Nil tibi claudetur, hortus quod meus

                 producit, esset lautius vellem mihi

                 quo sin tibi gratus.

Gloc.   Quid imperii status

                 salusque regni poscat, et patriae decus: [25]

                 vestris adhuc jactate consiliis patres.

                 abesse cogunt paululum negotia.

                 ne sit molestus forte discessus precor.

Hast. heros   Operam navare maximam patres decet

                 ut dum gerit rex sceptra puerili manu   [30]

                 pellamus omnem fortiter discordiam,

                 quae scissa nuper regna dira exercuit.

                 hoc flagitat secura patriae salus.

                 claraque poscit mollis aetas principis

                 et ultimo fides sacramento data,   [35]

                 regi sepulto. magis hoc nullum fuit

                 regni satellitium, ergo proceres si invicem

consentiant: florebit hoc regnum diu.

sin invicem dissentiant: brevi ruet.

purgare tandem patriae maculam decet,   [40]

et scelere nosmet liberare pessimo.

sed ecce retro dux venit dubio gradu

quassans caput, torvo supercilio furit

duro labellum dente comprimit ferox

et pectore irato tegit dirum malum.   [45]

Gloc.   Quas destinatis his patres poenas, suis

qui nunc veneficiis mihi exitium parant

qui sum superbo regius ortus sanguine

tutorque declaratus hujus insulae?

Hasting Quas patriae perferre debet proditor   [50]

nec moror honorem altum, nec excuso decus,

Gloc.   Sensus mihi omnes fratris vxor fascinat.

Hasting Verbes stupentes triste demittunt caput:

Justas luat regina poenas pessima.

parum tamen placet quod aures haec meas   [55]

adhuc latebant. fraude captivi mea

erant propinqui matris. hodie jam meis

---

53 Verbes] ed.; verbis ABCEFGHI; virbis D

	hi Pontefracti capite plectuntur dolis.	
Gloc.	Comitata modo regina Shori conjuge	
	suis venefica cantibus me prodidit	[60]
	fluit tabo corpus, oculi somnum negant	
	stomacho invidet lentum sibi fastidium	
	venas hiantes deserit pulsus cruor	
	exangue brachium exaruit, officium negat.	
Hastingus	Heu frigido cor palpitat tremulum metu	[65]
	num pulcra destinatur heu morti mea?	
	pereunt amores? concubinam conjugis	
	regina nunquam consuleret usquam sui.	
	timent loqui: securus alloquar ducem.	
	Si fecerint, gravissimas poenas luent.	[70]
Gloc.	Si fecerint? itane mihi? si fecerint?	
	quin dico factum, quod tuum luet caput,	
	sceleste proditor.	
Satelles	Proditio, proditio.	
Gloc.	Te perduellionis esse aio reum.	
Hasting.	Me? mene?	
Gloc.	Proditor sceleste patriae.	[74a]
Eliensis Epis.	Percussit heu clarum satelles Stanleium,	[75]
	an occidit? stillans rigat genas cruor.	
Gloc.	Vos perduellem date neci servi statim	

             sacra morituro mox sacerdos finiet.

             Juro sacrum Paulum, prius non prandeo,

             poenas mihi quam pendat abscissum caput.   [80]

             patremque Cardineum, Eliensem praesulem,

             Dominumque Stanleium coerce vinculis.

             scelerisque poenas Shora pellex impudens

             damnata persolvet jubente judice.

Hasting.   Quis nostra digne conqueri potest mala?   [85]

             heu quas miser voces dabo? quae lachrymis

             nostris Aedon exhibet luctus graves?

             O machinator fraudis, et dire artifex

             sceleris, meorum prodidit fallax amor.

             blandaque tectum fronte secretum malum   [90]

             cur invident severa fata vitam? in mea

             quid morte tam potens erit versutia.

             suumque cumulat gaudium luctu meo?

             sed parce demens lachrymis. testor sacrum

---

92 morte] nocte AC

heu numen adversum mihi, simul voce   [95]

quocunque defugistis intus inferi

terris opacis, innocens morti trahor

supplex fides non intrat aulum, nec pie

didicit superba pompa vivere, in meam statim

fortuna poenam mutat inimicas dotes.   [100]

Gloc.   An luctus attonitos muliebris commovet?

tantas moras suadere lachrymae queant?

non abripitis huic impio ferro caput?

auferte, quid cunctamini istum perdere?

Hasting. Gaudet dolor sua fata multis spargere   [105]

nec solus impoenam placet vestras colos

saevae sorores impetrant. ludunt genus

mortale caeca fata. praemonstrant malum

vitare quod vetant tamen perterritus

somno nihil Stanleius heros commovet   [110]

heu visus est lacerare caput vtrique aper

frendens cruente dente, longus diffluit

cruor per humeros, insignia dederunt apri

nomen Glocestrio: ter lapsus insidenti equus

---

107 genus] genas AC

cecidit, senatum dum nefandum viserem.   [115]

Gloc.   Isti malum sibi quaerunt satellites

          qui dum moras faciunt inanes fletibus

          demetere cessant impium ferro caput.

Hasting. Hei mihi salutis nulla spes, nunc ad necem

          trahite quibus fortuna jus in nos dedit   [120]

          quid lachrimis miser moror? pio manus

          cruore spargite, vltimum solis vale

          coeleste jubar perditum reparans die

          vale cohorte nobilis nitida soror

          phebi quieta: longa jam nox obruet.   [125]

          [V. vii] Dux Gloc.   Cives lond.   Nuncius

Gloc.   Cives peroptati hic adestis, prope licet

          sero nimis nobis, in arce quod modo

          Hastingus impiique consortes sui

          sceleris peremissent, deus si non opem

          tulisset: idque licet diu celaverint   [5]

          astu: ante decimam solis (ut sit) istius

---

121 lachrimis] lachrymas ACEH

  3 impiique] impii C; imperii A; impusque F

  4 peremissent] perimissent ACF

perceptimus, metuque subito perciti

quaecunque casus arma dedit, (ut carnitis)

miseri induimus, ipsique jam opprimuntur: aut

virtute nostra, gratia vel coelitum   [10]

magis doli hujus principes in pessimos

ac sceleris autores redundabit malum

nunc ergo vos jussu vocati estis meo

immane quia constaret omnibus nefas.

per vos ut innotesceret quaeventibus.   [15]

Cives   Jussus fideles exequemur sedulo.

O pertinax scelus, mendatio cedem tegens,

blandaque tantum fronte contentum malum

quis nescit immanes dolos saevi ducis?

dubitatque captum fraude nobilem virum?   [20]

suum scelus plerunque in authorem redit

prius in alios postquam crudelis saeviit.

Nuncius Coruscus Hastingi hausit casis spiritum.

Cives   Ut gesta res est queso paucis expedi.

Nuncius Postquam ad locum durus satelles traxerit   [25]

ad astra tollit clarus heros lumina

---

11 principes] principis ACDFGI

16 Cives] Cives speech begins at l. 17 AC

26 tollit clarus heros] tollit CLARUS heros C; tollit heros DEFGI

ex ore casto concipit deo preces

quaecunque nostra contumax superbia

supplicia meruit (inquit) o numen sacrum

vtinam meo jamjam luatur sanguine [30]

vix ultimas moratur carnifex preces

quin solvit illico ense corporis obicem.

Cives   Extinxit Hastingum suorum ingens favor

animusque laetis credulus rebus nimis

nec triste suspicatur integer scelus [35]

auctore donec misere amico plectitur.

Sed huc gradum confert ad arma serviens

quid civibus clamare quaerit publice.

Serviens ad arma. Cives

[Serv. ad arma] Caeptis nefandis hic scelestus proditor

Hastingus, horrendi caput primum mali, [40]

et turba perjuro gerens morem duci,

Struxere tectos principis Glocestrii

[vitae dolos, altique Buckinghamii,]

vtrique dum sacro senatu consident

ut sic ruinosae peremptis Angliae [45]

---

33 Extinxit] exstinxit C; extinguit DEFGI

42 principis] principes AC; principis > principi H

43] This line is omitted in AC .

rectoribus, sedis supraemae culmina

scandant superbi summa, celso vertice

quamvis inepti qui ruentis maxima

regni gubernarent Britanni pondera

quis nescit Hastingum parentem principis   [50]

traxisse secum turpiter quis regium

nescit malis faedasse nomen moribus

splendore vel spoliasse regnum pristino,

dictis suis, factis quis turpem virum

quis nescit? Hastingi libido perdita   [55]

quot virginum passim pudorem perdidit

lectique rupit conjugalis faedera

amplexus infamis adulter pellices

nam Shora pellex nota, scortum nobile

hujusque caedis particeps, et conscia.   [60]

hunc nocte polluto suprema lectulo

accepit amplexu parum caste suo

ut morte poenas jure pendat maximas.

turpem gravi qui scelere vitam polluit

	ne si diu dilata damnati foret	[65]
	mors traditoris Marte funesto suum	
	Jurata poscat turba demens principem.	
	quae poena festinata fallet singulos	
	dirosque jurantum tumultus comprimet.	
Civis	Praeceps agendi magna perturbat modus	[70]
	foetumque festinans parit caecum canis	
Civis alter.	Haec scripta sunt alto prophaetae spiritu	
	nam tantulo qui tanta possunt tempore	
	vel cogitari dicta, vel sic exprimi	
	pulchrae mihi sane videntur literae	[75]
	pulchreque depingi videtur chartula.	
	et pulchra postremo, loquendi formula.	
	Illud tamen mirum videtur maxime	
	tam pulchra tam parvo parari tempore.	
Cives	En Shora tremulum careum gerens manu	[80]
	induta, poenas linteo infames luit	
	Regum inclyta meretrix tyranno dat truci	
	poenas. Pater descende Jupiter et thoro	
	tam grata pignora nunc tuo rape. nam tuam	
	Laedam vel Europam puta, desere polum.	[85]

---

79 parari] parare AC

80 Shora] Shori AC

Oh misera, me miseret tui, piget, pudet

licet impudica mulier et minus proba

privare vita dum nequit dux Claudius

spoliare fama quaerit iratus tibi

Processio solennis

Chorus   Preces deo fundamus ore supplices   [90]

ne sit nota polluta mens adultera

1   Fidem tuere conjugum

lectumque probro libera

defende privatos thoros,

furtiva ne laedat venus.   [95]

2   Quemcunque facti poenitet

purga solutum crimine.

exempla sanent posteros,

furtiva ne foedat venus.

Epilogus.

Quas dirus admovit Richardus machinas   [100]

quantisque regnandi, libido luctibus

affecit afflictam videtis patriam

ut celsa regni scandat altus cul͡mina

frendens aper regni lues Glocestrius

illustris Hastingi cruor diffunditur   [105]

quod regulis vivus faveret parvulis.

regno repugnantes novo Riverius,

Vaghanus et Graius repressi carceris

horrore laethali premuntur vulnere.

*[The Shewe of the Procession.

   a Tipstaffe

   Shores wife in her petticote haveinge a

            taper burninge in her hand.

   The Verger

   Choristers

   Singinge men

   Praebendaries

   The Bishope of London

   Citizens.]

   finis primae actionis

---

108 Vaghanus] ed.;   Vahamus CFH;   Vahannis AE;   Vahanus BDI;
                       Vaghamus G

* The Shrewe of the Procession with the list of marchers is found in DEFGH.

Actio Secunda

Dramatis Personae

Dux Glocestrensis

Dux Buckinghamiae

Lovellus heros

Praetor Londinensis

Fitzwillam Recordator ut vulgo Recorder.

Civis Amicus Shai

Doctor Shawe

Civis primus

Civis secundus

Hospes

Nobilis

Servus unus et alter Buck.

Argumentum

Postquam hos omnes in potestatem suam Richardus

Dux Glocestrensis redigisset, quorum erga regem

fidem metuebat, quorum Hastingum nobilem morte

affecit, caeteros in carcerem conjecisset, in id studium

sedulo incumbit ut sine tumultu civium in regni   [5]

Injustum possessionem veniat. Itaque at Londinenses

fraudem induceret, ut ultro cum caeteris nobilibus

regnum sibi deferant, regis ortum fratrisque sui du-

cis Eboracensis parvuli damnavit: regem Edwardum

fratrem suum, non ita multo ante defunctum   [10]

adulterii per ducem Bucking. in curia praetoris

accusavit, neque suiipsius matri ducissae quondam

Eboracensi pepercivit. Tandem delatam sibi

majestatem quam tantopere inhiabat, aegre ut

videbatur assumens, solennibus comitiis coronatur.   [15]

Actus Primus

Dux Gloc.   Dux Bucking.

[I.i]   Lovellus heros.

[Gloc]   Illustris heroum propago, ducem genus

insigne Buckinghamiorum. particeps

nostrique consilii Lovelle nobilis:

quin rumpimus segnes moras. strenuum decet

fore, magna quisquis cogitat. res nihil habet   [5]

isthaec periculi audere decet haud amplius

quis influentis dona sortis respuit?

regem potest creare Buckingamius.

honor ducis erat semper hic amplissimi

virtute te natura firma robarat,   [10]

et corporis vestivit anxia dotibus

tibi rursus aciem inclusit ingenii parem,

nec te magis Minerva quenquam luminat.

segni decet, natura quo praestans vocat.

tantum potest excelsa Buckingamius.   [15]

---

6 isthaec] ishas C

tolluntar hostes ecce suspecti mihi,

reosque diri carceris vincula premunt

regis favor quos armat in regnum meum.

jubere cunctos voce licet una mori.

Hastingus interemptus heros occidit.   [20]

Stanleius heros continetur vinculis,

et Eliensem Episcopum carcer domat.

reliqui jacent tetro specu clausi, meis

quicunque coeptis impii favent parum.

Bucking. Puerum levem regnare: fortunae jocus,   [25]

lasciva ridens sceptra miscet litibus,

victus suo succumbit infans ponderi.

tu cogita quosnam struis regni dolos

nunquam tuos jussus relinquam pertinax.

res expediri magna nescit illico.   [30]

Gloc.   En ipsa temporum jubet securitas,

audacter aggredi, prius quae consulis

animis oportet praevidere singula

res arduas nec aggredi temere decet.

Quis exitus rerum futurus, cogitat   [35] sapiens prius. Gerenda cuncta provide.

quicquid timendum juncta consilia explicent.

Lovellus En temporis nimium premunt angustiae.

quo regium caput corona cingeres,

nunc ergo cunctis imperandum publice   [40]

ut non sacris statim comitiis confluant.

regni moras persuadet occasio gravis.

ne cingat ante caput corona reguli,

quam luceat secunda Novembris dies,

hic destinatus est dies, solennibus.   [45]

dum cogitant mora tarda quid velint sibi,

patrios lares procul relinquentes, suis

dum viribus nudati adessent nobiles:

incerta dum dubios opinio torqueat:

mutuamque suspicentur incerti fidem   [50]

agitata mente consilia nec digerant:

suam priusquam vim rebelles jungerent:

tu rapta pueris sceptra tutus posside.

tractes habenas Angliae facili manu.

mox numini devicta succumbet tuo   [55]

---

36 Gerenda cuncta provide] GERENDA CUNCTA PROVIDE C

46 velint] velit C

invidia, dum fero revellat principem.

Bucking. Ferat licet decepta nobilium cohors:

animusque prudens fero tentaret nihil

at arma junget pertinax populi furor

motuque caeco rapitur, in praeceps ruit   [60]

quocunque fertur. verba convenient feris

Injusta factis. victa nec cedet metu

concepta rabies temere qualis turbine

sevo Meander funditur rapiens, pati

nequit resistentem sibi, et dirum fremit.   [65]

Lovellus Mulcera blandis plebis ingenium ferox

decet, sequitur lubens et ultro pellitur

at quem suorum civium favor beat

inter suos nec parva micat authoritas:

tractare mollius rudem mentem potest   [70]

tuumque persuadere regnum civibus

urbs Angliae praeclara Londinum tuis

inducta votis si faveret: vicimus

errore capti caeteri procedent pari.

possessa regna facile ferro munies.   [75]

---

56 fero] sero C

58 fero] sero C

61 fertur] fortitur C

63 rabies] rabido C

At quis color regni probetur civibus

ne decipi captos sagaces senserint?

irata se plebs graviter illudi feret.

Bucking. Infausta gens tot lassa vincitur malis.

stragemque majorem minantur parvuli   [80]

lasciva regna. Anglia novas lites timet.

et matris haud cessabit in poenas furor,

tua regna luctus auferent teterrimos,

qui natus esses regum superbo sanguine,

tantamque regni sustines molem sagax.   [85]

Lovell Istum facile plebs sentiet callida dolum

causamque regni credet injustam fore.

Gloc. Quidni dolis facilis patet nostris via?

palam fratris damnentur infames thori

pudica sceptra non ferunt lecti probrum.   [90]

spurios vetant regnare jura filios.

Amore postquam rex flagraret Luciae

aetate tum calcante: dum notas prius

iterum Venus furtiva delicias petat

et libido sevis nec modum flammis dedit: [95]

---

85   molem]   malem C

temere spospondit Luciae regni thoros,

illamque participem sui regni vocat.

experta saepe Venus parit fastidium,

sordent amores Luciae tum principi,

nec furta lecto quaerit obscuro improbus [100]

decepit animum conjugi obstrictum suae

nec possidet regina promissos thoros.

tum Lucia locum pulsa pellici dedit,

adhuc rapaces nil timens fati minas,

hinc filios generi suo infames pater [105]

genuit adulter, vulnus et regni grave.

nec hanc thronus maculam tulit solam patris:

lectum priorem lusit impudens amor

nostri parentis Eboracensis ducis.

thalamis ducissae turpe mentiti viri [110]

vestigium secretus invenit comes.

coitus nefandos nec dolus tegere potest.

Socium tedae scit, pudetque criminis,

faedaeque matris faeda proles rex fuit

Edwardus. ignoto deceptus filio [115]

---

113 scit] ed.; sciunt ABCDEFH; sciuat I

infesta sceptra detulit falsus pater.

diversa fratris ora patrem denegant,

moresque degeneres fratris meos pater

vultus habebat, talis aspectu fuit.

imago dissimilis fratris stuprum docet [120]

amoris haeres turpis, haud regni fuit.

Bucking. At jure vendicas dolos, quid querimus?

fatetur aequitatis istud plurimum.

iter patet caeptis. quid utendum artibus

quomodo ista turbae verba constabunt levi? [125]

aut cujus in tantis dolis sequeris fidem?

Gloc. Nil frigidus cor torqueat tremulum metus

quae non secreto vincitur praetio fides?

civem potentem facile Londinum dabit,

et qui dolos tegere sagax nostros potest [130]

animosque blandus commovere civium,

multisque vincere Londinensis praemiis.

Inter suos praetor valet plurimum,

vanos honores ambit, et fluxas opes,

multumque avarae mentis instigat furor [135]

reddet fidelem spes honoris improba

et pellet usque longa nummorum sitis.

Lovellus Falsis sacris nihil fallacius fuit,

plebem facile mentita ludunt numina,

animus statim devotus impetum dabit   [140]

si praeco scripturae fidelis (dum sacra

insculpit auribus piis oracula

divina vel praecepta populo personet)

commemoret olim fraude deceptos thoros

lectique probrum, vulnus et clarae domus.   [145]

Bucking. Vix literis insignis est Doctor Shaa

praetori eadem matre conjunctus frater

hunc laude ditarunt frequentes literae

fucata cives sanctitas mire allicit.

cujus tamen mente facile labes sedet   [150]

hoc munus exequi fidele qui potest.

Gloc. Aliquis meorum accersat urbis Londini

Praetorem honore inter suos magno virum,

summisque doctum litteris fratrem Shaum.

ubi praetor animos civium demulserit   [155]

---

148 laude] tamen C

149 mire] jure C

154 doctum] H; [DOCTUM] C; doctrina B

et nostra regna civibus persuaserit:

hoc convenit pleno senatu te alloqui.

minatur illustrem ducem vulgus rude.

fulgore populus captus attonitus stupet

lapsumque caelitem deum putat sibi   [160]

vultu tuo plebs victa succumbet statim

dulci veneno mox stupentes opprime

ut filios pari insequantur et odio.

promitte libertatis alta praemia

urbem beabit laeta civium quies,   [165]

et fine nullo crescit immensum decus

si vindicent lecti stupro infamem domum

et sceptra nobis jure reddant sanguinis.

Lovellus Dum praedicat coitus nefandos, et fratris

novos amores, matris et probrum tuae   [170]

domusque regis dedecus sanctus pater:

donec tuarum praeco laudum, maximis

virtutibus decorat intentus Shaus

quasi caelitus repente lapsus advola

te principem divinitus crearier   [175]

populus levis putabit, atque numine

---

160 caelitem] ed.; caelitus ABCDEFHI

176 numine] H; (NUMINE) C; numen B

ductum sacro dictasse te regem Shaum

credet, levemque distrahet mentem stupor.

[I.ii] Dux Gloc. Praetor Lond.

Doctor Shaa.

Gloc   Praeclare praetor urbis illustrissimae

et sancte preco, diisque sacratum caput,

en magna molimur futura commoda,

et maximam regno quietem quaerimus,

hujusque laudis magna vobis pars erit   [5]

quos novimus regni precari prospera

uterque votis anxius si pareat

nunc ergo vestram posco secretam fidem,

tam magna quibus arcana regni pandimus,

honoribus magnis fidem pensabimus   [10]

largisque fidos praemiis ditabimus.

Praetor Protector illustris propago splendida

regis: tibi lubens fidem consecro meam

quod imperas fidele munus exequar.

Gloc   Contrita mutuis caedibus Britannia   [15]

heu terret, et majora suadent vulnera

_____

15 caedibus] aedibus C

infirma pueri sceptra, matris et furor.

sceleri mederi quis facile demens potest?

deponat animo justa qui reges timet,

et male parebit regis imperio pudor.   [20]

viro potenti vera laus non contigit,

fortuna quos impellit invitos male,

vetatque saepe facere, quod cupiunt pie.

justus facile erit, cui vacat pectus metu.

suadent mihi decora regni nobiles,   [25]

regnare quem regalia jubent stemmata.

Vos civium suadere mentibus velim

in urbe quorum fama tanta splendide

celebratur ut mihi sceptra regni deferant.

Praetor Quo jure tu regnum nepotis vendicas?   [30]

ne temere plebs irata turbas concitet

ubi senserit spoliatum honore principem.

Gloc   Talia tuis clam sparge Praetor civibus

lecti stuprati natus incestus fuit

Edwardus olim frater, alienos thoros   [35]

dum matris amor avarus admisit, ducis

---

22 quos] D;   [NOS] C;   nos B

32 senserit]   senserint C

36 ducis] DUCIS C

atque soboli falsos nepotes miscuit

lecti probrum pudebundus invenit comes

stuprumque secretum fatentur famuli.

imago dissimilis, patris nothum vocat   [40]

moresque degeneres fratris. me filium

legitimum imago nota persuasit ducis

iidemque mores patris et voces pares.

neque tulit hanc solam labem infaelix genus

majore dedecore domun infamen gravat   [45]

matrem secutus frater Edwardus suam.

Nam conjugali Luciae junctus fide,

repudia sponsae nunciat amator novus

thalamisque primis [ludit] injunctam fidem

Elizabetha sero regali face   [50]

uxor secunda juncta principi fuit

possidet iniqua mater alienos thoros

faedosque patri filios pellex tulit.

Sum populus ista cogitat secum, statim

---

42 legitimum] legitime C

49 [ludit]] ludit omitted C

    injunctam] in junctam C

in curia cives tua, dux inclitus [55]

coram decebit ista Buckingamius.

procerumque quas sit omnium sententia

splendore populus captus insignis viri

me forte principem suis suffragiis

clamabit, et regem clamabit Angliae. [60]

haec cruce Pauli sacra fundens dogmata

populo simul divine praeco edissere

sed turpe probrum matris invitus quasi

perstringe nostram cautus offensam gravem

metuisse fingens: laudibus ubi nos tuis [65]

copiosis ornabis subito quasi caelitus

princeps datus Britanniae, laudes meas

stipante pompa intercipiam, [miraculum]

dum creduli meditantur: illico numinis

spes falsa seducet. facile, nunc exequi [70]

vox expedit fideliter qua jussimus.

Doctor Mox tua fidelis imperata persequar
Shaa
nunquam meam damnabis incertam fidem.

---

68 [miraculum]] miraculum omitted C

69 numinis] nominis C

[II.i] Actus Secundus

Civis primus, Civis secundus

Primus Quosque scinditur Britannia litibus?

luctusque cumulat luctibus fatum grave?

dirum premit recens malum. paene modum

severa fata nesciunt. nunquam domus

irata, plaena caedibus pacabitur?   [5]

haeresve nullus sceptra impune gerit?

at jam nihil stirpem timent Lancastriam

erepta ferro regna. Iam novum scelus

infausta sibi domus parat. quantam luem

praesagit assuetus malis animus? fides   [10]

est nulla regni, nec suis parcere potest

ambitio demens. Glocestrium ducem

ambire regnum murmurat secreta plebs.

patrui nefas crudele, tetrum, parvuli

latent in obscuro nepotes carcere.   [15]

En comitiis defertur ascriptus dies.

---

3 paene] paenae C

Glocestrii tantum ducis frequens cliens

attrita pulsat limina. illic emicat

illustris aulae splendor. istuc confluit

mitiora quisquis supplici implorat prece [20]

quicunque regis nuda calcat limina

et principes servus fidelis viserit:

illum nimis edocta vulnerat cohors.

Civis sec   Charum caput, duraeque sortis particeps

fidelis: heu quam nos premunt casus graves. [25]

fessam repetit en turbo saevus Angliam

viresque triste reparat amissas malum.

Primus   Effare quae cives manent lassos mala?

Secundus   Brevi scelus complectar horrens impium.

dum rebus otiosus intentus novis [30]

vagarer, et commune regni gaudium

revolvo: praeceps ecce fertur impetu

insana plebs, caeco frequens cursu ruit:

denso statim miscebar agmini stupens,

ad templa rapimur dubius aures porrigo [35]

expecto sacra. cogitabundus steti.

---

18   limina] lumina <u>C</u>

19   confluit] <u>ed.</u>; confluunt <u>ABCDEFHI</u>

22   principes] principis <u>C</u>

Divinus ecce praeco scandit pulpitum

quem literis lucere clarum jactitant,

sordere faedis moribus, Doctor Shaa

mox e sacris sic ortus est oraculis   [40]

Semen beatum thorus adulter denegat,

proles nec altas spuria radicos dabit.

postquam diu regni decus quam vulnerat

lecti probrum, premonstrant et falsae faces

thori fidem quantum beabunt numina   [45]

lectique decepti scelestos filios:

peccata testantes patris quantum horreant

bona falsus haeres quamvis occupat patris:

furtum tamen mox prodit ignotum deus,

suoque restituit sua haeredi bona.   [50]

quod possidebat regis infandos thoros,

fidemque lusit conjugalem pellace

Elizabetha falsa mater, impio

declamat ore: quodque primum Luciae

promissus olim lectus Edwardi fuit   [55]

Ergo thoros hac possidebat Lucia

Injusta mater Elizabetha, liberos

---

52 pellace] ed.;   pellica ABCH;   pellucca DF;   pallaca EI

et polluit macula suos adultera.

nec filios mentita faedebat fides

solum regis: patris polluta mater arguit   [60]

spurcosque natales, suis dum liberis

adulteros furtiva miscuit Venus

summique ducis falsumque patris filium

diversa suadent ora: solus exprimit

Richardus effigiem patris. regem vocat   [65]

vultus ducis. nunc ergo jure vendicat

amissa patris regna. mox Glocestrium

ad astra laudibus ferebat, regius

quod splendor hic lucebat, hic versus nitet

vultus patris, virtus frequens quantum beat   [70]

hunc intueri jussit hunc solum coli

omnes stupent, vultumque demittunt, fremunt,

mox intuentur invicem. Venit Glocestrius,

suas laudes serus amittit, comes

stipabat ingens. ubi ducem vidit Shaus   [75]

rex Angliae quasi lapsus esset caelitus.

```
               en (inquit) en chari Britanni, en principem

               hunc intueri rursus, hunc coli jubet

               periisse quasi frustra blanditias pudet

               Iam tum priores, dux prius quod abfuit.          [80]

               haec vera imago patris, hic vultus ducis

               nescit mori pater Richardo sospite.

               stipante pompa, spiritus altos gerens

               per densa perrumpens virorum civibus

               spectanda praebet ora dux:  alto sedet.          [85]

Civis primus   Quis hujus at sermonis eventus fuit?

Secundus       Postquam Shaus periisse laudes cerneret

               populum nec acclamare laetis vocibus

               Rex vivat aeternum Richardus.  (nam stupet

               tum populus, admiratur infandum nefas)           [90]

               coepti pudet, seroque cognovit scelus.

               Reparare vires quaerit amissus pudor

               frustra, prius spretamque virtutem timet

               en civium vultus miser fugiens, domum

               subducit ipse se clam.  at hic quid vult sibi    [95]

               in curia corona tanta civium.
```

---

85 praebet] probet C

88 laetis] laetum C

Primus   Coire cives praetor huc jussit suos

de rebus ut nos consulat gravissimis

propago Buckingamiorum nobilis.

Secundus   Avertat omen triste propitius deus.   [100]

    [II.ii]   Dux Bucking.   Praetor Lond. Nobilis

         Servus vnus et alter Buckingami

Buck   Amore vestro ductus (o cives mei)

de rebus alloquar hodie gravissimis

Sunt ista patriae decora maxime

vobis, nec auditu seorsim tristia.

Quos haec beat fortuna laetos undique   [5]

quae namque vestris expetita saepius

votis, diuque frustra defessis erant

sperata tempora, pretio quae maximo

parasse vel labore summo non piget:

oblata vobis gratis adsunt omnia,   [10]

si tanta tamque optata quae sunt quaeritis,

tranquillitas secura vitae, liberum

dulcis tutela, salusque conjugum.

heu quis prius tot explicatis seculis

vos perculit metus gravis? nam per deos   [15]

coelumque quicquid possidet: quis tot dolis

tantisque, tuto perfrui rebus suis

potuit? quis esse liberis solatio?

quis in suis regnare solus aedibus?

mens horret illam persequi tyrannidem,   [20]

per ima quae grassata regni viscera,

exhausit aedes, neque pestis invida

insontibus novit parcere, quid explicem

exacta quanta sint tributa saepius?

extorta vi, quanta visa luxui,   [25]

nec grande civis ferre vectigal potest

exhaustus, mulcta crevit immensum levis

paenaque gravis percussit offensam brevem.

meminisse Burdetti arbitror (cives mei)

cui quod jocatus est lepide, demi caput   [30]

Rex jussit indigne, nefas judex licet

horreret infandum, [locusque] nobilis

urbis senator qui diu vestrae fuit,

---

32 [locusque]] locusque omitted C

heu quam graves perpessus est paenas miser,

viris quod illis ipse multa debuit,   [35]

quos intime rex invidebat impius?

non est necesse caeteros ut persequar.

adesse pene neminem virum puto,

qui tam cruenti temporis non sit memor,

metusque non sit ipse conscius sui: [40]

quem non nefandus regis injecit furor

vel civium tot improborum ingens favor

Rex namque ferro nactus imperium grave

hunc victor iratus decora laedere

regni putabat impie, qui sanguine   [45]

affinis esset, aut amoris vinculo

conjunctus his, princeps prius quos oderat

at huic malo quin majus accessit malum

vitae dubius haerebat, haud belli exitus

quod vexat incertus modo, sed (quod faedius)   [50]

urget tumultus civium, esse maximus

qui tum solet, cum nobiles odio invicem

tacito ardeant nec optimates acrius

---

42 improborum] D;   improbor C;   improbi B

se maximis exulcerabunt litibus

quam sceptra cum gestaret infesta manu [55]

Edwardus, intestina tandem praelia

sic aestuabant undique ut tristi nece

pars interiret maxima civium

haec, haec fuit tam faeda strages civium

qualem vidit devicta nunquam Gallia. [60]

haec praepotens exhausit Anglorum genus,

haec pristinis spoliabat illos viribus,

sumant tot urbes tanta clades omnium.

dubia minatur pax pares bello minas.

nummos luunt domini, atque agros quisquis tenet, [65]

mactatur, iram principis quisquam fugit?

Iam nemo non timore languebat miser,

nec ulla non plena periculis erant tempora

at at quis illi charus esse creditur

cui frater odio erat suus? confidere [70]

Quibus potest, cui frater esse perfidus

videtur? aut quibus pepercit mitior

fratri suo qui toties damnum intulit?

---

61 genus] gena C

at quos colebat intimus: nihil moror,

honore vel quales decoro pinxerat? [75]

quis nescit unam plus potuisse pellicem,

regni viros quam totius primarios?

Invitus sane ista vobis affero.

sed nota quae singulis: quid attinet

tacere? quo non impulit libidinis [80]

immanis aestus? amoris et caecus furor?

quae virgo paulo pulchrior? quae femina

plus caeteris decora, matris e sinu,

quam, vel mariti, non rapuit amplexibus?

ubivis at licet tyrannus ingruat: [85]

hujus tamen prae caeteris sensit minas

urbs vestra, cujus potius ornasset decus

quod prima regni sedes est, et praemia

defensus olim saepe princeps debuit

majora. benefacta vivus spreverat, [90]

nec mortuus referre gratiam potest.

alter en eodem restat ortus sanguine

rex gratior suis futurus subditis

---

86   sensit]   vincit C

88   praemia]   prima C

quique meritis referre vestris debita,

votisque respondere possit affatim.   [95]

nec animis illa (credo) vestris excidunt

doctus sacrorum praeco quae sparsit prius

nunquam fidem fefellit interpres dei:

patruum sacerdos fratris ad regnum vocat.

Glocestrium regnare, quin jussit deus.   [100]

nec sceptra patris tractet impurus nepos.

aut polluat regni decus lecti probrum.

Richardus haeres fratris unicus fuit.

huic civium decrevit et procerum cohors

magnanima: supplex ut rogaret patruum,   [105]

regni velut decus tueri principis,

sumeret onus pollentis haeres insulae:

facturus est aegre, scio: regni labor

deterret ingens, certat invidiae capax.

Ingrata pacem sceptra nequaquam colunt   [110]

Quantis cietur fluctibus fallax decor?

(mihi crede civis) non potest tantum puer

onus tueri. pulsat aures vox sacra

---

104 huic] hunc C

Infausta regna sunt quibus puer praeest.

faelix acumen invidum decet thronum [115]

aetasque plena: patruum qualem vides.

Si chara vobis ergo civium salus,

aut si juvent optata pacis faedera:

tam fausta procerum vota laudetis simul.

uno creetur ore rex Glocestrius, [120]

tantum laborem promptus assumet magis

si vox fatiget vestra nolentem prius.

mens ergo quae sit vestra palam dicite.

altum quid hoc silentum? plebs cur tacet?

Praetor Vix forte populus aure dicta concipit. [125]

Bucking Affabor illos ergo rursus altius

Clausa sunt iniqua (cives) tempora.

pax alma tandem sorte faelice viget,

nisi suo demens quis invideat bono,

aut nescit uti: cum premebat Angliam [130]

Edwardus atrox saeviens vultu truci:

insula quibus jactatur usque fluctibus?

non vita tuta civium, nunquam bona

---

114 sunt] H; [SUNT] C; sceptra B

130 cum] dum C

sunt clausa cuique dissipatque singula

luxus nefandi tum libido principis.   [135]

quae virgo fuit intacta? quae conjunx labe

carebat injusta, licet, quicquid lubet,

misera fuit cunctis potestas civibus:

sed Londinensibus longe miserrima

Illis licet benigna persuasit locus   [140]

sed unus est, pericula qui tot vindicet,

Dux ipse regio creatur stemmate

quem singuli colunt Glocestriae decus.

Regnare quem leges jubebant patriae,

haeresque solus regiae manet domus.   [145]

furtiva proles matris injustae, patris

frustra sibi vendicant thronos adulteri.

vir nuper ista vos docebat optimus

Dum sacra vobis praeco pandit dogmata.

divina nullus ora damnabit pius.   [150]

hinc nobilis commota magnatum cohors

et magna civium corona, supplices

orare statunt patruum, haeres ut suum

---

149   pandit] [PANDIT] C

capessat imperium, decus nec patriae

falsus nepos corrumpat. id faciet lubiens   [155]

si sponte vos id exoptare senserit.

clamore ergo publico mentem diffundite.

quid hoc? adhuc tacet? mirum nimis.

Praetor   Unus solebat ore jussus publico,

de rebus alloqui cives magnis suos.   [160]

hinc forsitan responsa querenti dabunt.

Affare cives urbis interpres tuae.

[Recordator Quam sorte faelici cadant magis omnia
Fitzwilliam]
quam fratre quondam rege quis demens negat?

mihi nec esse necesse singula persequi.   [165]

memoravit haec dux omnium clarissimus.

estis duorum facile testes temporum

quantum prior premebat aetas, postera

quam grata lucet, quem latet? cupit

magnanimus heros ergo nunc cognescere

regnare num Glocestrium placet ducem   [170]

quod singulos statuisse constat ordines.

regemque proceres Angliae verum vocant.

---

158 s.d.: The mayor and others going to the duke DEFH

163 [Recordator Fitzwilliam]] Recordator Fitzwilliam omitted C

vir ille quis quantusque sit quis nesciat?

quo jure poscat haeres imperii decus   [175]

admonuit omnes doctus interpres dei,

et arte qui pandit polum doctor Shaa.

edatis ergo voce mentem publica.

Bucking.   Est pertinax istud nimis silentium.

de rebus hiis (amici) longe maximis   [180]

vos alloqui, non jure quaero concitus,

amore sed commatus, ignotum bonum

vobis adhuc referre quod cupio lubens.

hoc singulis erit salubre civibus.

manifesta mentis signa precor aedite statim.   [185]

Servus unus   Rex vivat aeternum Richardus.
  et alter

Praetor   Aula levi tota susurrat murmure.

Cives tacent, spectant retro, quae vox fuit

mirantur. acclamant nihil regnum duci.

Bucking   Vox hercle laeta, clamor atque maximus   [190]

dum nemo voce contra quicquam murmurat.

vox ergo civium una cum sit omnium

pariter mihi comites (precor) cras jungite,

---

177 s.d.: Rounding the mayor in the eare DEFH

186 s.d.: These words are spoken by a few of the dukes servantes. I

precemur una supplices ducem, velit

nomen deinde sustinere principis.   [195]

Nobilis   Heu quid genas fletu rugas miser? dolos

juvat nefandos plangere? haud parcis tibi

furtum pium, sit lachrymarum, sed tamen

laethale solus fata mundi qui vides

tremende pater, insontibus miseris necem   [200]

averte tristem, sed sequor comes ducem.

[III.I]   Actus Tertius

Dux Bucking.   Cives.

[Bucking.] Veneranda civium cohors, quos affatim

urbs possidet praeclara londinum en sua

Iam quisque sponte contulit faustum gradum,

et quilibet confluxit ordo civium

ut dempta sceptra adulteris nepotibus   [5]

Glocestrio gerenda reddant patruo,

---

197 s.d.: Weepinge behinde the duke turninge his face to the wall BDEFI

198 sit] ed.; si ABCDEFHI

200 miseris] misere C

1 s.d.: Let the mayor come first accompanied with citizens, then the
          duke with other nobles they assemble at Bernhardes Castle DEFH

4 quilibet] quaelibet C

ne regiam mentita proles inquinet.

Sed tu prius nostri ducem adventus mene

ne tantus anxium tumultus illico

perturbet, illum supplices cives petunt   [10]

Quos Angliae torquent graves casus, sui

dignetur aditum subditis fidelibus,

de rebus illum maximis dum consulunt.

Ingens onus, regni labor, nec allicit

statim bonos blandum venenum; qui furor   [15]

vexabit intestinus aeternis minis

en delicatas eligunt fraude domos

et nulla cingunt tela principem satis.

tantumque licet at serme popularis premit

sed ista quorsum persequor? quod si pium   [20]

onus coronae cura commendat gravis,

nihilque suspectum facit ducem fides:

At illum metuo deterreat nepotibus

vivis adhuc, infame regnum patrui.

Honore plenus est, latere dux cupit   [25]

a turbidis semotus invidiae malis.

---

8 s.d.: He sendeth his man into the palace BI

15 qui] ed.; quos ABCDEFHI

aditum negat Protector (o cives mei)

tantamque turbam suspicatur, nisi prius

adventus hujus causa quae sit, audiat.

quod magna procerum turba supplex consulit   [30]

cinctusque multo cive praetor, nuncia.

Domesticum torquet malum, quod auribus

tantum suis sollicita mandabit cohors.

At nos Glocestrium rogemus supplices

rogamus numani. reluctantem prece,   [35]

ut sceptra regni justus haeres occupet.

Sed nunc duobus cinctus ecce episcopis

apparet in summa domo princeps pius.

ah sola dux divina faelix cogitat.

Cives   O fraude pugnans pervicax audatia   [40]

colore dum ludit alieno, nil timet

secura, sed nescire caeteros putat

tectum malum, sibique blanditur nefas.

---

27 s.d.: His servant returninge and to him secretlye reportinge. To his servant whome he sendeth again. BDEFHI

35 numani] inani C

[III.ii] Dux Buckingamiae, Dux

Glocestrensis, Chorus civium

[Buck.] Te civium profusa flagitat cohors

excelse praeses ut tuam de re gravi

praestantiam alloqui liceret, afferunt

ignota regno bona, decus magnum tibi,

non audet eloqui jussus pios tamen,   [5]

id nisi licere voce testaris tua.

Gloc. Quaecunque mens jussit, licebit, dicere

publica juvat decreta scire civium.

Buck. Diu nimis perpessa plebs tyrannidem

laetatur haec luxisse tandem tempora   [10]

se pristino quibus timore solveret

vitaeque grata sit suae securitas.

De rebus ergo dum coiret publicis,

statumque regni plena civium cohors

tractaret, haeres unicus, regni decus,   [15]

Vt vendices, sanxere sacris jussibus.

nec sceptra prolem fratris impuram ferunt

Injusta quam matris Venus suae premit

---

2 re] te C

nunc ergo turba civium frequens adest

ut voce supplex publica multum petat   [20]

ut pristino cives timore liberes.

regnum et sagaci debitum tractes manu.

Gloc. Quam vera cives finxerint licet sciam

fratris tamen manes veneror olim mei,

nec in meos ferox nepotes patruus   [25]

demens ero, verbisque nec populus feris

pulsabit iratus, thronum quod ambiam

fratris mei, nec exterae probris simul

gentes lacessent si dolis patruus meis

nepotibus regnum scelestus auferam.   [30]

aut sceptra tollam dubia cognati laris.

potius latebo tutus invidiae malis

nec caecus animum pulsat ambitus meum

satis premunt sceptri propinqui munera.

Vos at mihi dixisse non tamen piget,   [35]

cogit potius amor referre gratiam,

nec vos colatis nepotem nunc minus obsecro

cujus magis privatus imperium feram

---

22 debitum] debitam C

regnare qui puer licet novit parum:

laboribus meis adjutus is tamen   [40]

regni decus puer satis tuebitur.

viguisse quod nuper magis nemo negat,

tutela postquam tanta regni traditur

veterata cessat ira, franguntur minae,

bonoque languent pulsa consilio odia,   [45]

partim, dei sed maximi nutu magis.

nil sceptra damnate regis optimi viri

debet mihi nomen placere subditi.

Bucking. Da pauca rursus alloqui (o dux inclite)

regnare non sinunt nepotes subditi,   [50]

summi vetant proceres vetat vulgus rude

regnum student purgare adultera labe.

Sin justa regni sceptra non via pertinax

at posse flecti nobilem sperant prece

qui regio splendore cultu gaudeat   [55]

de rebus hisce quid ergo statuas audiant.

Gloc.   Quod invident regnum paternum liberis

dolen, fratris qui honoro manes mortui.

---

47 damnate] ed.; damnes ACDEFH;   ferte BI

50 sinunt] sinant C

53 non vis] H; (NON VIS) C; renuis B

utinam queant nepotis imperium pati,

sed regere populum nullus invisum potest [60]

haec quia video statuisse consensu pari,

regnumque spuriis auferunt nepotibus,

cum jura regni solus haeres vendico

quod filius relictus unus sum patris

cum fuit necesse civibus cedere meis [65]

vota sequor. en regna posco debita

votis creari subditorum principem

magis reor, curam Angliae accipimus simul

et Galliae, rex gemina regna vendico.

sanctius habenas Angliae princeps regam [70]

magis pacata civium quies monet.

tum nostra discet fraena victa Gallia

haec Angliae subacta ditabit decus,

cujus miser si gloriam non quaerem

utinam sorores fila rumpat perfida. [75]

Chorus Richardus rex, Richardus rex, Richardus rex.

Quaerit colorem triste virtutis scelus

pudet sui deforme vultus vitium,

---

76 s.d.: The duke and noblemen go into the kinges palaice the maior
and citizens departe away. BDEFHI

heu quis secretos nescit ignarus dolos?

et mille patrui machinas? quis sibi prius   [80]

promissa fratris regna fraude non videt?

dolis petitum publice regnum negat,

Inventa damnat sceptra, ficta sanctitas.

qualis negat bis consecrari pontifex

qui sacra tamen ambit colenda forsitan: [85]

talis sua rex sponte compulsus gerit

erepta pueris sceptra sed decet magis

spectare tantas plebeios tragaedias.

quicquid libet regi licet, nec legibus

semper piis rex vota metitur sua.   [90]

crebro juvat nescire, quod scias tamen.

                    Actus Quartus

[IV.i]   Doctor Shaa.   Civis amicus

Civis Cur sic pigro miser gradu moves stupens

       dubiusque sese pes incerto tenet?

corpus cupis referre progressum licet?

haeret animus, ponisque nolentem pedem

quid triste consilium diu torques? modum   [5]

nec invenis? quid civium vultum fugis

insane? vince quicquid obstitit, expedi

mentem tuam, teque restituas tibi?

Shaa   Heu mihi animus semet scelere plenus fugit

vetat quiescere pectus oneratum malis,   [10]

mentisque consciae pavor. dolor aestuat

Animus non potest venenum expellere,

scelerisque mordet saeva conscientia.

quis, quis coegit daemon adversus mihi,

faedare stupro regis Edwardi thoros,   [15]

heu mihi tuos Edwarde natos prodidi,

et ore nuncio nefando adulteros.

tuam coronam possidet jussu meo

Richardus. hei mihi voce faedavi mea

natos tuos, mendatiis sacra miscui,   [20]

et ore scripturas inani pollui.

Civis Cur te ipse paenis gravibus infestus gravas?

---

9   semet] plenus C

nutritus alios colligit dolor faces.

renovatque durum nolle sanari malum.

fraenos capit prudens dolor et extinguitur. [25]

vincit dolorem quisquis eximere cupit,

et perfidum sanare conatur malum.

Shaa   Praeceps monentem mens fugit, redit statim

concepta frustra consilia repetens sequi

cogit scelus pejora, virtutem timet [30]

accendit ipse semet infestus dolor.

lapsaque vires integrat. nunquam meas

cessabit in paenas scelus. nunquam quies

nocturna curis solvit, aut altus sopor

noctu diem voco, repeto noctem die [35]

semper memet fugio, non possum scelus.

Civis   Malum nequis sanare.

Shaa   Si possim mori.

Civis   At dedecus demi licet magnum potest.

Shaa   Nisi turpis haeret usque vestigium labis.

Civis   Mors sola maculam demere infandam potest?

Shaa.   Faedata nescit vita crimen ponere. [40]

---

39 sola] ista C

Civ. At paenitenti sera parcunt numina.

Sha. Sceleris novi mater prius natum scelus.

Civ. Sanare cessas qui nimis vulnus times.

Sha. Sanare non potes facile vulnus grave:

Civ. Nulli pepercit, quisquis haud parcit sibi.   [45]

Sha. Prius ipse crimen solus accusa tuum.

Civ. Absolve te, quem judicas ultus satis.

Sha. Nemo satis ulcisci scelus dirum potest.

Civ. Crimen nimis durum judex acerbus vindicas.

Sha. Nisi mordent acre, faeda sordent vulnera.   [50]

Civ. Dum cogitas severa nil curas reum.

Sha. Dolor doloris est medela, nescit parcere,
      caelum crimen vidit nefanda, conscia
      tanti fuit dedecoris et tellus vaga.
      ruina mentis faeda tam me disparem   [55]
      fecit mihi, ut memet nihil fugiam magis,
      et factus infaelix mei sum perfuga.
      animusque serum corporis divertium
      precatur anxius, necat quisquis jubet
      vivere mori quisquis jubet, vitam dedit.   [60]

---

50 mordent] ed.; mordet ABCDEFHI

tantum potest placere quicquid displicet.

de me viri quid loquuntur futiles?

Civis   Te sceleris arguunt nefandi conscium .

Sha.   Sed quis tumultus civium isthuc convolat?

Civis   Ubi civium regnare Jussu caeperat   [65]

princeps Glocestrius: loco primum studet

rex pius ab illo subditis fari suis

ubi voce lex Anglis loqui viva solet

nunc ergo ad aulam commigrat Westminsteri

rex ut pius legum peritis imperet   [70]

ne prava mens legum minas adulteret.

discessit infaelix, pati nec civium

vultus potest. huic verba pandam principis.

[IV. ii] Dux Gloc.

[Gloc.]   Juvabat Astreae locatum sedibus

et hoc tribunali tremendo Minois

auro caput sepire primum fulgido

Justaque cives lege regere patriae.

---

3 sepire] sepirae C

Rex providere debet id potissimum [5]

ut urbium columna lex firmissima

in curia dominetur aequali potens

vestrum domare pectus haud metus decet

quorum superbum claruit titulis genus.

non caeca regnat ira vinci nescia. [10]

nunc ense fessum miles exonerat latus

omnes amoris vinculo jungere juvat.

contempta nec patrum jacebunt stemmata.

vos laudo patres jure doctos patrio

qui continetis legibus rempublicam: [15]

ne jurgiis lacerata mutius Anglia

languescat: amplo vos honore persequar.

et mente cives gaudeant lassa licet,

e sordidis qui nutriuntur artibus.

nec causa vos agitata judici premet, [20]

nec fera clangore bella perstrepent tubae.

nam concidunt res prosperae discordiis.

hinc falsa mens vultu minatur integro

hinc omne fluxit civitatibus malum.

---

12 amoris] amores C

13 patrum] patrui C

18 gaudeant] gaudeat C

sedabit hos fluctus, amor, pietas, fides, [25]

his vinculis faelix cohaeret Anglia.

quae nec furor contunderet domesticus,

nec robur hostium potest infringere?

odii recentis pereat omnis memoria

statim mihi Foggum satelles libera, [30]

supplex asylo qui metu nostri latet.

sit finis irae, nec minas jactet furor.

summo laborat impetu mens anxia,

a subditis vultu benigne conspici.

heu quam velim fides vigeret aurea [35]

tantum vetustis nota quondam saeculis

aut quae fucos experta virtus non fuit.

mox sit decorum numen adversum mihi

si lingua mentis fallat interpes suae.

Noli timere Fogge concedas prope [40]

sociemus animos, pignus hoc fidei cape.

conjunge dextram, et me vicissim delige.

---

30 libera] liberat C

[V. i]   Actus quintus

Hospes. Civis.

[Hospes.] Domesticum narras malum, tetrum, grave,

Immensa regni moles invidiae capax

quantis cietur fluctibus. victum licet,

potuisse vinci non sibi credit tamen.

graves procellas concitat regni fames,   [5]

dum caeca quassavit libido principis:

quot urbium projecta sunt cadavera?

qualem maris salsi secantem gurgitem

puppim benignam turbo concussit gravis

et volvit horrens concitum flatu fretum,   [10]

dum latera scindit, geminat minas:

talis premit vehemens statim mutatio.

affare quaeso, cur frequens huc convolat

populus? notatque proximos oculis locos,

theatra stupidus spectat, usque splendida   [15] et stragulis sternuntur omnis fulgidis.

regale splendet atque solium principis.

Civis   Hospes, fideli mihi corona cingitur

rex Angliae Richardus, assensu pari

cujusvis haeres approbatur ordinis.   [20]

Hospes Hoc sparsit olim rumor ambiguus.

Civis   Locus

hic maximus datur comitiis; imminet

hora.

Hospes   Bona, dum pius creatur rex: mala

si nequior, rex si bonus sit, civium salus.

rex si malus sit, civitatis pestis est.   [25]

Civis   Qui regio natus superbo stemmate,

duos nepotes principes tutor suam

suscepit in fidem patruus, en Angliae

rex ipse conventu creatur maximo.

Hospes Ubi reguli duo? nefas regere patruum,   [30]

hi dum supersunt.

Civis   Hoc facit regni sitis.

in arce regni carceris caeci luem

patiuntur.

Hospes   O scelus.

Civis   Sed principis tamen.

Hospes Magis hoc nefandum.

Civis   Propter imperium simul.

Hospes Pietas decet regem, nec impio licet   [35]

---

17 splendet atque] sibi det alta C

parare regnum praetio.

Civis   Semper tamen

Imperia constant praetio bene quolibet.

Hospes   Nunquam diu male parta succedunt.

Civis   Satis

semel est regere.

Hospes   Statim labi duplex malum

faelicitas brevis, labor regni gravis   [40]

Civis   Prout lubet regendo minuitur labor.

Hospes   Crescit magis odium.

Civis   Hoc metu restinquitur.

Hospes   Potius fide.

Civis   Quin deme tantos spiritus

lacerare dictis principem diris grave est,

statimque suspectos sibi mori jubet   [45]

Jam parce dictis: tempori decet obsequi,

nuper nimis blande salutat obvios.

objicere se cogit mali mens conscia,

regemque vultus pene serviles docet.

Hinc liberavit cardinalem vinculis   [50]

et Stanleium emisit solutum carcere.

hujus timebat filium Lancastriae,

ne saeva patris vindicaret vincula.

At Eliensem praesulem clausum domi

retinere Buckinghamium jussit ducem.   [55]

---

45   jubet]   jubent C

sed regis adventum sonat clangor tubae

Comites, ducesque, Marchiones, Praesides,

praeire torquibus micantes cernimus.

Hospes Effare (civis) nitida quid calcaria

aurata signant, quae comes manu gerit?   [60]

Civis   Sunt bellicae virtutis haec insignia.

Hospes Baculum quid?

Civis   Edwardi fuit regis pii,

id illius nunc memoria perferunt.

Hospes Sed absque cuspide gladius, quem fert caput

nudus quid indicat?

Civis   Clementiam.

Hospes   Aureas   [65]

clavus quid?

Civis   Officium comestabulis Angliae

aequitum magister, publico hunc caetu gerit.

Hospes Ensis quid a dextris feruntur principis

et a sinistris fulgidi duo simul?

Civis   Sunt arma justitiae: scelus celeri simul   [70]

Laicique puniunt salubri vulnere.

Hospes Nudi duo feruntur enses cuspido

nullo. Cives.

Hospes Quidnam loquuntur sceptra?

Civis   Pacem.

Hospes   Quid globus.

cujus super crux elevatur verticem?   [75]

---

65 nudus] calvus C

73 nullo. Civis] All manuscripts give these two words and then leave the rest
    of the line blank.

Civis   Monarchiam,

Hospes   Ecce alius vagina conditum

Et arte summa fulgidum gladium gerit,

itemque magnum.

Civis   Summa dignitatis est

honore summo spatha.

Hospes   Sed dic quis locum

splendore medium maximo radiis quasi   [80]

nitidis micans rubroque tinctus murice

tenet?

Civis   Iste faecialis est sui ordinis

primus atque regis ipse nomine.

Hospes Virgula quid alba prae se fert ducis?

Civis   Hanc similis Angliae archicamerimis gerit.   [85]

Hospes Quid alba reginae columba denotat?

Civis   Notat avis innocentiam nihil nocens.

[*After they have thus declared what everythinge
signifieth let the singers singe. Or being placed
on the toppe of some of the houses in the meane
season lett such ceremonyes be used for the cororation
as the chronicle declareth. and after let them departe
in this order followinge.

        The Shewe of the coronation.

First trumpets and heraldes. Then singing men,
priests in surplices and graye amesies
or silk hoodes, Bishops in Rochets and
chymers, and last the Cardinal. Then Noblemen
Lordes, Earles, Dukes. Then gylt spurres
caried by the Earle of Huntingdon. Then St.

---

79 sed dic] (SED DIC) C

80 maximo] maxime C

* Line 87 ends Part II in C. The stage direction and The Shewe of the
   Coronation are found in BI.

Edwardes staffe caried by the earle of
Bedforde. Then the pointles sworde naked by
the Earle of Northumberlande bare headed.
Then the greate mace by the L. Stanley. Then
two swordes together naked by the Earle of
Kent and the L. Lovel. Then the great scepter
the Duke of Suffolke. Then the ball with the crosse
the Earle of Lincolne. Then the sword of estate
with a rich scaberd the earle of Surrey. Then
three together that is the king of heraldes in
the middest, on the left hand the Mason of
London with a mace, on the right hand the
gentleman usher. Then the kinges crowne
the Duke of Norfolke. Then the king under a
canapy betwixt 2 Bishoppes. Then
the Duke of Buckingham with a white staffe
bearing up the kinges trayne. Then Lordes
and gentlemen before the queene. Then the
Queenes scepter. Then the white dove with
a white rodde. Then the Queenes crowne.
Then the Quene with a circlet of   on
hir head under a canapy with four belles
hanginge on it and one lady bearinge hir
trayne. Then a troupe of Ladyes. Then
Knights, Esquires, gentlemen, Tipstaffes.]

**[During the solemnity of the Coronation lett this
   songe followinge be songe with instruments.

   Festum diem colamus assensu pari

   quo principis caput corona cingitur

                 Decora Regni possidet

                 Regis propago nobilis

                 Illustre principis caput   [5]

                 fulva corona cingitur

                 Nunc voce laeti consona

                 cantum canamus principem.

                 Regnum premebat dedicus

                 Libido Regis polluit.]   [10]

** This stage direction and song are found in DEF.

Actio Tertia

Argumentum

Furor

Quorsum furor secreta volvis pectora

minasque spiras intimas, nec expedis

faces tuas? scelus expleas Glocestrium.

Glocestrios invise rex olim tuos

et sceptra jactes, pretium saevae necis   [5]

dubiosque regni volve fraterni metus.

decora spectet ora Eboracum stupens,

miretur excelsum decus vulgus leve.

quorsum moras trahis leves? totus miser,

fias, magisque saeviat negas breve.   [10]

Aude scelus, mens quicquid atrox cogitat,

---

7 spectet] spectant C

regnumque verset ultimum regis scelus.

nondum madebant caede cognata manus.

nondum nepotes suffocantur regii:

et frustra poscas neptis incestos thoros.   [15]

Imple scelere domum patris tui: illico

discat furor saevire Buckinghamius.

macta tyrannum, deme sceptra, si potes:

sed non potes, poenasque dignas perferes

tanti tumultus. en venit Richmondius   [20]

exul venit promissa regna vendicat,

regnique juratos prius thoros. age

stringantur enses, odia misce, funera

diramque stragem, impone finem litibus.

en regnet exul, rex nec exilium impetret   [25]

tuaque cadat (Henrice) Richardus manu.

actum est satis. parcam, furor, Britanniae

posthac. novasque jam mihi quaeram sedes.

Dramatis personae

Rich. rex	Dux Norfolciensis.
Dux Buck.	Rhesus Thomae Walliae
Elizab. regina.	nuncius
filia Ed. major.	mulier, 1. 2.
Ancilla	Anus.
Episcopus Eliensis	Hungerford ⎫
Brakenburius prefectus arcis	Bourchier ⎬ equ.
Tirellus generosus	Miles
Ludovicus medicus	Stanleius heros.
Anna regina vxor Rich.	Dux Straunge fil. Stanlei.
Nuncius 1	Centurio
Nuncius 2	Braa servus comitissae Richmond.
nuncius 3	Dighton carnifex. a big sloven
nuncius 4	
nuncius 5	Muti
Lovellus heros	the yong k. and his brother
Catsbeius	lyenge dede on a bed.
Henricus comes Richmondiae	4 daughters of kinge Edw.
Comes oxonii	Souldiers unarmed and
	armed.

Actus Primus

[I.i.] Brakenburius ordinis equestris. Tirellus

[Brakenburius] O rector alme caelitum, et terrae decus

quisquis gubernas: parce Brakenburio.

clemens furorum siste duri principis,

paenaque certam libera gravi fidem.

horrere nunquam cessat imperii sitis   [5]

curis nec unquam solvitur aegra ambitio.

Regni metu Rich. aestuat ferox,

injusta sceptra possidet trepida manu,

novasque suspicatur insidias sibi.

stipante dum magna caterva rex suam   [10]

inviseret Glocestriam, famam aucupans:

incerta sortis cogitans ludibria,

quamque facile injusta ruit impetu potentia,

regnique lubricum nimis statum tremens,

dum spiritu vescatur aethereo nepos: [15]

mox ut suo reddat dolori spiritum

geminus nepos, et sanguine extinguant suo

regni metum pueri, ferox patruus studet.

nuper Johannes Greenus intento sacris

mihi, traditas a rege literas dedit.

parare tristem jubet regulis necem, [20]

et principibus adferre crudeles manus,

quos vinculis praefectus arcis comprimo.

Solus potest mactare Brakenburius

natos tuos Edwarde? solus perdere [25]

stirpem tuam? mandata regis exequar

lubens, tibi Richarde promptus servio:

necare stirpem fratris (ah) pietas vetat.

[intus] jacent squallente miseri carcere,

solusque captivis ministrat carnifex. [30]

O principis dirum nefas, tetrum, ferox,.

inter metum animus, spemque dubius volvitur,

mentemque distractam tumultus verberat.

nunc regis horreo minas: notus mihi

animus satis, vetat timere conscius [35]

nihil mihi, quo fata vellicant, sequor.

---

29 [intus]] intus omitted (blank space) C

quid in tuum Richarde subditum paras?

crudele quid spiras? quid atrox cogitas?

pius fui: cruore regum pollui

nunquam manus meas: quid incusas? fidem   [40]

tuebar: ulcisci bonum immensum paras?

Testor deorum numen, innocens eram,

insons eram. solumne regnum non timet

maculam? quid aulam pertinax fugis pudor,

humilemque casum quareris? aulam deserat   [45]

quisquis pie vivet, micans splendor nimis

sortis beatae, lumen impedit pium

et turpiter collisa mens impingitur.

sin fata me morentur: at veniam lubens

tibi de tuorum caede tristis nuncius   [50]

Edwarde, perculsus miser ferro simul.

a rege sed Tyrellus huc quid advolat?

an non perimus? heu metu cor palpitat.

quam, quam parat paenam gravem fide mihi

foram libenter quicquid est, ruam licet.   [55]

Tirell. Ignava mens quid jussa regis exequi

dubitas? inanes et metus fingis tibi?

---

43 solumne] solume_C

haud leve timebit, quisquis triste cogitat.

quid principe Tirelle gratari times?

rex imperat: erit innocens necessitas. [60]

magna anxium cura Richardus liberas,

et longa te regis beabunt praemia,

principe suo Eborum domus contenta erit,

prolesque regiae spiritum inimicum expuant

pro mortuis pugnare quis stulte cupit? [65]

aut principum demens tueri cogitat

exangue corpus? quicquid est audendum erit.

malus minister regis anxius pudor.

equestris ordinis decus Brakenburi,

regis parentis adulterum vivit genus? [70]

Brak.   Tantum moratur ultimum vitae diem.

Tirell. Nihil tremendam horrescis iram principis?

Brak.   Sequor lubens quocunque fata me vocant.

Tyrel.   Annon decet mandata regis exequi?

Brak.   Nunquam decet jubere regem pessima. [75]

Tirell. Fas est eos vivere quos princeps oderit?

Brak.   Nefas eos odisse, quos omnes amant.

Tirel.   Regni metu angi principem non aequum putas?

Brake.   Scelere mederi vulneri, scelus reor.

Tirel.   Constare regnum illis nequit viventibus.   [80]

Brak.   Illis mortuis invisum erit.

Tirel.   Ars prima sceptri posse te invidiam pati.

Brak.   Quem saepe casus transit aliquando opprimit.

Tirel.   Regnare non vult, esse qui invisus timet.

Brake.   Invisa nunquam imperia retinentur diu.   [85]

Tyrellus Tua interest vivat puer vel occidat?

Brankenb Parum: nisi ut occisere me non occidat.

Tyrel   Tua ecquid imbelles timet pueros manus?

Brankenb Qui castra non timeo seclus tamen horreo.

Tyrel.   Hanc immemor regi reponis gratiam?   [90]

Branken   Quod in scelere nullam repone gratiam.

Tyrel.   Nil saevientis principis iram times?

Braknen   Generosa mens terrore nunquam concidit.

Tyrel.   At multa rex tibi minatur horridus.

            En serus alto jungitur Phaebus salo,   [95]

nudumque lustrandum sorori deserit

caelum, ergo sume regis ad te literas,

claves ut arcis illico mandes mihi

hac nocte regis exequi jussa ut queam.

[I.ii] Brakenb. Tirellus. Joannes Dighton.

[Brak.] O caeca regnandi libido, o scelus

regis furentis triste nimis, o patrui

nefanda sceptra, quae suorum sanguine

madent. propinquae vos manus heu destruunt

o nobiles pueri pupillos opprimunt. [5]

hostemque dare solum genus vestrum potest.

amissa postquam regna cognovit puer,

et possidere rapta sceptra patruum:

sic fatur infaelix lachrymis genas rigans,

ab intimo pectore trahens suspiria, [10]

regnum nihil moror, precor vitam mihi:

hanc patruus ne demat, heu quis Caucasus

lachrymis potest, aut durus Judus parcere?

nunquam deinde ornare se miserum juvat

nullo solutae diffluunt vestes modo.   [15]

Imago semper errat ante occulas mihi

tristis gementis principis, nec desinit

pulsare maestam animam querela reguli

sed huc refert Tyrellus infaustum gradum.

Tyrell.   Caedis fidele munus intus occupant   [20]

vastusque Dighton et Forestus carnifex

mortem morabor principum dum perferant.

Brak.   Vterque fato cessit inimico puer?

Tyrell   Vivunt adhuc, illis tamen necem parant.

Brak.   Aliter placari regis ira non potest?   [25]

Tyrell   Regem metus, non ira crudelem facit.

Brak.   Effare, quo rex ore responsum tulit

cum sibi referret talem Greenus nuncium

quod ense nunquam principes caderent meo?

Tyrell   Vt ista primum novit, ingenti statim   [30]

stupore torquet, sanguis ora deserit,

totusque cineri similis expallet simul.

Suspiria imis efflat praecordiis

levique cordi proximum feriens latus

---

34 levique] ed.; levoque CH; leveque A; levaque BDF; laevaque EI

regale subito deserit solium, furens   [35]

graditur citatis passibus, quassans caput,

tacitoque secum dirus immugit sinu

ubi sanguis e fornace veluti denuo

proruit adustus fervidas torret genas.

rubetque totus (puniceo velut mari   [40]

immersus, aut minio fuisset perlitus)

Oculi scintillant, flammei obtuitu truci,

veluti setis horret erectis coma.

his tanquam Orestes facibus accensus fuit

nam de suorum caede convellunt pares   [45]

vtrumque furiae. Discrepant uno tamen

agitatur umbra matris illo mortuae

gravi nepotum ast ille vivorum metu.

et graviter in te exarsit ira turbida.

responsa rex qua nocte percepit tua.   [50]

coram tacendae functionis assecla.

ingemuit, et in hos maestus erupit sonos:

Proh cui quis ullam sanus adjunget fidem?

ubi gratus animus? quove pietas exulat?

---

37 immugit]   immangit C

terras relinquens scelere pollutas latet.   [55]

viris nec ullis jam licet confidere.

quos ego velut gnatos parens enutrio,

quos arbitrabar fore mihi fidissimos,

si quando tristis urgeat necessitas,

hi me parentem deserunt, violant fidem,   [60]

meoque jussu prorsus audebunt nihil.

responsit illico principi astans assecla,

at proximo stratus cubili vir jacet,

(audacter istud audeo nunc dicere)

id esset arduum nimis quod is neget   [65]

vnquam subire placeat hoc modo tibi.

Cum rex ab illo tum quis esset quaereret,

me dixit. ad cubile rapitur illico,

ibi me fratremque offendit in lectum dates,

rex tum jocose: tum cito (inquit) vos thoro   [70]

componere juvat? tum seorsim vocat

Panditque mentis triste consilium suae

de regulorum celeri et occulta nece.

ego quis moneret intuens, qualis simul

---

62 responsit] D; responsa C; respondet B

72 suae] suum C

ipse fuerim, lamenta nec regis ferens   [75]

meam ultro regi tum lubens opem tuli

quocirca primo mane, mihi literas dedit

ad te notatas, quas mea ferrem manu.

jussitque claves turris excelsae mihi

ut traderes, quo regis exequar cito   [80]

fidele mandatum nocte commissum mihi.

Dighton   Vterque suffocatur exanguis puer.

Brak.   Hei mihi per artus horror excurrit vagas.

Tyrell.   Quo sunt perempti genere laethi parvuli?

Dighton   Cum triste caelum stella lustraret vaga   [85]

serasque gallus cecinit umbras pervigil,

en dum nepos vterque lecto sternitur

dulcesque somnos caperet geminus puer:

cubile nos intramus occulto pede.

fratesque subito stragulis convolvimus,   [90]

summit volutos viribus depressimus,

vbi plumea clauduntur ora culcitra

vocemque prohibent pressa pulvinaria:

mox suffocanter adempto vterque spiritu

_____

80   cito] [CITO] C

quia pervium spirantibus non est iter, [95]

en ambo caesi lectulo strati jacent.

Brak. Videone corpora regulorum livida?

funestus heu jam caede puerili thorus.

quis lachrymas durus malis vultus negat?

heu mihi perempti fraude patrui jacent. [100]

quis Colchus haec? quae Caspium tangens mare

gens audet? sedis incertae scytha?

nunquam tuas Busiris aspersit ferox

puerilis aras sanguis, aut gregibus suis

expulanda parva membra Diomedes dedit. [105]

Tyrell. Bene est. fratris Richarde nunc solium tene

securus, et decora regni posside.

saepilite tetri carceris gradu infimo

satis profunda fossa fratres contegat

et saxeo mox obruantur aggere. [110]

De morte sparsim sparge rumores vagos,

quod fata sponte trina convulsit soror,

periisse subita morte finge regulos.

sunt regis haec mandata, cura sedulo.

Jam sume claves, (pertinax Brakenburi.) [115]

Brak. O saeva nostri temporis crudelitas,

o regis animus dirus, o mens barbara,

secura turbans jura naturae ferox,

tu innocentes principes, pueros pios

monstrum procustes tune mactasti duos? [120]

o terra, coelum, maestumque regnum tartari,

scelus videtis triste, sustines nefas

tantum trisulco horrens Saturno fulmine?

Acheronte toto merge sidereum caput

radiante Titan: pereat et mundo dies [125]

quisquis suo generi hostis infestus fuit

adeo ut cruent et caede puerili manus?

Jam Nero pius es scelere materno madens,

nefande Pelops cede, majus hic nefas,

sola teneros Medea mactat liberos. [130]

jugulare civem semper indignum fuit,

privare luce faeminam tetrum nimis

at innocentes, parvulos, infantulos,

(qui vita quid sit non per aetatem sciunt)

spoliare vita, facinus horrendum nimis. [135]

quid parcet aliis, qui suos ferox necat?

qui morte pueros mulctat atra innoxios,

quos summa charos cura commendat sibi?

heu, heu, quibus jactaris Anglia fluctibus?

discede pietas, et locum quaerat fides.   [140]

en longa sanguinis sitis regno imminet.

[I.iii]   Regina. Ancilla.

[Regina] Eheu recenti corda palpitant metu,

gelidus per artus vadit exangues tremor,

nocturna sic me visa miseram territant,

et dira turbant inquietam somnia.

at tu pater qui clara volvis sydera,   [5]

et igne flammiferum vago regis jubar,

omen nefandum averto, funestum, tetrum.

Jam cuncta passim blanda straverat quies,

somnusque fessis facilis obrepsit genis

Vidi minantem concito cursu heu aprum,   [10] natosque frendens dente laniavit truci,

vtrosque saevus mactat. aethereae potens

dominator aulae, fata si quid filiis

dirum minantur, in hoc caput erescat furor,

matremque prius jam fulmen irati petat.   [15]

Ancilla Quando vacabit tempus ullum cladibus?

modumque ponet matris attonitae dolor?

num triste matri nuncium demens taces?

totas an animus gaudet aerumnas suas

tractare, longos et dolores claudere?   [20]

O regio quondam tumens fastu, potens

regina.

Regina   Misera voce quid media stupes?

exire jussus non reperit viam sonus,

fusisque turpes lachrymis genae madent?

Ancilla Saevit cruento dente frendens aper.

Reg.   Adhuc   [25]

quicquam me sceleri restat?

Ancil.   Ah gnati tui

Regina Audire cupio miserias statim nostras.

Ancilla Heu ambo scelere, suffocantur principes,

labefacta mens succumbit, assurge, heu mihi

rursus cadentem misera spiritum leva.   [30]

---

30 leva] laeva C

spirat, revixit, tarda mors miseros fugit.

Regina   Regnare nunc sceleste patrue potes, nihil

timebit imbelles ferox pueros furor.

scelesta vibres sceptra, adhuc unum deest

sceleri tuo, jam sanguinem nostrum pete,   [35]

tui furoris misera testis haud ero.

quem defleam infaelix? propinquos? liberos?

an me? malis superesse fata quam sinunt.

tantis? ego meos mater occidi, latus

Edwarde quando comite nudavi tuo,   [40]

et tunc asylum deseris dulcis puer.

toto precor supplex mater genibus minor

qui vindices flammas vibras tonans pater,

in hunc vibrentur tela perjurum tua,

spolies Olympum irate fulminibus tuis   [45]

et impium caeli ruina vindicet.

Ancilla   Quin placida cogites, animumque mitiga,

mentemque sana turbidam, curis leva.

Regina   O patrui monstrum nefandum, quale nec

dirus procustes novit, aut Colchos ferox.   [50]

---

39 tantis? ego meos] tantis ego meis C

43 vindices flammas] vindicas flammis C

O cardinalis impii fallax fides,

cui filium vesana mandavi meum,

o filii charissimi, o liberi,

quos patrui crudelis ensis eripit,

suo nec unum sufficit sceleri nefas.   [55]

vestrumque matri funus invidet mihi.

Actus Secundus

[II.i] Dux Bucking. Episcopus Eliensis

[Buck.] Venerande presul Eliensis insulae,

depone maestitiam, prius liber, licet

nunc aedibus captivus haereas meis.

nam te meae cum crederet fidei ferox   [5]

princeps, parum promitte severus fore

parem tibi potius amicum possides.

Jam pristinae vitae status reminiscere,

et non quis es, sed quid fuisti, cogita.

---

56 invidet] invident C

Eliensis   O me beatum (pace quod dicam tua)   [10]

carcere quod isto liberum me sentiam.

sed fata quid non graviter incusem mea

quod mentis Juditium benevolae defuit?

virtus sed animi rebus afflictis tui

solamen est, quae non potentis respicit   [15]

tam copiam quam quae voluntas indigi.

Buck.   Gratum est voluntatis tunc iuditium mihi,

adversa quamvis singula videntur tibi

cum sic amice me colis, indignum tamen:

conabor ut quae voce jactentur mea   [20]

haec vera tandem expertus affirmes fore

nec fata damnes dura, quin potius probes.

tantum nec aestimes malum, te liberum

non esse, quantum est gaudium vita frui,

duras Tyrannus regni habenas dum tenet.   [25]

quin capite quod non plecteris, lucrum puta.

vitam dedit, dum non adimit audax furor.

quot caedibus cruentat insanas manus?

quot destinavit ad necem mentis furor?

---

21 haec] hac C

dicere nequeo, nec verba sufficiunt mihi. [30]

dolor tacere jussit, o nullo scelus

credibile in aevo, quodque posteritas negat,

Patruus nepotes patris heu regno expulit.

tantum expulit regno? necem miseris dedit.

fraenos dolor vix patitur, ulcisci cupit. [35]

Eliensis Praeclara suades inclytum ducum genus

hoc patribus percrebuit olim pristinis

Imperia scelere parta solvuntur statim.

tanto medelam vulneri nisi feceris:

queret lues secreta regni vulnera. [40]

perdere tyrannum laus, vel hostem aequalis est.

Buck. At sceptra tutus ut regat potius velim

(cujus furor paucis nocebat forsitan)

quam sede dimoveri pulsum regia.

nec talis est ut in suos sic saeviat. [45]

stimulo coegit ira, quae nescit modum.

cujus tamen regno scio prudens caput

consulere, pax florebit aequa civibus:

laudandus ergo, cura quem regni tenet,

---

33 regno] ragno C

36 Praeclara] Praeclarae C

et cui suorum civium chara est salus. [50]

Eliensis Superbus eructat animus nec continet

sese, secretam miscet iram laudibus,

sic regis illi cautus odium concita

ut se tamen sequi puteris nunc magis

stultum est occultare, quod prodas statim. [10]

nullam mihi fidem dabis certo scio,

diversa modo juvare si vellem tibi

Testor deum si non fuissent irrita

vota mea: et Edwardo quod obtigit duci,

stetisset Henrico stabile regni decus,: [60]

Henrice partes non reliquissem tuas.

sed cum serus tulere fatorum vices,

sceptraque regi deferunt Edwardo, magis

quae volueram Henrico remansisse integra:

non sic furore percitus miser fui [65]

ut mortui patronus illudar pius.

calcare victorem quis audet invidus?

post ego sequens victoris arbitrium sagax,

in gratiam receptus illico fui,

---

63 sceptraque] sceptrumque C

vivoque nunquam tibi fefelli tum, fidem   [70]

Edwarde, liberis praecabar et tuis

Decora regni sceptra, longas Angliae

tractent habenas, regis orti stemmate

at quae deus contexuit, retexere

non est meum: sed qui fuit regni modo   [75]

protector, et nunc regio fulget throno:

Cohibebo me, quin sacra praesulem vocant

senem magis, non studia regni, jam meis

doctus malis satis, at praeces decent modo.

Buck   De rege fatus obmutescit, audio   [80]

lubens, sagax de rege quidnam cogitat.

quin perge pater, egressa verba ne premas,

animique tutus vota persequere tui:

hinc non modo periculi nihil, sed gratius

votis tuis mox commodum eveniet tibi,   [85]

consultor eris in rebus incertis mihi,

quod cogitabam a rege cum precibus meis

impetro, tuam domi meae custodiam:

alterius esset forte carcer tibi magis

molestus, hic te liberum potius puta.   [90]

Eliensis Factis parem habeo gratiam (dux inclyte)

at non placet tractare gesta principum:

hic saepe blanda tecta fronte fraus latet.

quae dicta sunt bene, saepe torquent non bene.

curamque fabula suadet Aesopi Phrygis.   [95]

Legem tulit princeps feris talem Leo

passim necis paenam minatur horridus

corunta sylvas bellua nisi deserat:

tantum tumens vesana fronte bestia,

jussus tremens regis, parat misera fugam: [100]

forte properanti vulpes occurrit sibi,

causamque mirabundus exquirit fugae:

sylvam fugio, leonis (inquit) horreo

mandata, ridet vulpes, affatur feram

falso times demens, nihil de te leo   [105]

tantum tumet frons [tibi] gerit cornu nihil.

satis (inquit) hoc inermis, et novi fera:

Sin esse cornu dixerit frendens leo,

quid tum? perempta, pulchra sane disputo.

---

106 [tibi]] tibi omitted (blank space) C

subridet, omnia sorte faelici cadent.   [110]

Buck   Nihil time, leo nil nocebit rugiens,

Aperve dente vulnus infliget tibi

nil audiet corum princeps, quae tu mihi

narras secretus.

Eliensis   Hercle aures si suas

hic sermo pulset, ipse nec sumat male.   [115]

nil tum timerem, forsitan grates daret.

sin mala (quod auguror) potius affectio

interpres esset, veritas nec penditur,

vtrique verba grande conflarent malum.

Buck   Hoc quicquid est audire mens avida cupit.   [120]

culpam lubens praestabo quamlibet, haud time

tantum meis morem geras votis pater.

Eliensis Nihil Hercle dico, sceptra quando possidet

Protector, haec quo jure princeps vendicat

praecarer (at supplex tamen) quod patriae   [125]

salus requirit, cujus ille fraena jam

moderatur, et pars ego fidelis extiti:

dotes ad illas addat clemens deus

(his licet abundet, laude nec nostra indiget)

quod in tuo numen benignum fusius　　　　　　　　　　[130]

sparserit honore:　dotibus abundet magis

regnique tractet melius habenas sui.

Cohibebo me:　haec tacere me decet magis.

Buck　　Miror quid haeret.　voce quid media stupet.

quin serio cum patre tremulo colloquor.　　　　　　[135]

Venerande pater animum quid incertum tenes?

seseque vox egressa continet statim

dum fundis interrupta, concludens nihil

et crebro spiras.　qua regem fide colas

neque scio, neque tuus amor in nos quis fuit　　　[140]

nostras quod ornas praeco virtutes licet

in me reperio laudibus dignum nihil,

id me magis nunc mentis incertum tenet,

sed tuam odio mentem ardere suspicor,

vel amore ductus ista caeco concipis.　　　　　　　[145]

obstat hoc ut audeas, vanus timor,

vel impedit pudor senem parum decens.

effare:　honorem pignero dubio tibi.

Tuti recessus, surdus audiam.

Eliensis　　　　　　　　　　　　　　　Quid est.

Promissa cernis, dux nimis fastu tumet.   [150]

Avidus honores haurit, odit principem,

secretus huic aperire mentem quid times?

aut regis exitum paras, vel dum faces

accendis irarum duci: tuam fugam

Captivus ex quo regis arbitrio tuus   [155]

fueram (liceat hac voce pace uti tua)

quanquam molesti carceris sentio nihil

libris levabam pectus attonitum malis.

sententiam didici revolvens optimam:

quod nemo liber nascitur solum sibi   [160]

victurus, at partem parentes vendicant,

partem propinqui, maxime sed patria

debet parens communis allicere pium

dum mente volvo: debitum patriae juvat

praestare, cujus (heu) statum dum cogito   [165]

quantum micabat summa regum gloria.

tantum tyrranus nunc jugo premit gravi.

Regni ruinam sceptra promittunt sua.

sed magna miseris non deest spes civibus,

dum corpus aspicio tuum, pulchrum decus   [170]

ingens acumen, vimque dicendi parem,

summas opes, raramque virtutem ducis,

prae ceteris cui chara patriae salus.

patriae labanti gratulor, cui contigit

heros, mederi qui malis tantis potest   [175]

qui regni habenas tractet aequali manu.

quas nunc tyrannus occupat Glocestrius.

(namque illud nomen antiquum novum

parum placet, quod jure sceptra non tenet)

nec invideo regnum, pios si non honor   [180]

mores simul mutasset effrenos ducis,

novamque mentem nomen acciperet novum.

O gravia passum nobile imperium Angliae

graviora passurum, tyrannus si imperet,

Immanis usque scelera quid persequar?   [185]

agnosco qualem stravit ad regnum viam,

en optimatum caede faedavit manus,

obstare votis quos putabat improbia.

O sacra regnandi sitis, quo animos trahis

mortalium? scelestus at pergit furor.   [190]

---

178 namque illud] H;   [NAMQUE ILLUD] C; retinest ille B

Quantumque libuit, audet, sceleris haud modum

ponit, patravit majus et fide scelus.

ætasque credet ulla, matrem filius

quod damnet infamis probri solus suam?

impius inurit criminis falsi notam   [195]

fratresque geminos spurios falso vocat.

nec non nepotes impia notat labe.

stirpemque fratris damnat ambiguam sui.

hoc est familiae nobile tueri decus?

sed cur queror, num sceleris hic finis fuit?   [200]

gradus mali fuit hactenus non stat nefas

Jam regna fratris possidens, non timet

audere majora, miser heu implet manus

funere suorum patruus, insontes necans.

Erumpat ergo vis corusca fulminis,.   [205]

an parcet aliis, qui suos mactat ferox?

sperare quis meliora nunc demens potest?

majora menstra triste praesagit nefas.

nunc ergo moneat temperum tandem status

per numen aeternum, per Anglorum decus   [210]

titulis superbum si genus charum tibi,

succurre miseris, rumpe fatorum moras,

capesse regnum, sede pulsum deprime

tyrannum. ademptum vindica regni decus.

nec justa dubium causa terreat nimis,   [215]

defende cives chara sit patriae salus,

comes laboris haud deesse jam potest

plebs tota defectum rebellis murmurat

magis subibunt barbari Turcae jugum,

quam rex suo impius cruore luderet,   [220]

quanto magis nunc te crearent principem

in quo genus refulget excelsum. meis

quiesce votis, Angliae oblatum thronum

nec respuas, prodesse multis dum potes.

nec te labor deterraet, si quem putas   [225]

inesse, sed sit arduum: minime tamen

pro pace patriae deserendum publica.

quod si recusas pertinax, nec te sinas

vinci precibus: adjure per verum deum

per maximi ducis fidem, sancto simul [230]

quondam per astrictam fidem Georgio.

Insignis ascitus eques ordinis Garterii

quando fuisti primum, ut in nostrum caput

sermonis hujus culpa grassetur nihil.

hoc publicis imploro precibus civium. [235]

sin alterius aptanda sceptra dexterae

queris: throno Lancastriae pulsum genus

reddas paterno. aut filiam Edwardi patris

thoro superbo nobilis jungas viri.

sic impium tyrannus exitium feret [240]

et cladibus defessa gens ponet modum.

habes meam de rebus his sententiam,

Cur sic tacet? miror. metuo multum mihi,

suspirium ducit, fidemne decipit?

Buck Video timore distrahi pectus, pater [245]

doloris ansam doleo quod tacens dedi.

tu macte sis virtute, non fallam fidem.

O magne caeli rector, et mundi arbiter

quantum tibi devincta gens est Anglia?

qui fluctuantem saepius regni statum   [250]

clemens deus manu benigna protegis,

Jam statue tandem gravibus aerumnis modum.

clementem animis spiritum inspira, pater

ut principem queramus auspiciis tuis,

qui justa tractet sceptra regali manu,   [255]

statimque rebus collocet lassis opem.

Reverende sedis praesul Eliensium

specimen dedisti mentis erga me tuae

clarum satis,: amoremque testor patriae.

par culpa nostri, quare nil time dolos.   [260]

de rege mentis sensa prorsus eloquor,

vires cur illi adjutor adjunxi meas,

retinere postquam non potest fati colos

Edwardus ejus nominis quartus, mori

sed fata cogunt liberis parum suis   [265]

fui benevolus: ille quod meritis parum

dignum referret praemium generis mei

titulos nec altos aestimavit invidus.

---

256 collocet] collocat C

260 par] parva C

261 mentis] mensis C

Ergo minus orbos tum colebam liberos

patris inimici, vulgo jactatur vetus [270]

dictum. Facile regnum labi cujus tenet

rex puer habenas. coepta tum comes tua

Richarde foveo, judicabam tum virum

fuisse clementem, atque nunc video ferum.

hac fraude plurimum allicit mentes pias, [275]

ut publico protector assensu Angliae

renunciatus esset, et regis simul:

accensa sic honore mens fuit novo

ut cum secundum possidet regni locum

tantum placere sceptra ceperunt statim [280]

regni decora poscit ad tempus sibi,

teneros nepos dum complet annos debilis.

dubitare postquam nos videt, regni fidem

nec fallimus: spurios nepotes tum probat

patruus scelestus, credimus tandem sibi [285]

statimque nostri fraena regni tradimus.

Damnavit haeredem ducis Clarentiae

crimen paternum jura perdidit [sui]

regni, thronum Richarde sic paras tibi,

ruisque tandem, quo furor traxit tuus,   [290]

regnare liceat (ut lubet) jam nominem

aequum est metuere, nullus est hostis ferox,

obstare coeptis nemo jam potest tuis.

at quis minister funeris tanti fuit?

tu, tu tyrannus natus ad patriae luem   [295]

tu prole matrem saevus orbaris sua,

nec abstines a caede cognita miser,

teneros nepotes patruus injustus necas,

quorum necis cum fama penetrasset meas

aures, trementes horror occupat vagus   [300]

artus, venas deserat hiantes intimus

cruor, soluta membra diffluunt metu.

nobis salubre pollicemur inscii

incerta cum sit propriae domus salus?

mihi damnat injustum frequens injuria   [305]

[oblata frustra jure posco praedia]

summique [nomen] vendico comestabuli

graviter repulsam laesus ingratam tuli

---

306 [oblata...praedia]] This line is omitted, with blank space left in C.

307 summique [nomen]] suumque (nomen omitted with blank space left) C

     comestabuli] comestabulis C

nunquid dabit nova, qui suum nunquam dedit?

at si dedisset: non tamen gratis daret.   [310]

ope namque nostra possidet imperii decus.

Agnosco culpam. quin mea carens ope

nunquam feroci sceptra gestasset manu

fratris, redundat in meum crimen caput.

namque patriae vulnus inflixi meae.   [315]

hoc expiabo si medelam fecero.

modebor ergo, sicque decrevi prius,

Justam quaerelam durus ubi tum respuit,

non amplius me contineo, dicam ordine

quodcunque mente absconditum tacita latet.   [320]

Cum regis animum scelere plenum cernerem,

in odium amor immutatur, ulcisici paro.

quem sum passus, ejus aspectum tamen

tuli moleste, ferre nec vultum queo

Aulam relinquo regiam, domum peto   [325]

dum caepi iter, mea facile tum dextera

erepta posse sceptra transferri puto,

quo mihi placebam lubrico titulo diu

---

326 dum...dextera] D;   dum...dextere C;   dum capio iter, mea puto

manu statim B

et justus haeres domus Lancastriae

mihi falso videor, ambiens regni thronum [330]

haec cogitanti subito me rogat obvia

Richmondiae comitissa, reditum filio

precarer exuli, si rex benignus annuat.

Tum regis Edwardi relictae filiae

natum suum despondet ad castos thoros. [335]

dotem nihil moratur vna dos erit

Regis favor, nec amplius mater petit.

hinc nostra pereunt regna, tum mihi

exciderat animo, filio primum suo

matrique jus patere regni, somnium [340]

thronus fuit, regnumque frustra vendico.

Contemno primum vota comitissae pia

mens altius dum cogitat matris preces.

tum spiritu impulsam sacro matrem, bonum

sensisse regno huic Angliae immensum puto. [345]

infensa si domus thoros jungit pios,

quae sceptra jure dubia vendicat suo:

aeterna ferret civibus tranquillitas,

---

330 videor] videar C

340 matrique] matrisque C

345 huic Angliae] H;   [HUIC ANGLIAE] C;   nesciam B

346 infensa] imensa C

348 civibus] civibo C

         solidamque pacis alliget certam fidem.

         haeresque dubiae certus esset Angliae.   [350]

Eliensis O certa   patriae spes, salus, solatium,

         respicere caepit mitis afflictos deus,

         O sancta lecti jura legitimi Angliae

         tibi gratulor, lactare: solamen venit

         nunc tanta quibus arcana tuto pandimus.   [355]

Buck.   Matris prius mentem decet cognocere.

Eliensis Jam nostra votis caepta succedent satis

         servus, fidelis ecce Commitissae venit

         et nos licet lentus juvat miseros deus.

         Brai potentis serve Comitissae, tuae   [360]

         dominae salutis gratus esto nuncius

         .Jactata pacis appulit portum rates.

         mox natus Her. sceptra gestabit manu:

         si jurejurando suam astringet fidem,

         quod face velit sibi jugali jungere   [365]

         quae nata major regis Edwardi fuit.

         nati ergo faustos mater ambiat thronos,

         ut sede pellatur sua rex impius.

---

361 dominae] domina C

Brak.   Tam laeta dominæ nuncius foram, lubens

         quamcumque vobis atque praestabo fidem.   [370]

Buck.   De rege tandem memet ulciscar probe

         de sede male parta triumphabit parum.

         nunc saevus infensum inveniet aper sibi

         fortem leonem, qui vnguibus tantum valet

         quantum ille dente, jam scelere cumula scelus,   [375]

         crudelis imple caede funestas manus,

         adhuc inique jura detineas mihi,

         dominare tumidus, spiritus altos gere,

         Sequitur superbos ultor a tergo deus.

         reddes coactus, sponte quae negas mihi,   [380]

         nuper superbus Eboraci fastu tumens

         cinctus corona vestibus claris nitens

         spectanda prebet ora stupidis civibus.

         Diadema pariter cinxit vxoris caput.

         celebratque plebs honore divino levis.   [385]

         portendit excelsus ruinam spiritus.

Eliensis Tu tu tyrannum morte culctabis ferox,

         si liber essem, vinculis nudus tuis

---

386 excelsus] excelsas C

```
        meaque septus insula tota satis:

        nihil furentis horream regis miras.                    [390]

        nunc liceat ergo pace discedam tuae.

Buck.   Dispersa perdit turba vires debilis,

        unita fortius minatur hostibus manus.

        morare paulum, milites dum colligo.

        defendet armatus tuam miles viam.                      [395]


             [II. ii]   Lodovicus medicus.


        Comitissa mater lacta Braii nuntia

        postquam sui nati de nuptiis acceperat,

        ut regis Edwardi priori filiae

        si sacra lecti jura sponderet comes

        Richmondius, speraret amissum thronum:                 [5]

        adire reginam jubet celeri gradu.

        tentare mentem sponte quasi pulsum mea,

        ut qui peritus arte medicorum fui,

        faedera medelis sacra miscerem meis,

        lectumque promissum comitis Richmondii.                [10]
```

---

389   meaque] meque C

nunc ergo Lodovice jussus exoqui

decet fideles, vince matrem ne thoros

comiti negaret conjugales filiae.

[II. iii]   Episcopus Eliensis fugiens

Deserere nolens cogor hospitium ducis.

turbata magnum consilia cogunt metum.

Nunc ergo consulam mihi celeri fuga.

quam nunc manus miser hostium saevas tremo?

sed cautus incedam, insulam petam meam,   [5]

sulcabo salsa nave mox et aequora,

hospesque tutus bella spectabo procul.

te te potens mundi arbiter supplex precor

ab hoste servum protegas saevo tuum.

[II. iv]   Lodovicus. Regina.

[Lodovicus]   Regina servans conjugis casta fide

lectum jugalem, siste misera lachrimas,

---

12 thoros]   thronos C

13 filiae]   filio C

3 ergo]   ego C

adesse spero jam malis finem tuis.

parumper aure verba facilis percipe

vocato nostris precibus: inveni modum   [5]

quo trux tyrannus debitas paenas luat

tracentque rursus sceptra felici manu

tui nepotes,: rege dejecto truci.

Procerum sibi plebisque concitat odium

Richardus, invisum eximere regnum student.   [10]

Jam vulgus insano crebescit murmure.

quam ferre possunt, gravius imponi jugum

an sceptra speremus benigna principis?

neci nepotes patruus infantes dedit,

querela civium frequens pulsat Jovem.   [15]

amare nequeunt quem execrantur publice

servile collo populus excuteret jugum

si notus haeres esset imperii sibi

Richmondiae (nunc exul) Henricus comes,

haeres familiae certus est Lancastriae,   [20]

huic filiae sociare si thalamos jubes,

de jure regni nullus haeres disputat.

Regina	Quod populit aures nuncium laetum meas,?
	quid audio? num misera mens est credula?
	hoc facile credunt quod minus miseri volunt. [25]
	[sed quod volunt fortuna contumax vetat]
	prona est rumori semper in pejus fides.
	regnat tyrannus, exul Henricus comes,
	Est vulgus anceps, dubius et populi favor,
	quae filiae facilis patet meae via [30]
	ad sceptra?
Lodovicus	Voto tremulus obstabit timor
	confide causae civium pugnat salus.
	prudens familiae consulas mater tuae.
	caedis recentis immemor sobolis jaces?
	cur sic inultam te sinis? stimulet dolor [35]
	caedis tuorum, et conjugis chari probrum.
Regina	Spem pollicetur animus, invitam trahens,
	dotare thalamo filiam Elizabetham velim,
	sed spernet illam forsan Henrici parens,
	illam petas, scrutare num maneat vetus [40]
	domus simultas, exulis gnati potest
	flecti malis, ut fieret ex misero potens

---

26 [sed...vetat]] This line is not in C

38 Elizabetham] ed.; Elizabeth BCDF; Elizabethae AEH; Elizabethe I

Lodovicus   Regina peragam jussa.

Regina.   Respiciat deus

consilia laeta pergo non dubio gradu.

[II. v] Dux Buck. ad milites.

Ultrice dextra, milites, saevus cadat

communis hostis ille, tum quisquis comes

fueris tyranni, jaceat et paenae comes.

quid ira possit, durus exprimat dolor.

vtinam cruorem capitis invisi deo   [5]

libare possim, nulla mactatur Jovi

opima magis, arasve tinxit victima

quam rex iniquus, aut tyrannus impius

violenta nemo imperia continet diu.

aperare tanto scelere quis demens potest   [10]

regnum salubre vel fidem tutam diu?

vobis scelestae mentis exponam dolum.

Bellus parari dum videt, mox literas

mittit benignas spondit agros, nil negat.

sensi dolum, moram traho, veniam peto.   [15]

---

44 pergo] perge C

8   aut tyrannus impius] H; [AUT TYRANNUS IMPIUS] C; aut tyrannus impius
                          omitted B

aegre repulsam passus, imperat statim

venire, adhuc recuso, sed veniam tamen,

veniam Richarde, sed male tandem tuo.

et ultor adero inimicus infensus tibi

miseris Britannis pacis autor publicae.   [20]

fugiens asylum Marchio Dorcestrius

vim militum magnam Eboraci colligit

Ducem sequuntur Devonienses Courtneum

viresque fratris adjuvat sacrum caput

Episcopi Excentrensis,. infesto agmine   [25]

Gilfordus impium tyrannum eques petit.

frequensque Cantii caterva militum.

mactetur hostis, bella poscunt impias

dirus suorum carnifex poenas luat.

ergo tyrannum patriae pestem suae   [30]

trucidate, cum sit grata civibus hostia.

praesidia cum sint tanta, quae partes student

nostras tueri, et patriae vitam dare.

omnesque dux feram lubens angustias

ut hostis pereat vester, et ferox Hero   [35] quid desidemus? arma cur cessant pia?

cadendo vinci ut perfidos hostes putes

stultum nimis votisque pulsando Jovem

vibrentur enses copias jungi decet.

ad arma ruite vos ferox hostis manet. [40]

pugnate validi, vir viro inferat manus.

tollantur alte signa, bellum tuba canat

et excitetur classico miles truci.

[III. i]   Actus Tertius

Richardus rex

O saeva fata semper, o sortem asperam,

cum saevit et cum parcit ex aequo malam.

fortuna fallax rebus humanis nimis

insultat, agili cuncta pervertens rota.

quos modo locavit parte suprema, modo [5]

ad ima eosdem trudit, et calcat pede

subitio labantis ecce fortunae impetu

quis non potentem cernit eversam domum.

heu gnatus heu primo vnicus periit meus

(O dura fata et lugubrem sortem nimis)   [10]

qui clara patris regna speret mortui

ut ille magni parvus armenti comes,

primisque vix dum cornibus frontem tegens,

cervice subito celsus et capite arduus

gregem paternum ducit, et pecori imperat.   [15]

o suave pignus, o decus domus

Regalis, o Britanniae fumus tuae,

o patris heu spes vana, cui demens ego

laudes Achillis bellicas et Nestoris

annos praecabar, luce privavit deus.   [20]

nunquam potenti sceptra gestabis manu

faelix, Britanno jura nec populo dabis.

victasque gentes sub tuum mittes jugum.

Non Franca subiges terga, non Scotos trahes,

In tua rebelles imperia, sine gloria   [25]

jacebis alto clausus in tumulo miser.

---

21 gestabis] gestabas C

23 mittes] mittas C

porro exul haerens finibus Britanniae

dirum parat bellum comes Richmondius.

viresque cogit, sceptra rapturus mea.

domi cruorem populus en nostrum petit [30]

incendit animos pertinax nimium furor,

sceleris ministera armat in nostram necem.

quidam minantem viribus Richmondium

juvare, quidam firma praesidia arcibus

locare, quidam clanculum armatos domi [35]

servare quidam subditos fidem ut suam

fallant, rogare precibus infensi student.

nescire volui, cuncta simulavi lubens

dum caeca potui coepta, consilia, dolos

sentire militumque vires jungere. [40]

hujus furoris cum ducem Buckinghamium

caput esse scirem, et totius fontem mali:

vel marte aperto trahere vel precibus pie

allicere caepi, ne fidem mutet suam.

addi benignas ad ducem item litteras. [45]

faelix ad aulem convolet celeri gradu

---

33 quidam] quidnam C

34 quidam] quidnam C

35 quidam] quidnam C

36 quidam] quidnam C

45 item] H; [ITEM] C; mox B

Sentit dolos dux, texuit causas morae

stomachique se dolore fingit compremi:

omnem statim moram jubebam rumpere:

venturum ad hostem patriae sese negat [50]

et milites cogens suos dux pessimus

in me nefanda bella demens commovet

quid facio,? amicus qui mihi summus fuit

auferre regna querit: odit maxime

qui maxime colebat. a scelus impium, [55]

et dux profundo devovende Tartaro.

At plebs velut procella ventis turbida

agmine scelesto principem neci petit.

solus Richardus causa cantatur mali.

quid nunc agendum restat? aut quem consulam? [60]

infecta facta reddere haud quivis potest.

si populus odit, pereo: sed populi favor

servetur: isto macula tolletur modo,

qua nomen indui scelestus heu meum,

ut in Britannos si quid erumpat malum: [65]

damnent nihil, Jam mitis, humanus, pius

et liberalis civibus meis ero,

---

48 stomachique...compremi] H; stomachique se dolore [FINGIT COM] PRIMI
      C; stomachique dixit se premi morbo
      gravi B

et scelere vindicabo nomen impio.

centum sacrificiis alta surgent maenia,

curis soluti ut precibus incumbant piis   [70]

legesque patriae utiles feram meae,

fortasse nostras populus in partes ruet,

pietate falsa ductus auri montibus

blandisque verbis ducitur vulgus leve.

    [III. ii]   Nuncius. Rex Rich.

[Nuncius] Adfero ducem figisse Buckinghamium

          magnaeque quod nunc dissipantur copiae

Rex Rich. Quae causa subito terga vertendi fuit?

Nuncius   Ubi Wallicorum numerat ingentem manum

          qua sylva sese porrigit danica, viam   [5]

          pandit superbus, et Sabrinam nobile

          superare flumen properat, agmini suo

          Vt Courtenorum jungat agmen, at minas

          dum spirat horreas impio dux agmine

(annon genus mortale curant numina)?   [10]

dum militos vicina spectant flumina,

altasque ripas non datur adhuc tangere,

subito gravis terram ruina caeli verberat

divesque pluviis laxat imbres humidus

Auster, et agros altum tegit frequens aqua   [15]

en piscis ignotas in auras tollitur.

lectis jacentes arboribus haerent, agris

atque mediis mirantur, vndis, vndique

eversa tecta, vagit in cunis puer

passim per agros, montibus natant ferae   [20]

Terram diebus obruunt aquae decem

stupet miles cum Courtneorum copiis

jungere perfusus agmen haud fluctus sinet

at Wallicorum turba nullo premio

invita serviens duci, carens simul   [25]

misera cibariis statim illum deserunt

nullis minis gens Cambra adduci potest

aut precibus, ut maneat simul belli comes

               aut pergat ultra: praeda nudus hostibus

               suis relictus caepit infaelix fugam. [30]

Rex Rich. Faelix ad aures nuncius nostras venit.

               prius labantam fausta tollunt numina.

               portus ad omnes miles vndique sepiat

               dux exterasne erumpat ad gentes. Comes

               Richmondius quidam parat, querat simul [35]

               num caepta linguat, an minetur amplius

               Princeps honorem testor, illum qui mihi

               captum reducet, praemium dignum feret

               si servus ille fuerit, emittat manu:

               sin liber: illum mille ditabo libris. [40]

               Classis Britannum armata sulcabit mare

               ne perfigus premat Angliam Richmondius

               aude scelus, ne crescat malum

               exprimere jus est ense, quod nequeunt preces

               quicunque sceleris socius in nostras manus [45]

               veniat, piabit sanguine inceptum nefas.

---

39 emittat] emittant C

[III.iii]   Nuncius, Rex Rich.

[Nuncius]   Captus tenetur vinculis Buckinghamius.

Rich.   Sacris colamus prosperum votis diem.

            o mihi propitios, sed tamen lentos deos.

            Hostis quibus captus dolis sit: explica.

Nuncius   Ubi Cambrio dux milite orbatum vidit   [5]

            obstupuit illico, atque sorte tam gravi

            perculsus, animum pene despondit suum,

            consilii egenus, sed sibi fidit tamen.

            Banisteri tremens ad aedes clam fugit

            cui dux amore fovebat eximio prius   [10]

            et semper auxit dignitate plurimum.

            hujus latere clam studebat aedibus

            donec cohortem repareret, et belli minas

            nudusve mare, fugeret, secans Britannicum

            comitique sese jungeret Richmondio.   [15]

            at male deorum si quis invisus duci

            fuerit, paratum non potest fugere malum.

            Servus Banister, seu timens vitae suae,

---

7   pene]   penae C

tuisve ductus praemiis: Solopiae

preconsul tum Mittono prodit ducem. [20]

is militum stipante pergit agmine.

servi praehendit ab aedibus sui haud procul

dum fata silvis dira solus cogitat

tibique vinctum fidus adducit virum.

Rich Si non fides me sacra regno continet: [25]

tentabo mea stabilire sceptra sanguine,

et regna duro saevus imperio regam.

nunc ergo dux paenas gravissimas luat.

obrumpat ensis noxium, tristis caput,

nullamque paenae carnifex reddat moram. [30]

regnare nescit odia qui timet nimis.

non tua mihi Stanlei dubia fides fuit.

Comes sitit Richmondius honores meos.

gener tuus sibi sceptra despondit mea.

vxor suo Comitissa quaerit filio [35]

victrice dextra rapta sceptra tradere.

Rapidis volabis gressibus Lancastriam.

Illam intimis reclude mox penetralibus

---

21 pergit] perdit C

25 sacra] sacro C

pateat nec ullum faeminae servorum iter:

ad filium nullas mater det literas: [40]

ne patriae demens luem tristem paret.

et sceptra mihi mulier rebellis auferat.

at Straungeum praestantem honore filium,

fidei tuae mecum relinques obsidem

testabitur puer patris coastantiam [45]

natura mentem faeminae pronam dolo

dedit, dolisque pectus instruxit, negat

vires, malum ut tantum queat vinci.

[III.iv] Dux Buck

O blandientis lubricum sortis decus,

o tristis horrendi nimis belli casus,

heu, heu, fatis mortale luditur genus

quisquamne sibi spondere tam firmum potest

quod non statim metuenda convellat dies? [5]

---

44   tuae]   meae C

cujus refulsit nomen Anglis inclytum

modo, pallidus nunc ad lacus trudor miser.

quid, (heu,) juvat jactare magnos spiritus?

fallacis aulae fulgor, heu, quos perdidit?

heu blanda nimium dona fortunae, mare   [10]

non sic aquae refluentibus turget, aut vadia

turbatus ab imis. pontus Euxinus tumet

ut caeca casus heu fortuna magnatum notat.

funestus heu, dirusque Richardi favor.

quid illa deplorem miser tempora quibus   [15]

fretus meo consilio aper frendens, sibi

regnum cruento dente raptum comparat?

en hujus ictu nunc atroci corruo,

natale solum, illustre decus, o Angliae:

horrenda quae te fata nunc manent? ferox   [20]

postquam jugo tyrannus oppressum tenet,

heu heu miser stygias ad undas deprimor,

crudelis et collo securis imminet.

---

12 turbatus] turbata C

    Euxinus] Exinus C

23 et] ut C

    imminet] <minuet> C

[IV.i]   Actus quartus.

Richard rex.   Nuncius.   Lovellus
heros.   Catsbeius.

[Richardus]   Quid me potens fortuna fallaci nimis

blandita vultu, gravius ut ruerem, aedita

de rupe tollis?   finis alterius mali

gradus est futuri, dira conspirat manus

in me rebellis, torqueor metu miser   [5]

disrumpor aestuante curarum salo.

Richmondiensis ille perfidus comes

in transmarinis ambit heu regnum locis

in cujus arma jurat turba civium

inimica mox hujus mali tanti metu   [10]

famulos cruenta morte mulctavi meos.

at fama vexat turbidum pectus magis

thalamos jugales Richmondio filiae

comiti student regina mater jungere.

rediret ut domus inimica in gratiam   [15]

suasque vires geminet Anglicana gens

erepta ferro sceptra promittunt sibi.

o triste facinus, hostis in nostra potens

regnabit aula, meque fatis destinat.

Nuncius   Richmondiensis incubat ponto comes.   [20]

Rex   O flenda fata, gesta quae sunt explica.

Nuncius   Vbi ter quatuor implesset october dies,

oculis profundum mane spectantes fretum,

vagas carinas vidimus appellere

portum petunt Dorcestriam, quem Polum   [25]

vocant, dubia nos turba spectantes diu

manemus illic nave tum praetoria

comitem ferocem novimus Richmondiae,

auxilia forsan alia sperantes manent

aliquot diebus, utque nos celsas vident   [30]

ripas tenentes littus appellant simul.

num simus hostes, miles an charus duci

querunt. vafros nos fingimus vultu dolos

ibi milites locasse Buckinghamium

Vt comitis adventum manerent exulis,   [35]

---

16 Anglicana] [ANGLICANA] C

35 manerent] maneret C

dubiumque mox ad castra deducant ducis,

junctae facile possent phalanges vincere.

Rex maximo sepultus obruitur metu

hi blanda verba suspicantes, carbasa

complente vento, laxa committunt mari   [40]

velisque pansis advolant Britanniam.

Rex   Cur ludis inconstans nimis miserum dea?

nuper locatum me levas summa rota,

auraque molli prosperas adfera dies

illico supinum lubrico affigis solo.   [45]

quam varia? quam maligna? quam levis dea?

Lovellus   Cur vexat animum cura vesanum gravis?

ubi prisca virtus? pellat ignavos metus

excelsus animus fortis haud novit metum

nullo periculo nobilis virtus labat.   [50]

quorsum ducis manes tremiscis mortui?

quorsum rebelles caeteras? annon jacent

terra sepulti? pulverem demens times?

promissus himen? et fides Scotis data

illos fideles pacis officio tenent.   [55]

---

37   junctae]   juncte C

43   levas]   laevas C

49   fortis haud novit metum] [FORTIS HAUD NOVIT METUM] C

mandata legati duci Britannio

tua deferunt: agros sibi rebellium

promittis armis sceptra si juvet tua

quem non movebunt ampla promptum praemia?

desine timere: quod satis tutum est times. [60]

Catsb   Si praemiis dux pertinax ductus tuis

non excitetur, aliud inceptum manet.

Richmondio disjunge promissos thoros

neptis tuae. Lancastriis si non opem

ferat domus Eborum (fremat licet ferox) [65]

frustra minatur disseca connubium

Richmondii nec filiae Edwardi faces

celebrat jugales, si frui voto velis.

Rex   Rapietur illico, finietque nuptias

districtus ensis. Tartaro nubet prius. [70]

Lovellus   At est Asyli grande violati nefas.

meliora cogita, ista non prodest tuo

medicina morbo, culpa non sanat reos

Nec est aperto scelere purgandum scelus.

et nuper allectus tibi populus fuit [75]

quam plurimus dudum modis colere studes,

	statim scelere perculsus immani oderit.	
Catsb	Quod impetrari mollibus precibus potest	
	non est minis duris parandum voce vel	
	saeva tyranni neque frigido metu.	[80]
Rex	Taedas ne demens patiar invitas mihi,	
	meaque sceptra contrahi? nunquam accidet.	
	scelesta nostrum firmat impietas thronum.	
	audebo quodvis scelere vincendum scelus.	
	violare jura facile regnanti licet.	[85]
	in rebus aliis usque pietatem colas.	
	stringatur ensis, regna tutatur cruor.	
Lovellus	Regina tenera. mollibus verbis potest	
	utrinque torqueri facile, mox deferant	
	jussus tuos legati ad illam ut filias	[90]
	suas in aulam adduci mater sinat.	
Catsb	Si socia thalami forte moriatur tui,	
	neptem statim vince ducendam tibi	
	illoque pacto fracta spes comitis erit.	
Rex	Placet quod inquis potius quam regnum ruat	[95]
	tentanda cuncta, triste consilium tamen,	

---

82 meaque] H; meoque BC

	dum vivit uxor, hanc decet letho dari.	
Lovellus	Frequentet illam rumor esse mortuam.	
Rex	Cum salva fuerit illa, quid rumor potest?	
Lovell	Fortasse longa oppressa curarum tabe,	[100]
	morietur. atque mors sit illi certior.	
	Illico suborna qui susurret clanculum	
	fecunda quod non sit, fore funestam tibi	
	arcenda thalamis sterilis uxor tua est.	
	aulam beare sobole faelici decet,	[105]
	regem. doloris saeva perpetui lues	
	matura timidae fata faeminae dabit.	
Rex	Mactabo potius ense, lethali prius	
	tollam veneno, quam mei pestis throni	
	cladesque fuerit. vosque quos semper colo	[110]
	faciles amici, fida magnatum manus	
	Adite templum, tum meis verbis pie	
	matrem salutetis, colere me dicere,	
	vitaeque sordes esse mutatas meae.	
	contendo, quaevis opprimat silentium	[115]

populi favore nequeo nancisci prius

quam fratris ut complectar olim filias.

quorum duos miser fratres neci dedi.

natumque Marchionem honore persequor.

amplos agros promittite, magnas et opes [120]

si gratus Angliae exul illico venerit.

Richardus rex solus.

Animum tumultus volvit attonitus, rapit

regni metus, quiescere nec usquam potest.

sanare nunc malum queo solum, face

neptem jugali si maritus jungerem [125]

vxor sed obstat scelera novimus prius.

quid conjugem cessas veneno tollere?

aude animo. num peccata formidas tua?

sero pudet, peracta pars sceleris mei

olim fuit maxima: pium esse quid juvat [130]

post tanta miserum facinora? nihil

facis, patravimus nefanda, parva nec placent.

Regnum tuemur, omnis in ferro salus.

---

128 animo] animo C

[IV.ii] Lovellus: Regina Eliz. Rex Rich.

[Lovellus] O socia thalami regis olim faemina

illustris, ad te non legatos principis

fecere jussus, ut soluta sacro carcere

aulam sequaris splendidam, mater potens,

non moveat ante regis immensum scelus,   [5]

quem tantopere vitae scelestae paenitet.

matura sancte suadet aetas vivere.

vitam cupit mens lapsa spurcam ponere.

serumque caepit vitii fastidium.

dum vincere cupis: arma delectant magis.   [10]

nescit modum sibi strictus ensis ponere.

at placida victori magis pax expedit

quem civium quivis tumultus territat:

partam prius ne perdat iterum gloriam

A plebe rex quaesivit ardentur coli: [15]

hoc efficere nequit prius princeps pius

nisi te, tuasque filias sancte colat.

et splendidas illas locaret nuptiis

---

12   at] et C

cujus necavit filios heu turpiter

en concidet dolore confectus gravi,   ⌈20⌉

fletu rigantur ora sceleris vindice

vitaeque tantum corrigendae defuit

honos tuarum filiusque Marchio

Dorsettus heros, qui per oras nunc vagus

incognitas pererrat exul, si domum   ⌈25⌉

reversus arma deserat Richmondii

florebit alto clarus imperio statim

illustris heros, sibi patebunt omnia

fulgentis aulae dona: nil frustra petet

Nunc ergo quaeras lumen aulae splendidum,   [30]

in gratiam regina cum principe redi,

nec regis animum sperne tam charum tibi,

sed dulce pignus filias animi tui

mittas ad aulam, adhuc nec obscuro horreant

loco, pius quas diligit rex vince.   [35]

quid maesta terram conticescis intuens?

errore quid pectus vago versas tuum?

Regina Ergo filiorum sanguine. madentes manus?

---

36 conticescis] conticessis C

38 Ergo] D;   ego BC

non liberos crudelis occidit fratris?

nostrosque conspersit thoros falsa labe?   [40]

at non potest matri scelestus parcere,

infame generi vulnus afflixit suo.

saevire ferrum cessat ubi regnat furor?

quisquamne putat ullum deesse nequitiae modum?

saevire cum ratione num quisquam potest?   [45]

strictus tuetur ensis, immitis tuis

quicquid tenere te scias. quicquid scelus

peperit, tuetur magis admissum scelus,

haud dulcis aula cruore quae meo fluit

quas nuptias sperem meorum sanguine?   [50]

an filiarum nuptias celebret? prius

reddat sepulchrum filiorum, plangere

funera meorum mater aefflagito prius.

suisque debetur atque mortuis honor.

Lovellus Sepulta quid renovas odia? pectus premit   [55]

aeterna vesanum ira? patratum liceat

scelus expiare. quid juvat genitu adeo

_____

51 celebret?] celebret C

opplere caelum, vel lamentis aethera

pulsare? toties vulneri quid heu manus

adfers? medelam nec pati potes mali?   [60]

si quisque quoties peccat, illico Jupiter

iratus ignes vindices jaculabitur

orbis jacebit squalido turpis situ

et tanta damna sobole repararet sua

nunquam, venus cunctis petita viris. adhuc   [60]

ferrumne terret?

Regina	Cujus ictu concidi.
Lovell	At melius infligens medetur vulneri,
Regina	Ad arma nova perrumpit ira saepius.
Lovell	Despecta magis irascitur clementia.
Regina	Veteratus at nescit furor clementiam. [70]
Lovell	Quid arma metuis ira quando extinguitur?
Regina	Haud sanguine saties sitim nisi expleas.
Lovell	At in cruore quod est necesse sufficit.
Regina	At triste furioso necesse quod libet.
Lovell	At ira vana luditur sine viribus, [75]

caeptique mox temerarii nimis pudet

quod si furore pectus attonitus times

et regis horres impias adhuc minas.

---

77 attonitus] attonitum C

haec sola spes relicta: pugnandum prece,

luctantibus nihil valebis viribus. [80]

sed fortius commota mens ebulliet,

nullamque vim patitur sibi resistere.

Regina   Heu mihi mulier, heu, heu, quid infaelix agam?

animus vacillans fluctuat timet omnia.

sperare rursus jussit amissus thronus. [85]

tradamne regi filias? egone meas

honore privabo? nula filias decet.

at quid facis? cui credis insontes tuos

mactavit, an parcet sorori? jus idem

utrique regni cujus heu thoro meas [90]

rex filias commendat, has qui turpiter

matre aeditas mentitus est adultera.

Lovellus Errore quorsum pectus uris anxium?

sin vita regis sancta nil persuadeat,

sed hujus animum adhuc ferocem somnias: [95]

quantum tibi iratus minetur, cogita,

hujus benigna vota si contempseris.

Regina   An morte quicquam minatur amplius?

Lovellus Exosa vitam, filias nunc destrues?

Regina   O filiae charissimae, heu, heu filiae,   [100]

         dotare vos thalamis beatis rex parat.

         abite, vos fortuna quo miseras jubet.

         et supplices ad genua patrui sternite:

         dedisce regnum infausta proles principis,

         privata vos decent magis regnum nocet.   [105]

         facere juvet, quicquid necessitas jubet.

         omnia timore plena, metuendum tamen

         palam nihil: nunquam preces spernit leo

         timidae ferae nec supplices temnit sonos:

         si sors beabit fausta. jussit en parens   [110]

         vos ire: sin credele fatum perderit,

         ulciscar ipsa morte eadem me simul,

         meique paenas mater incepti feram.

         adsis fidelis partipceps mentis meae

         celeri gradu oras Galliae mox advola   [115]

         gnatoque Marchioni reditum suadeas:

         dubium nihil rerum exitum pavescerit

         nec horreat minas cruenti principis.

sceleris sui regem nefandi paenitet.

deflet cruenta miser nepotum funera   [120]

sibique larga pollicetur praemia,

magnosque honores, atque liberam malis

vitam, ergo praeceps vela pandat prospera.

charamque rursus patriam reddat sibi.

Rex Geminas sorores video, o faustum diem.   [125]

compone vultum, amplectar illas arctius.

neptes amandae, quam libens vos osculor.

vestrae miserandam doleo fortunae vicem.

itaque sacro aegre carcere inclusas tuli.

quapropter hunc mutabo luctum flebilem   [130]

in gaudium atque veste praeclara induam.

vobisque magnatum parabo nuptias.

Jam gaudet animus, pace sperata fruor.

has nuptias uxoris invisum caput

perturbat: Anna huc confert tristem gradum.   [135]

concepta mente scelera, vultu contegam.

aegramque verbis molliam mentem piis.

[IV. iii]   Regina Anna.   Rich. Rex.   Nuncius.

[Regina Anna.]   Heu quantis curarum fluctibus aestuo?

quid mihi horrendi animus praesagit mali?

in lugubres rumpamne suspiria voces?

et quaerulis feriam corusca sydera planctibus?

quid misera faciam? fata deplorem mea?   [5]

en rumor percrebuit vitam ablatam mihi

et garrula volavit fama funeris mei

ergo vivae mihi sepulchrum queritur,

et nostra lachrymis viva decoro funera,

cogorque justa nunc mihi persolvere.   [10]

cur mihi meus minatur ingratus necem?

nihilque nostros amores crudelis aestimat?

Cardinalis antistes mihi gravis pater

fletu genis madentibus mihi nunciat.

rex inquit jamdudum, saturavit amorem,   [15]

nec dabit amplexus, aut oscula figet dulcia.

te sterilem esse, regali nec aptam thoro.

talem regiae conjugem poscunt faces

qualis liberorum procreare possit magnum decus.

qui tenera patris sceptra gestabit manu.   [20]

Variis animus curarum fluctibus aestuat.

rumorque vexat scelestus augur fati mei,

quid faciam misera? en querunt neci,

nostraeque vitae ultimos claudere dies

vitaeque rupta [fila] eripere sororibus.   [25]

Illustre Britanniae decus, rector potens

quid misera merui? quid ad mortem trahor?

En mortuam perstrepunt garrulae voces,

et ad sepulchrum funesta turba vocat.

si non placet thalamis fides tuis data   [30]

aut si tuum demens honorem lesi invida:

at manibus pudica moriar tuis

et scelesta tuus fodiat ensis viscera.

nec populi millies suis vulnerent vocibus.

et sordidis regina civibus occidam.   [35]

Rex. Nunquam miser charae pararem conjugi

mortem, castasque tuo cruore manus spargerem

nec te minae perturbent, cum futilis

erroris esse populus magister solet

---

25 [fila]] fila omitted C

nec principi plebs novit garrula parcere.   [40]

jam siste lachrymas, teque cura mollius:

en nos graves premunt curae Britanniae,

motusque turbidos cives rebelles concitant.

hos maximum decet ducem compescere,.

post, mutuis simul fruemur amplexibus.   [45]

Nuncius   Fugit manus Richmondius comes tuas.

Rex   Effare carcerem cur evasit tetrum.

Nuncius   Postquam sinus complente laxos vincerent

impulsa vento vela fluctus turbidos

littusque puppis tangeret Britannicum: [50]

mandata monstramus duci statim tua

hujus dolor premebat artus languidos,

nec rebus ullis aeger animus sufficit.

hinc jussa rerum cura thesaurario

soli fuit: Petrum vocant Zandisium.   [55]

huic mox agros promittimus rebellium,

fortuna vel benigna quicquid addidit,

si patriae restituat exulem suae

Richmondium, comitesque caeteros fuga

---

43   turbidos]   turbidus C

promissa vincunt ampla thesaurarium.   [60]

Anglisque tanti gaudet autor muneris

quo se tueri possit Anglorum potens

viribus, et hostis frangat iras invidi

mox concito querit gradu comitem velox

At sensit astus callidos comes prius   [65]

furtoque se subduxit illo Parisiis

tum dura quos fortuna junxit transfugas

comites sequuntur at dolet Zandisius

praedam sibi ereptam esse. sed sero dolet

celeri cupit vi praevertere elapsum licet,   [70]

terramque calcantes pede ruunt concito

hastasque vibrantes dextera equites, si queant

tardare fugientum tamen redeunt statim

illisque tantus cessit incassum labor.

nam rege fretus Gallico tutus satis   [75]

implorat adversus tua sceptra opem.

nec finis hic mali: solutus carcere

Oxonii fugit Comes Hamisiis

comitique jungit supplici supplex comes.

Rex   O nuncium infestum, o nitida palatia   [80]

passura graviorem exitum, Oedipode

o luce splendens principis falsa decus.

o sors acerba. o fata regnis invida.

sed parce diis demens, scelere quos irritas,

opaca regna ditis, et caecum chaos   [85]

exangue vulgus, numen abstrusi? Jovis

et quicquid arcet, huc novos spargite dolos.

vestras manus Richmondium vocat nefas

ut spiritus illico scelestos expuat.

nisi graviores expetat paenas dolor.   [90]

[IV. iv] Nuncius. Rex.

[Nuntius] Regina florens Anna dudum mortua est.

Rex   O dira fata, saeva nimis o numina

res possident mortalium certi nihil,

consors vnica vitae et chara conjux vale.

crudele tristis indica exitii genus.   [5]

Postquam lugubris sedisset maesta diu

suspiria gravibus mista cum singultibus

heu saepe fundit, saepe falsis lachrymis

diris querelis conjugem ingratum premit

tandem inquietus cepit attonitus furor   [10]

Nuncque huc et illuc currit erranti gradu

tanquam tumultum patiens in se turbidum

statimque querit (vocis infractae sono)

quae cor revellit dextera crudelis meum?

Ann est maritus (inquit) heu fidele cor.   [15]

valde est ineptum munus ingrato viro.

postea pupillae prorsus occultae latent.

et solum aperta pallide albugo micat.

vomitiones inde crebras extulit.

animaeque in altum saepe deliquium cadit.   [20]

artus per omnes frigidus sudor meat.

orisque subito nitidus evanuit color.

frons flava mercet, livida ardent tempora.

et palpebrarum defluunt omnes pili.

cerulea turpi labra liquescent situ,   [25] et lingua (visu horribile) specie lurida

prominet, hiante ex ore solito grandior.

unguesque nunc haud amplius clare nitent.

sed quasi veneno pelliti pereunt. cadit

tandem misera luctata fatis faemina. [30]

Rex   Nunc fausta neptis ambio connubia.

neptisque fallam frustra promissos thoros

sed neptis huc dubio venit gradu mea.

tentare procus hujus instituam thoros.

[IV. v]   Rex. filia Edwardi major

[Rex]   O regia de stirpe derivans genus

et digna sceptris virgo. postquam (proh dolor)

rapuere fata conjugem. tam tristia

quae sit magis mihi juncta regali face

quam genere quae regis superbo nascitur. [5]

sociemus animos, et thori sponde fidem.

accipe maritum. quid truci vultu siles?

Fil. Ed.   Egone? o nefandum scelus, expiandum rogis

nullis, egone manus misera conjux meas

rubente mortuorum sanguine imbuam? [10]

---

29 pelliti] ed.;   peliti C;   polit A;   perliti DEI;   perciti F;
           politi H

Olympus vxori deerit ante suae

[lunaque gubernabit diem noctemque sol]

prius Aetna gelidas emittet ardens aquas.

Nilusque vagus ignitas laminas vomet.

Egone silebo parvulos misera invidos   [15]

tibi nepotes, at mihi charos fratres

crudeliter tua peremptos dextera

sceleste patrue? prius ab extremo sinu

Haesperia Thetys lucidum attollet diem.

lepus fagabit invidum prius canem.   [20]

punit nefandum quamvis abditum scelus

Jupiter, et astutos sinit nunquam dolos.

humeros premebant saxa Sisiphi lubrica

saevus procustes asperam paenam luit,

quoniam suos vivi necarunt hospites,   [25]

non hospites tu, sed nepotes heu tuos

nuper relictis fasciis miser necas.

Rex Agedum efferatas virgo voces amove

ne ob unum seclus corpora pereant duo

---

12 [lunaque...sol]] This line is omitted in C.

cruore solium fateor acquiri meum,   [30]

et innocentum morte; sic fatis placet.

cecidere fratres? doleo facti paenitet.

sunt mortui? factum prius nequit infici.

num flebo mortuos? nihil lachrymae valent.

quidvis facerem: an fratrum geminam necem   [35]

hac dextra effuso rependam sanguine?

faciam: paratis ensibus pectus dabo.

et si placet, magis moriar ulnis tuis.

ignes, aquas, terram, aut minacem Caucasum

petam, petam tartara, vel umbrosum nemus,   [40]

atrae stygis: nullum laborem desero

si gratus essem tibi, virago regia.

1. Ed. Sit amor, sit odium, sit ira, vel sit fides,

non curo. placet odisse, quicquid cogitas.

tuus prius penetrabit ensis pectora,   [45]

libido quam cognata corpus polluat,.

O Jupiter saevo peritus fulmine

cur non trisulca mundus ignescit face?

Cur non hiulca terra devorat illico

_____

ago regia] H;   [VIRAGO REGIA] C; virago regia omitted B

	immane portentum ferocis principis	[50]
	terrore superans Gorgonum genus?	
Rex	Pessima, tace. solum silet in armis fides?	
	nihilne valet amor? nihil thorus movet	
	regius? acerbae neque lachrymae valent?	
	est imperandi principi duplex via,	[55]
	amor et metus: utrunque regibus utile	
	cogere.	

Fil. Ed.   Si cogas mori, sequor lubens.

Rex   Moriere.

Fil. Ed.   Grata mors erit magis mihi

et praestat aerumnis mori oppressam statim

quam luce curis obsitam frui diu.   [60]

Rex   Moriere demens.

Fil.   Nil minoris amplius?

mallem mori virgo, tyranno quam viro

incesta vivere, diis hominibusque invida.

Rex   Heu, quid agis infaelix? thoros spernet tuos

regina viva, sis mea miseros sile   [65]

fratres.

Fil.   Miser non est, mori quisquis sciet.

Rex   Anne lubens, en nullus est ferro metus,

strictusque nescit ensis unquam parcere.

Fil.   Neronis umbrae atque furiae Cleopatrae

truces resurgite, similem finem date

his nuptis, qualem tulit Oedipodae domus.

nec sufficit fratres necasse principes?

et nobili faedare caede dextram?

quin et integram stuprare quaeris virginem

maritus? o mores, nefanda o tempora. [75]

at saeva prius invadat ales viscera,

in me prius tuas atrox manus

emitte, vel quod triste monstrum nutrias:

quam casta thalamos virgo sequar adulteros.

Rex   Discessit, et nostros fugit demens thoros. [80]

negligit amores stulta virgo regios.

nunc ista differam, minae forsan cadent

rabidae puellae, patriae dum consulo.

[IV.v]   Nuncius. Rex

Nuncius⌋   Gerebat altos nuper animos insolens

Richmondius: celso superbus vertice

tumebat, at cecidit miser tandem, sui

sero pudet caepti, atque franguntur minae.

---

71 Oedipodae] Aedipodae C

Rex   O grata lux, quae sceptra confirmat mea.   [5]

jam solida certe pacis emergit fides.

at cuncta narras, namque spes miseros alit.

Nuncius Adhuc juventae flore vix primo viget

Rex Galliae, nec prima depinxit genas

barba, nec sceptra puerilis manus   [10]

satis tuetur, quin tenera tutoribus

curanda datur aetas, viribus post vigor

dum regna discat, hos frequens pulsat comes

votis iniquis, rebus et fessis opem

implorat ardens, nec praeces frustra sinit   [15]

perire, dum multos fatigat anxius

multo labore, nec pati potest moras

mens lassa, planctus atque frustrari suos

aegre tulit tam saepe, dum longam pati

cogit repulsam, multiplex procerum favor;   [20]

desperat animus, optat exul vivere

potius, inanis et laboris paenitet.

Rex   Festum diem celebrare jam laetos decet.

o mihi dies albo lapillo nobilis,

jam sors beatis mitior rebus fluit.   [25]

quot modo procellas concitat frustra comes:

et quam graves nuper minatur exitus?

quin in suum redibit authorem scelus.

Jam frustra placido classis incumbit mari,

Richmondios jam falso reditus excubat.   [30]

ergo rates haerere nunc ponto veta.

milesque quisque adversum [portum] cavet

deponat arma, finis hic malorum erit.

tuto licet regnare: jam cessit timor,

nisi quod timendum non sit id timeas tamen.   [35]

Actus Quintus.

[V.i]   Nuncius. mulier, mulier, anus.

[Nuncius.] Quis me per auras turbo raptat concitus

fuge, fuge civis haeret a tergo comes.

---

30 Richmondios] Richmondius C

32 [portum]]   portum omitted (word is crossed out completely leaving a
                 blank) C

minatur horrendum furor Richmondius.

dum comitis arbitramur extinctos faces,

fractamque belli spem ducis Richmondii.   [5]

portum pedite Milfordium immani premit.

totamque calcat proditam sibi Walliam.

furens comes toti minatur Angliae.

Mulier   Quo, quo fugis charam marite conjugem?

frustraque tot perire patieris preces.   [10]

vxoris en fletu genae multo fluunt.

miserere: sin fugere lares dulces juvat

eat simul conjux, itineris parvum onus.

Alia Mulier   Te per deorum numen, et datam fidem

thori, per annos filii teneros precor   [15]

ne deseras immitis ah tristem domum.

Anus   Matris tuae solamen o fili mane.

sin hostibus domum relinques perfuga

scrutetur ensis nota quondam filio

ubera, tuo mater peribo vulnere.   [20]

---

14 s.d.: Heare let divers mutes run over the stage from divers places
    for fear. DEF

[V.ii]   Henricus, Comes, Rhesus Thomae Wallicus.

[Henricus] Optata tandem tecta cerno patriae

           miserisque nosco maximum exulibus bonum.

           o chara salve terra, sed salve diu

           frendentis apri dente lacerata impio

           da patria veniam bella si geram pia   [5]

           da queso veniam: causa commovit tua

           dirumque principis nefas bellum vocat.

           rex est peremptus. occupat regnum Nero

           cum rege fratre parvulus periit puer

           solum tuentur templa reginam sacra.   [10]

           regum cruoris ultor adveni pius.

           Paenas dabit Richardus Henrico: dedit

           si nostra clemens vota concedat deus.

           Rhesum Thomae de stirpe video Wallica.

Rhe. Tho. O clare princeps regia stirpe edite   [15]

           honore praecellens comes Richmondiae

           heros Britanniae gentis auxilium unicum

           optatus Anglis civibus venis tuis.

           post multa vota, et temporis longas moras.

---

14 video] vidio C

Henr.   Natale semper mente complector solum   [20]

servile collo strenuus excutiam jugum.

Rhes. Tu patriae nunc columen, et verum caput

tu solus affers rebus afflictis opem,

et rege tanto laeta gaudet Anglia.

Henr.   Non quem fatentur ore principem suo   [25]

hunc corde semper intimo cives colunt.

Rhes. Deus trisulca qui quatit flamma polos,

et in profunda perfidos Proserpinae

detrudit antra, me premat vivum nigra

tellure, si datam fidem fallam tibi,   [30]

si signa Campis Cambriae ponere jubes,

in Wallicum agrum messor impius ruam.

quoscunque velles disjici muros cito:

hac aries actus saxa disperget manu.

nec miles in meis castris erit ullus   [35]

qui te sequetur.

Henr.   Rhese grata est mihi fides

si caepta numen prosperet mea, spondeo

te praesidem toti futurum Walliae.

---

29 vivum] vivum <u>C</u>

[V.iii]   Burcher. Hungerford. Miles.

Hung.   Splendens equestri clare burcher ordine

laetus scelestas hostis effugi manus

agmenque lubens duci Brakenburio

per noctis umbras abstuli densas miser.

Burch.   Quot per recessus labimur Hungerford vagi   [5]

huc usque nostro terga vertentes duci.

at o quieta noctis almae tempora,

tuque miseris praebens opem Phebi soror

adhuc tuere: differas Titan diem

donec tyranni tuti ab armis inclyti   [10]

tentoria Henrici comitis attingimus.

Miles   Faelix tuas fugio per umbras caeca nox

mactetur ense quisquis obstabit mihi.

Henr.   Quis hic locus? quae regio? quae regni plaga?

ubi sum? ruit nox. hei ubi satellites?   [15]

inimica cuncta. fraude quis vacat locus?

quenquam rogabo? tuta sit fides vide.

nativus artus reliquit internos calor

rigore frigent membra vix loquor metu

---

12 s.d.: Let here divers mutes armed souldiers run over the stage one
            after an other to the Earle of Richmond BDEFH

13-14] Between these two lines, there are five or six blank lines left
        in C, probably to indicate a short lapse of time between the speech
        by Miles and the speech by Henr. who enters here.

tremisco totus: cura mentem concoquit   [20]

hos vitricus luctus dedit meus mihi

Stanleius: illum lenta quae tenet mora?

dum varia sortis cogito ludibria

dubiamque solus civium volvo fidem,

exercitum praeire jussi. tam moras   [25]

damnare lentas vitrici caepi mei

postquam metus cor, spesque dubium verberat

et quicquid obstat mente dum volvo satis,

densas per umbras lapsus aspectum fugi.

exercitus suo errat orbatus duce.   [30]

sum nudus hostibus relictus perfuga.

Comes oxon   Ingens premebat cura sollicitos (comes

illustris) animos horror excussit gravis

dux milites quod absens deseris

dum nocte caeca summa montium juga   [35]

vincunt nec ullus jussa privatus facit.

mox triste pectus maeror invasit gravis

nunc voce miles frustra compellat ducem.

```
            nunc civium timemus incertam fidem
            laetique sero fruimur aspectu licet                    [40]
            animus adhuc turbatur excusso metu.
Henr.       Quorsum times?  pellatur ignavus metus
            solem juvat secreta saepe volvere.
Hunger.     Saevi tyranni ereptus insidiis miser
            supplex tuo vivere sub imperio  Comes,                 [45]
            illustre atque signa dux cupio sequi.
Henr.       Propago clara, equitumque generosum genus
            Jam vos sequetur digna facilis gloria
            me grata delectat voluntas civium,
            vestramque  tantam laetus amplector fidem              [50]
            at quas tyrannus copias ducit:  doce.
Hunger.     Pauci sequuntur sponte signa milites
            et cogit arma jungere Richardi metus
            sese magis dubius metuit exercitus
            suis nil armis miles audet credere.                    [55]
Henr        Tu transferas ad castra milites sua.
```

---

40 aspectu] aspectum C

[V.iv] Henricus Comes. Stanleus heros.

[Henricus] Nisi vota fallunt vitricus venit meus,

domus suae Stanleius eximium decus.

verumne video corpus? an fallor tua

deceptus umbra? spiritus vires capit,

exultat animus, et vacat pectus metu.   [5]

Stanl. Et nostra dulce membra recreat gaudium

generum juvat videre, complexus mihi

redde expetitos, sospitem qui te dedit,

det tua vicissim cepta perficiat deus.

Henr. Dabit tuo si liceat auxilio frui.   [10]

Stanl. Utinam liceret quae velim.

Henr.   Quid ni potes?

quid non licebit?

Stanl.   Saepe quod cupis tamen

non absque magno perfici damno potest.   [15]

Henr. Quidnam times, dum patriam juvas tuam?

Stanl. Quod vita chara filii fuit mihi.

Henr. Servat Richardus obsidem fidei tuae?

Stanl. Ne te juvarem pignori datum tenet.

Henr. O subdolum scelus, o tyrannum barbarum,

---

1 meus,] meus. C̲

	amore quos fidos parum credit sibi,	
	horum fidem crudelis exprimit metus.	[20]
Stanl.	Iram coere, pectus et nobile doma.	
	palam juvare si nequeo: furtim tamen	
	subsidia nunquam nostra deerunt tibi.	
Henricus	Discessit. heu me lenta vitrici fides	
	perturbat. hujus quanta spes fulsit mihi?	[25]
	[Frustra at quaerelis pectus uritur anxium],	
	vanisne juvat implere caelum quaestibus?	
	quin triste praeciptare consilium decet.	

[V. v]   Dux Norfolciensis   Rich. rex.

[Dux Norf.]	Armatus expectat suum miles ducem.	
	bellum ciebunt aera, nec moras sinent.	
	Richardus huc dubio venit princeps gradu.	
	secreta solus volvit, et curae premunt.	
	quae subita vultus causa turbavit tuos?	[5]
	quid ora pallent? mente quid dubia stupes?	
Rex	Norfolciae charum caput, dux nobilis	

---

25 perturbat...mihi] perturbat. at querelis pectus uritur anxium C

26 [Frustra...anxium]] This line is omitted in C. C has obviously combined
    11. 25-26

1 s.d.: Speaking to his< > E

cujus fuit mihi semper illustris fides.

falsaque nihil celabo fronte perfidus.

horrenda noctis visa terrent proximae.   [10]

postquam sepulta nox quietem suaserat,

altusque teneris somnus obrepsit genis:

subito premebat dira furiarum cohors,

saevoque laceravit impetu corpus tremens.

et faeda rabidis praeda sum demonibus.   [15]

somnosque tandem magnus excussit tremor.

et pulsat artus horridus nostros metus.

heu quid truces minantur umbrae tartari?

Norf.　Quid somnia tremis? noctis et vanas minas?

quid falsa terrent mentis et ludibria?   [20]

Jam strictus ensis optimum augurium canit.

aude satis, nec vota formides tua.

tibi rebelles spolia tot cives dabunt.

vinctae fatebuntur manus victoriam.

Rex　Nil pectus ullus verberat tremulum metus   [25]

ignava nec quassat tumultus corpora.

audere didicimus prius. telis locos

---

19 Norf.] Norf. appears beside l. 18 in C.

hostes vicinos jam premunt, bellum vocant.

acies in armis nostra, ex adversis stabit.

Norf. Quid agimus? heu quid caeca fata cogitant?   [30]

quidnam parat suspecta civium fides?

inventa nuper scripta me talia monent.

               Norfolciensis inclyte,

               nil caeperis audacius,

               nam venditus rex praetio   [35]

               Richardus herus proditur.

At nulla nostrum macula damnabit fidem.

Richardi nunquam signa vivus deseram.

      [V. vi]   Oratio Richardi ad milites.

Comites fideles, milites, et subditi

crudele quamvis facinus et dirum scelus,

olim patravi, lachrymis culpam piis

satis piavi, sceleris et paenas dedi

satis dolore crimen ultus sum suo,   [5]

vos tanta moveat ergo paenitentia.

---

1 s.d.: Lett them put on the head peacis and exhort one another E

partum tueri melius est, quam quaerere.

pugnate fortes, regna parta viribus

vestris studete fortiter defendere.

non est opus cruore multo. Wallicus   [10]

oppugnat hostis, regna vendicat impudens.

illum sequuntur perfidae Anglorum manus

sicarii nequam, genusque prodigum,

vestraeque flamma patriae gens Gallica.

at civium me credidit manibus deus   [15]

quorum fides spectata mihi semper fuit.

quorum paravi viribus regni decus.

orisque nisi decipiar interpres, truces

victoriam vultus ferunt, dandam mihi

oculi necem diris minantur hostibus.   [20]

vicistis, inquam, vicit Anglorum manus.

suo video cruore manantes agros.

simulque Gallos, Cambrios simul leves.

mox faeda victos strages absumet mea

sed fata quid moror? cur his vocibus   [25]

vos irruentes teneo? mihi veniam date

---

14 Gallica] Wallica C

19 vultus...dandam mihi] H; vultus...[DANDAM MIHI] C; vultus truces
                                 laetam ferunt victoriam B

nunc quanta clemens ultro concedet deus

si vincat ille. vos manent dirae cruces

ferrum, Cathenae, et dura collo servitus

et nostra membra quaerit ensis hostium [30]

me nil morabor: recta sit vestri salus.

consulite vobis, liberis, uxoribus,

prospicite patriae, haec opem vestram petit.

estote fortes victus hostes occidat

dubiumque martis exitum nemo horreat [35]

nobis triumphi signa dantur maxima

non vos latet, summa ducis prudentia

niti salutem militum, nullos habet

en vultus Henrici minas, frustra times

et robur invictum ducis Richmondii [40]

infesta quare signa campis fulgeant

cursu citato miles infestus ruat.

et hostis hostem vulneret, ferus ferum.

vos, vos triumphus nobiles socii manet

hac namque dextera spiritum ejus hauriam [45]

qui causa bellorum fuit civilium.

aut moriar hodie aut parabo gloriam.

[V. vii]   Nuntius.   Rex Rich.   Dux Norf.

[Nuntius]	Magnanime princeps jussa perfeci tua
	respondit ore Sanleius duro nimis:
	si filium mactes suum, plures habet.
Rex	Detractat ergo perfidus jussus meos
	ingratus hostis et scelestus proditor? [5]
	mactabo gnatum, vota persolvam statim
	te digna patre, tam diu cur filius
	vivit scelesti patris? o patiens nimis
	o segnis ira post nefas tantum, mea
	tu jussa perage, mitte qui velox mihi [10]
	ejus perempti referat abscissum caput.
Norf.	Animum doma, nec impius vexet pater
	jam bella poscunt, tempus aliud petunt
	signis vicina signa fulgent hostium.
Rex R.	Parcamne nato invultus impii patris? [15]
Norf.	Post bella gnatus patris expiat scelus.
Rex R.	Ergo nefandi patris invisam prolem
	in castra ducite, Marte confecto statim
	capite paterni criminis paenas dabit

---

6 mactabo] magtabo C

16 gnatus] gnato C

[V. viii]   Oratio Henrici comitis ad milites

O sceleris ultrix, signa quae sequeris mea

Britanna gens, vanos metus nil somnies

sin ulla justus bella curet Jupiter

nobis favebit regis excusso jugo.

quos liberam videre patriam juvat.   [5]

en rapta fraude sceptra jure poscimus

quae causa belli melior afferi potest?

quam patriae hostis, regiae stirpis lues?

ergo tyrannus morte crudeli cadat.

scelere Richardus impios vincit Scythas   [10]

te Nero vicit caede matris nobilem

suos nepotes ense mactat impio

matris probro nihil pepercit filius.

stuprare neptem audet libido patrui.

sic fratris exhibes honores manibus   [15]

cesset timor et infestus hostem vulneres

nil arma metuas tanta media ducem

linquent arena, quos sequi cogit metus

parum ducem tuentur inimici suum.

at sint fideles, nec spernant ducem. [20]

pugnent acriter et millibus multis ruant.

non copiarum numerus at virtus ducis

victoria potitur et laudem feret.

hujus timebis arma qui scelus timet

nullum? nepotes morte confecit suos? [25]

[pietas in illo? sanctitas? pudor? fides?]

Asyla rupta, frater occisus, stupro

tentata neptis, falsa cui denique fides

quid non patravit patriae pestis suae.

adversus hostem corpus ense cingite. [30]

in bella ruite, agmenque strenue rumpite

tollantur alte signa. quisquis occidet

bello fidelis, perfidos, pius impios:

placidus tyrannum, mitis immitem petis.

quod si liceret (salvo honore principis) [35]

ad genua vestra volverer supplex petens

ut verus haeres Anglici Henricus throni

vincat Richardum sceptra qui furto tenet.

---

26 [pietas...fides] This line is omitted in C.
32 quisquis occidat] H̄; ⌊QUiSQUIS OCCIDAT⌋ C̱; quisquis occidat
     omitted B

sin vincat ille: vester Henricus vagus

patria exulabit, aut luet paenas graves,   [40]

et vox pudebit colla victori dare.

petatur ultro dum parat vires modo

aut perdat, aut peribit, hoc certum mihi.

Upon his returne let gunnes go of and trumpets
sounde with all sturre of souldiers without the
hall vntil such tyme as the Lord Stanley be on
the Stage redy to speake as followeth.

    Stanleius ad milites

Properate solvite patriam tyrannide

infesta ferte signa pugna dum calet   [45]

ut verus haeres regna teneat Angliae

pugnabit adversus scelus virtus pia

pugnate tantum, vestra nunc victoria

si vincitis, patria tyranno libera.

medios in hostes ruite passu concito.   [50]

    Let here the like noyse made as
before, as sone as the lorde Stanley
hath spoken, who followeth the rest
to the fielde. After a litle space,
let the L. Northumberland come with
his bande from the fielde, at whose
speach let the noyse cease.

---

43 s.d.: Here the battle is joyned DEF

45 ferte] furta C

46 s.d.: The battel ACDEF

[Oratio] Comitis Northumbriae ad milites.

Northumbreorum illustre nil damnes genus

nostramve lunam miles ignavam putes.

quod tela fugiens hostium terga dedi,

immane regis exercror tandem scelus.

horreo suorum sanguine madentes manus.   [55]

suasit vetustas fatidica regi fore

victoriam, manus prius si conferat

mutata quam sit luna nos sumus

mox ergo lunam milites mutavimus

tyrannus ut dignas scelere paenas luat.   [60]

Let here be the like noyse as before,
and after a while let a Captayn runne
after a soldier or two with a sworde
drawne, drivinge theim ageane to the
field, and saye as followeth.

Centurio

Ignave miles quo fugis? nisi redis

meo peribus ense.

---

54 s.d.: The battel ACDF

61-62] Note the use of singular verb in 1. 61 (redis) and plural verb
(peribis) in 1. 62.

After the like noyse ageane, let soldiers runne
from the field over the stage, one after another,
flinginge of theire harnesse, and at length
some come haltinge and wounded. after this
let Henry earle of Richmond come tryuphinge
havinge the body of king Richard dead on an
horse, Catsbey, Rattlife, and others bounde.

[Nuncius]   Sedata lis est, juditium Mavors tulit

Jacet Richardus at Duci similis jacet

postquam feroces mutuo se acies vident.   [65]

et signum ad arma classicum cecinit tuba

saevus paratum miles in bellum ruit

fugiente tandem milite comitem videns

equo Richardus admisso in illum ruit,

Catulis Nemeus ut furens raptis leo   [70]

per arva passim rugiens saevus volat

vexilla comitis forte Brandonus tulit

cruore cujus hastam tepefacit suam

hinc se Richardo Cheneus armis valens

offert: Richardi hic viribus una cadit   [75]

ventum est ad hostem, quem valide solum petit

in comite solo commorabatur ferox

---

70 furens] ferens C

contra potenti dextera sese comes

defendit. aequo marte pugnatur diu

donec tot hostes convolent illo simul   [80]

ut ille multis vulneribus fossus cadat

o laude bellica inclytum vere ducem,

si saeva Gallus arma sensisset tua

vel perfidus fallas datam Scotis fidem

sed sceleris ultor caelitum potens pater   [85]

est sero vitam sed satis ultus tuam.

Oratio Henrici comitis

Rector potens Olympi Astrorum decus,

terrestrium qui pastor es fidelium.

et principum cujus est potestas cordium

tu laeta regibus trophaea collocas.   [90]

nitida caput cingis corona regium

solus deorum falsa vincis numina

hostesque generi affliges invidos suo.

ingens honor debetur et gratia tibi

qui splendidum [nobis] triumphum indulseras   [95]

cedit tuis armata jussibus cohors

---

95 [nobis]] nobis omitted C

si strage quis saeviret Astyagis ferox

Phrygiove Pelops rege natus Tantalo:

expectet ille Cyrum, et ultorem tremat.

Henricus audebit Richardum pellere [100]

at tu nitentis o gubernator poli

quem terra colit, et vasta mundi fabrica

dum corpus aura vescitur nec ultimum.

diem fati claudunt sorores invidae

teneros levis dum nutrit artus spiritus [105]

te laude perpetua canemus, debitas

tibi afferemus gratias potens deus

tu belluam meis domandum viribus

mitis dabas heu civibus pestem suis

at vos graves passi dolores milites [110]

curate mox inflicta membris vulnera

crudele ne quo serpat ulcus longius

reliqui sepulchra mortuis mites date,

et inferis debetur excellens honor.

---

97   saeviret]   saevierit C

     Astyagis]   Astyages C

99   expectet]   expectat C

111 curate]   curata C

[V.ix] Straunge heros puer. Henricus comes.

Stanleius heros

[Straunge] Non semper aequor fluctibus rabidis tumet

nec semper imbre Jupiter pulsat mare

non semper acres Aeolus ventos ciet

nec semper humiles caeca calcat sors viros

aliquando fluctus sternitur rabidi maris.   [5]

illico caput radiatus, et Titan micat.

pressosque tollet aequa sors tandem viros

Rex exul olim Gallicis et Britonum

latens in oris victor en potens suo

regno potitur, regis o charum caput   [10]

salve, tuoque laetus in solio sede.

multos in annos Angliae verum decus

faelix deinceps subditis vivas tuis

fideique captivos tuae hos clemens cape.

Henr. O Stanleiorum chara progenies mihi   [15]

O Straunge nobilis en libens te conspicor

quos mihi dedisti reddo captivos tibi

Stan Rediisse charum patri salvum filium

    crudelis elapsum tyranni dexteram

    exultat animus laetus o fili mihi   [20]

    pericula post tam dira quod [sospes venis.]

Henr Regno mihique gratulor. regno gravi

    quod sit tyranno liberum. pars mihi

    quod sceptra regni tracto regalia mei

    quare supremo, regna qui dedit, deo   [25]

    laudes canamus ore supplices pio.

Epilogus

Extincta vidistis Regulorum corpora

horrenda magnatum furentum funera.

funesta vidistis potentum praelis

et digna quae caepit tyrannus praemia.

Henricus illustris comes Richmondius   [5]

turbata pacavit Richardi sanguine

Antistitis commotus Eliensium

sermone faelici sagaci pectore

---

21 [sospes venis.]] D; These words omitted in C, with blank spaces left; et plurimos B

 1 s.d.: Let a noble man put on the crowne upon k Henryes head at at the end of [t]his action ABCDEFHI

et gloriosi Marte Buckinghamii

tum Margaretae matris impulsu suae   [10]

illustre quae nostrum hoc suis collegium

christoque fundavit dicatum sumptibus.

quae multa regalis reliquit dexterae

nunquam laudatae. satis mentis suae

praeclara cunctis signa quondam seculis   [15]

his stirpe regali satus Lancastriae

accepit uxorem creatam sanguine

Eborancensi sic duarum faedere

finiunt aeterno domorum iurgia.

hinc portus hinc anglis quietis perditis   [20]

finisque funestae fuit discordiae.

hinc illa manavit propago nobilis

heresque certus qui Britanni cardinem

regni gubernans iure rexit iam suo

Henricus, henrici parentis filius: [25]

qui verus afflictae patronus patriae

tum singulis vnum reliquit commodia

praestantius multo, licet quam plurimis,

---

15 cunctis] cunctra C

cum tam potentem procrearet principem

Elyzabetham, patre dignam filiam   [30]

canosque vincentem seniles virginem

quae regna tot phoebi peractis cursibus

commissa rexit pace faelix Anglica

quam dextera supremi tonantis protegat

illius et vitam tegendo protrahat.   [35]

    Finis. <α>une. Januaryis

      ANTHONIUS CADUS.

finis Tragediae tripartitae actionis, tribusque noctibus
   actae Collega Divi Johannis Cantabridg.
     factaeque a Tho. Leg, juriscivilis
        Doctori, Gonvilli et Caii
         Collegii rectore.
      α, φ, ω, γ. [i.e. 1583]

TRANSLATION

OF

RICHARDUS TERTIUS

By Thomas Legge, Doctor of Laws, of Caius and
Gonville College in the University of Cambridge, master
and director, Richard the Third, a tragedy in three parts,
performed in the College of St. John the Evangelist at the
Bachelors' Commencement in the year 1579.

Anthony   Cade

Written down from the autograph of the author by the hand of A. Cade.

Printed U.C.   1582   January 1.

Richard the third

A Tragedy divided into three parts

Dramatis personae

Queen Elizabeth

Cardinal Archbishop of Canterbury

Messenger

King Edward, 15 years old

Duke of Gloucester, afterwards King Richard

Duke of Buckingham

Rivers

Hastings

Stanley   Barons

Howard, afterwards Duke of Norfolk

Lovell

Bishop of Ely

Servant of the Queen

Catesby, a lawyer

Howard, a knight

Servant of the Duke of Gloucester

Servant of the King

Hastings, a follower [of Lord Hastings] commonly called a pursuivant

Citizen of London

Chorus of turbulent citizens

Guards

Archbishop of York

Mayor of London

Chorus of turbulent nobles

Sergeant-at-arms, commonly [called] a servant at arms

Messenger

Chorus of London Citizens

Fizwilliam, Recorder of London commonly called the Recorder

Doctor Shaw

First citizen

Second citizen

Foreigner

Servant of the Duke of Buckingham

Citizen, a friend of Shaw

Older daughter of King Edward

Brackenbury, Superintendant of the Tower

Tyrell, a nobleman

Lewis, a doctor

Queen Anne

Messenger 1.

Messenger 2.

Messenger 3.

Hungerford ⎤
         ⎬ knights
Burchier ⎦

Soldiers

Lord Strange

Captain

Bray, a servant

Dighton, a murderer

Mutes

Richard, duke of York

Grey, a young noble

Vaughan

Wife of Shore

Hawte, a knight

Priest

Five daughters of Queen Elizabeth

FIRST PART

Argument of the First Part

Edward IV, King of the English people, has died. He has left two sons,

the elder of whom Edward, Prince of Wales, was fifteen years old: the

other, Richard, Duke of York, has completed eleven years of life. When

the brother of the dead Edward, the Duke of Gloucester, a man swollen

with too much ambition, perceived the still tender age of his nephew,

he thinks an easy access to the kingdom lies open to him. Therefore he

first recommends to the Queen through [her] friends that she should pro-

tect Edward's march without an armed band when he hastens from the

borders of Wales. Meanwhile he himself communicates secretly to [his]

friends how much danger would be thenceforth made for them if the guar-

dianship of the young king should be demanded by the Queen's kinsmen

alone, who, since they might despise the other nobles, can readily to

their destruction take full advantage of the King's name. Therefore, he

cast into prison Lord Rivers, uncle of the King, and Grey, his [i.e. the

King's] half-brother, [both] snatched from the King himself; who not so

long afterwards are punished severely at Pomfret. The Protector, pro-

claimed by the illustrious Parliament, receives the King himself under

his guardianship. Next from the Queen who had at that time [i.e. at the

capture of Rivers and Grey] fled to asylum [i.e. sanctuary], he carried

off the little Duke of York with the help of the Cardinal Archbishop of

York [who] at that time suspected nothing. When he had confined the

royal youths in the Tower, just as if in a prison, he first punishes Lord

Hastings, unjustly condemned to death because [the Protector] suspects

that he is too concerned about his nephews. The Cardinal, the Bishop

of Ely [and] Lord Stanley are thrust into prison lest they obstruct his

enterprises, because he greatly fears their loyalty to the princes.

Finally, the wife of Shore, since he could not condemn her to death, is

punished as a harlot with a disgraceful penance.

Dramatis personae of the First Part

Queen Elizabeth

Cardinal

Messenger

King Edward

Duke of Gloucester

Duke of Buckingham

Rivers

Hastings

Stanley   } Barons

Howard

Lovell

Bishop of Ely

Servant of the Queen

Catesby

Howard, a knight

Servant of the Duke of Gloucester

Hastings, a follower

Citizen of London

Chorus of turbulent citizens

Chorus of turbulent nobles

Archbishop of York

Guards

Sergeant-at-arms

A Noble

Mutes

Richard, Duke of York

Lord Grey

Vaughan

Hawte, a knight

A priest

Five daughters of Queen Elizabeth

ACT I [scene i.]

Queen Elizabeth. Cardinal. Messenger.

[Queen.]   Whoever credulously trusts too much to happy affairs and

greatly desires to rule in a great castle, he seeks to obtain an

alluring evil. Although [my] noble birth bade [me] to hope for

nothing [too] great, yet was I married [lit. joined to the marri-

age bed of] to King Edward, after a harsh destiny had offered me

your bedchambers, noble Grey.[1] Credulously I was eager for

sweet poison and [my] renowned beauty seized high titles [for

itself] until a noble kinsman of the King [i.e. Gloucester]

scorned my lowly family and [as an] enemy prepared a sad ruin

for my kinsmen, because, to these [i.e. my kinmen] the chief

care of [my] son [in Wales] is given over and the maternal

uncle [Rivers] takes care of [his] royal nephew.[2] I wanted

my kinsmen to join the King [in Wales] as companions so that

[his] affection might cleave more deeply to [their] excellent

minds, when [his] tender age grew greater. Nor was cruel fate

happy with this plague.[3] The earlier evil was [but] the bottom

rung of a greater evil. [My] husband died [lit. exhales his

---

[1]Because of her inferior birth, King Edward's marriage to Elizabeth
Grey, the widow of Sir John Grey, was considered ill-advised by the King's
closest associates, especially since the Earl of Warwick was at the time
in France arranging for the marriage of Edward to the sister of the French
Queen. See Hall, pp. 263-264; and Holinshed's Chronicles of England, Scotland
and Ireland (London, 1808), III, 223-224.

[2]Gloucester turned the fact that only the Queen's kinsmen surrounded
the new King to their ultimate destruction. See Hall, p. 347; More, p.
408; and Hol., p. 365.

[3]I.e., the Queen was not happy with Edward's decision to send her older
son to Wales.

sick spirit], and the cruel sisters [who] begrudged me [my] husband broke off with impious power the natural term of the King's
life. Mankind is toyed with by the fates. Fortune cannot promise
anything so stable that it does not turn around uncertainly. The
humble home alone remains happy, while great [worldly] power fears
ruin. After I, a mother, enriched the home of the King with a
double heir, remote Wales sought an heir, nor did the Welsh nation lack its prince willingly: From there [i.e. from Wales] to
here [my] son [now] hastens his journey. A small company of my
[kinsmen] accompany [him] so that they might encircle his head
with the royal diadem. Even though the happy sceptre of [my] son
urges [me, his] mother, to rejoice, yet [my] ardent mind does not
dare to hope for itself the promised joy; it fears a good [when]
obtained, and fear once born breeds fear, and [hence] my anxious
heart burns with many cares. But [even] if up to now no external
force has threatened anything disloyal to [my] sons, and the
royal power has not been wrested from them, [still] the House of
Lancaster is envious of Edward and cannot endure the sceptre once
taken from [its] victorious hand. Moreover [my] native fear
oppresses [me] and [my] mind inured to evils dreads a greater
villainy, and fear and hope divide [my] torn mind with manifold
confusion. O the acclaim [that goes with] royal power [is] in-
auspicious for many [people]: [for] having reversed [itself],
after it has deceived credulous man for a while, it hastens [them]
unto their punishment.

Cardinal.   [Most] excellent Queen Elizabeth, why do you turn cares

about in your anxious heart and weigh down the public joy with

your sorrow? Rather spurn the mockeries of [your] turbid mind

and joyfully leave off [your] mournful mother's sighs when the

head of [your] son is encircled with a crown.

Queen.   [O] holy one, distinguished with the honor of a Cardinal,

and eminent Archbishop of Canterbury, may you remain ignorant

of anything more miserable than [my] sorrows! That time has

ever been without tears for me? I do not lament the cruel death

of King Edward, nor do I foolishly complain of the sad hatred of

the nobility [toward me]; this [is an] old evil. When Edward's

heir, [in] leaving his Welsh [home], should have returned sur-

rounded by an armed band so that he might possess the realms of

his father in his own right, the oft-repeated talk [i.e. advice]

of many[4] wearied [my] ears, and [still] does not cease to advise

[me] that the Prince [should] protect his march without arms,

[and that] he should entrust himself bare [of arms] to his sub-

jects; [for] if the House of Grey, solely attendant upon the

King, should surround [lit. encompass the sides of] the King with

its armed band, when the Prince can fear no evil, the nobles will

at once think that so many soldiers are armed to their [i.e. the

nobles'] destruction. The recently extinguished threats will

readily support [their] belief and they [will] immediately sus-

pect that the [old] wounds not well healed have broken open

---

[4]See Hall, pp. 348-349; More, p. 407; and Hol., p. 365.

again. Therefore since they [i.e. Rivers and Grey] fear to expose themselves unarmed to [their] enemies, [and] at the same
time defend [their] lives[s] with the sword, the entire country
will overflow with the fury of war; the earth, being terrified
by the treading cavalry, will groan; a wounded England will
rage with the tumult of war, and immediately the league of
friendship [which was] fashioned [by King Edward IV][5] will be
broken. Then calamity will punish the perfidious instigator
[of the war] and the fallen house of Grey will pay the penalty.
At first [when I heard these things], a cold fear ran through
[my] body; at length trembling at its warnings to [my] mind, I
at once made known everything in letters to [my] brothers[6] so
that they might encircle [lit. surround the sides of] the King
with no armed band and [so that] they might free the march of
the King from a large retinue. [Now] when alone I wisely recall
[my] secret fears, a new worry weighs down [my] mind with dread,
lest the prey may be exposed to armed enemies. A mighty hatred
oppresses our house; blind ambition rages when it fears no disgrace. The youth [lit. slight age] of [my] son does not protect
him. Gloucester has brought about the death of his own brother
[i.e Clarence]: how [then] will the ambition of the uncle spare
[his] nephew?

---

[5]On his death bed, Edward IV had effected a league of friendship between
the Queen's kinsmen and their enemies. See Hall, pp. 344-345; More, pp. 404-
405; and Hol., pp. 363-365.

[6]The Queen's reference to her "brothers" is puzzling since Lord Rivers
was her only brother. Grey was her son. Shakespeare (Richard III, III.1.138)
makes a similar error in describing Grey as Prince Edward's "uncle."

Cardinal.   Let the unhappy love of a mother cease to fear and desist
from falsely speaking [these] foolish deceits. Grief is an unfair judge of things. Does it profit [you] anything to terrify
[your] heart with a foolish fear? The worst prophet of evils
[is] fear: it always threatens itself falsely, and predicts its
own ruin, though unknown before. The nobles promised at the
death of King [Edward] a long quiet to the quarrels [already]
buried, and an England [with its wounds] healed does not fear
menaces [now] dead. Whoever fears former hatreds will move new
hatreds to a renewal of war.

Messenger.   The king has reached the half-way point of his journey
safe and sound.

Queen.   What way now detains my weary son?

Messenger.   Twice late day [i.e. two evenings] had vanished in the
starry sky when [his] weary limbs reached Northampton.

Queen.   And how great a band [of soldiers] surrounds the King?

Messenger.   When he hastily removed from [his] abode in Wales, a numerous
guard was protecting the Prince and the continued work [of re-
cruiting by Rivers and Grey] joined many [men] to him. After
Lord Rivers had received your letters, he stripped the person of
the King of every soldier; only Rivers, [and] Lord Grey, united
with his uncle [Rivers], go with [the Prince].

Queen.   Has the Duke of Gloucester [met] the King along the way?

Messenger.   He sent a greeting to the King by letters. He prayed eternal
honor to his reign and with many a prayer blessed [their] common
joy. The Duke of Buckingham, eminent in honor, addressed the
Prince with the same courtesies; and they [both] promised that

they would [soon] be companions of the young King. Gloucester
has written often to Rivers, and he has visited [his] nephew
Grey with letters; he liberally promised all things in [his]
messages, and a large group of the nobles has been importuned
[by Gloucester] in like manner.

Queen.   After the favor of a gentle following breeze has moved a
boat far [from shore], abating, it leaves the same on the deep
sea, and [the boat] tosses about on many waves; thus when prosperous
affairs bid [me] to be happy, I revert to [my] fears, and my mind
does not cease to fear, even though it should perceive joyful
things.

Cardinal.   Fear readily believes in sinister prophecies.

Queen.   He knows nothing who little experienced knows.[7]

Cardinal.   That which the wretched fear too much, they readily believe
in.

Queen.   Whoever is beware of future events is less upset [by the
turns of Fortune].

Cardinal.   Great virtue never ceases to hope.

Queen.   To the extent you falsely hope for more things, the more
you are upset [by Fortune].

Cardinal.   Do the dead hatreds of the nobility still frighten [you]?

Queen.   Ancient wounds are not healed immediately.

Cardinal.   The Prince [i.e. Edward IV] has consecrated [by his death]
the promises made [to him] at his death.[8]

---

[7]I.e., one without experience in evils really knows little about them.

[8]See Footnote 5 above.

Queen.	Dubious promises seek to die along with the Prince.
Cardinal.	The commonweal overcomes private hatreds.
Queen.	Private ambition destroys public peace.
Cardinal.	Does it please [you] to be always wretched?
Queen.	Whoever has stood high [in life] has Yearned to fear, and

deep sleep is shut off from [those concerned in] great affairs. Poison is [often] drunk from a golden goblet; evil [is] unknown to the humble cottage and the highest roofs tried by every wind shake at their highest point.

ACT II [Scene i.]

Richard, Duke of Gloucester. Henry, Duke of Buckingham. Lord Rivers. Lord Hastings.

Gloucester.   [O] splendor and honor of the House of Rivers, [O] guardian of the orphan King, [O] noble lord, just as Electra protected [her] brother [by] taking [him] from the menaces of [his] bloody mother into the kingdom of [his] father,[9] so you, [who have been] protecting [your] nephew in the Welsh lands, have faithfully brought [him] back to his own country unharmed. Behold, England thanks you for its Prince and [its] sweet pledge of love [who has been] restored to [his] native land. The numerous populace rightly celebrates your loyalty. Behold, this deed [is] pleasing to all of Britain, and we pay equal thanks to you. Welsh homes know of your unselfish labors. The long journey, after Wales had

---

[9]Electra rescued her brother Orestes from the fury of Aegisthus by sending him to the court of her uncle Strophius.

cared for its Prince, testifies to [your] equal care. But when

Titan with radiant hair renews his day in the world and puts to

flight the transient shadows, we will together on the morrow

unite with the flank of the Prince's [army] under whose direction

he is led to Stony Stratford. At the break of day we will hasten

with a quick pace because now one place [i.e. Stony Stratford]

should not contain so many nobles.[10]

Rivers.   O Claudian,[11] Protector of [our] illustrious country, [o]

famous Duke and descendant of the royal family, my duty bade [me]

to support the King with whatever excellent qualities our fortune

has given [us]. A life owing to the King must be laid down in

battle if the menaces of the enemy can in no other way be broken.

Because your tables have spread feasts for me this night, I am

rightly indebted to you [very] much. Now a pleasant sleep [will]

relax my languid limbs and my weary legs [will] rejoice to be

placed in bed. I long for the quiet peace of the most recent

night [i.e. last night]. [Rivers goes off to bed.]

---

[10]Gloucester is here deceiving Rivers as to his purpose in staying with
him at the inn in Northhampton rather than pressing on to stay with the King
who is at Stony Stratford: "On whiche day, the two dukes and their bende came
to Northampton, fainyng that Stony strafford could not lodge them al, where
thei found the erle Riuers, entendynge the nexte mornynge to haue folowed the
kynge..." (Hall, p. 349). See also Mirror for Magistrates:

"The kyne that nyght at Stonystratford lay,
A towne to small to harbar all his trayne:" (p. 250, 11. 393-394).

[11]The name "Claudian" applied to Gloucester throughout this tragedy is
apparently a term of praise, meaning here "emperor-like."

Gloucester.   Illustrious duke, and star of Buckingham, to whom in former

times the buck has not secretly [i.e. has apparently] given its

name, and Hastings born of a famous line of ancestors, behold,

the sun summoned by night, forsaking its reins, dips [his horses']

manes steaming with sweat in the sea, and the moon shines through

the empty sky, bidding silence in men; moreover a glittering

throng [of stars] follows [the moon], spreading a hazy light in

the heavens. A place a [little] farther on will be free for all

[our] decision[s]; no attendant will exhibit secret ears [i.e.

no attendant can be trusted not to listen if we remain here].

Do you not see how miserable the states of the nobles is? and

[do you not see] that for a long time noble virtue has been

despised? Although we are joined to the King by the closest

blood-ties, and [our] distinguished ancestry shines forth with

famous titles, still no approach to the King lies open to me,

and they [i.e. the Queen's relations or his blood-ties] prevent

[me] the uncle from living in the company of [my] nephew. To

what end does such impudence of the mother proceed? Now the honor

of England succumbs to a woman! Lo, our faith is doubted, due

 honor is buried, and our noble blood, scorned, is despised.

Hereafter the sacred charge of the King will be given [over] to

the kinsmen of his mother. Since, however, we do not yield to

them in honor and [our] equal loyalty to [our] nephew is mani-

fest, it was ill fitting for the lowly family of [his] mother

(lowly except that [her] desire for rule urged [her] marriage)

to refuse his illustrious uncles [i.e. Richard and Buckingham][12]

---

[12]Buckingham was married to Catherine Woodville, the Queen's sister, and
hence was an uncle by marriage to Edward V.

access to the King and to surround [him] with a less noble retinue. It will be little proper for the Prince or for us.
Rather a mightier retinue will protect [him] because evil awaits
us if those who desire evil for us may shut off the royal person
[from us] and anticipate the chief desires of the Prince so that
they might grow old in the favor of that one [i.e. the Prince].
In whatever direction the tender mind is steadfastly bent (and
even trifles entice fickle youths nor do they reject with mature
minds whatever formerly has been pleasing to their affections
and earliest delights), mature age will approve and will not
correct itself. Formerly Edward IV (even though he was of more
mature age [than the Prince is now] and [even though his] step-
mother had for a long time recommended much severe discipline
[for him]) condemned his many former [evil] deeds and [yet his]
later behavior did not mend [his] earlier failing, as, alas,
noble Clarence knows. That one, that one, my brother knows
(alas) too well how the credulous King once submitted to his
wife. Too, too much, alas, did our rudenesses [to the Queen]
advise [against us] then because the wife shudders at whomever
the husband reverences.13 For how long a time did a cruel fate
depress our circumstances? How great a ruin would the perfidious
Queen have caused for me if my sagacious mind had not averted
[her] wickedness? The one who turns the heavens by his own hand

---

13In reference to Clarence's death, Hall writes: "...for were it by quene or
nobles of her blud, whiche highly maligned the kynges kyndred (as women com-
menly, not of malice but of nature, hate suche as their husbandes loue)...
heinous treason was laied to his charge...and iugded to death, and there vpon
hastely drowned in a butte of malmesey within the towre of London" (p. 342).
See also More, p. 401; and Hol., p. 362.

and avenges cruel evil with [his] harsh thunderbolts fortunately

delivered [me] by his powerful right hand. Alas, how often has

my brother [Edward IV], aroused in a brief anger, killed those

condemned by their [i.e. the Queen's and her kinsmen's] deceits

to a violent death, [while those condemned were] importuning

Jove with [their] hopeless speech? Never did [his] anger spare

his own blood. He added his own blood-relations (alas) to the

carnage. But we are complaining of ancient [evils]. Now evil

is imminent, for if our common enemy alone cleaves to the young

prince and if only the House of the Greys [which is] hostile to

us surrounds the throne, immediately the strength of the enemy

will heap destruction upon our head as soon as [that] savage

house will dare to use the sacred name of the Prince toward our

ruin. May [our] so provident father Jupiter prevent this [merely]

because Edward has consecrated the sacred leagues of peace by

[his] death and has healed the ancient wound of peace and [merely

because] we have also mutually joined [our] right hands in a

simulated pledge of peace? Did the sacred authority of the

King have greater validity at that time [i.e. at his death] than

[it did] at the peace fashioned by the dubious promises of the

nobles, [especially since] we [also] struck [that] pact [i.e.

the pact that ended hostilities between the House of Lancaster

and York] by order of the Prince.[14] Does such stupidity vex

anyone not insane so that he may madly trust him who is accepted

---

[14]Gloucester is arguing that the promises made to King Edward on his
death bed, just as the pacts that ended the War of the Roses, were more a
matter of "...the Kyng his pleasure...then the parties hertes or willes...,"
and hence can and should be broken for their "good prouision," that is,
their own protection (Hall, p. 348.). See also More, p. 406; and Hol., pp.
365-366.

as a new friend [after having been] so recently an ancient enemy? Will the brief goodwill of a month endure more steadfastly than a long hatred lasting for many years? Now, then, it is fitting to exchange [our] counsel. The longer evil increases, the stronger it is wont to become and it always gathers strength.

Buckingham.   O protector Claudian, and Prince of the royal line, unhappy because England seems [about] to rage again with wild rebellion and [because] civil wars have begun to rumble, I ordered my servant [i.e. Percival] so that he might put in your ear with a secret whisper [these] express words: "the Duke of Buckingham will follow your standards."[15] For a long time [thereafter], I wanted to mingle words [i.e. to converse with you] person to person so that I could speak together with you about these things. The haughty Queen abuses us. It is fitting to crush [her] villainy at once: as evil once born begets greater evil and knows no measure. It is proper that you restore to health the   great ruin of the kingdom. A mighty band of nobles will endure anything rather than that the Queen should play in our blood, and that [that] cruel person should arm against our son [i.e. his only son, Edward].

Gloucester.   Therefore, [o] Duke, I call you a deliverer of your country, and of weeping England, from the maternal treachery. I call to witness you, [the God] of heaven, and you, the troop of bright gods, who understand the rights of a king, [that] I seek only the ancient honor of Britain. The remedy of prison is profitable for a severe wound. The Queen is now absent: she cannot offer

---

[15]Hall is the only source of this passage (p. 347).

aid to her captive kinsmen. Now it is possible to remove safely
from the King all the disgraces of his native land. Yea, it is
right to suppress the sleeping Rivers and to shut the guest within
[these] dwellings. But if he has fled, then he proves his guilty
fear. Demand at once, servant, the keys of that place in which
the guest Rivers has recently retired. But if they [i.e. the keys]
are denied [you], urge the command of the King and do not let any
servant [of Rivers] run outside from there, but let each and every
one be locked carefully within; and secretly advise [our own] servants of our words [i.e orders]: even though the black night
should frighten [them], [since] the day has not yet been admitted,
yet they will defend our person because at daybreak we will approach [our] nephew.

Buckingham.   If you force the relatives of the King into chains and
boldly shut [those] captives up in a dark prison, the fickle
mob [i.e. the populace] will immediately stir up a storm [of
protest] when you do not set just trials for those accused and
[when] you convict them [but] little guilty of crime.

Gloucester.   They both offend the dignity of their Prince and they wish
to dishonor his noble blood: they seek to tear England with dis-
cords in spite of the commands of the hallowed senate [i.e.
Parliament] and of the senators [i.e. the legislators]. The
Marquis [of Dorset] the brother of the Greys, has sailed the
British sea with a long fleet. How many soldiers can he

cruelly arm to our destruction and to waste the distant hopes
of the princes.[16]

Hastings.   But if Lord Grey sees his uncle [Rivers] suppressed in
chains, he will surround Edward with a fierce army; a trembling
Britain will prepare [its] arms, [and] rebellion will drag off
[us] the wretched ones. All things will flare up in the heat of
war and the populace will purge [our] crime with our destruction.

Gloucester.   A careful watch guards the approaches of the roads so that
no one may break through from here to Northhampton and [so that
no one] may prevent our first journey to the King. We have decided that, after Lucifer has dispersed the light shadows and the
bright torch of Phoebus has ordered [our] flight [from here], we
[will be] the first to attend the King so that thus [our] loyalty
may appear gratifying to the Prince.

Buckingham.   Direct the sinews of [all my] strength; the noble ardor of
my mind cannot be overcome and no labor wearies [my] diligent
concern for the greatest Duke. I shall never let my loyalty [to
you] waver.

Hastings.   Sooner heaven will be joined to mournful hell, stars will
float on the waters, fire will be a friend to savage waters, [and]
night will conquer day before you may condemn my loyalty.

---

[16]Legge uses this accusation against Dorset twice, here and again at Stony
Stratford when Grey, Vaughan and Hawte are accused and taken captive. In the
chronicles, this accusation is made only once, at Stony Stratford before the
young King: "...in the kynges presence they picked a quarel to the Lord Richard
Grey the quenes sonne,...saiyng that he and the Marques [of Dorset] his brother
and the lord Ryuers his vncle had compassed to rule the kyng and the realme and
set variaunce betwene the states, and to subdue and destroy the noble bloude of
the realme. And towarde thaccomplishmente of the same, they sayde, the lord
Marques had entered into the towre of London, and thence had taken out treasure
and sent men to sea, which thynges these dukes knewe well wer done for a good
purpose and as very necessary, appointed by the whole counsaill at London..."
(Hall, p. 349). See also More, p. 409; and Hol., p. 267.

Rivers.   [To himself, having been roused from his sleep.]

I do not know what sad evil [my] mind forbodes; [my] legs
tremble with fear, [my] heart quakes with dread. I wonder why
these [men] are asking for the keys of the guest-chambers.
What great change of circumstances has occurred? They [i.e.
Gloucester and Buckingham] voluntarily filled [me] [with food]
at last night's banquet. Will they now punish [me who has been]
detained [from attending the King] with a shameful death? They
are friends to me: [my] faith does not like pretences. [My] mind
wavers; [it] is perplexed [and] not at ease with itself. If I
fly, no place of refuge is safe. If I hide, I will be wildly
conscious of [my] wickedness. Lo, [my] guiltless mind rejects
any [and all] fears. It is determined to remain: whatever
comes, I shall bear. I shall approach the dukes: I shall hear
what the reason [for all this] may be.

Gloucester.   O enemy of the King, [o] impious and bold person, you desire
to punish the nobles with wounds and you sow [your] haughty discords. You invoke the will of the Prince toward our destruction
and you senselessly entangle the kingdom in your disputes. Do
you think you will fulfill [your] abominable villainy?

Rivers.   Illustrious Prince, believe no such thing about me: May
this [so foul a] crime (I beg) be far removed from our loyalty!

Gloucester.   Such [a crime is] the infamous ruin of your King. Shall we
willingly allow that our blood be sought? Will you alone destroy
Britain's high honor? But you [soldiers] punish [this] captive
in a dark prison, and let our other associates surround us
[lit. our side].

Rivers.   Where are you dragging me? What punishment does mighty

                 Fortune command? What evils now await wretched me? If they

                 punish [me] with death, they will condemn [me] by public law

                 [i.e. they will have to give me a trial first]. What [other]

                 hope of salvation is left to me?

                        ACT II [Scene ii]

                 King Edward. Duke of Buckingham. Duke of
                      Gloucester. Servant of the King.

Edward.   Even though I, seized with a love of my native land,

                 [reluctantly] undertook [this] dangerous journey when I left my

                 Welsh estates, yet [now] I willingly leave Stonistratford because

                 [people] report that Gloucester is hastening hither since one

                 place does [i.e. should] not hold so many nobles.[17]

Buckingham.   Edward surrounded by his own relatives approaches [lit.

                 brings his pace hither]. Advance [ye noblemen] whom the noble

                 crowns of [your] ancestors bless: let the inferior ranks follow

                 [us].

Gloucester.   May the illustrious King of the Britains live eternally!

Edward.   Your sight, my uncle, is welcome to me after we have

                 just left [our] foreign estates, and I have a like gratitude for

                 [your] prayers so dear [to me].

Buckingham.   May God establish for you a happy rule!

Edward.   I likewise praise your loyalty, illustrious Duke.

-----

[17]See Footnote 6 above.

Gloucester.   A nature unable to be resisted [i.e. instinct] has consecrated me loyal to your commands, and [my] royal descent prevents
me from devising plots against [you] the King [even] when a common
duty urges my loyalty to others. The hostile fire will dwell with
the waters, a ship will sail through the stars, and an unknown oak
will grow up in the cruel sea when so false a loyalty may suborn
[me to be] forgetful of you. I shall willingly lay down [my] life
[fighting] in your battles; I earnestly wish to die, hostile to
your enemies. [Turning to Grey.] What ambition possesses you,
haughty Grey, or your brother and the cruel Rivers when you [three
wish to subject the Prince to yourselves and also to split the
nobles in an infamous contention? Lo, you entangle Englishmen in
the very worst kind of quarrel, and the high source of [our] blood
is derided. Why does the Marquis of Dorset constantly menace us?
He has boldly broken into the chest of war, [and] from thence the
money of the King is plundered by a devouring hand, and he has
burdened the long sea with a mighty fleet.[18]

Edward.   What my half-brother the Marquis has perpetrated against me,
I do not know, [but] the loyalty of my uncle and of my brother
Grey (believe me) has never been suspected [by me].

Gloucester.   Yea, so many deceits are hidden from your ears, illustrious
King, [that their] secret villainy exerts [itself all] the more.[19]

---

[18]See Footnote 12 above.

[19]The chronicles give this speech to Buckingham. See Hall, p. 349; More,
p. 409; and Hol., p. 369.

I declare that you, infamous Grey, are accused of treason and
I announce that you, Vaughan, [are] guilty of villainy; also I
call [you], perfidious Hawte,[20] a traitor to [your] native
land. Remove [them] at once to a squalid dungeon: let them
pay the [most] severe penalties of [our] country.

Servant of   [Aside]   [Behold] the unhappy boy [i.e. the King]: he
the King.
wets [his] checks with tears, seeing [his] brother carried off
to cruel bonds.

Gloucester.   Servant, we free you from your servitude and we do not want
you to cleave to the side of the Prince. [Addressing one of his
own servants.] You, as a faithful attendant, will assist the
Prince and [your] constant labor will bind you to the King.

ACT II [Scene iii.]

Servant of the King. Servant of the Duke of Gloucester.

Servant of   A feeble boy does not maintain the authority of [his] father's
the King.
reign: overcome by his own forces, at length, he falls. Sacred
majesty protected by its very name looks impiously [i.e. scornfully]
on [its] enemies [even] when [their] ambition secretly plans to
obtain [its] cruel destruction. Slight loyalty [is given to]
suspected royal authority [i.e. authority that is feeble] and the
secret struggle for the throne does not permit an anxious prince
to rest. He who remains in a lesser station [in life is] safer:

---

[20]Only Hall mentions Hawte by name (p. 349).

neither the fear of a lost crown nor honor unlike [i.e. honor
that does not equal] that of [his] ancestors burdens [him].
Thundering Father, you who turn the bright stars about and strike
the [very] spheres of heaven with your ligtning   defend in your
might the Prince of the Britains so that the true heir of England
may restore justice. What servant flies here at a speedy pace?
Whither now do you so stoutly hasten [your] step?

Servant of
Gloucester.
    Noble Rivers has sent [me] to his nephew [Grey].

Servant of
the King.
    [Are] you not the minister of that one's [i.e. Rivers's]
prison for the Duke?

Servant of
Gloucester.
    I assisted Claudian as a faithful associate.

Servant of
the King.
    Why do you come [as] a messenger of the uncle to [his]
nephew?

Servant of
Gloucester.
    When hunger knawed at a fasting Gloucester [and] excellent
feasts burdened the table of the Duke, he carefully surveyed the
entire banquet with [his] eyes and sent selected dishes to Rivers,
and he bade [him that he should] bear everything with a calm mind,
[and that] nothing of that one's [i.e. Rivers's] circumstances was
fearful [i.e. a cause for alarm].

Servant of
the King.
    Did he foolishly refuse the generous gifts [of food and
encouragement]?

Servant of
Gloucester.
    A long familiarity [with evil] urges [him] to endure upon whom
harsh Fortune has often raged: he desires less comfort for his
afflicted life. When he sent back [his] thanks with a full heart,
he ordered the sumptuous dishes brought to Grey (whom grief unknown [to him] before has dispirited, nor has the younger [one]

learned to endure bitter events) so that the gentle words of the
Duke [of Gloucester] might encourage the dispirited [Grey]
and [so that] the feasts might calm his distrubed mind. But
[now] it is fitting that I execute the commands of so great a
man.

Servant of   Perhaps deceit presented with a gentle countenance lies
the King.
concealed so that it may fix deep[er] wounds in the ignorant,
or does Fortune changed by a happy chance bless us, [by] freeing
the wretched ones [i.e. Rivers, Grey, and their associates] from
the fear of prison? May a happy result fall to such great
troubles!

ACT III [Scene i]

Servant of the Queen. Queen. Archbishop of York.

Servant [alone].   You who twirl in [your] hand the avengers of evil [i.e.
thunderbolts] and [who] mercifully direct aid to [our] weary
affairs, pity the overthrown House of York! What will be the
outcome of [these] evils? Alas! alas! how long will the Queen
burden her life with dreadful lamentations? What savage Alecto[21]
or what bloody Megaera[21] brandishing coiled snakes besets the
royal family? And [the Queen's] earlier sorrow calls forth
greater sorrow [now], and the Queen is scarcely able [to bear] such
great evils. What whirlwind will carry me taken up through the
heavens so I may not sorrowfully hear the   many sad complaints
of the mournful house and the lugubrious lamentations of the
mother?

---

[21]Alecto, Megaera and Tisiphone are the names of the three Furies.

<u>Archbishop</u> <u>of</u> <u>York</u> [<u>approaching</u> <u>alone</u>]. While night has not yet fled, the sun
renews the day, and the sister of Phoebus [<u>i.e</u>. Diana or the
moon] leaves [her] post to [her] brother; or black night, driven
from the heavens draws up [its] uncertain light. Why do you wish
to appear [here] in the shadows of the night? An immense evil
needs swift comfort [from me]: the sick mind [of the Queen] does
not permit delays [on my part]. Prepare to calm the troubled
mind of the mother. But what [is this] noise? How great [is]
the commotion in the palace! [<u>To</u> <u>the</u> <u>servant</u>.] Speak: what may
be the meaning of such great noises in the night?

<u>Servant</u>.   Archbishop of York, resplendent with honor, do you bid me
to repeat to you the dire happenings? After the waning moon had
urged sleep and [after] black night might frighten [anyone],
since the day was done, it became known in the palace that
Rivers and [his] nephew Grey are restrained in harsh bonds;
then [it became known] that no one knows who holds the Prince.
After such great evils had been made known to the Queen, [her]
mind disturbed by a sudden fear was stunned. [Her] limbs, alas,
were weakened by [her] uncertain breathing. After [this]
miserable [one] had gathered her trembling energies, lo, she
immediately struck the stars with such words: "O cruel fates,
spare [me]! What alas are you turning about [in your minds]?
How much evil will you breathe forth? If punishments please
[you], wrathful Father, avenge [yourself] by hurling [your]
lightning-bolts against this [my] head. What [crime] has the
innocent boy committed? What has he deserved? Why is a little
child ruined? You crush an entire house in a single ruin."

Soon she did not hold [her] tottering head [upright] on [her]

neck; [her] cheeks bathed in a great shower [of tears] grew wet;

[her] sad heart seethed with great sorrows; [her] sense of

decorum [made her] put away [her] regal clothing and [her]

purples of excellent hues. She was never at rest: here [and]

there, she flew. She ordered [her] substance [i.e. all her

possessions] to be lifted up and to be put down again, and im-

patient always of her own position, she was quickly altered and

struck the heavens with [her] complaints. Sometimes she lamented

[her] son, sometimes the ruin of [her] kinamen, and feeling [her]

late concern for and [her] so great wounds [on account] of [her]

dead companion [i.e. Edward IV], she re-echoed [them] in anguish.

Soon that one ordered [her] servants to take within the sanctuary

the purple cloth and the yellow gold, the household furniture and

the noble treasures of the King which she had [in her possession];

and lest slight delays might hinder the carrying [out of these

goods], she ordered the interior walls, by which the palace of the

King is shut off from the sanctuary, broken down so that a shorter

route might lie open from here to the Abbey;[22] and the mother

wildly clutching [her] beloved son to [her] breast and summoning

her five daughters, flew to the sacred temple, all the while

trembling with fear just as a small wild beast fleeing, fears to

be crushed in the vast jaws of the lion feeding on its prey.

---

[22]The Queen fled from the Palace of Westminster to the Abbey of Westminster,
which two buildings were joined by the common wall she ordered broken down to
speed the removal of her possessions to the sanctuary. See Hall, p. 350; More,
p. 410; and Hol., p. 368.

Queen.   [O] excellent Father of the city of York, what now can be
lacking to our ills? or who could [be] miserable [enough] to
outdo our fates? [Now] we fear in vain what we dreaded to fear
just lately. Of a great house, we, alas, are the small remains
and the sacred temples alone protect [us] unhappy [ones]. They
[i.e. the children] are prepared for the ruin of their blood-
relation, and the servants do not know what place holds the King
nor whether we [all] are going to die or not. Does any hope for
[our] house remain?

Archbishop of York. Dispense with [your] fear! Put off your anxious
worries! That [is] all wrong whatever the evil is. What heavy
sorrow ever uplifts wretched spirits? Rather think more mildly
about these affairs. Recently when black night recommended
sleep to me, a messenger aroused me buried in sleep. Lord
Hastings sent [him]; this one told me that the [dukes of Gloucester
and Buckingham] have gone back [with the King from Stratford] to
Northampton where the King [now] remains surrounded by his own
servants.[23] [Knowing this], no one at all may beguile my heart
with fear, for all things at length fall to a happy lot [i.e.
everything comes out all right in the end].

Queen.   That one, that cruel enemy of our kinsmen, Hastings, that one
prepares ruin for the Prince. Behold, I a mother, humbly pray
that the avenging gods may consign [his] cruel head to horrible
flames.

---

[23]See Hall, p. 350; More, p. 410; and Hol., p. 368.

<u>Archbishop of York</u>. Relax the troubled motions of [your] raging spirit

and prudently quench the unpleasant impulses of [your] mind. I

call to witness the majesty of the god [<u>i.e</u>. Jove] who twirls

the stars in his hand, if they [<u>i.e</u>. the dukes] crown anyone

besides your son, at once on the very next day we will hand over

to this one, his own brother, the insignia proper to the royal

authority; behold, I shall now return to you the Great Seal

(which your husband formerly offered to me), which you [will]

keep for your son.

<u>Archbishop</u> <u>of York</u> [alone].

O mighty ruler and thundering Father of Olympus, restore

now peaceful quiet to [our] native land so that the [rightful]

heir may wield the sceptre in his youthful hand lest the kingdom

fall by a cruel default to a conqueror and [lest] the Lancastrians

form a new hope of war while its enemy [<u>i.e</u>. the House of York]

sacrifices itself in impious slaughter. But what are you doing?

What oblivion of mind seizes you that you give the Great Seal

to anyone? to whom have you offered [it]? to a woman? Why has

she always been envious of [it]? The dukes will mock your

faith at the time when [it is learned that your] great charge

of royal authority has been rashly handed over [to a woman].

Do you put [your] faith in a woman? She is easily opposed and

only her violence [instead of that of the dukes] will rage

against your head. Now, therefore, I will send [one] who may

secretly demand the Seal so that the dukes may not condemn my

light trust.

[ACT III. Scene ii.]

Servant of Gloucester. Chorus of turbulent nobles.
Archbishop of York. Lord Hastings.

Servant.   Now, as you wish, a watch guards the way and boats in thick

array sail the entire Thames so that no one fleeing may break

forth to sanctuary. Fear not at all, Duke Claudian, the sacred

flight [of anyone]. But why do they take the treasures of the

mother away to the Abbey? What commotions do you evil men stir

up here? Where does the fury of Elizabeth drive [you] senseless

ones?

Chorus of nobles. City, city, (citizens) to arms, to arms! Behold, the

arms with which the rebels were secretly preparing ruin for the

dukes are carried forth concealed in barrels.[24] What evil will

so great a commotion produce? The water of the Thames burdened

with ships has been frightening. The Queen fleeing, moreover,

has carried many arms [with her]. What evil does the bloody

Queen prepare? But yet arms may protect [only]: if they threaten,

they do not ride [in wagons]. May the gods avenge the cruel

crime of the woman but yet may God protect you, little Prince:

Archbishop of York. [0] noble band of barons of a mighty kingdom, does

not a rash rumor, spreading new fears, delude the credulous or

increase the ancient evil in a [new] cause for sorrow? and does

---

[24]Gloucester arranged to have a cart go through the streets of London,
on which cart were barrels filled with the arms and harness of Rivers, Grey
and their allies as evidence of their proposed treachery to himself and
Buckingham. Some saw through the ruse, realizing that the proper place for
arms is on one's back and not in a barrel; others, however, were fooled.
See Hall, p. 351; More, pp. 411-412; and Hol., p. 360.

a raging ambition again seek a throne acknowledged [as legitimate] before and demand booty for itself? A dangerous tumult does not permit [only] slight restraints. The trembling mother lies suppliantly in the temple. The Queen suspects the rule [placed over her] son; several nobles are shut up in a black den whose loyalty has earned [for them the right of assuming] the protection of the King. The [still] weak youth of the King readily admits treachery, and however much anyone secretly stirs up evil toward the King, yet it is proper to exercise prudence until this trickery makes more manifest who does wrong. But [now] illustrious Hastings flies hither to me.

Hastings.   It is now unknown to you, [O] beloved gathering of citizens, with what affections King [Edward IV] tightly embraced me in times past; and the generous gifts of so great a King compel [me] to reverence his beloved pledges [i.e. his children], the life of whom unless I would expiate with my death, no name would shame [me] more than [that of] ingrate. I am grieved that peace is harmed by a foolish rumor and that Britians are disturbed by an uncertain murmuring. I, a stranger [to London], see subjects causing a tumult, robbers flying through every dwelling. Why does it please [you] to vex [your] foolish hearts with fear? What do prating mouths allege? The loyalty of Gloucester has been sufficiently ascertained by me. Lo, he conducts the Prince with a quick procession only so that he might gird [his] youthful head with the golden [lit. yellow] crown. Yet he restrains in harsh custody the nobles who perfidiously sought to destroy the Duke of Gloucester by shameful deeds, and they grow cold in a dark prison

[only] until the hallowed Parliament might settle the contention
[i.e. might try the case]. One thing I humbly beg (fathers): that
your [present] opinion might not prevent [i.e. prejudice] your
future mind [i.e. judgment], that [private] disputes might not
grow into public destruction, that a [single] rebellious man might
not incite you to arms. Even though the most just of wars can be
urged, a more just reason will be brought forth in support of
these [men] who enclose the Prince with their arms. When the
royal youth arrives at the walls [of the city], may a peaceful
city wish joy to its Prince!

[ACT III. Scene iii.]

King Edward. Mayor of London.

Edward. Whereas we have left the foreign estates of a wild nation, I
[now] return safe and sound to my paternal dwellings. Here the
bright splendor of the lofty city excels and [here] greater honor
of the famous kingdom shines forth. Hail beloved city! [There were]
never such great joys after the   great ruin of Asia by the Argives
when after   many long battles the [Greek] chieftains saw [their]
longed for native kingdoms and [their] Argolian treasures. So
joyous [is my] return to you [that] scarcely did the Cephalenes
prepare so many sacrifices for [their] guest, even though [their]
unfortunate duke had been saved from such great shipwrecks.[25] [O]
how [my] desire for [my] most country increased after I, a stranger,

[25]Neither sixteenth-century nor modern classical dictionaries throw any
light on this allusion to the Cephalenes.

was deprived [of it] for a long time and [after my] long journey
[away from it] had denied its sights to me.

Mayor.   [O] illustrious King, distinguished ornament of our country,
behold, the joyous crowd of citizens has spread itself [along the
way] so that it may wish much joy to its Prince. So that you may
happily shine forth as another sun in our heavens and [so that]
you the heir of [your] father may give [just] laws to the Britians,
the citizenry will anxiously importune God with prayer. Behold,
o my citizens, Edward our King, resplendent with regal honor:
behold the mighty youth. Beloved Britians, look upon your Prince:
be faithfully subject to one preeminent in virtue.

ACT IV. [Scene i.]
Lord Hastings [alone].

The mourning Queen resides in the sacred temples; [her]
kinsmen are restrained by harsh bonds; and Gloucester has been
declared Protector of England just now by our votes. The Great
Seal has been taken from the Archbishop of York. Claudian [i.e.
Gloucester] rebuked him greatly in a speech because he delivered
the Seal to a mere woman. A happy fate will bless everything.
[Our] enemies are overthrown and now await [their] sad destruction
at Pontefract [Castle]. Hurry, [ye] fates, let them pay at once
heavy penalties! But why do I delay from visiting the hallowed
Council?

[ACT IV. Scene ii.]

Richard, Duke of Gloucester. Henry, Duke of Buckingham.
Bishop of York. Bishop of Ely. Stanley. Hastings. Howard. Lovel.
Barons.

Gloucester. O illustrious gathering of noblemen, whom the noble English

nation has produced, does not the harsh evil of the Queen

move [you] at last? Can a noble mind still endure such great

infamy? Will the malice of a woman remain hidden for so long

a time? Lo, the hostile [Queen] holds captive [her] son in

sanctuary so that she [like] a rebel may with a plaintive murmur

stir up the nobles of Britian and [so that] the mob aroused to

a commotion might assail [us] with cruel words just as if the

loyalty of his protectors may be doubtful upon whom the careful

Parliament bestowed the care of the Duke of York. Neither a

far off enemy [i.e. removing him far from his enemy], nor well-

noted food [i.e. attention to his diet] will alone safeguard

the little boy [in sanctuary]: the more moderate recreations

attract a boy. An age equal to its own delight is pleased.

A boy associated with an old man never plays. A brother

[all] the more will insist on the play of his brother. Who

does not know that great things are wont to grow from small

things. Great might be the dishonor of the King and no slight

stain may damn our faith when a fleeting rumor murmurs to

Frenchmen that the brother of the Prince has fled to a sanctuary

out of fear. Nothing can fly faster than evil speech, nor does

an opinion [once firmly] established die at once. Therefore,

by [your] sacred assent, let men be sent whose loyalty to the

King was never doubtful, [and which has been even] less suspicious to the mother, [and well] enough known to the country so that she

may restore [her] son, freed from [his] sacred prison, to his own

brother. But so great a mission demands your loyalty, [o]

illustrious Archbishop distinguished with the title of Cardinal,

if your sanctity does not refuse to do [it]. The solace of the

King greatly demands this; and the health of [his] brother [and]

the assured peace of the country [all demand this]. But if the

Queen stubbornly detains [her] son, and [her] mother's love

unhappily makes a stay, the supreme commands of the King may

check [her] opposition. [Her] malice, [her] hatred, [her]

forwardness will [then] be evident. I will willingly listen to what

the opinion of your mind is, for, by the God supporting [my] life,

never will I urge my observations [so] stubbornly but [that] a

stronger [i.e. better] judgment may change [them].

<u>Duke</u> <u>of</u> <u>Buckingham</u>. Who [among you] is not moved by the solitude of the

Prince, the declining honor of the nobles, or the safety of our

country already for a long time cast down? As long as the insane

mother restrains [her] son within the sacred confines, the boy

[thus] separated [from the Prince] will bring great dishonor to

the Prince, nor will it be safe in the prison for [his] little

brother. The foolish mob [will] assail [us] with shameful abuses

just as if no concern for the King occupies [us] nobles. The

mother alone may not claim [for herself alone] the birth of [her]

son [since he is a Prince], and [yet] she foolishly thinks [him]

born for her delight alone. The honor of the kingdom demands

[him]: forgetful of the dear mother, it bids [us] to heal [our]

native land at once. That the holy Father, the excellent Bishop, can better urge these things, I agree. But if the fearful mother

does not know the [full] measure of [our] love, he should order

[her] son taken away from her by force.

Hastings. Why should a small child cleave to sacred [places]? or why

does she begrudge the triumph of the King to [his] brother? If

trembling she fears danger for [her] son, yet here at least the

numerous paternal members of [his] family will protect [him]; here

a Protector has been prescribed by [this] sacred Council, and

[here] the devoted servants of the King will care for [him]. Then,

[too], the mutual comfort of the brothers summons [us to take

forceful action]. If the stubborn mother refuses to send him,

the Cardinal Archbishop should carry off [the boy] taken [from her].

Archbishop of York. Inasmuch as the abode of [one] brother may also please

the [other] brother, or [inasmuch as] my labor may be pleasing to

England, I refuse nothing equal to my abilities. But if the

mother keeps [her] son in the sacred Abbey, and the lonely King

does not obtain his brother, it is yet never fitting to break the

privileges promised to a church: which [privileges] St. Peter,

so they say, first consecrated, [our] ancient faith at once

confirmed, and a long line of princes has [since] perpetuated.

It is well known that the sacred promises have safeguarded many

good [men]. Nor does any Isther [River] affording flight to the

savage Alani, nor the land freezing with perennial Hyrcanian snow,

nor sparse Scythia dare to violate [the sacred promises].[26]

---

[26]The Isther River, Hyrcania and Scythia are found in a region between
the Black Sea and the Caspian Sea, on the outermost limits of civilized
Europe. The Archbishop is arguing that not even the uncivilized people of
these lands would violate the rights of sanctuary.

No one sacrilegiously breaks a trust granted by the gods. But a mother's love [for her son] will grant a brother to the little Prince, and the parent will not begrudge the comfort of [her] son. But if the palace of the [one] brother may be forever unoccupied by the [other] brother, and the mother keeps [her] son in the sacred prison, my devout labor will be in no way blamed inasmuch as [lit. and] the blind love of the mother alone will impede [it].

Duke of Buckingham. Nay rather the stubbornness of the mother will impede [it]. I will dare to place my life in wager [that] she may think of no reason for fear either for herself or for [her] son. No one will willingly fight with a woman. I might wish for the womanish sex in [her] kinsmen likewise (it would trouble England less) whose own villainy alone has caused [our] hatred [of them] [and] not because they derive their origin from her blood. But [even] if the Queen or her kinsmen were not dear to us, yet what does it profit [us] to hate the brother of the King to whose [family our own] noble family has joined blood-ties.[27] But unless [our] honor were hateful to her and [unless] she may [want to] menace us with an infamous censure, she would never refuse [to us] her son to whom the loyalty of the nobles has never been suspected. The nobles will leave her son to her if she, the mother, will remain in [any] place suitable to her [station in life].

Duke of Gloucester.[28] Now, then, if she refuses [her] son to us whose loyalty is sufficiently [well] known to her, this will be [due to]

_____

[27]See Footnote 8 above.

[28]Legge apparently assigned the rest of the argument on sanctuaries to Gloucester, although the chronicles agree in assigning it to Buckingham. See Hall, pp. 352-355; More, pp. 413-418; and Hol., pp. 371-373.

the stubbornness of an inhuman woman, [and] not [to] the fear of [her] frightened mind. But if the unhappy mother, who can fear [her own] shadow, still fears, so much the more the [inordinate] love of the mother [for her son] bids [us] to beware lest the suspicious Queen send her secret stolen love, [that is], her son, to foreign lands. A thousand times better it is to break the privileges promised to a church than [that] the Council suffer so great a dishonor and that others who can see the brother of the Prince cast away [under our very noses] should laugh at our noble person[s].[29] Therefore, it will be proper that her son, freed by force from [his] mother, be taken from the Abbey lest we are rightfully [held] in scorn by outsiders. Neither would I willingly violate the right of sanctuary to which long [continued] custom has granted very much force, nor would I, [were I] a chief in former times, have granted its privilege to churches; or perhaps now [i.e. today] I would agree to [such] places of refuge if a creditor persistently rages against [his] debtors and cruelly threatens chains to those whom adverse Fortune has condemned or [to those whom] a foreign sea has overcome with a profuse wind [i.e. those who have suffered shipwreck]. Inasmuch as a place of refuge protects a person snatched [from the sea], it [is] certainly a virtuous [practice]; but [is] it not an evil [practice] to spare impious citizens, or robbers and murderers whom no fear can ever restrain? But if the privileges granted to a sanctuary protect

---

[29]The Duke is afraid that the Queen might embarass the Council and England in general if she should send the Prince to France: ". . . And if she might hap to bring that purpose to passe, as it were no great mastery to do, we letting her alone, all the world would say that we were a sorte of wyse counsaillers about a king to let his brother to be cast away vnder oure noses" (Hall, p. 353). See also More, p. 415; and Hol., p. 372.

only [those] whom an unjust Fortune upsets, why do the sacred
[privileges] extend [also] to robbers? why to murderers? why
to worthless citizens? The sacred [place] also overflows with
evil men. Will any god be a patron to wicked men? Did [St.]
Peter stipulate these rights for thieves? The holy place prompts
prodigals to snatch other men's goods and to entrust to it [i.e.
to the sanctuary] the things taken by stealth. A wife will
leave [her] husband laden with his goods, mocking [her] husband
[after] she has stored up [her] stolen goods in the church. Many
a thief issues forth from here to [commit] a murder, and having
committed [his] crime, considers the place a safe [refuge].
Therefore, it does not violate the right of sanctuary to take
its sacred favors away from robbers, and [moreover] it will be a
[deed] holy and pleasing to God. Since a too merciful pope, or
a tender-hearted (yet not sufficiently wise) prince (I know not
who) [long ago] granted these privileges to sanctuaries and since
[their] posterity [i.e. the princes and popes that followed them]
led by superstition never [dared to] attack [the sacred privileges],
let us still preserve their promises to the sacred places. However,
the sacred [promises] in no way support the Duke [who has been]
shut within [the Abbey]. Right, Nature, Law forbid unjust
punishments; ([in saying this,] we say nothing against either a
prince or a bishop [i.e. we speak no disparagement of their
respective powers to forbid unjust punishments, a king by his laws,
a bishop by providing sanctuaries]), [for] any place is sufficiently
safe against [physical] violence.[30] The sacred laws [that have been]

---

[30] The argument is more fully developed in Hall: "The conclusion is,
sithe it is so long a goo I wote not what pope and what prince more piteous

granted may prevent the menaces of the law [i.e. legal threats] if

a harsh necessity has recommended their indulgence [i.e. the

indulgence of the sacred laws]. But what cruel necessity oppresses

the Duke? [His] royal birth proves [him] loyal to the King; [his]

age ignorant of evil urges [his] guiltlessness. Why should an

innocent boy obtain sacred protection? Another [person] requests

the sacred font [of baptism] for the infant, but whoever obtains

the rights promised to sacred places must request [them] himself

by an impulse of his own mind. How may the guiltless boy request

[sanctuary]? [How] has he merited [it]? [His] mature age [i.e.

if he were older] would never endure prison. The enraged boy

would forthwith abhor [all] refuges. If anyone who has plundered

another's goods flies here, the sacred privileges do [and should]

protect [his] person, but he should be made to [lit. will] give

up the [stolen] goods. Neither pope nor prince can change these

things [i.e. that a man should not be allowed to keep in sanctuary

goods with which he can discharge his debts].[31]

---

then politique, hath graunted it [i.e. the right of sanctuary], and other
men sence of a religious feare haue not broken it, lette vs take a paine
with it, and lette it stande a Goddes name in his force,. . . whiche is not
so farfurthe as may serue too lette vs of the fetching furthe of this
noble manne [i.e. the little Duke] to his honoure and wealthe out of that
place in the whiche he nether is nor can bee a sanctuarye. . . man. A
sanctuarye euer seruethe too defend the body of that manne that standeth
in daunger abrode, not of greate hurte onely, but of lawfull hurte: for agains
vnlawfull hurtes and harmes no pope ner kynge entended to priuilege any one
place wherein it is lawfall for one manne to doo another manne wronge. That
no manne vnlawefully take hurte that libertie the kynge, the lawe and verie
nature forbiddeth in euery place and maketh too that regarde for euery
manne euery place a sanctuarye: but where a manne is by lawefull meanes
in perell, there nedeth he the tuicion of some speciall priuilege, whiche
is the onely ground of all sanctuaries, from whiche necessitye this noble
prince is far, . . . whose innocence too all the worlde, his tender youth
affirmeth, and so sanctuarye as for hym is not necessary, ner none he can haue
(p. 354). See also More, p. 416; and Hol., pp. 372-373.

[31]". . . for nether kynge nor pope can geue any place such a priuilege
that it shall discharge a man of his debtes beeyung hable to paie" (Hall, p.
354). See also More, p. 416; and Hol., p. 373.

Bishop of Ely. Divine law has urged that the rights promised to a church

protect free from their creditors the persons of debtors whom by

chance a harsh lot bids to lie concealed. Also the decrees of

[various] popes grant sacred refuge [lit. flight] to those wretched

[in fortune] provided that they surrender another man's property

to their creditors so that the debtor free from prison with [his]

goods taken away may rise again by his own labor and may the sooner

restore [his] loss by [his] assiduous care. Who would cruelly

rage at [them if their] backs [are] naked?

Buckingham. This opinion is indeed approved by me. If a wife [in] leaving

[her] husband flies to the [sacred] altars, cannot this one be

taken out of a church of Peter with the approval of Peter? [If]

a sportive boy hating school loiters in the sacred places, shall

[his] teacher allow him [to do so]? But he [i.e. the schoolboy]

at least fears the rod: this one [i.e. the Prince] has nothing

to fear at all. I have heard of the sacred privileges granted to

men, [but] not to boys. A refuge may be a protection as long as

it is agreeable to those guilty. To him the sacred promises are

denied because [his] weak mental ability does not know [enough]

to request [them], nor does his honest life permit [him] to deserve

[them], nor could the Prince safe from evils need [them; and moreover]

he will in no way violate the sacred privileges who removes [a

person from sanctuary] so that he can benefit [him].

Lord Stanley. Because it is expedient to the King, to the British people,

to England that [one] brother should play with the [other] brother

in a single palace, a doubtful mind after this cannot cling [to

its doubt]. I expect that [his] mother's mind will be easily

pacified. Led by sane advice, she will readily surrender him.
But if the mother stubbornly detains [her] son and refuses to
obey [our] sacred commands, let an armed guard deliver the Duke
to [his] brother and restore the boy to his play.

Lord Howard.[32] The infancy of the son has been given over to the mother,
and his sportive age has turned to its own delights. Now [our]
beloved country demands the rest of [his] years. I care nothing
for the bitter complaints of the mother. If she refuses that her
son [be] freed from prison, soldiers should deliver him to [his]
brother.

Gloucester. The Council with a single voice demands that you, Archbishop,
[be] the messenger to [his] mother, [and] and [our] sacred command
be executed. [You], Duke of Buckingham,[33] join yourself to the
Bishop as a companion, and [you, too,] Howard, illustrious in
descent. But if [his] mother places no limit at all on her love
[for her son] and she foolishly wants to keep [her] son from us,
robust soldiers will at once take [him] from the asylum, and [then]
in vain will [his] mother, unhappy and excessively wanton with
regard to her son, complain of [her] offspring taken from her. A
heavy duty now summons you, Archbishop. We near relations [of the
boy] will wait upon the responses of [his] mother.

---

[32]The person, designated here as Lord Howard, was "one of the priueyest
of the lord protectors counsaill and dooyng" (Hall, p. 361), and should not
be confused with his son, a knight, of the same name who appears in scene iv
and v of Act V (Part I).

[33]In the next scene, Legge apparently forgets that Buckingham was directed
to accompany the Cardinal, for Buckingham's name is no where mentioned in this
scene. The chronicles are not specific here, mentioning only that "certain
lordes" or "divers other lords" accompanied the Cardinal. See Hall, p. 355;
More, p. 417; and Hol., p. 373.

[ACT IV. Scene iii.]

Queen Elizabeth. Archbishop of York. Lord Howard.

Archbishop of York. Illustrious person, mighty Queen Mother, even though

the words are now spoken by [my] mouth, do not believe [them] to

be ours. The full Council of nobles, and the Protector Gloucester

also, has decreed [what I am going to say]. Although your natural

inclination advises you [lit. although with your native urging]

that the boy should cleave to the sole embrace of [his] mother,

and [although] his early age is more suitably spent with [his]

parent, yet the honor of the kingdom does not allow [it to be so].

Foolishly you stain the honor of your son [Edward]. Now, indeed,

the peace of Britian, shaken at its very roots, is falling down

while you, trembling with fear, remain mourning in a needless

[lit. false] sanctuary. If the only brother of the Prince is kept

shut up in a prison, deprived of the sweet solace of his own brother,

[then] the populace will at once suspect [there is] hatred between

the brothers on the grounds that [this] boy has fled in fear to

the sacred altars. Therefore, return your son freed from [his]

prison. Thus you may free your children from [their] bonds and

[thus] you may cause great comfort for the Prince, and the band of

nobles secure [again] will rejoice.

Queen.   [O] excellent Father with the very great honor of the furred

cap, that it is proper that [one] brother live together in the home

of [the other] brother, I do not deny, although one of the two

[boys], whose tender age still bids [me] to fear, might more safely

cling to the gentle bosom of [his] mother, [especially since] his

younger age protects [him even] less since the time when a malicious

disease oppressed him for a long while; and [his] great danger [still] calls for the [constant] care of [his] mother [because] a relapse [l̲i̲t̲. a disease returning] menaces the one [who has been] sick so much more; nor will [his] health [l̲i̲t̲. his nature] oppressed before bear up strongly under a second wound nor can it protect itself sufficiently [from a second visit of the disease]. I know how hard many a matron, who may sedulously care for my son, will work; yet it is more fitting that my son be left with me since I, in whose arms the little boy has always remained, know how to nurture him better; nor can anyone sustain him more tenderly than [his] mother who sustained [him] in the womb.

Archbishop of York. O Queen, no one senselessly can deny that [your] son is better [off] left in your care. The distinguished band of nobles might [even] now wish that the boy live in the embrace of [his] mother if you would remain together in a place suitable for both of you [i̲.̲e̲. a place befitting your station in life]. But if you, [who are] mature in understanding, [want to] consecrate your life to things sacred and [if] hereafter [your] devout mind will zealously strive in prayer, yet [one] brother--the boy [who has been] freed from the temple--should play in the palace of [his] brother, nor may the pious theft of his mother remain in the sacred prison. In all wisdom, the boy is taken from the arms of [his] mother, [for] an infant will not always prate pertly at [his] mother's breast. That savage Wales should nourish the [young] King and [that that] son might shine forth among foreigners, your Majesty was recently content.

Queen.   Content never: Besides, the same worry [now] for the one son did not hold back the mother [then for the other son]. At that

time, the health of the [young] King [when he went into Wales]
bade [me] to fear nothing. [But] the legs [of this one here],
weakened by much disease, are useless to him, and the tottering limbs
of his body scarcely support [him]. What so great concern for [my]
son possesses [his] uncle? [For] if the untimely fates carry off
[my] son and [if] the covetous sisters cut off [his] dear threads
[of life], a death [in any way] suspicious will still accuse the
Duke of Gloucester, [as the] guilty [one], nor will he escape the
rumor of fraud.34 Or does he perhaps think that his own honor or
[the honor] of the King will be damaged if he [i.e. the little Duke]
remains in this extremely safe place? The trust of no asylum has
ever been suspected. Here he may permit the son to live with [his]
mother. I have decided that [it is] safer to lie hidden in a temple
than to fear the punishments of a harsh prison with my kinsmen whom
I would prefer to have hidden now in sanctuary [with me] than to
have [them] surrender [their] right hand to your bonds.

Howard.35   Do you then know privily something that these [men] have perpetrated?

Queen.   I neither know anything they have done nor why chains may restrain [them], but [my] fear has not been slight that those who did
not delay for a pretext for the imprisonment [of my kinsmen] will

---

34"...I maruaill greately why my lorde protectour is so desirous to haue
him in kepyng, where if the child in his sicknesse miscaried by nature, yet
might he ronne into slaunder and suspicion of fraud" (Hall, p. 356). See also
More, p. 419; and Hol., p. 375.

35Hall, in his text, attributes this question to "lord Haward" (p. 356).
More (p. 419) and Holinshed (p. 375) mention "another lord" as asking the
question. Holinshed, however, has in the margin: "The lord Howard, saith
Edw. Hall."

likewise not overlook any reason for [their] death [i.e. for putting my kinsmen to death].

Archbishop of York.   [Aside to Howard.] [Her] anger is aroused: after this
[say] nothing about her kinsmen.   [Aloud to the Queen.]   [Their]
case [when] disputed before a judge will spare your kinsmen, nor
does any fear of the nobles threaten you.

Queen.   Yea, rather, what prevents [me] from fearing [these] upright
nobles when a guiltless life does not protect [my] kinsmen, or
perhaps I the Queen, who has been the grievous cause of [many]
evils [to my enemies], am more dear to my enemies [than my
kinsmen are]? or [perhaps my] noble descent allied to the King
will spare [me] the mother? Does not close descent commend my
kinsmen less since that uncle of the King [i.e. Rivers] is a
brother here [to me]? Yea, rather, [my] son will delay here
together with me unless a more intelligent mind recommends something different. For I suspect the faith of the nobles [to be all]
the more unfriendly because they without cause greedily demand
[my] son.

Archbishop of York. But they suspect this mother's affection of [yours all]
the more lest a cold fear laying hold of [your] stout heart urges
[you] to send [your] son to foreign lands. But if it is pleasing
[to you] to deny [your] son to [his] native land, a violent band
[of soldiers] will thereupon wrest [him] from you and too late you,
beaten down, will surrender [him] to just forces. The rights promised to a sanctuary do not protect him nor [does his] immature age
which has not [yet] learned to demand [these rights], and [besides
his] innocent life has bid [him] to fear nothing.

[The nobles] do not consider the faithful protection promised to
a sanctuary [would be] broken if they should set [your] son free
from the sacred places; and with you unwilling, [this decision of
the nobles] menaces the sacred power [of sanctuary].[36] Such is
the love of the uncle [Gloucester] toward [his] nephew that he
would [undoubtedly] tremble at the disgraceful flight of the Prince
[to a foreign land].

Queen.   Was the loving uncle [when you talked to him] glowing with
such tender affection for [his] nephew that he dreaded nothing more
than that [his] little nephew might escape his hands? Does he think
[the boy's] mother will urge a flight upon [her] son whose long ill-
ness forbids [his] departure? [Besides,] what place can protect
[my] son more than sanctuary which neither a cruel Caucasia nor a
savage Thrace has ever once violated?[37] But [you say] a guiltless
boy cannot be deserving the sacred rights, [and that] now, therefore,
[my] little boy seeks the Abbey in vain. Your empty head consults
the notorious oracles of the Protector: [do you mean to say that]
the sacred rights protect a thief not at all virtuous, but a little
boy whose innocent life forbids [him] to fear [anything] and [whose]
youth ignorant of evil has bade [him] to be free of [all] fear does
not deserve the sacred rights? I pray that God will at length banish
[my] justly conceived fear from [my] heart! Does the Protector (but
may he be, I pray, a protector of these [my children] and may he not

---

[36]The subject of "minatur" is not clear. The chronicles offer no help.
Apparently the statement is the invention of Legge.

[37]See Footnote 20 above.

[as] a bloody enemy rage against his own relations!) think that
[my] son clings to [this] Abbey disgracefully or that [one] brother
may only play in the home of the [other] brother? For a long time
now a sad disease and a weakening plague has prevented [him] from
playing; or perhaps there may be lacking to the little [Prince] those
[playmates] with whom [his] earliest age longs to play, but only on
condition that only those equal in honor and joined to the high
blood of kings are presented [to him to play with]; this age in
those [children of equal rank] is wont to be less harmonious?[38]
The illustrious band [of nobles] falsely assures itself that the
comfort of the two brothers [will be] mutual. While a nature vying
for its independence plays harmlessly [enough], it might fashion
brotherly hatreds. Domestic contentions are more pleasing to boys,
and the troubled hearts of brothers immediately feel their wound
and can endure it less. A boy is more eager to play with anyone
related [to him] than with his brother, the pleasure of whom [i.e.
brothers] [since it has been readily] afforded grows dim quickly;
and [besides] domestic delights cannot please [a boy] for a long
time. But [you say] the boy unaware did not demand the sacred privileges? What messenger has proclaimed these secrets [to the Pro-
tector]? Ask [him]? Let Claudian ask [him]? He will hear [him
ask for the privileges]. But suppose [he] did not ask for [the sacred

---

[38]"...but if his brother which hath no luste to plaie for sicknesse,
must come out of sanctuary...to play with him as though that princes so young
as they bee, could not play without their peeres, or children coulde not play
without their kyndred, with whom for the more parte they agree much worse
then with straungiers" (Hall, pp. 356-357). See also More, p. 420; and Hol.,
p. 376.

privileges] or [suppose] the little boy cannot safely desire to

leave the sanctuary, he will still remain [here, though] unwilling.

If I demand the [rights of the] church only for myself, it will

protect my goods also. No one sacrilegiously snatches a horse from

the sacred places: cannot a boy remain safe in a church? Indeed,

British law has [always] referred the son as a ward to [his] mother.

If it [i.e. the British law] may refer to the credit side of no

one the goods possessed [by him], [then certainly] the laws will en-

trust the love of her own [child] to the mother as a ward.39 What

force hostile to the sacred places would carry off from the guardian

her very own wards? When poor Edward -- overcome by the mother [i.e.

the Queen Mother, Margaret],40 [and] the sceptre taken from his

hands -- fled the hostile forces, leaving [me to face] his enemies,

I big with child fled at once to the sacred altars where the [pre-

sent] King was born into the light [of day] and [where] the boy

reached the first of his sacred birthdays. Not little was the fear

in the enemies of [his] father inasmuch as [lit. and] he [i.e. the

boy] caused a doubtful confidence in the uncertain peace. [Yet]

[this same] sanctuary afforded a safe dwelling place for us both

until I might [upon] leaving the Abbey joyfully deliver [my] son

to the embraces of his returned father.41 Would that the

39See Hall, p. 357; More, p. 420; and Hol., p. 376.

40For a brief time in 1471, the forces of Queen Margaret were victorious. Edward IV fled to France, and Queen Elizabeth to sanctuary in Westminister
Abbey.

41This passage is not in Hall, nor in More's English History of Richard
the Third. It is found in More's Historia Richardi Regis Tertii (fol. 50r)
and is translated and included by Rastell in his edition of More's Richard
the Third, pp. 420-421. See also Hol., p. 376.

trustworthiness of his royal dwelling place were as certain! And

let no one ask what the cause of my fear may be! The boy will re-

main with me in the sacred Abbey. Let whoever may break the rights

promised to the sanctuary, let [that] impious one, I pray, have the

advantage of a sacred refuge: I will not begrudge the sacred aid

[even] to my bitter enemies.[42]

Archbishop of York. [Aside.]   What shall we do? Anger distracts her blinded

mind and meanwhile she fiercely pricks at Gloucester, and an angered

breast is not turned with a slight entreaty.   [Aloud to the Queen.]

It is not pleasing [to me] to argue. I bring the sacred commands

of the very great Council, which [commands] you fear to obey in vain.

Great is the torment of suspicion: it is bitterly twisted by its own

deluded false opinion. If you, the Queen, will entrust the beloved

nephew to [his] uncle and to the others whose noble families have

for a long time spread their noble sons abroad in England, I shall

never fear to place [my] life [and soul which are] dear to me in

pledge to you for [your] son. But if you, [his] mother, deny your

son to us, I will not again after this be an advisor to you, and

yet constrained you will surrender [your] son. [Aside.] She trem-

bles. Undecided, she is thinking. Have we won?

Queen. [Aside.][43]   A terrible fear has struck our limbs, and [our] blood

---

[42]The Queen is not so magnanimous in the chronicles: "...but whosoeuer
he be that breaketh this holy sanctuary, I pray God sende him shortely nede
of sanctuarye, when he maye not come to it, for I woulde not that my mortall
enemie shoulde bee taken oute of sanctuary" (Hall, p. 357). See also More,
p. 421; and Hol., p. 471.

[43]This entire "speech" by the Queen must be read as an interior monologue
in which the Queen debates whether she should or should not surrender her son.
Her "divided mind" (1. 191) shifts from one alternative to another, at times
offering arguments for surrendering her son, and then obstinately refusing to
accept these arguments. See Hall, pp. 357-358; More, pp. 421-422; and Hol.,
p. 377.

restrained by a cold fear torments [them]. What are we going to

do? An uncertain fear divides [our] mind: on this side [my] son

strongly urges, on that side [his] uncle [urges]. I call to wit-

ness the true God and whatever happiness in heaven the shades of

my husband possess, I do not now seek for myself anything in behalf

of my son than that he should mightily bear your sceptre, Edward,

in the royal palace, [and] that he should give justice to the

Britons, and that the family of the King live in eternal happiness.

Why are you wavering? Do you then betray [your] son? and will you,

[his] mother, give [him] up who is sought for destruction? Do not

the unjust chains of your kinsmen terrify [you]? Even if the Pro-

tector does consider the honor of the English, lo, he [already] has

the elder son of the Prince [Edward IV]: let him be content with

that one [son]: let him allow to the mother her [only] comfort.

The country does not demand this one. He [the Protector] asks for

[this] one; I, the mother, ask for both. I, to whom he has been

obliged for the two [boys], demand that one be granted [me]. But

do you foolishly fear none of his threats, and will you submit to

the   great force of the nobles? Nevertheless you [will] send

[your] son and you [will] see your children die by your own wound.

The Father Cardinal does not put a stop to [lit. cause to accelerate]

the brief delays [made by your] mother's lament.[44] The uncle firmly

threatens that force [is] nearby and the rights promised to the

asylum will not protect [my] child. A soldier will never give way to

---

[44]The Queen here interrupts her mind's debate to note the patience of
the Cardinal who never once interrupts her long silence.

hasty flight [when] an armed enemy occupies all places [of retreat],
[for] what trustworthy place [will] keep [him when he has] retreated?
[Yet] the loyalty of the Cardinal has by no means been doubtful [to
me], and authority of the Father was always sacred [to me]. Deliver
your son to him, [or] rather can you, [his] mother, see [your] son
torn from [your] breast and the final destruction of the house of
[his] father, the King? Rather let the cruel Gloucester strike at
things worthy of reverence: I will bear [it], I will endure [it],
provided [my] son remains [with me]: You are mistaken! You [will]
lose both [your] son and your kinsmen together, and [yet] you can
not submit to the Gloucestrian.

Archbishop of York. While [your] blind rage gathers strength, your unhappy
love rashly arms [itself] to your ruin. Why do you deny the beloved
nephew to [his] uncle to whom the chief care of England is entrusted?
Do you likewise unjustly charge us with ignorance and argue that we
are foolish when we fear none of these things such as you foolishly
fear. Yet [our] serious concern for the kingdom joined us with the
Duke of Gloucester, nor has the life of Duke Richard been known by
anyone better [lit. more] than [by us].

Queen.   I have never been so foolish or weak of mind that I [might]
consider you all to be foolish and that I might offend your
trustworthiness by my suspicion. I deeply desire [your] wisdom
and at the same time [your] loyalty: if either of these is absent
in you, it will precipitate great harm against our person and
it [will] cause great destruction to the country. [But] an
insane desire for rule has no regard for the sacred compacts
of Nature: noble ambition gives itself up [even] to the

slaughter of brothers, nor does it fear dishonor. A feigned loyalty [to one's brother] recommended [itself] to a few of the ancients:

   Roman walls were [often] wet with fraternal blood. But if
rulers fear to spare their own brother[s], does a nephew fear [his]
uncle in vain? If the royal brothers dwell apart, there will be
safety for both: let us take care of one and you will care for the
other. You can protect both with the life of one. Nor will it be
safe for both to live together in the same dwellings. A merchant,
whom many a storm bids to fear, and [whom] violent hurricanes are
not wont to threaten in vain, does not put several incomes in a
single ship. Although conscious of my right [that] I might expect
that I could keep [my] son in [this] sacred place, however much
[his] savage uncle may roar harsh things [at me] and may thunder
at that which is worthy of reverence [i.e. the sanctuary], behold
[that] nevertheless I entrust [my] son to your hands at the same
time that I entrust to you the brother of that one, [both of] whom
it will be fitting for you to protect dutifully. I, [their] mother,
will again repeat this [my charge] to you at the time when after this
[life] all flesh is summoned together before the throne of highest
judgment by the sounding trumpet. [Although] trembling, [yet] I
know how your loyalty waxes far and bright, how far-reaching is the
might of [your] right hand, [and] also [your] practical wisdom
attested to by so many deeds   that no safeguarding may be lacking
to my children. But if your power has [ever] been suspected by you,
by the gods and by the chaste faith of King Edward's wife, leave him
with me, and just as much as you say that I fear too much, it is
little fitting for you to fear so much less [than I do]. [To her

son.] O [my] sweet pledge of love, the second [greatest] honor of
the kingdom, [and] the vain hope of a mother for whom I will foolishly pray in vain for the acclaim of [your] father [i.e. the acclaim
that your father enjoyed while living] [and] for the long days of
[your] grandfather, may God, the ruler of the many storms of the
world, be [ever] present to you as a defender and may he direct
[your] wind-driven sails to a safe harbor. Unhappy [youth], receive
the kisses of [your] sorrowing mother, fixed upon your lips. He
alone who holds the reins of [earthly] affairs knows when another
dawn when our kisses will again be impressed upon your lips. Now
you will [begin to] fear that which your birth has given [you].[45]
If you do not miserably feel the hurt [yourself, then] put on the
mourning of your mother. But if [your] noble mind denies tears to
you, yet at least grant to [your] mother her causes of sorrow: we
knew how to weep before. Lo, assume the tears of [your] mother
[to be] whatever has remained from the unhappy burial of [your]
father, for can anything be more lamentable than the death of King
Edward? But there was still another Edward, who might strongly uphold the proud sceptre of [his] father's kingdom. The younger son
of Edward formed [his] [first] words here [with me], but at the time
when my elder son was about to start talking, a noble band of my
kinsmen supported [him in Wales], and fate had not [yet] shattered
anyone [of them; i.e. Rivers, Grey, and her other kinsmen] with a

---

[45]The chronicles do not have this sentence. The Queen probably means
that her son will now begin to fear his high birth which puts him second in
the order of succession to the crown, and, therefore, makes him an obstacle
to be overcome by anyone seeking the royal power.

single death. Now the harsh custody of a prison has taken away [my]

brother, [and now] the loyalty (which must be feared) of Richard

holds the King himself. Behold the only remains of the father: the

one [remaining] hope of [our] fallen house was [put] in this [sanctu-

ary], in which all [our] goods have now been brought together. What

sad end awaits you, [my] son? To what troubles, alas, is [your]

guiltless life exposed? If the cruel fates seek [the life of my]

little boy, [and with you] the final ruin of your house, I, [your]

mother, will at once ask [the fates] that I may shut with my own hand

your eyes [while you are still] living and [that] you, [my] boy, may

die in the bosom of [your] mother. Farewell, [my] son, farewell:

farewell, solace of [your] mother! Just as a savage lion, champing

with enormous bites, carries off in [its] mouth [its] smaller prey

from the distant mother, so [too] the savage uncle has torn [his]

nephew from my bosom.

Howard. [Aside.] Behold her shining eyes filled with tears: she enfolds

the tender limbs of her son with several embraces, covering [him]

with [her] final kisses, and [her] weeping does not permit the

wretched [mother] to speak any [more] and her voice broken off in

the middle of [her] throat has ceased to issue forth [her] commands

[to her tongue], and her unhappy love does not find expression [lit.

find its way out]. Why have you disturbed the dear heart of the

mother so?[46] At length, turning [her] back, she leaves [her] son.

Archbishop of York. Do not fear, noble Prince! You will play together with

---

[46]The chronicles provide no hint of remorse in Howard. See Hall, p. 358;
More, p. 422; and Hol., p. 377.

your brother; [though] deprived of [your] mother's embrace, suspect
not the home of the King.

Gloucester.[47]   O beloved offspring of King Edward, I gladly enfold your body
in my embrace. Lo, I imprint sweet kisses on your lips. May eternal
honor increase your happiness!

ACT V. [Scene i.] [48]

Catesby. Duke of Buckingham.

Catesby. [Alone.]   A joyous Gloucester [now] exults that the feeble wild animals [i.e. the two princes] are held in [his] nets: the hoped for
prey has fallen into his hands. [His] deceit is turned in a safe
direction. Each nephew is held in a dark cell; now it pleases [him]
to promise himself the thing befitting royal authority [i.e. the
sceptre and crown] and the throne of [his] dead brother. Just as a
wise dog (sensing wild beasts by [their] distant odor), after he has
perceived [his] prey nearby, attacks at the quick neck[49] and with
his precise mouth searches for the windpipe [of its prey], so
[Gloucester now] strives by every means to fit the sceptre of [his]
brother to [his] right hand, and he covets the almost expected royal

---

[47]Legge does not list Gloucester as appearing in this scene, yet the inclusion of these four lines at the end of this scene in the most trustworthy manuscripts indicates that Legge did not hesitate to violate dramatic conventions
when he felt the need. The chronicles also support the inclusion of these lines
see Hall, pp. 377-378; More, pp. 422-423; and Hol., p. 358.

[48]The material on which this scene is based is found in More, pp. 423-424
and in Hol., pp. 378-379, but not in Hall. It is in More's Historia Regis
Richardi Tertii (fol. 50^v) and is translated and included by Rastell in his edition of More's English History of Richard the Third.

[49]The neck is called "quick" because the wise dog can effect the instant,
or quick death of its prey by attacking its neck.

authority of Britain. The seeds of [his] future rule have already

been sown. An angry group of nobles cannot endure the family of

the Queen: he [Gloucester] will cruelly demand their punishment

[i.e. of the Queen's kinsmen] while they [the nobles] are anxiously

struggling in legal action [i.e. while they are debating the legal-

ity of the imprisonment of the Queen's kinsmen]; the Duke plans to

kill secretly whoever obstructs [his] enterprises. But, without the

[help of the] Duke of Buckingham, he fears to plot his strategies and

he fears [to plot his] frauds. He has ordered [me] to incite the

proud mind of the Duke [of Buckingham] and to arouse [his] hatred

of the royal offspring so that the sceptre may be lost to the little

infants, and [so that] Buckingham may assist the frauds of the uncle

and so that the dangerous Duke [of Gloucester] may acquire the royal

power for himself. Meanwhile, so that the nobles may suspect nothing,

these [i.e. the nobility] commanded [by Gloucester to do so] are con-

ferring about the crowning of the king. Catesby, why do you hesitate

in preparing the throne for the Duke? I see that Buckingham approach-

ing [lit. brings his step hither]. Haughty in spirit, he is puffed

up. I will plot deceits for him [i.e. I will deceive him]. [To

Buckingham.] Flower of England, famous progeny of Jove and the

greatest ornament of troubled Britain, why do you, forgetful of your

own safety, [so] securely promote hatred [of yourself]? How great a

wound would the collapsed state of the kingdom receive if the aroused

anger of a youth should rashly crush [you] unaware; the anger of a

raging youth will in no way be appeased.

Duke of Buckingham. But if anyone [at all who is] mighty in a lofty palace,

[and] immune from the sway of the fickle goddess [Fortune] can boast

that his happy estate [is] by no means in a transitory position, the
elevated Lord Buckingham can [boast] that.[50] But why, then, do you
darkly cast that warning of yours from [your] doubtful mouth? or
perhaps [our] enemy does not rage in vain against our person in the
dungeon of a black prison?

Catesby.   But [first] let [this] place be free for every opinion.

Buckingham. [To his attendants.]   Ye young servants, free my side of your
commotion [i.e. leave me].

Catesby.   The noble nature of [any] high-minded [person] fears nothing so
long as [his] great power denies that he can be overcome. Lord Rivers
and Grey are suffering the rewards of their arrogance. [But] this is
[only] the first approach of evil [to us]. The King brandishing the
sceptre in [his] youthful hand [now] rages. Often he has threatened
that their injuries would not be unavenged, and he has not accepted
[as right] the cruel chains of his brother [Grey] nor of his maternal
uncle [Rivers]. [His] mother [too] having torn [her] hair seeks vengeance: Whoever among [her] kinsmen may be inferior in birth [to
you], she considers him to be [the more] esteemed. Now, then, wisely
consider these things with regard to yourself. For if the [King's]
power spared your enemies and the kinsmen of [his] mother drew [their]
arrogant breath [again], they will accuse [you] of crime before a
King related [to them] by marriage: their fury at your punishments
[of them] will never cease. But if they should die because of your
fear of them [lit. if they cast out their spirit for your fear], and

---

[50]Although no direct relationship can be shown, the idea here recalls various passages of Buckingham's complaint in the Mirror for Magistrates, pp. 318-
345.

if they [should] extinguish [your] just wrath [at them] with their
blood, you will fear the King [himself] as long as evil will overcome with evil and [as long as] the house of his blood-relations
demands [your] cruel destruction.

Buckingham.　The brief anger of a boy is immediately quenched.

Catesby.　But [even] the slight anger of a boy is the more dangerous.

Buckingham.　A day will diminish [it]: what is violent will dissipate
[lit. haste away] at once.

Catesby.　The tremendous sorrow of [his] parent will never permit [it]
to die: the chains of her kinsmen arouse [his] mother, and [his]
mother's complaints [will arouse[the son.

Buckingham.　Gloucester has been a sharer in this crime.

Catesby.　Anger is satisfied [only] by revenge: it ignores [who is]
guilty; it punishes [only] the crime.

Buckingham.　The authority of the Duke can diminish the wrath of a boy.

Catesby.　[Only] while he is a boy.

Buckingham.　But he will always fear his own uncle.

Catesby.　[One] worthy of rule does not know how to fear anyone.

Buckingham.　What plan can safely protect us?

Catesby.　That [plan] alone which denies to the Prince your destruction.

Buckingham.　Will the wrath of the mother urge [her] son so far [as my
destruction]?

Catesby.　[Her] dead son can harm nothing.

Buckingham.　Is the sole remedy of evil to kill the Prince?

Catesby.　Evil cannot be overcome except by a new evil. Necessity
makes certain kind of crime justifiable [lit. honorable]. A
captive wild animal is restrained with nets just as each nephew
is held in bonds. They will die at a slight nod of Duke Claudian.

They would die at once, if you will [only] have regard for your
self now. A guard secretly protects the Duke of Gloucester.
[His] secret watch (of such a kind that you may consider [them]
the least false of [all] your servants) notes your habits,
especially [to see] if you may prepare anything against him.[51]
If you see nothing that must be feared, yet fear the doubtful
loyalty of many [men]: nothing [is] stable: believe all things
hostile. A troubled look is wont to counterfeit many things
and it [often] fashions frauds. The father Thyestes, [by] en-
trusting his children to [his] brother, drank the mingled blood
of his own children.[52]

Buckingham. [To himself.] What now? Why do you remain rooted to the spot?
What plan do you insanely turn about [in your mind]? or will perhaps you [now] repent [that] the nobles [have been] put in prison?
This is cowardly in a man whom the wrath of the King frightens.
Do you fear a boy? or a woman? for the fates oppress [her] blood-
relations. From the Queen's party [lit. from that side] is initiated
the hatred [lit. are put in motion the hatreds] of the splendid
Duke [of Gloucester], whose power, which all [men] fear, [is] most
great. Do you seek safety? You will be safer with him. Trust in
the greatest [of persons] and put your faith in the Duke [of Gloucester

---

[51]". . . the Protector had provided a privy guard for himself", so had
he spials [i.e. spies] for the Duke [of Buckingham] and trains [i.e. schemes]
to catch him, if he should be against him, and that, peradventure, from
them whom he least suspected. . ." (More, p. 423). See also Hol., p. 378.

[52]Thyestes was banished from Mycenae for having seduced his brother
Atreus' wife. Atreus, pretending to be reconciled, recalled him to Mycenae,
killed his two sons, and placed their flesh before their father at a
banquet, who unwittingly partook of the dreadful meal.

Catesby.　　　If the fates, hastened [by us, should] free the King from
　　　　　life, noble Richard will provide the sceptres for himself. You
　　　　　[are] the sole support of the troubled country. The Duke of
　　　　　Gloucester can readily seek the rule of the kingdom with your political
　　　　　influence. [In so doing,] you will secure the life of both [your-
　　　　　self and Gloucester].

Buckingham.　　The royal youth, who will pay for his threats [to me] with
　　　　　[his] head [lit. whose head snatched away will appease his threats],
　　　　　will never sport with my blood. The sacrifice of a king [is]
　　　　　slight if you can [thereby] save your own life. The things proper
　　　　　for ruling little befit boys. This would be a rule not of the King,
　　　　　but of [his] spiteful mother [instead], at whose instigation the
　　　　　enraged boy will be armed only toward the destruction of his
　　　　　own kinsmen.

[ACT V. Scene ii.]

Duke of Buckinham. Duke of Gloucester. Catesby.

Buckingham.　　O Protector Claudian, the only hope of the House of York,
　　　　　and sharer of my danger, your nephew prepares a severe ruin for
　　　　　us. The family-ties of [King] Edward [i.e. because of his family
　　　　　ties, Edward] mournfully bewails the fall of his kinsmen and
　　　　　mixes serious threats [to us] with [his] tears. The unfortunate
　　　　　offspring of the [dead] King must be removed to the chains of a
　　　　　dark prison or [else] their house will appease the avenging gods
　　　　　with our destruction.

Gloucester.　　The mighty torches [i.e. lighting bolts] of the avenger and
　　　　　the violent thoughts of the enraged King compel [me] to shudder.
　　　　　[Your] sound advice bids [me] to hasten. The longer evil grows,

the stronger it is wont to become and brief [indeed] is the delay
given [to evil] by deliberations [i.e. by talking about it].

Buckingham.   A harsh remedy is provided for the enormous evil: lo, evil
cannot be easily overcome. The blind anger of the Prince will
always threaten [us hereafter], [and] vengeance [when] armed with
a sceptre fights most harshly. I call to witness the true God and
the highest honor of the heavens, [that] whatever you plan, I will
follow as the guide of my life.

Gloucester.   A vague fear runs through my trembling limbs. The youthful,
cruel, untaught nature of the new King cannot be turned, cannot be
broken. If we allow [him to live] he will prepare a harsh end for
us. It is right to free the life of the King of [its] chains; yet,
alas, it would be shameful to weaken the royal powers coming from
[my] brother, [for if we allowed the weak King to rule,] many of
the House of Lancaster, laughing on all sides, will rejoice at the
fallen house of its rival. But since it is proper to have regard
for one's own life and [since] it is not proper to burden the
country with [needless] causes for sorrow, I demand the fraternal
sceptre by right of blood and I summon you [to be] defenders of
your own safety. If you pledge your loyalty to our enterprises
(I swear by the supreme gods who uphold the heavens), my son, [my]
sole comfort, will [as] a husband take your daughter [as] a wife
to himself. [And] because you claim [the title already], you will
be the Earl of Hereford; the treasures, the household furniture,

whatever the palace [of Hereford] contains, [o] illustrious one, everything will yield to your desires.[53]

Buckingham.   I swear to the same gods, the sea [will be united] with the stars, and the waves with flames and the savage wolf with sheep, [and] the black night will be united with the sun as an eternal companion [and] the surface of the Thames will lack [enough] water for fishes before I unfaithfully leave your part.

Catesby.   [To Gloucester.] Now, then, [while still] aroused perform the promises undertaken, and first of all transfer the princes to the Tower and substitute servants now to [your] nephews, [servants] whom you esteem [to be] listeners to your speech, and henceforth no approach to the King will lie open. Transfer the rumbling of the people to your doorstep and turn from the King the eyes of [his] subjects and after this clients [i.e. petitioners] may tread on your thresholds.[54]

Gloucester.   Yea, rather, it is necessary to conceal [our] fraud from the nobles of England until the seized sceptres should come into our hands.

Catesby.   Messengers sent forth [by you] will advise [the nobles] that the royal head could not be girded by the crown till now, and

---

[53]"Then it was agreed that the Protector should have the Duke's aid to make him King, and that the Protector's only lawful son should marry the Duke's daughter, and that the Protector should grant him the quiet possession of the Earldom of Hereford, which he claimed as his inheritance and could never obtain in King Edward's time" (More, p. 424). See also Hol., p. 378.

[54]"...for litle and litle all folke drewe from the tower where the kyng was and drewe to Crosbies place, so that the protectoure had all the resorte, and the kyng in maner desolate. Whyle some made suyte vnto theim that had the doyng, some of theim were by their frendes secretly warned, that it might happely turne them to no good to be to muche attendaunt on the kyng without the protectoures apoinctemente, whiche remoued diuerse of the kyng his olde seruauntes from him, and sette newe in their roumes aboute hym" (Hall, p. 358). See also More, p. 424; and Hol., p. 379.

[then] let a group of nobles gather at your command for the coronation proceedings [lit. so that a great assembly of the British
people may celebrate the coronation]. While musing much [about
our proceedings], they [will be] taking their journey [to London],
and they will remain in the city bereft of [their] forces, and
before the thoughtful ones may join arms [with each other] (since
trust among themselves is mutually uncertain), [you may] safely
take possession of the sceptres snatched from the boy.

Buckingham.   But [this] stratagem will not deceive Lord Hastings; and Lord
Stanley, who lives in the city, [and] the Bishop of Ely will [also]
comprehend [our] cunning if they should notice that [we] secretly
meet apart [from them].

Gloucester.   Lest [some] eager mind anticipate our enterprises, several
nobles will assemble at my command [on the pretext] that they will
confer about the most serious affairs of England [i.e. about the
plans for Edward's coronation].[55]

Buckingham.   But who else will be a confederate of your plan? A great
undertaking cannot be executed by a few [men].

Gloucester.   Whom will not the sceptres [once they have been] taken constrain with fear? [Then] authority for [whatever] our desire [may
be] cannot be lacking [to us].

Buckingham.   Prevail upon the fickle mob with many rewards, and heap with
many gifts [those] who can be easily induced so that they will
adhere to your policies. Fear will constrain [those] whom money
cannot conquer.

---

[55]See Hall, p. 358; More, p. 424; and Hol., pp. 378-379.

Catesby.   [It is] difficult to determine immediately the minds of

noblemen [i.e. to know whose side they are on].

Gloucester.   Just as if extremely concerned about public affairs, I shall

solicitously ask the advice at every point of those [nobles whom]

I am suspicious of; while I will ambiguously propose many things

and [while] we consider the secret [affairs] of the kingdom, my

[true] mind will lie hidden. Only Hastings openly sides with the

Prince and offers [all] the respect due to the princes. This [man]

[is] beloved by the English people and [is] very powerful. First

[before we do anything else], it is fitting that [either] this

[man] rejoice at my [prospect of taking the] sceptres or die.

Catesby.   He strongly favored Prince Edward [when last I talked to him].

His promised loyalty can never be weakened.

Gloucester.   It is well to try his obstinate mind [once] more. Perhaps

you may break [this] resisting [man] by fear. I, meanwhile, will

ask advice [from various nobles] on Britian's affairs [to sound

out their loyalties].

Catesby. [Alone.] What do you do now, Catesby? Why not confer with yourself?

Summon now the cunning of your mind, now the frauds, the deceits,

and [indeed] the entire Catesby. [Even] if Hastings, as a sharer

in the frauds of the Duke [of Gloucester] procures the throne [for

Gloucester], you will take credence away from yourself, and after

this it will be less relied on.[56] If having been slain he spews

---

[56]"But Catesby, whether he assayed him [i.e. Hastings] or assayed him
not, reported vnto hym [i.e. Gloucester] that he found him so fast, and
herde him speake so terrible wordes that he durst no farther breake. . . and
therefore, he fearyng leste their mocions might with the lord Hastynges
minishe his credence. . . procured the protectour hastely to ryd him and much
the rather, for he trusted by hys death to obtayne muche of the rule whiche
the lord Hastynges bare [in the counties of Leicester and Northampton]. . ."
(Hall, p. 359). See also More, p. 425; and Hol., pp. 379-380.

forth his hostile spirit (just as if [his] obstinate love reverences the boys too much), you alone, the successor of Hastings, can be preeminent in Leicester: the dukes will trust [you] more. It is well that he dies so that our glory may increase. May a cruel sword break through [his] unfortunate flesh. I shall counterfeit that the adverse one [i.e. Hastings] strongly favors the princes, and [that] the obstinate [man] can be swayed by no entreaty.

[ACT V. Scene iii.]

Stanley. Hastings.

[Stanley.]   My heart is terrified, and dispirited by a vague fear is agitated; here, there it turns nor cannot it extricate itself: [my] mind augurs some kind of evil. What is the meaning of [their] consultations separated in locations [from ours]? When part [of the nobility] deliberate in the Tower and another part in the palace, [only] that thundering father [i.e. Jove] knows what [that] distant nobleman [Gloucester] turns about in his cunning mind. He may long for the royal power through us, or he can plot death for us or treacheries to the [young] King. Whatever it is, I greatly fear this [man].

Hastings.   Illustrious descendant of Stanley, put off [your] fear, and do not let a foolish suspicion torment [your] mind. They can perpetrate nothing against us so long as my Catesby is together [with them], (who is never wont to be absent from them) because just as if not absent, as it were, I hear what has happened from his [i.e. Catesby's] mouth.

Stanley.   But an impure faith is not rarely hidden by a becoming brow. Shameful deceit fights under the guise of virtue, and a few days does not expose a false appearance.

Hastings.   A faith heaped with rewards remains firm. The people of

           Leicester greatly reverence my command, and it avails very strongly

           with the people of Northampton; [and] I place the greatest of my

           affairs [in these two counties] upon this man [Catesby].

Stanley.   In the midst of evils, the time for taking precautions is

           [too] late. [Gloucester's] blind desire for power fears no

           strength. As soon as the feeble youth is overcome, [Gloucester's]

           secret villainy will afterwards rage against whomsoever of us any

           sharer of his villainy fears, and we will be naked [i.e. unarmed]

           plunder for [our] faithless enemies. But, with a quickened pace,

           let us return to our paternal homes where [our] followers may defend

           [us] with their forces. [Then] a treacherous sedition will especially

           fear [its own] beginnings.[57]

Hastings.   Unnecessarily we fear a prosperous enough fortune. The fair-

           spoken dukes are wont to address [me] with kind words and have

           always favored me very much; and [besides] the very wishes, rumors,

           [and] fears of the people I have communicated to my Catesby a

           while ago. [I knew then while talking to Catesby that] my great

           concern for the Prince was troubling the others [i.e. Gloucester

           and Buckingham]; [also that] the citizens [have begun to] seek

           out the Duke [of Gloucester when they have petitions and that] they

           neglect [to seek out his] nephew.[58] Because he [i.e. Catesby] hid

           these things from me, it is not agreeable [to me] to fly like a

           wild animal? Flight will prove us guilty, and [his] greater wrath

           would ruin [us when we are] called back to the bar of justice. A

---

[57]Lord Stanley feels that if he and Hastings were in the country surrounded
by their chief sources of armed strength, then Gloucester would fear to undertake
his seditious enterprises.

[58]See Footnote 41 above.

guiltless life will keep those safe who remain. But if there were

evil in us, I would [still] desire that [our] guilty mind should

not further condemn [us] by our flight. This deceit (believe [me])

is not as bad [lit. nothing] as you foolishly fear. Sooner will

unwrought Chaos be changed into a heaven, sooner may the stars

cleave to the earth, [and] the ocean to fire than [may] Catesby

falsify [his] iron-clad loyalty [to me].

Stanley.   Soon the outcome will give belief to such great evils.

[ACT V.   Scene iv.]

Duke of Gloucester. Catesby. Howard, a knight.[59]

Gloucester. [Alone.] Hope and fear agitate my troubled mind, and [my] fearful

heart wavers because of [lit. in] the double effect [of my mind upon

it]. [My] dream of ruling always wanders about before my eyes, and

[my] deep ambition always drives [me] on uncertain, and my heart is

in a turmoil. Desire for rule [once] aroused cannot be stilled:

now the sceptres alone [will] satisfy [me]. I shall not stop until

I have attained the highest of [my] desires. The uncertain loyalty

of the nobility greatly troubles [me]. To whom I shall safely

confide our plans, I do not know; nor have [all] my frauds been

put in a safe place [i.e. been entrusted to completely trustworthy

accomplices].

Howard.   Why do you in a turmoil beat your anxious breast? Whoever

dares great things does not know how to fear. Soon you [will]

seek the royal authority: Fortune assists [only] the brave. The

foremost skill of ruling [is] for you to be able to keep the

citizens in fear. He who fears [his] citizens incites rebellions.

---

[59]See Footnote 32 above.

Whoever rules with authority and wields a harsh sceptre in his
royal hand, will dare all things.[60]

Gloucester.   Cowardly fear disturbs [my] heart not at all. Begone, piety,

if you lie hidden in our mind. [My] sword will support whoever

you [i.e. Howard and Catesby] consider opposed [to us]. It is

now fitting to open the way of [my] fraud with [my] sword. Let

whatever enemy will obstruct me be punished.

Howard.   Why do you hold the kinsmen of the [Queen] mother captive in

chains at Pontefract, and not order [them] put to death at length?

[One] life indulged will give courage to others, and besides a

mild punishment calls into question punishments [in general].

Let them, slain by the sword, spew forth [their] hostile spirit[s].

Make [your] friends secure, [and] the others [not your friends will]

waver with fear.

Gloucester.   I want [my] present enemies to die at once which [enemies] I

have prudently recognized as standing in the way to my sceptres

[i.e. they prevent my becoming King] so that a single fear may

in like manner seize all whose doubtful mind opposes [our] slightest

desire. Soon cruel chains will hold those captive [who oppose our

slightest wish]. Where does Hastings turn [his] mind?

Catesby.   Against your great person.

Gloucester.   Does he refuse to be an aid to my designs?

Catesby.   Sooner will the narrow strait of Ithaca flow profusely and

the raging water of the Sicilian Sea stand still and the black

night give brilliance to the earth [than will Hastings aid you].

---

[60]The chronicles provide no basis for the Machiavellianism apparent in this
speech and underlying much of this entire scene.

Fiercely shaking [his] head he deprecates the frauds. He swears
that he will always be loyal to the sons of Edward [and] a severe
enemy to the enemies of the King.[61]

Gloucester.   He will learn what the arms of an angry king can do, and he
will extinguish our wrath with his very blood. Let [others] learn
to obey through fear of their prince. But by what means shall I
afflict [this] foolish person?

Catesby.   Seized by [his] love for Shore's wife, he rages, nor does
his desire restrain [his] raging flames [of passion]. You may
charge that this one [Shore's wife] plotted death to your person
by sorcery; if her unfortunate patron [Hastings], blind with love
and aroused in anger, defends the cause of his mistress, you may
on the spot accuse [him of being] guilty of a wicked crime; and
[then] accuse [him as] a traitor to his own country. Immediately
[thereafter] let an axe cut off [his] unhappy head.

Gloucester.   The nobles will assemble in the Tower at once. Openly I will
oppress [those] whom I know to favor the King, and I will accuse
[Hastings of being] guilty of crime. A guard with a two-edged
sword will at once cut off [his] head, and the Council stunned
[by the speed with which it is all done] will not [have time to]
comprehend my deceits.

Catesby.   But if the sly Lord [Hastings] stays away from the sacred
assembly, a new method of deceit must be sought.

Gloucester.   You, at least, Howard,[62] visit the famous person at once and urge
the delaying man with flattering words. I am unwilling to allow
that [he] be absent from the sacred assembly.

---

[61] See Footnote 43 above.

[62] In Shakespeare, Buckingham plays the role that Howard plays in Legge
and the chronicles.

Catesby.   Do you ask a cruel death for Hastings only?

Gloucester.   Lord Stanley and the Father Cardinal, [and] the Bishop of Ely,

will be clamped in chains so that a cell of the prison may conquer

their mind[s] loyal [to the King]. But if anyone with a wild spirit

stubbornly refuses [to submit], and [if] the sad death of Hastings

does not move him [to submit to me], a cruel sword will cut off his

guilty head. A harsh sword will pierce [all] disloyal bodies.

Moderation in villainy is indeed a foolish thing.

[ACT V. Scene v.]

Lord Hastings. Howard. Hastings, a common solider, [or pursuivant].

[Lord] Hastings. [To himself.] I wonder why my horse has now shamefully

stumbled [thrice] on the ground here. May God avert [this] evil

omen. But why do the foolish tricks of fate affect [me]? And

[indeed] Stanley was afraid of [his] cruel dreams. He told me

that a boar seen by him in a dream cut off [our] head[s] with

[its] teeth: blood at once flowed down [our] shoulders, and

[therefore] he foolishly advised a shameful flight for me. A

sportive Fortune delights in playing with us and laughs at men

troubled by a slight mishap to whom the envious [Goddess] never-

theless threatens nothing at all.[63]

Howard.   Hurry, [o] noble Hastings: speed [your] pace!

Lord Hastings. [To a priest who is walking by.][64] Pray, then, will you,

[o] happy Father, sacred to the gods, come to [me for a moment]?

Lend [your] secret ears to me for a little while.

---

[63]I.e., the Goddess Fortune often delights in sending a man an ill omen,
not to warn him of impending disaster, but only to laugh at his fear of the
omen.

[64]See Hall, p. 361; More, p. 428; and Hol., p. 382.

Howard.   Leave off at last: why do you speak to the priest for [so]

long a time? At present, [there is] no need for a confessor.

[Aside.] The unfortunate man, secure in himself, sees nothing

[ambiguous in my remark]. How great the need for a priest will

soon be for him [when he has been] condemned [to death].

Hastings. [To a pursuivant named Hastings.] Does the once evil and extremely

sad day never slip from [your] mind when I, all atremble with fear

of a harsh death, last saw you under the walls of that prison

[i.e. the Tower]?[65]

Hastings, the common soldier [or pursuivant]. O sole ornament and famous

offspring of your name, an event so grave or sad never slips from

me; yet there was (thanks to the gods!) no harm [done] to you then

nor was there [any] advantage to those [i.e. to Lord Rivers and

his kinsmen who had accused Hastings before King Edward IV]. There

was equal fortune on both sides.

Lord Hastings. [To himself.] Nay, rather, you would say more than this if

you might know the secrets of our mind, which several will know

after this, but [which] no one [knows] now. [Aloud.] Ah, Hastings,

as far as I know, I was never more doubtful of [my] life than on

that day. Now the course of the times has changed. [To himself.]

[Our] enemies are dragged out to [their] death on this very day.

They make inviolable our peace with their very blood. [Aloud.]

Never, Hastings, have I lived more secure in my own mind, and

[never] has my life, disturbed by no troubles, been more free from

fear.

65" . . . vpon the very towre wharffe, so neare the place where his
was of, so sone after, . . . a pursyuaunt of his awne called Hastynges mette
with hym, and . . . he was put in remembraunce of another tyme, in which it
happened them to mete before together in the place, at which tyme the lorde

Hastings, the soldier. May God prove it so!

Lord Hastings. Why do you doubt [that it is so]? [66]

Hastings, the soldier. I [only] pray [that it is].

Lord Hastings. I know well enough [that].

Howard.   Why not, noble lord, break off [these] slowing delays [i.e.

stops that slow down the journey], for the wise Council has expected

you for a long time [now] so that it [lit. they] may consult [you]

about   many   matters [having to do with the coronation]? [Alone.]

The noble person has departed [for the assembly of nobles]. Alas,

the poor [man] does not know that a cruel destruction is ready

for him. Ah, [Hastings,] why do you favor the boys too much? [67]

The false loyalty of Catesby has deceived you and you, wretched

[man], are caught [like] prey captured in nets.

Hastynges had bene accused to kyng Edward by the lord Ryuers. . . . , insomuche
that he was for a while. . . highly in the kynges indignacion as he now mette
the same pursiuaunt in the same place, the ieoperdy so well passed, it gaue
him great pleasure to talke with him thereof, . . . (Hall, p. 361). See
More, p. 428; and Hol., p. 382.

[66]Hastings is aroused to anger by the pursuivant's ambiguity: See
Hall, p. 362; and Mirror for Magistrates, p. 286, ll. 485-487. More and
Holinshed omit this final interchange between the two Hastings.

[67]Again (See Footnote 37 above) Howard's remorse has no support in
the chronicles.

[ACT V. Scene vi.]

Duke of Gloucester. Duke of Buckingham. Lord Hastings.
The Bishop of Ely. Guards. [Stanley.]

Duke of Buckingham. Who, fathers, does not know how great a concern for

the kingdom weighs upon the Protector and troubles Duke Claudian?

[All] England gazes at him alone and demands that the Duke [be]

the guardian of its affairs. He has especially chosen [you for]

your wisdom, whose wise old heads he may dutifully consult so

that he may carry out the many great affairs [of England] with

care. He anxiously desires an assembly for honoring the King

wherein he might gird the royal head with the diadem so that

it may be pleasing to [his] dead brother, the son of which buried

[one] he [will] dutifully adorn [with the crown].

Gloucester [entering]. O assembly of fathers worthy of reverence and the

highest honor of [our] powerful kingdom, may God grant now a

happy outcome to these proceedings. [Jocularly.]^{68} Truly, I was

too late a dreamer who am so late [in coming] to [this] full

assembly. Sleep is a grievous counsellor to my business affairs.

Have you, Bishop of Ely, an old man, come [here already], having

slipped from [your] bed so early in the morning? Rest, old man.

[Your] work befits a youth. They say that your garden produces

most agreeable strawberries. Order, I beg, that a few be picked

for my lunch.

Bishop of Ely. Nothing that my garden produces will be kept from you. I wish

it were [something] more splendid in myself wherein I am pleasing

to you [than my strawberries].^{69} [He goes out.]

---

^{68}See More, p. 426; and Hol., p. 380.

^{69}With a note of good-humored raillery, the Bishop is implying that
Gloucester likes him not for himself but for the delicious strawberries he grows.

Gloucester.   What may the condition of the kingdom, the safety of the

realm, and the honor of the country demand? Busy [yourselves]

still with your deliberations, fathers, I pray (business affairs

compel [me] to be absent for a little while) lest my departure

may be especially annoying [to you]. [He goes out.]

Lord Hastings. It is fitting, fathers, to render a very great effort so

that, when the King bears the sceptre in his youthful hand, we

might vigorously expel all discord which has recently wearied the

cruelly divided kingdom. The secure well-being of [our] country

demands this, and [both] the bright youth of the weak Prince and

[our] faith to the last oath pledged to the buried King demands

[this]. None of the safeguards of the kingdom has been greater

than this pledge [to Edward IV]. Therefore, if the nobles on

both sides agree, this kingdom will flourish for a long time.

But, if on both sides they disagree; [this kingdom] will be ruined

in a short while. At length, it is fitting to purge this stain

of our native land and to free ourselves from the very worst evil

[i.e. civil war]. But, behold, the Duke returns with a hesitating

step. Shaking [his] head, he rages with a knitted brow. Savagely

he presses [his] lip with a harsh tooth and he hides dire evil in

[his] angered heart.

Gloucester.   What punishments do you, fathers, resolve for those who are

with their sorcery now preparing death for me who has been regally

born of the highest blood and [who] has been declared protector of

this island?

Hastings.   [Those punishments] which a traitor of [his] country is obliged

to suffer; nor do I care anything for [his] high honor nor do I

excuse [him on the ground that he is] worthy.

Gloucester.   My brother's wife bewitches all my senses.

Hastings.   [Your] astonishing words deject me [lit. cast down my sad

head]. May the most wicked Queen suffer just punishments. [Aside.]

Yet it little pleases [me] that these things were concealed until

now from my ears. The mother's kinsmen were captured by my fraud;

already today these have been severely punished at Pontefract due

to my deceits.[70]

Gloucester.   The Queen, accompanied only by Shore's wife, effected her

sorcery on me by her incantations. My body has become weak with

disease; my eyes refuse [me] sleep; an apathetic aversion for food

grudges [my] stomach; pulsating blood deserts [my] open veins;

[my] bloodless arm has dried up [and withered]; it refuses [its]

function.

Hastings [Aside]. Alas, my trembling heart shakes with a cold fear. Is my

beloved destined, alas, for death? Do [our] loves perish? Never

in any case would the Queen plot with the [former] concubine of

her husband. They [i.e. the rest of the nobles present] fear to

speak. [At least] I may address the Duke safely. [Aloud.] If

they have done [this], they will pay the severest of penalties.

Gloucester.   If[71] they have really done [this] to me? If[71] they have done

[this]? Yea, rather, I say [this] was done, which your head will

pay for, wicked traitor!

Guards.   Treason! Treason!

---

[70] ". . . at these woordes . . . hys hart grudged that he [i.e. Hastings]
was not afore made of counsail of this matter as well as he was of the takyng
of her kyndred and of their puttyng to death,whiche were by hys assente before
deuysed to be beheaded at Pomfrete, this selfe same daye. . ." (Hall, p. 360).
See also More, p. 426; and Hol., p. 380.

[71] Italics are added here to indicate emphasis.

Gloucester.   I declare you to be guilty of treason.

Hastings.   Me? Not me?

Gloucester.   [Yes, you,] wicked traitor to [your] country!

Bishop of Ely. [Returning]. Did a guard, alas, strike illustrious Stanley

or did he fall down? Dripping blood wets [his] cheeks.

Gloucester.   You, servants, put the traitor [Hastings] to death immediately

after a holy priest has finished with [him who is] about to die.

I swear to St. Paul [that] I will not breakfast before [his]

decapitation pays [his] penalties to me; put the Father Cardinal,

the Bishop of Ely and Lord Stanley in chains; and [furthermore]

the impudent wench Shore, condemned by a prescribing judge, will

pay the penalties of [her] crime.

Hastings.   Who can worthily bewail our evils? Alas, what sounds shall

I wretchedly utter? What bitter laments will Aedon[72] produce for

our tears? O contriver of fraud and cruel author of villainy,

the false love of my own [friends] and [their] secret evil

concealed by a mild countenance have betrayed [me]. Why do the

cruel fates envy [my] life? Why should there be such great cunning

in my death, and [why] does their joy increase with my sorrow?

But, foolish one, spare [your] tears! I call to witness, in

whatever voice [or incantation] ye dead have fled from into the

dark earth, that the sacred will of the gods is, alas, adverse to

me. Guiltless, I am dragged to [my] death. [My] humble loyalty

---

[72]Aedon, envying the wife of Amphion her six sons, sought to slay one of
them in the night, only to slay her own son by mistake.

has not entered the palace, nor has it learned to live virtuously
with proud display; yet Fortune changes [her] hostile gifts into
[my] punishment.[73]

Gloucester.   Will he give way to the senseless laments of a woman? Can
[his] tears urge such great delays? [To the guards.] Are you
not going to drag this man away? Remove [his] head with a
dreadful [lit. impious] sword! Why do you delay to kill this man?

Hastings.   Grief rejoices to disperse her calamities among many [men],
nor is she alone pleased with [your] punishment. The cruel
sisters effect their dominion.   The blind fates sport
with human kind: they point out the evil to shun which yet they
forbid [you to shun]. Lord Stanley terrified by a dream will
effect nothing [now]. Alas, a boar, grinding with bloody teeth,
was seen [by him] to lacerate the head of us both. A long stream
of blood flowed down upon our shoulders. [His] insignia of the
boar has given the name [of the boar] to Gloucester. Three times
by slipping [my] horse fell when I was coming to visit the impious
Council.

Gloucester.   Those guards are asking for evil for themselves who, when they
foolishly make delays for [his] tears, stop from cutting off [his]
impious head with a sword.

------

[73]The chronicles offer no help with this passage. Hastings is apparently
lamenting a fickle fortune which has reversed itself. Usually fortune overturns
those who seek the palace, and the proud display that goes with it. Hasting's
devoted loyalty to Edward IV sought none of this. Hastings lived modestly on
his own estate in the country, apart from the honor and display that his
friendship for Edward might have commanded, and yet, fortune turned this gift,
his loyalty, into his punishment.

Hastings.   Alas, there is no hope of safety for me! Now, you, to whom

Fortune has given jurisdiction over us, drag [me] off to [my]

destruction. Why do I, a wretch, delay [you] with [my] tears?

Bedew [your] hands with [my] pious blood! Farewell [to you,] the

last celestial ray of the sun, completing the spent day; farewell,

quiet sister in the glittering band of noble Phoebus: the long

night will now bury [me].

[ACT V. Scene vii.]

Duke of Gloucester. London Citizens. Messenger.

Gloucester.   Beloved citizens, you are near at hand [now], however too

late [to be of aid] for us whom Hastings and his evil partners

in crime would have killed just now in the Tower if God had not

offered his aid; and although they had concealed it [i.e. their

villainy] for a long time in [their] cleverness, before a tenth

part of this sun (as it were), we, aroused by a sudden fear,

perceived [their villainy]; and whatever arms (as you perceive)

the occasion afforded, we unfortunates put on,[74] and now they

themselves are crushed either by our strength or by the grace

of heaven. A greater evil will fall upon the most wicked originators

of this deceit and upon the authors of [this] crime. Now, therefore,

since the monstrous crime should be well known to all, you have

been summoned [here] by my commander so that [this crime] might

be made known through you to those asking about [it].

74"... the Protectoure... (entending to set some colour vpon the matter
[i.e. Hastings' death and the imprisonment of Stanley and the bishops]), sent
in all the haste for many substancial men out of the cytie into the Towre,
and at their commyng him selfe with the duke of Buckyngham stode, harnessed
in olde euill fauored briganders, such as no man would wene that they would
haue vouchesafed to haue put on their backes, excepte some sodeyne necessitie
had constraigned them" (Hall, p. 362). See also More, p. 429; and Hol., pp.
382-383.

Citizens.   We loyal [citizens] will sedulously execute [your] command.

[Then after Gloucester departs.] O obdurate villain, hiding

[your] slaughter with a lie and [hiding] such evil confined by

[your] mild aspect; who does not know about the monstrous deceits

of [this] savage Duke? and [who] doubts that the noble man

[Hastings] has been taken by fraud? A crime generally comes back

upon its author before it afterwards cruelly rages against others.

Messenger.   A bright sword has drawn out the spirit of Hastings.

Citizens.   I want explained in a few words exactly how [lit. as] the

deed was done.

Messenger.   After a stern guard had dragged [him] to the place [of

execution], the famous noble lifted his eyes to the stars [and]

from [his] chaste mouth he began [his] prayers to God: "Whatever

punishment our stubborn pride has merited, o holy God, (he says)

would that it be expiated now by our blood." The executioner

scarcely waited for the final prayers. Rather he at once penetrated

the barrier of [his] body with a sword.

Citizens.   A great indulgence of his own servants, and a mind too trusting

in [his] happy affairs have killed Hastings, nor did the blameless

one suspect the cruel villainy until he was wretchedly punished

by [its] well-wishing author [i.e. Gloucester]. But a sergeant-

at-arms directs [his] step here. What does he seek to cry out

publicly to [us] citizens?

Sergeant-at-arms. Citizens.

[Sergeant-at-arms.]   Having undertaken villanies, this wicked traitor,

Hastings, the chief source of terrible evil ([Aside.] and I, observing the will of the Duke, swear falsely to [this] crowd),[75]

[and his associates] devised secret plots against the lives of

Prince Gloucester and of exalted Buckingham while both were

sitting together in the hallowed Council, so that, having thus

slain the protectors of ruined England, they might arrogantly

ascend the highest summits of supreme authority, even though [these]

who would rule over the great burdens of the ruined kingdom of

Britian [would be] unsuitable for [their] high elevation. Who

does not know that Hastings disgracefully drew the father of the

Prince after himself [i.e. evilly influenced King Edward IV]? Who

does not know that he polluted the royal name with his evil habits?

or who does not know that [this] base man by his words, by his

deeds, has despoiled the kingdom of its pristine glory?[76] Of how

many virgins has the abandoned lust of Hastings promiscuously killed

the shame? and [how many] vows of the marriage couch has [this]

infamous adulterer, who has embraced wenches, broken? For the

notorious mistress Shore, a celebrated prostitute and a conscious

---

[75]This parenthesis has no basis in the chronicles, although the general
skepticism of the people toward Gloucester's words at the beginning of this
scene does: "Euery man answered fayre [Gloucester's injunction to make known
the nature of Hasting's death to those asking about it], as though no man
mistrusted the matter, which of trueth no man beleued" (Hall, p. 362). See
also More, p. 429; and Hol., p. 383.

[76]". . . muche matter was deuised in the same proclamacion to the
slaunder of the lord Hastynges, as that he was an euyll counsailoure to the
kynges father, entisyng hym to many thynges highly redoundyng to the
diminishyng of hys honoure and to the vniuersall hurte of his realme by his
euyll compaignie and sinister procuryng and vngracious example, . . ." (Hall,
p. 362). See also More, p. 430; and Hol., p. 383.

sharer of his [planned] slaughter [of the dukes], [only] last
night received him in her unchaste embrace in [her] dishonored
bed so that he who has polluted his life by a serious crime
rightly has paid the supreme penalties by [his] death. Truly,
if the death of the condemned traitor were delayed for a long
time, [his] band [of followers] sworn to deadly war might madly
demand their leader. [His] punishment which [has been] hastened
will make everyone ineffective and will crush the cruel tumults
[of those who have sworn oaths to Hastings].

Citizen.   A hasty manner of acting disturbs great affairs and a hurrying
dog produces a blind litter.

Second Citizen. These things have been written by the profound spirit of
a prophet,for how else could so many [beautiful] words be thought
up or so [well] expressed in so short a time? The documents seem
extremely beautifully [done] to me, and the little proclamation
seems to be delineated beautifully, and finally the arrangement
of words [seems] excellent for speaking [purposes]. Yet it seems
especially wondrous that so many beautiful things were prepared in
so short a time.

Citizens.   Behold Shore carrying a flickering taper in [her] hand;
dressed in a linen [kirtle], she pays [her] infamous penances.
The famous harlot of King [Edward] pays [her] penalties to this
savage tyrant. Descend, Father Jupiter, and take now to your bed
so pleasing a pledge of love: for consider [her] your Leda[77] or
Europa[77] [and] leave [your] heaven. O wretched [woman], I am sorry
for you, I am ashamed [for you], I feel regret [for you], even

---

[77]Jupiter carried off both Leda and Europa.

though [you are] an incontinent and a none-too-virtuous wife.

While Duke Claudian refuses to take your life, enraged he seeks

to ruin [your] reputation [completely].

Solemn Procession.

Chorus.　　　Let us pour forth from [our] mouths suppliant prayers to God

lest [our] mind be polluted by the notorious adultress.

　　1.　Protect conjugal faith

　　　　and free [its] bed from dishonor;

　　　　defend private marriage beds

　　　　lest furtive Venus shame [them].

　　2.　Whoever repents of [his] deed,

　　　　purge free of his crime.

　　　　May [good] examples make posterity [morally] sound

　　　　lest furtive Venus defile [it].

Epilogue

What stratagems cruel Richard has directed, and with how much strife

his desire for rule has affected the afflicted country, you are [now]

seeing.　So that exalted Gloucester, the teeth-gnashing boar, the

plague of the kingdom, may ascend the hightest summits of the

kingdom, the blood of illustrious Hastings has been poured forth

because, [while] living, he favored the little princes.　[Those]

opposed to [his] new rule, Rivers, Vaughan, and Grey repressed in

the horror of a prison, have been crushed with a deadly wound.

[The Show of the Procession

    A Tipstaff

    Shore's wife in her petticoat, carrying a burning

        taper in her hand

    The Verger

    Choristers

    Singing men

    Prebendaries

    The Bishop of London

    Citizens]

End of Part One

SECOND PART

Dramatis Personae

Duke of Gloucester

Duke of Buckingham

Lord Lovell

Mayor of London

Fitzwilliam, the Recorder [of London]

Citizen, a friend of Shaw

Doctor Shaw

First citizen

Second citizen

Foreigner

Lord

A few servants of Buckingham

346

Argument

After Richard, Duke of Gloucester, has reduced to his sway all
those whose loyalty to the King he [had] feared and has thrown into
prison [all] others whose [loyalty] to Lord Hastings he [had] aroused
[by putting Hastings] to death, he sedulously applies himself to this
[one] desire, [namely,] that he may come into the illegal possession
of the kingdom without [causing] an uprising of the citizenry. Therefore, in order that he may perpetrate [his] fraud on the Londoners so
that they, together with certain nobles, may voluntarily offer the
kingdom to him, he has damned the birth of the King [Edward V] and
of his brother the Duke of York; [and] his own brother, King Edward
[IV], who [had] died not so long before, he caused to be accused of
adultery by the Duke of Buckingham in the council hall of the Mayor
[of London]; nor did he spare his own mother, the former Duchess of
York. Finally, taking, as it were unwillingly, the kingship offered
to him (which he [had] coveted so greatly), he is crowned in solemn
assemblies.

ACT I. [Scene i.]

Duke of Gloucester. Duke of Buckingham. Lord Lovel.

[Gloucester.] Illustrious offspring of noblemen, [and] eminent descendant
of the dukes of Buckingham [and] noble Lovel, a sharer of our
counsel, why don't we break through [these] lingering delays? It
is fitting that he who contemplates great affairs should be prompt.
This very same business holds no danger: is it not fitting to venture
further? Buckingham can create a king: this has always been an
honor of the very greatest duke [in the land]. Nature makes you
firm in virtue and has carefully vested you with bodily

endowments. Moreover, she has included an equally strong keenness
of mind in you, nor does Minerva[78] enlighten anyone more than [she
does] you. It is only fitting to follow where [your] excellent
nature calls [you]; Buckingham alone can [accomplish] high honors.
Lo, the enemies suspicious of me are destroyed and the chains of
a harsh prison oppress those culprits whose partiality toward the
King arms against my authority. It is possible to kill [them] all
with a single word. The slain Lord Hastings has fallen. Lord
Stanley is restrained by bonds and jail subdues the Bishop of Ely.
The rest who undutifully favor little [our] undertakings lie shut
up in an abominable dungeon.

Buckingham. That a little boy rules is a jest of Fortune. Lasciviously
laughing, she mixes sceptres with contentions. The little child,
overcome, succumbs to her oppressive weight. Consider whatever
deceits you plan for the kingdom: never will I obstinately
disobey your commands. [But this] great affair cannot be executed
immediately.[79]

Gloucester. Lo, the very security of the times commands [us] to begin
audaciously rather than what you counsel. It is necessary to
provide [our] minds with a single [purpose], nor is it fitting to
begin difficult undertakings rashly. What will be the future
outcome of events, the wise man considers first. All things must
be executed prudently. May [our] joint counsels unfold whatever
must be feared.

---

[78]The goddess of intelligence.

[79]The chronicles offer no basis for Buckingham's advising Richard here
(and in the rest of the scene) to proceed slowly with his plans for usurpation;
nor do they offer a basis for Lovel's urging swift action.

Lovel.   Lo, the shortness of the time wherein you might encircle your

royal head with the crown presses [us] too closely [already].

Therefore, it must be publicly proclaimed now to all that they

should not assemble as yet for the coronation [lit. sacred ceremonies].

An opportunity of great moment for seizing the royal power recommends

delays so that crown may not encircle the head of the Prince before

the second day of November dawns. This is the day determined for

the solemnities. While [the nobles, who] are [here in London] far

away from [their] ancestral homes, are considering what the delays

mean, while [these] nobles are present [here] deprived of their

strength, while an uncertain opinion torments the doubtful [ones],

and [while these] uncertain ones are suspicious of [their] mutual

loyalty [to the King], and [while] they have not set in order [their]

harassed deliberations, before [these] rebels might join their

strengths, take safely the sceptre seized from the boys![80] Handle

the reins of England with a skillful hand! Then the [people's]

subdued hatred will yield to your command when it destroys the

Prince with a sword.

Buckingham.   Although the band of nobles may profess [itself] deceived and

[although] the wise mind may attempt nothing by the sword, yet

the persistent rage of the mob [lit. people] will join arms and

will be carried away by its blind impulse: it rushes forth

dangerously wherever it is carried. [Its] unfair words will

---

[80]The chronicles credit Richard with this shrewd opportunism: ". . .then
the protectour caused it to be proclaymed that the coronacion for diuers
great and vrgent causes should be deferred till the seconde daye of Nouember,
for then thought he, that whyle men mused what the matter meant, and while
the lordes of the realme were about him, out of their awne strengthes, and
while no man wyste what to thynke nor whom to truste, or euer they should
haue tyme and space to digest the matter, and make partes, it were best
hastely to pursue his purpose and put hym self in possession of the croune,
or menne could haue tyme to deuyse any wyse to resyste" (Hall, p. 364). See
also, More, p. 433; and Hol., p. 385.

correspond to [its] savage deeds, nor will a rashly conceived fury [that is] conquered by fear submit [completely]; just as the hurrying Menander is routed by the savage whirlpool: he cannot permit the opposition to himself and he rages against the cruel [whirlpool].

Lovel. It is fitting to appease the savage nature of the mob with flattering [speeches]; [the mob] is willingly led [by flattering speeches] and besides is touched [by them], nor may slight authority shine forth among his own [subjects in him] whom the goodwill of his own citizens blesses. It [i.e. a flattering speech] can manage the rude mind [of the mob] more gently and can recommend your rule to the citizens. If the city of London, the most illustrious of England, persuaded to your wishes, should be favorable [to you], we have won. Others taken in by a like deception will advance [your cause]; you will easily defend with the sword the royal power [once it has been] taken. But what pretext for [your] rule will be approved by the citizens lest they wisely sense that those taken in have been deceived? The angry crowd will be greatly vexed with itself that it has been deluded.

Buckingham. An unhappy people so wearied with evils is [easily] subdued, and the wanton rule of the little boy threatens [the country with a] great catastrophe. England fears now strifes and the mother's rage will not end in [mere] penalties. Your rule will remove disgraceful battles, you who have been born of the highest blood of kings and who will wisely sustain the great power of the kingdom.

Lovel. The cunning mob will readily sense this deceit and will believe that his reason for [assuming] the rule is unjust.

Gloucester. Why doesn't an easy way lie open to our deceits? Let the

infamous beds of [my] brother be publicly condemned: Virtuous

sceptres do not permit a disgrace to the marriage bed. Laws

forbid bastard sons to rule. After King [Edward IV] had become

inflamed with the love of Lucy, then in the treading season when

furtive Venus first sought again [his] sweet shame and [when]

desire assigned no measure to [his] savage flames, he rashly

promised the beds of the kingdom to Lucy and named her a sharer

of his kingdom. [But] Venus [i.e. carnal love] often experienced

produces loathing: then [his] affections for Lucy became sordid

to the Prince, and he no [longer] shamefully sought [his] stolen

love in a dark bed. He deceived [her] mind bound to her husband,

and the [rightful] Queen [i.e. Lucy] never did possess the marriage

beds promised [to her]. Then, the ill-treated Lucy, in no way

fearing the violent threats of fate up to that time, gave [her]

place to a mistress [i.e.Elizabeth Grey]. From hence, from her

loins, the adulterous father gave birth to [his] bastard sons and

[caused] a severe wound to the royal authority;[81] nor did the

throne of [their] father bear only this stain. The shameless love

of our parent [i.e. the Duchess of York] made a mockery of [her]

former marriage bed. A secret companion found the footprint of a

shamefully false man in the bed-chambers of the Duchess. Nor

could [any] deceit conceal [such] wicked unions. The [innocent]

---

[81]Although Lucy was one of Edward's early mistresses, the chronicles
state that she was never betrothed to Edward, and hence there was no impediment
to his marriage to Elizabeth Grey as Richard argues here. For the complete
Lucy affair, see Hall, pp. 365-367; More, pp. 434-437; and Hol., pp. 386-389.

partner in the marriage became acquainted with and was ashamed of [his spouse's] crime, and [hence] King Edward was the dishonored offspring of a dishonored mother. Deceived, the spurious father [i.e. the Duke of York] bestowed the insecure sceptre on [his] ignoble son. Different mouths and the unworthy habits of [my] brother deny the [supposed] father of [my] brother. [My] father had my features: he was such in appearance. The dissimilar appearance of [my] brother reveals the pollution [in his birth]. The descendant of a shameful love was not of royal blood.

Buckingham. But you rightly claim [the throne]: why [then] do we look to deceits? That [claim] admits of much greater justice. The path lies open to our undertakings. What need is there for tricks? [But] how shall these words be made known to the fickle mob? Or will you seek [its] loyalty with great deceits?

Gloucester. Let no cold fear torment my trembling heart: What loyalty is not won by a secret reward? London will readily grant [its] mighty citizenry [to our cause], and [indeed anyone] who is wise can conceal our deceits and enticingly influence the minds of the citizens and win over the Londoners with many rewards. The Mayor has very great influence among his people; he seeks vain honors and inconstant political power, and the desire of [his] greedy mind incites [him] greatly. [His] insatiable hope for honor will render [him] loyal, and [his] deep thirst for money will always move [him to do our bidding].

Lovel. Nothing has [ever] been more deceitful than false holy [men]. [Their] false divine commands readily delude the people. [Even] a devout mind will yield to violence if a faithful preacher of

Scripture (when he impresses the holy prophecies on pious ears or
when he voices divine precepts to the people) recalls the marriage
beds once deceived by fraud, and the infamy of the bed and the
damage [done to] the famous House [of York].

Buckingham.   Dr. Shaw is a man eminent in letters. He is the brother to
[lit. joined to] the Mayor by the same mother. Many letters have
enriched this man with praise. [His] false sanctity, the shame
of which rests easily on [his] mind, wonderfully attracts citizens
to this [man] who will [lit. can] faithfully perform [this] service
[for you].

Gloucester.   Let one of my [followers] summon the Mayor of the city of
London, a man of great honor among his own people, and [his]
brother Shaw, [a man] learned in the highest sciences. When the
Mayor has reassured the minds of [his] citizens and has recommended
our rule to [his] citizens, it will be fitting that you, [Buckingham,]
proclaim this to the entire Commons:[82] "The rude mob marvels at
the illustrious Duke. The awe-struck populace, dazed by his [glory],
is stupefied and thinks that a heavenly god has fallen to their
[lot]." The mob will be won over at once by your look. While they
are dazed, stifle [them] immediately with the sweet sorcery [of words]
so that they may censure [Edward's] sons with appropriate hate.
Promise [them] the highest advantages of independence, [that] a
happy peace of the citizens will bless the city, and [that] great

---

[82]"Then on the tuesday after. . . foloyng this sermond. . . there came to
the Guyld hall of London the duke of Buckingham. . . And at the east ende of
the hal . . . the duke and the maire. . . sat downe, and the aldermen also, all
the commons of the citee beeynge assembled and standynge before theim" (Hall,
pp. 368-369). See also More, pp. 439-440; and Hol., p. 390.

honor [will] increase without end if they deliver [our] disgraced
house from the shame of [its] marriage bed, and [if] they rightfully
give to us the sceptre of [our] family.

Lovel.   While the holy Father [Shaw] makes known the evil unions and
the recent loves of [your] brother, and the shame of your mother
and the dishonor of the King's house, while the preacher of your
glories, Shaw, intently adorns [you] with the greatest of virtues,
fly [to the place where he is speaking] like a heavenly being who
has suddenly descended [to earth]. The fickle mob will think you
a divinely created prince, and it will believe that Shaw has proclaimed
[you] a king sent by the sacred will of the gods, and amazement will
distract its fickle mind.

[ACT I. Scene ii.]

Duke of Gloucester. Mayor of London. Doctor Shaw.

Gloucester.   Distinguished Mayor of [this] most illustrious city, and holy
preacher and person sacred to the gods, behold, we are striving
for great future prerogatives, and a great part of this honor will
be yours (whom we know to pray for prosperous affairs for the
kingdom) if each [of you] will carefully comply with [our] wishes.
Now, therefore, I request your secret loyalty. So great [are] the
secrets of the kingdom which we are announcing, we will compensate
[your] faithfulness with great honors and will enrich those [who are]
loyal with large rewards.

Mayor.   Illustrious Protector, splendid offshoot of the King, I
willingly consecrate my loyalty to you. Whatever you command, I
will perform [as] a faithful duty.

Gloucester.   A worn-out Britain is already terrified (alas) by the [recent]

carnage on both sides, and the infirm sceptre [i.e. the weak rule]

of a boy and [his] mother's madness will urge [even] greater wounds

[to the kingdom]. Can anyone certainly mad [such as the Queen is]

cure [this] evil? He who fears a king [lit. kings] renounces in

[his] mind the respects due [to him], and [he who has] shame in

the rule of a king will wrongfully submit [to that rule]. Genuine

praise has never reached a mighty man, [because] Fortune impels

those who are unwilling [to act] evilly [to act evilly] and often

forbids [them] to do [honorably] what they want to do honorably.

He is [lit. will be] certainly just whose heart is free from fear.

The nobles urge the things befitting a rule upon me whose princely

ancestry bids rule. I would like you, whose great fame is celebrated

in [this] splendid city, to persuade the minds of the citizens so

that they may offer me the sceptre of the kingdom.

Mayor.   By what right do you claim the kingdom of [your] nephew lest

an angered populace rashly stirs up riots when it comprehends that

the Prince has been robbed of [his] title?

Gloucester.   Mayor, spread secretly such [as follows] to your citizens.

In times past [my] brother Edward was sinfully born in an infamous

bed when the greedy love of [my] mother sent [her] to strange beds,

and [thereupon] she mixed bastard children with the progeny of the

Duke. A modest attendant discovered the shame of [her] bed, and

[other] servants [too] confessed the secret infamy. The different

appearance of [my] father and the degenerate habits of [my] brother

call [attention to] the bastardy. A marked likeness has persuaded

me [that I am the only] legitimate son of the Duke [of York], and

[also] habits similar [to those] of [my] father and [our] like

voices. Nor did my unhappy family endure only this disgrace.

[My] brother Edward, following after his mother, burdened [our]

disgraced house with an [even] greater shame. For [already]

faithfully joined to [his] wife Lucy, [as] a new lover, he repudiated

[lit. announced the repudiations of] [his] vow and mocked the faith

enjoined to [his] first marriage. Elizabeth [Grey, his] second

wife, was joined to the Prince by a late royal marriage. [This]

wicked mother [i.e. Elizabeth Grey] took the beds of another [i.e.

Lucy], and [as] a mistress produced bastard sons for the father.

When the people consider these things among themselves, immediately

the famous Duke of Buckingham personally will inform the citizens

of these things in your council hall and [also] what the sentiment

of all the nobles is. The populace, captivated by the splendor of

[this] distinguished man, will loudly proclaim me Prince with its

approval and will call [me] King of England. [Turning to Dr. Shaw.]

Similarly, divine preacher, [while] pouring forth sacred doctrines

at Paul's Cross, explain these things to the people. But, as if

unwillingly, touch cautiously upon the shameful infamy of my mother,

feigning that [you] fear our grave offense. While you are honoring

us with your copious praises, suddenly as if a heavenly Prince has

been bestowed on Britain, I, attended by a retinue [befitting a god],

will interrupt my praises; while the credulous are considering

[this] miracle, [their] false hope for a divine being will readily

seduce [them] on the spot. Now it is expedient that you execute

faithfully what we command.

Doctor Shaw. I will faithfully follow out your commands at once. Never will you condemn my faith [as being] uncertain.

ACT II. [Scene i.]

First citizen. Second citizen.

First citizen. How long will Britain be torn with strifes, and how long will a harsh fate heap lamentations on lamentations? Will cruel evil oppress [it] anew? The cruel fates scarcely know of moderation. Will [that] maddened House [of York], filled with slaughter, never be pacified, or will no heir [ever] bear the sceptre with impunity? But at least, now, the realms seized by the sword in no way fear the Lancaster offspring. Now [instead] the ill-starred House [of York] readies new evils for itself. How great a ruin does my mind accustomed to evils presage! There is no faith in the kingdom, and crazed ambition cannot spare its own [kinsmen]. The populace secretly murmurs that the Duke of Gloucester seeks royal power. The villainy of the uncle [is] cruel [and] inhuman: [his] little nephews lie in a dark prison. Lo, the prescribed day for the [Coronation] ceremonies has been postponed. Many a client [i.e. petitioner] treads only the worn-out threshold of the Duke of Gloucester. There the splendor of an illustrious palace appears; in that place gathers whoever begs for less harsh treatment with a humble entreaty. Whoever treads the barren [i.e. deserted] threshold of the King, and [whatever] faithful servant might [happen to] visit the princes, a band of men, extremely well informed [as to who it is that visits the princes], wounds this man.[83]

---

[83]See Footnote 54 above.

Second citizen. Dear friend and faithful sharer of [my] harsh lot, alas,

[how very much] grave events oppress us! Behold, cruel turmoil

returns to an exhausted England, and cruel evil renews [its] lost

strength.

First citizen. Tell [me] what evils await the wearied citizens.

Second citizen. In a few words, I shall fearfully encompass the impious

evil. While I was idly wandering about, [thinking] intently upon

the recent events, and [while] I was considering the common joy

of the realm, lo, a dangerous mob was put in motion by a mad impulse;

many rushed forth in a blind course. [All] at once, I, to [my]

amazement, was mingled with the dense mass: we were carried along

to a church; I grudgingly bent [lit. extended] my ears; I expected

sacred things to [be spoken]. I stood [there] musing. Behold,

[that] divine preacher, Dr. Shaw, climbed [into] the pulpit, whom

[the people] say is famous for [his] learning [but] is despised

for [his] abominable habits. Soon he began to speak, according

to the Holy Scriptures, as follows: "The adulterous bed is denied

a blessed seed, nor will bastard sons gain deep roots. For how

long afterwards does the disgrace of a marriage bed," he points

out, "harm the honor of a kingdom, and do false marriages presage

[evil to a kingdom]? How much do the gods bless faith in marriage,

and how much are they horrified at the accursed sons of a deceitful

marriage [lit. bed] [who] testify to the sins of [his] father? Yet

soon God reveals the unknown theft and restores his goods to his

[true] heir. Since [that] false mother Elizabeth took possession

of the unchaste beds of King [Edward] and wantonly mocked conjugal

faith," he [i.e. Shaw] declaimed from [his] impious mouth, "and because the bed of Edward had been once promised first to Lucy,

therefore the mother Elizabeth took possession of the beds from

the said Lucy unjustly and defiled her children with an adulterous

stain. Nor did the deceitful faith [in this union] alone defile

the children of King [Edward]. An impure mother [i.e. the Duchess

of York] attests to the mean origin of [the Princes'] father

[King Edward] when [this] furtive Venus mixed [her] adulterous

[children] in with her [legitimate] children, and their different

mouths convince [me] that he [i.e. Edward IV] [was] a false son of

[his] father, the great Duke [of York]. Only Richard presents the

image of [his] father: the face of the Duke [of Gloucester] calls

[him the true] king. Now, therefore, he rightly claims the lost

realm of [his] father." Immediately he raised Gloucester to the

stars with [these] praises: "Here is the regal splendor which

used to shine forth; here shines forth the true appearance of

the father. How many a virtue blesses [him]." He [then] bade

[us] to look upon this man with awe, [and] to reverence this man.

All were dazed, and they stood agape [lit. they dropped their faces];

they began to murmur; soon they were gazing at each other. [Then]

Gloucester came: late, he missed his own praises. A mighty

retinue accompanied [him]. When Shaw saw the Duke, just as if he

were a heavenly king descended upon England, he said, "Behold the

Prince of beloved Britain." He again bade [us] to look upon this

man with admiration, and to reverence this man just as if he were

ashamed that [his] former flatteries had already died in vain because

the Duke was not [there] before. "This is the true image of the father.

This is the face of the Duke [of York]. The father in his favored

Richard does not know how to die." The Duke, producing deep sighs [in the people] because of his accompanying retinue, [and] making

his way through the dense [masses] of men, showed forth [his]

countenance that must be gazed at by the citizens: he sat high

[on a horse].

First citizen.   But what was the result of this sermon?

Second citizen.   After Shaw had perceived that his praises were wasted, and

that the populace did not shout with joyous cries: "Long live

King Richard" (for the populace was at the time dazed: it was

wondering about [this] infamous evil), he was ashamed of [his]

undertaking, and too late he recognized his villainy. [His] lost

[sense of] shame sought in vain to repair [its] strength, and he

feared for his virtue [which was] despised before; lo, miserably

fleeing the looks of the citizens, he withdrew himself secretly

homeward.   But what is the meaning of so great an assembly of

citizens in the council hall?

First citizen.   The mayor has ordered his citizens to gather here so that

the noble offspring of Buckingham may advise us about [some] very

serious matters.

Second citizen.   May a propitious God avert an evil omen!

[ACT II.   Scene ii.]

Duke of Buckingham.   Mayor of London.   A Noble.

A few servants of Buckingham.

Buckingham.   Inspired by [my] love for you, o my citizens, I will speak [to

you] concerning very serious matters.   These [matters] will be

exceedingly propitious to the country, and [I trust will be] not

particularly sad matters to be heard by you whom this fortune will bless in every respect. For [those] times which have been often longed for and [which] have been vainly hoped for for a long time in your weary prayers, [and those things] which it does not shame [anyone] to have procured with a great amount of money or with very great labor, all [these] things are at hand for you deserving [people], if the so great and hoped for things you seek are a secure peace for [your] live[s], the sweet protection of [your] children, and the safety of [your] wives. Alas! what grave fear did not dispirit you before for so many years past? For only through [the grace of] God and heaven did [a man] possess anything: who [indeed] could safely enjoy completely [even] his very own possessions amid so many and such great frauds? What peace [could] there be [even] for [your] children? Who [could] rule alone in his own home? [My] mind shudders to describe that tyranny [of Edward IV] which cruelly impoverished the homes of [this] realm of [their] deepest means, nor did [this] hateful plague know how to spare the innocent. Why should I expound [to you people who know already] how many taxes have been exacted more often [from you], how many have been extorted by force [from you], how many luxurie[s] have been seen [by you]? Nor can the [financially] exhausted citizen bear the great tax[es]. Light fine[s] have increased immensely, and severe penalties have [recently] afflicted [even] small offense[s]. I think you remember Burdett, my fellow citizens, whose head the King unjustly ordered cut off because he jested wittily, although Judge [Markham][84] shuddered at the [King's] wicked crime, and [you

---

[84] See Hall, p. 369; More, p. 440; and Hol., p. 391.

remember also] [your] noble Mayor [Thomas Cook], who was an alderman

of your city for a long time. Alas, how [that] wretched [man]

suffered severe punishments because he himself was bound for many

things to those men whom the impious King strongly envied.[85]   It

is not necessary that I describe other [men who met similar fates].

I think that there is hardly anyone present who is not mindful of

so bloody a time and is not himself conscious of his own fear,

which either the King's wicked anger or his great favoring of

many evil citizens has caused. For, after the King obtained his

cruel authority by the sword, the enraged victor impiously considered

that any man [lit. this man] harmed [his] prerogatives of rule who

was connected [either] by blood to [those] relations or [even]

by a bond of affection to those whom the Prince had hated before.

But to this evil he also added a greater evil. Fearful of [his]

life, he did not firm up the end of the war, because he, uncertain

[of his authority], not only vexed [himself], but also (what [is]

more detestable!) encouraged riot[s] among his citizens which

were wont to be of the greatest [severity] at that time when the

nobles on both sides were burning with silent hate; nor did the

nobles [lit. aristocracy] aggravate themselves more bitterly with

the greatest of contentions than when Edward bore the sceptre in

his wicked hand. Finally civil wars so raged on all sides that a

very great part of [our noble] citizens died in a sad ruin. This,

---

[85]"What nede I to speke of syr Thomas Cooke Alderman and mayre of this
noble citee. . . his wonderfull spoyle and vndeserued distruction, onely
because it happened him to fauour them whom the prince fauoured not" (Hall,
p. 369). See also More, p. 440; and Hol., p. 391.

this [very] carnage of [our noble] citizens was so horrible [that] a twice-conquered France never saw the like of it. This [carnage] has exhausted the highest stock of Englishmen; this [carnage] has despoiled those [who have lived] of their pristine strength, so great a destruction has destroyed [lit. burned] so many [of their] cities. And [even] the uncertain [periods of] peace threatened [all with] menaces equal to those of war [times]. The lords paid the penalty [for having great] wealth and whoever held [great] fields [i.e. estates] was afflicted. Did anyone escape the Prince's wrath? So, indeed, no one was not miserably languishing with fear, nor were any times not full of dangers [for all]. But, indeed, who was trusted to be dear to him who hated his own brother [lit. whom his own brother was in hatred]? Could he to whom a brother seemed to be disloyal trust others? or perhaps he who condemned [lit. brought damnation upon] his own brother could be more gently sparing of others?[86] But I will say nothing against [those] whom he intimately reverenced, or [against those] such as he adorned with handsome honor[s]. Who does not know that a single mistress [i.e. Shore's wife] had more influence [upon him] than the foremost men of the entire realm? Extremely unwillingly do I bring these things before you! But of what avail is it to remain silent about what [is well] known to several people [already]? Where did not

---

[86]This passage is ambiguous. The "he" probably refers to Edward IV, and the "brother" to the Duke of Clarence, but in the context it can refer to the mistrust that was common between brothers who fought on opposing sides during the civil war. The chronicles are equally ambiguous: "For whom mistrusted he that mistrusted his own brother? Whom spared he that kylled his brother?" (Hall, p. 370). See also More, p. 441; and Hol., p. 392.

the great fervor of [his] passion and the blind raging of [his]

desire urge [him]? What virgin, a little prettier [than another],

[or] what woman more becoming than others, [is there] whom he did

not snatch from the bosom of [her] mother or from the arms of [her]

husband? But although [this] tyrant assaulted everywhere, yet

your city felt [his] menaces above [all] others, [your city] whose

worth he should rather have honored because it is the chief seat

of the kingdom and [because] the oft-repulsed Prince formerly owed

[it] greater rewards [than he paid it]. [While still] living, he

spurned [its many] benefactions, and [now] dead he can not pay [his]

gratitude. [But], behold, another born of the same blood remains

alive. The future King [should be] more gracious to his subjects,

and [one] who can repay what is due to your merits and [who] can

sufficiently answer [your] desires. Nor have those things, I

believe, which the learned preacher of things sacred proclaimed

[to you] before, vanished from your minds. Never has an interpreter

of God['s] [word] falsified [his] faith. The priest has called

the paternal uncle to the throne. Yea, rather, God has bade

Gloucester to reign. Neither may [his] bastard nephew manage the

sceptre of [his] father, nor may the shame of [his mother's marriage]

bed defile the honor of the kingdom. Richard is [lit. was] the only

[true] heir of [his] brother. A high-minded group of the nobles and

the commons has decided on this: that it should humbly ask the

uncle that, just as if [he were called upon] to defend the honor

of Prince's kingdom, he should [now] as heir take upon himself

the burden of this mighty island. He would do [it] unwillingly, I

know. The task of ruling will deter [him] greatly: [since it is]

prone to envy, he will strive [not to accept it]. Thankless
sceptres by no means cultivate peace [for a king]. To how many
battles is the deceiving elegance [of kingship] summoned? Believe
me, [o] citizenry, a boy cannot attend to the great burden [of
ruling]. A sacred utterance strikes [my] ears: "Unhappy are
the kingdoms in which a boy is king." A fertile intelligence and
a mature age befit the envious throne: such an uncle you see. If,
therefore, the safety of the citizenry [is] dear to you, or if the
long-awaited leagues of peace [will] please [you], you will at once
acclaim the   fortunate wishes of the nobles. Let Gloucester be
created king with a single shout! More promptly he will assume
the   great labor [of ruling] if your voice[s] will weary the
unwilling [man's ears] before [we ask him]. [Now], then, openly
proclaim what your mind is! [Aside to the Mayor.] Why this deep
silence? Why is the citizenry silent?

Mayor.   The people scarcely received [your] words strongly in [their]
ear[s].

Buckingham.   Then I will address them again louder. Iniquitous times, [my]
citizens, have passed. Gracious peace, at length, flourishes by
a happy chance, unless anyone madly begrudges his own good, or does
not know how to make use of [it]. When Edward, cruelly raging
with a violent appearance, was oppressing England by [those]
contentions by which the island was everywhere disquieted, then
the lives of the citizens [were] not safe, their goods were never
shut off from anyone, and the desire of [that] wicked King for
debauchery dissipated everything. What virgin was untouched? What
wife avoided an unjust disgrace [at his hands]? Whatever pleased

him was lawful. [His] authority was miserable to all the citizens, but by far most miserable to the Londoners, although [his] position [as King] recommended [many] kindnesses to them. But there is one [man] who may avenge [these] so many perils, the Duke of Gloucester, himself born of royal stock, whose [great] honor many [men] reverence, whom the laws of the country has ordered to reign, and [who] is the only remaining heir of the royal house. The furtive offspring of an infamous mother [and] of an adulterous father vainly claim the throne for themselves. An excellent man recently informed you of these things when, [as a] preacher, he expounded sacred dogma to you [last Sunday]. No one pious will condemn [his] divine words. Hence, an aroused band of nobles and a great assembly of citizens will suppliantly stand firm in begging the greatly esteemed uncle that [as the true] heir he may take in hand his royal power, and that the bastard nephew may not corrupt the honor of the country. He will willingly do [this] if he should perceive that you of your own free will desire this. Therefore express [your] mind with a public clamor! [Aside to the Mayor.] What is this? Are they still silent? What a great wonder!

Mayor.   One [citizen] with a public voice [i.e. the Recorder, or Public Crier] has usually addressed [all] commands concerning great affairs to his own citizens. Hence, perhaps they will give responses to him asking [them]. Mediator of your city, address the citizens!

[Fitzwilliam, the Recorder.] How much more all things fall to [his] happy lot than to [his] brother the former King, who insanely denies? Nor is it necessary for me to expound [his] many [virtues]. The

distinguished Duke has [already] recalled these things for all [to
hear]. You have [all] certainly been spectators on the two occasions
[on which he expounded these things]. How much the former time
oppressed [us], how pleasantly the future time will shine forth,
to whom is this unknown? Now, then, [this] great-hearted noble
wishes to know whether it pleases [you] that the Duke of Gloucester
reign because it is well known that several classes have decided
[it], and [because] the nobles of England call [him] the true
king. Who that man is and how great he is, who does not know?
By what right does [this true] heir demand the title of rule?
Doctor Shaw, [who is] the learned interpreter of God's [words]
and who expounds upon Heaven [itself], has advised [us] all [on
his right to rule]. Therefore, state your mind with a public shout!

Buckingham. [To the Mayor.] That silence is extremely persistent [Aloud to
the citizens.] Concerning these, the greatest affairs by far, I
seek to address you, [my] friends, inspired not by [my] right, but
inspired by [my] love [for you], because I freely desire to present
[to you] a good unknown to you till now. This will be good for
every citizen. Pour out immediately, I pray, manifest signs of
[your] mind!

A few servants [of Buckingham]. Long live King Richard!

Mayor [Aside]. The entire hall hums with a low whisper. The citizens are
silent; they are looking back; they are wondering whose voice it
was; they in no way acclaim the kingdom for the Duke [of Gloucester].

Buckingham. By Hercules, [one] voice [is] joyful, and [its] clamor [is]
great when no one with [his] voice murmurs anything contrary.
Therefore, since one may be the voice for all the citizens, join,
friends, together with me tomorrow, I pray. Let us together humbly

beseech the Duke: then he may be willing to take the name of

Prince.

Noble [Aside]. Why, alas, do you miserably bedew your cheeks with weeping?

Does it please [you] to lament [these] wicked deceits? Will you

not restrain yourself? [Your] secret tears may be honorable, but

may still be deadly! Awe-inspiring Father of the world who alone

perceives [our] fates, turn a cruel destruction away from the wretched

infants! But, [as] a comrade, I [must] follow the Duke.

ACT III. [Scene i.]

Duke of Buckingham. Citizens.

[Buckingham.] [O] gathering of citizens, worthy of reverence, whom the

famous city of London abundantly favors, behold, everyone of his

own free will has now directed his joyous step[s] [here], and

every rank of citizens has gathered [here] so that they may

present to Gloucester the sceptre [which has been] taken away

from [his] adulterous nephews [and which] must be borne by [their]

uncle lest a false posterity defile the royal palace. [To a

servant.] But, you first advise the Duke of our arrival lest so

great a crowd in this place make [him] anxious. The suppliant

citizens whom the harsh events of England have tormented seek him.

He may consider [this] approach by [his] loyal subjects worthy of

himself when they consult him about the greatest affairs [of England].

Mighty [is] the burden, the labor of ruling, nor does the sweet

poison [of rule] steadfastly allure good [men]; lo, [those] who

choose by deceit luxurious dwellings [for themselves], civil war

will torment with [its] constant threats, and no [amount] of arms

will sufficiently defend [lit. surround] [such] a prince [as the
one who chooses the luxurious allurements of rule]. But even
though [I know] a popular speech only depresses [you people], why
[then] do I expound these things to you? Because, [even] if [his]
grave concern renders the pious burden of the crown agreeable [to
him], and [even if our] loyalty [to him] makes the Duke in no way
suspicious [of our motives], yet I fear that the rule of the uncle
[considered] infamous [by a single person], because the nephews
still live, may deter him from accepting [our petition]. He is a
[man] replete with honor: the Duke wishes to remain far from the
turbid evils of the [slighest] reproach. [After his returning
servant has whispered in his ear.] The Protector denies access
[to himself], to my citizens, and will remain suspicious of so
great a crowd unless he first hears what the cause of [our] coming
may be. [To the messenger.] Tell [him] a great band of nobles
and the Mayor surrounded by many a citizen [would] humbly consult
[him]. A domestic evil troubles [us] which [this] solicitous band
will entrust to his ears alone. But let us humbly entreat Gloucester
ourselves. We shall entreat the reluctant one with a prayer to
the divine will so that the rightful heir may take the sceptre of
the kingdom. But, now, behold the pious Prince surrounded by
two bishops appears in the upper part of [his] home. Oh, fortunately,
the Duke considers things only divine.

Citizens [Aside]. O [his] stubborn impudence striving [to fool us] with
  [this] deceit, when he mocks [our intelligence] with this foreign
  outward appearance. Secure he fears nothing, and [lit, but] thinks
  that others do not recognize [his] concealed evil, but [lit. and]
  [his] villainy deceives [only] himself.

[ACT III. Scene ii.]

Duke of Buckingham.   Duke of Gloucester.   Chorus of Citizens.

[Buckingham.]   [This] profuse crowd of citizens asks for you.   Remain present,

illustrious one, so that they [lit. it] might be permitted to speak

to your excellency about a grave matter.   They bring good things

unknown to the kingdom [before, and] great honor to you.   They

[lit. it] do not dare to speak out their pious charges, however,

unless you declare by your own voice that it is permissible.

Gloucester.   Whatever [their] mind[s] have bade [them to speak], it will

always be permissible [for them] to speak.   It pleases [me] to

know the public resolutions of the citizens.

Buckingham.   For too long a time the people have steadfastly endured

tyranny.   They [now] rejoice that these times in which they might

free themselves from their former fear have dawned at last, and that

there may [now] be a pleasant security in their lives.   Therefore,

inasmuch as an entire band of citizens has [already] assembled

[to talk] about the public affairs and has discussed the state

of the kingdom, [the citizens] have sanctioned by [their] sacred

commands that you as sole heir [should] claim the title of royal

authority.   Nor will the sceptre tolerate the impure offspring of

[your] brother [anymore] than Venus [i.e. carnal love] will check

the injustices of his mother.   Now, therefore, a numerous crowd

of citizens is here so that humbly, by a public acclamation, it

may beg very much that you may deliver the citizens from [their]

former fear and [so that] you may direct by [your] wise management

the kingdom bound [to you].

Gloucester.   Although I know how much the citizens have formed true [conclu-

sions concerning Edward's children], yet I have formerly reverenced

the shades of my brother. Neither will I foolishly be cruel an

uncle to my nephews, nor will an enraged populace agitate [me]

with [their] savage speeches because I seek the throne of my

brother; nor will foreign nations likewise become provoked by [my]

infamies if I, [their] uncle, will [not] wickedly take the kingdom

from my own nephews by frauds, or if I will [not] receive the

dubious sceptre of the related house.[87] Rather I will remain safe

from the evils of envy; nor does a blind seeking [for rule] strike

my mind. The offices of my related sceptre [i.e. of my protectorship

weighs [me] down sufficiently. Yet, however, there is no shame in

your speaking to me [about this matter]; rather my love [for you]

urges [me] to thank [you], and, I implore, may you not now reverence

my nephew less, the greater [part] of whose power I privately bear.

Although he [is] a boy who knows little about ruling, yet he is

an aid to my labors. The boy will [soon be able to] protect

adequately the honor of a kingdom which no one denies has recently

been in [much] greater repute [than formerly]. After the great

protectorship of the realm was assigned [to me], the ancient hate[s]

ceased; [all] menaces were smashed; hatreds, driven away, have

languished, partly due to [my] good policies [lit. foresight], but

[even] more to the good-will of the greatest God. [O] best of

men, in no way condemn the sceptre of the King. It is pledged

[by me] that the name of subject satisfy me.

---

[87]That these statements should be read negatively is apparent from the
chronicles. See Hall, p. 373; More, p. 446; and Hol., p. 395.

Buckingham.   Grant, o famous Duke, that [I] speak a few words [to you]
again. The subjects will not permit [your] nephews to rule; the
highest nobles will forbid [it]; the untaught mass[es] will forbid
[it]. They [all] wish to purge the kingdom of [its] adulterous
stain. But if you firmly do not want [your] just sceptre of rule,
yet they hope at least that [some other] nobleman who may rejoice
in the respect paid to the royal splendor can be swayed by their
entreaty. Therefore, speak so that they may hear what you have
decided concerning [these] affairs.

Gloucester.   Because they begrudge the paternal kingdom to the children,
I, who honor the shades of [my] dead brother, am grieved. Would
that they could permit the rule to the nephews! But no one can
rule a hostile people. Because I see that [they] have decided
these things by common consent, and [because] they will take the
kingdom from [my] bastard nephews [anyway], I, within [my] right
[as] sole heir of the kingdom, claim that I am the only remaining
son of [my] father. Since it has [always] been necessary [for me]
to yield to my citizens, I will submit to [your] wishes: Behold,
I demand the kingdom which is my due. I esteem greater the prince
[who has been] created by the wishes of [his] subjects. We accept
the [full] care of England and also of France. [As] King I claim
the two [noble] kingdoms. [As] Prince I shall sacredly direct
the government of England. The [present] peace of the citizens
prompts [even] more peaceful [measures]. Then, a conquered France
will become acquainted with our reins. This subjugation [of France]
will enrich the honor of England, the glory of which, if I miserably
fail to seek, would that the [fatal] sisters break [our] perfidious
threads [of life].

Chorus. King Richard! King Richard! King Richard! [Aside.] [Every] cruel villainy seeks the pretext of virtue, [and every] horrible crime is ashamed of its own appearance. Alas, who ignorantly does not know about the secret deceits and about the thousand stratagems of the uncle? Who does not see that the kingdom of [his] brother was promised to him by fraud before [we came here]. He publicly refused the kingdom which he sought by frauds; [his] feigned sanctity disapproved of the sceptre [which he] sought: just as a bishop twice refuses to be consecrated who still perhaps desires strongly the sacred things worthy of reverence,[88] so [too] the King, impelled by his own will, will bear the sceptre snatched from the boys, but [still] it is more fitting that the lower classes view such great tragic scenes. Whatever pleases a king is permitted [to him]: a king is measured according to his wishes and not by his pious laws. Frequently it is well not to know what you nevertheless [cannot help to] know.[89]

---

[88]"For at the consecracion of a bishoppe, euery manne perceiueth by paiment of his bulles that he entendeth to be one, yet when he is twise asked whether he will be a bishop, he must twice say nay, and at the third tyme take it vpon him as compelled thereto by his awne will" (Hall, p. 374). See also More, p. 447; and Hol., p. 398.

[89]Compare with Hall: "And in a stage plaie, the people knowe right well that he that plaieth the sowdaine, is percase a souter, yet yf one of acquaintaunce perchaunce of litle nurture should call him by his name while he standeth in his maiestie one of his tourmentours might fortune breke his hed for marying the play. And so they [i.e. the people in reference to Richard's acceptance of the crown] saied, these matters be kynges games, as it were staige playes, . . . in which poore men bee but lookers on, and they that wise be, will medle no ferther, for they that steppe vp with them when they cannot play their partes, they disorder the plaie and do theim selues no good" (p. 374). See also More, pp. 447-448; and Hol., p. 396.

ACT IV. [Scene i.][90]

Doctor Shaw. A Citizen, friend [of Shaw].

Citizen.   Why do you wretchedly move in a daze with so sluggish a pace,

and why does your hesitating foot hold itself in uncertainty even

though you wish to move [your] advanced body backwards. Your

mind is perplexed, and you are putting forth an unwilling step.

What sad deliberation has tormented [you] for a long time? And

do you not find [its] limit? Why do you madly fly the face[s] of

the citizens? Conquer whatever obstructs [you]; set your mind

free and restore yourself to your [former] self.

Shaw.   My mind, alas, filled with crime flees itself. [My] heart

burdened with its evils refuses to remain quiet, and the trembling

of my guilty mind [and my] grief rage [inside me]. [My] mind cannot

expel [its] poison, and the cruel consciousness of my crime stings

[me]. What, [o] what demon, hostile to me, compelled [me] to defile

the marriage [lit. bed] of King Edward with [my charges of] pollution?

Woe to me! Edward, I have betrayed your sons, and I have proclaimed

[them] bastards [lit. adulterous] by [my] evil speech. Richard

possesses your crown by my command. Woe to me! I have defiled

your sons by my voice. I have mixed sacred things with lies, and

I have defiled the Scriptures with [my] foolish mouth.

---

[90]For Legge's inclusion of this scene, and for its approach to genuine
emotional expression, this scene is worth study in any assessment of Legge's
dramatic abilities, first because he departs from his usual method of consecu-
tively following Hall paragraph by paragraph (here he backtracks eight pages);
secondly because the scene is essentially original, Hall providing only the
slightest basis for it: ". . . after [the sermon was] once ended, the preacher
got hym home and neuer after durst loke out for shame but kept him out of
sighte as an owle and when he asked any of his olde friendes, what the people
talked of him, although that his awne conscience well shewed hym that they
talked no good, yet when the other answered hym, that there was in euery mannes
mouthe of hym much shame spoken it so strake him that in a few dayes after he
withered awaie" (p. 368). See also More, p. 439; and Hol., p. 390.

Citizen.   Why do you hostilely burden yourself with [such] heavy

punishments? A nourished grief gathers other torches [i.e. other

things that kindle grief] and renews a harsh evil unwilling to be

cursed. A prudent grief will seize restraints [lit. bridles] and

[hence] will extinguish [itself]. He overcomes [his] grief who

wants to free [himself] from [it] and strives to cure the perfidious

evil.

Shaw.   [My] rash mind flies [anyone] advising [it]; [then] it returns

immediately repeating the advice [which it has] received in vain;

[its] evil urges [it] to follow [its] worse [advices]; it fears

virtue. Inimical grief increases itself and [constantly] renews

[its] weakened strength. [My] crime will never cease to punish

me [lit. never cease unto my punishments]. Never does nocturnal

rest, nor does a deep sleep dissolve [my] cares. At night I call

for the day; I ask for the night during the day. I fly from myself

always; [my] crime I cannot [fly].

Citizen.   Can you not cure [this] evil?

Shaw.   If I can die.

Citizen.   But shame, although great, can be removed.

Shaw.   Not if a vestige of the shameful disgrace always cleaves [to

the person].

Citizen.   Can only death remove the accursed stain?

Shaw.   A polluted life does not know how to put off [its] crime.

Citizen.   But [even] the late beckonings [of God] will spare the penitent

[man].

Shaw.   The crime effected earlier [will be] the mother of a new crime.

Citizen.   Will you who fear a wound cease from healing [it]?

Shaw.   You cannot heal a grave wound easily.

Citizen.   Will he who has injured no one not spare himself?

Shaw.   First, accuse yourself that [it was] your crime alone.

Citizen.   Absolve yourself, you who decide [when a person] has been
             sufficiently punished.[91]

Shaw.   No one can sufficiently punish [my] terrible crime.

Citizen.   [Like] a harsh judge you punish [your] crime too severely.

Shaw.   Unless they [lit. it] sting bitterly, horrible wounds are
             scorned.

Citizen.   While you are considering [your] harsh [deeds], you have no
             care at all for the culprit.

Shaw.   Grief is the medicine of grief: it does know how not to
             restrain itself. Heaven has seen [my] wicked crime, and [even]
             the inconstant earth has been aware of [my] great shame. The
             shameful rule of [my] mind has made me so unlike my [true] self
             that I fly nothing more than myself, and I have been made an
             unhappy deserter of myself that [lit. and] [my] careworn mind
             prays for a long-lasting separation from [my] body: he kills [me]
             who bids [me] live; he gives [me] life who bids [me] die: what
             displeases, alone can please [me]. What are worthless men saying
             about me?

Citizen.   They accuse you [of being] guilty of a wicked crime.

Shaw.   But what commotion of citizens gathers in this place?

Citizen.   When Prince Gloucester began to rule at the command of the
             citizens, [this] pious King desired to speak first to his subjects

---

[91]As a priest, Shaw has often decided the penance or punishment a person
must pay to atone for his crimes.

from that place where the law is customarily spoken to Englishmen
by a living voice. Now, therefore, [the crowd] gathers at Westminist⊕
palace so that [its] pious King may give orders to those experienced
in legal matters [i.e. to judges] lest [someone with] a perverse
mind should corrupt the menaces of the laws. The unhappy [Shaw]
has departed: he cannot stand the faces of the citizens. I will
relate the words of the Prince to him [later].

[ACT IV. Scene ii.]⁹²

Duke of Gloucester.

[Gloucester.] It has [always] been pleasing [to me] that [this place], given
over to the seats of justice and to this awe-inspiring tribunal of
Minos, ⁹³ first encircled the head [of a king] with a glittering
[crown of] gold, and [first] ruled the citizens of [our] country
with just law. A king ought to have [great] care for this best
of all places so that Law, the strongest pillar of cities, may rule
powerfully on an equal basis with the Parliament. It is not at all
fitting that fear [should] dominate your heart[s], the high birth
of which has become clear by your titles of honor. Wrath not
morally blind [i.e. justifiable anger] rules, not knowing how to
be subdued. Now [every] soldier will remove [his] sword from [his]
weary side. All will be pleased to join in a bond of love, nor will
the despised offspring [of Edward] overthrow [their] uncle. I
commend you, fathers, learned in ancient laws, who uphold the state

---

⁹²The basis for this scene is not found in Hall, nor in More's English
History of Richard the Third. It is found in More's Historia Richardi Regis
Tertii (fol. 56ʳ⁻ᵛ) and is translated and included by Rastell in his edition
of More's Richard the Third, p. 448. See also Hol., p. 397.

⁹³Minos, a mythical king of Crete, was the reputed framer of the oldest
Cretan constitution. In Homer (Od. xi, 568), Odysseus sees him in Hades with
a golden sceptre in his hand, judging the shades.

by [your] laws lest a torn England be weakened by civil strife
[lit. by mutual contentions]. I shall follow you with full respect.
And even though [some] citizens who are sustained by their base
deceits may delight in [your] slow manner of coming to a decision
[lit. your weary way of thinking], neither will a case argued
before a judge press you closely, nor will wild battles resound
with a blast of trumpets, for the [present] prosperous affairs will
overthrow [all] discords. From this cause [i.e. from the recent
discords], a false mind has threatened [the citizens] from behind
an innocent face; from this cause, every evil has flowed to the
citizens. Love, piety, faith will settle these disturbances. A
happy England will adhere to these bonds [of friendship] which
neither domestic rage may break, nor the strength of [our]
enemies can impair. May every memory of the recent hatred perish!
Guard, set free to me at once Fogg who suppliantly lies in sanctuary
in fear of us! May there be an end of wrath, and may rage [no longer]
hurl forth [its] menaces. My anxious mind will labor with a very
great impulse to be beheld by [my] subjects in a kindly aspect. O
how I wish [that] virtue, which has never tried deceits, might
flourish [again in this realm]! May the divine will of the gods be
adverse to me if my tongue, the mediator of [my] mind, deceives [you]!
[To Fogg, who has been brought in from sanctuary.] Do not fear, Fogg!
Stand close by [me]. Let us unite [our] minds; take this pledge of
[my] faith. Join [my] right hand and love me in turn [as I do you].

ACT V. [Scene i.]

Stranger. Citizen.

[Stranger.]   You have told [me] of the domestic evil, horrible [and] grave.
By how many storms will the immense might of the kingdom, which
attracts much envy [lit. capable of envy], be agitated? Although
subdued [many times before], it [i.e. domestic evil] still does
not believe that [it] could be [completely] subdued. The hunger
for rule will [always] incite severe storms. [And] when the blind
desire of a prince has shaken [a kingdom], how many ruins of cities
have been spread forth! [Many] a severe hurricane has beaten upon
a gentle ship as if it were sailing through a whirlpool in the
salted sea, and has horribly churned the stirred up sea with [its]
blast (when it splits the sides [of the ship], it doubles [its]
menace): such a violent change will crush [it] at once. Tell [me],
I pray, why does many a citizen gather here and observe the nearby
places with [his] eyes? Dazed, [each one] looks constantly at the
splendid hall [lit. the theatres for the coronation], and all kinds
of [rich] things are lying [there] on shining carpets, and the royal
throne of a prince shines forth brightly [there].

Citizen.   [O] stranger, faithful to me, King Richard is being crowned,
whose inheritance of the title has been approved by mutual agreement.

Stranger.   An uncertain rumor had formerly spread this [news abroad].

Citizen.   This place is given over to [those] very great assemblies.
The time [for the crowning] is imminent.

379

Stranger. When a pious king is created, things [will be] good: if a
worse [king is created], things [will be] bad. If the king is
good, [there will be] security for the citizens: if the king is
evil, [there will be] a plague on the state.

Citizen. The uncle, who was born of the highest royal stock, [as]
Protector took into his faithful charge [his] two princely nephews.
Lo, the King himself was created by the very highest assembly of
England.

Stranger. Where [are] the two princes? Is it [not] a crime that the
uncle rules while these [two] are alive?

Citizen. [His] thirst for power has done this! They suffer the loss
of [their] kingdom in the cell of a dark prison.

Stranger. O [such] villainy!

Citizen. But yet [it is the villainy] of a Prince.

Stranger. This is [even] more infamous.

Citizen. Also, because of the person exercising authority.

Stranger. Piety befits a king, nor is it permissible to procure a
kingdom at an impious price.

Citizen. Yet, kingdoms [obtained] in any way at all may still continue
prosperously.

Stranger. Property procured evilly will never prosper for long.

Citizen. It is enough to rule [even] briefly.

Stranger. Evil [is] immediately doubled for the fall [from power]. The
joy [of ruling] is brief, the labor of ruling heavy.

Citizen. Inasmuch as one is pleased with ruling, [his] labor is lessened.

Stranger. [All] the more he will increase the hatred [of himself].

Citizen. This is subdued through fear [of him].

Stranger.   [It is subdued] preferably through loyalty [to him].

Citizen.   Yea, rather, remove [your] great animosities [toward our King]! It is a serious thing to asperse [our] Prince with harsh words, and at once he will order those suspicious of him to be killed. Now restrain [your] words! It is fitting to comply with the condition of the times. Recently he saluted those [people] along the way very mildly. A mind guilty of evil will [hardly] offer itself [to public view] and hardly teaches a king [such a] humble appearance. Then, too, he has liberated the Cardinal from [his] bonds, and has set Stanley free from prison, whose son of the Lancastrian [party] he feared lest he should avenge the cruel bonds of [his] father. But he ordered the Duke of Buckingham to keep the Bishop of Ely locked up in [his] home. But the blast of trumpets sounds the arrival of the King. Let us watch the courtiers and the dukes, the marquis [and] the nobles, glittering in [their] chaplets, proceed [along the way].

Stranger.   Tell [me], citizen, what do the glittering gilt spurs signify which the courtier carries in his hand?

Citizen.   These are the signs of strength in battle.

Stranger.   What [does] the staff [signify]?

Citizen.   It was St. Edward [the Confessor's]. They carry it now in his memory.

Stranger.   But what does sword without a point, which the bare-headed [man] carries, indicate?

Citizen.   Mercy.

Stranger.   What [is the meaning of] the golden spike [i.e. mace]?

Citizen.   [It stands for] the office of the Constable of England. The

Master of Knights carries this in [any] public assembly.

Stranger.   Why are two shining swords carried, [one] on right of the

Prince and [one] on [his] left too?

Citizen.   They are [his] weapons of justice: they punish with a healing

wound the crime[s] of the clergy and of the laity too.

Stranger.   Two bare swords with no point[s] are carried.

Citizen.[94]

Stranger.   What do the sceptres mean?

Citizen.   Peace.

Stranger.   What [is the meaning of] the globe upon which a cross is

raised?

Citizen.   Monarchy.

Stranger.   Behold, another [man] carries a shining and great sword placed

in a scabbard of very great art.

Citizen.   [This] two-edged sword represents the very great worth of the

highest estate.

Stranger.   But tell [me] who, tinged with red dye and shining with great

splendor as if with the glittering rays [of the sun], holds the

middle place [in this group of three].

Citizen.   That one is the chief of his own order of herald[s], and [goes]

by the name of King [of the Heralds] himself.

Stranger.   What does the white staff of the Duke [of Buckingham] carry

before him?

---

[94]All the manuscripts leave a blank space here for the Citizen's reply.
The chronicles offer no help. More omits the coronation procession entirely,
and neither Hall (p. 375) nor Holinshed (p. 399) mentions the "two" pointless
swords. They do mention the curtana, the sword of mercy, which has already
been referred to in lines 64-65 of this scene.

Citizen.   He carries this like the highest canopies of England.[95]

Stranger.   What does the white dove of the Queen denote?

Citizen.   The bird, not at all harmful, denotes innocence.

[After they have thus declared what everything means, let the singers, placed on the top of some of the houses, sing. In the meantime, let such ceremonies be used for the coronation as the chronicle presents, and afterwards let all depart in the following order.

The Show of the Coronation

First trumpets and heralds. Then singing men, priests in surplices and gray amices or silk hoods, bishops in [their] rochets and chimers, and finally the Cardinal. Then noblemen, lords, earls, dukes. Then gilt spurs, carried by the Earl of Huntington. Then St. Edward's staff, carried by the Earl of Bedford. Then the pointless, unsheathed sword, [carried] by the hatless Earl of Northumberland. Then the Great Mace, [carried] by Lord Stanley. Then two unsheathed swords, [one carried] by the Earl of Kent, [the other] by Lord Lovel. Then the Great Sceptre, [carried] by the Duke of Suffolk. Then the globe with the cross [on top, carried] by the Earl of Lincoln. Then the Sword of Estate [carried] in a rich scabbard by the Earl of Surrey. Then three [men] together, the King of Heralds, with the Mason of London, [carrying] a mace, on his left, and a gentleman usher on his right. Then the King's crown, carried by the Duke of Norfolk. Then the King, under a canopy, between two bishops. Then the Duke of Buckingham, [carrying] a white staff, holding up the King's train. Then lords and gentlemen before the Queen. Then the Queen's sceptre. Then the white dove on a white rod. Then the Queen's crown. Then the Queen with a circlet of   on her head under a canopy with four bells hanging on it, and one lady bearing up her train. Then a troop of ladies. Then knights, esquires, gentlemen, and Tipstaffs.]

[During the solemnity of the coronation, let the following song be sung to instruments:

The noble offspring of a King

possesses the things befitting a ruler.

The yellow crown encircles

the illustrious head of [our] Prince.

Now let us joyfully celebrate [our] Prince

in song with a harmonious chorus.

Dishonor oppressed the kingdom.

The desire of King [Edward] has defiled [the kingdom].]

---

[95]The Duke of Buckingham is following Richard, holding up his train on a white staff to form a canopy. See Hall, p. 375; and Hol., p. 399.

THIRD PART

Argument.

Fury.

Why do you, Fury, ponder [your] secret thoughts, and exhale [your]
inmost threats, and [yet] not dispatch [your] torches of vengeance?
[First,] complete the Gloucestrian evil. Hereafter, [o] hated
King, boast of your Gloucestrian [ancestry] and sceptre, [96] the
reward of [your] cruel destruction, and ponder the doubtful fears
of [your] brother's realm. Let the fickle mob, amazed, gaze at
[your] becoming features of [your father, the Duke of] York and
wonder at [your] excellent worth. Why do you make [even] slight
delays? Be completely wretched, and let [your] brief evil rage
further. Venture the crime which [your] cruel mind considers,
and let the worst crime of a king harass the kingdom. [Your]
hands are [lit. were] not yet wet with the slaughter of [your]
blood-relations (your royal nephews are not yet strangled) but
[lit. and] [yet] seek in vain the incestuous marriage beds of [your]
niece. Fill the house of your father with crimes. Then, Fury,
let Buckingham learn how to rage. Smite tyranny, [Buckingham]!
Take the sceptre if you can, but you cannot. Behold, Richmond comes!
The exile comes! He claims the promised kingdom and the marriage
beds of the kingdom sworn [to him] earlier. Come! let swords be
drawn; mingle hatreds, deaths and dire destruction, [and then] put

---

[96]Soon after his coronation, Richard visited the city of Gloucester, the
center of his strength, to show himself to the people "in his newe honour."
See Hall, p. 377; More, p. 449; and Hol., p. 401.

an end to the contentions. Lo, let the exile reign, and do not

let King [Richard] obtain a place of exile, and, Henry, let Richard

fall by your hand. [When] enough has been done, then I, Fury,

will spare Britain, and hereafter will seek new abodes for myself.

Dramatis Personae

King Richard	Duke of Norfolk
Duke of Buckingham	Rice ap Thomas
Queen Elizabeth	Messenger
Oldest daughter of Edward	Two women
Maid [to the Queen]	An old woman
Bishop of Ely	Hungerford
Brackenbury, Constable of the Tower	Burchier

knights (Hungerford, Burchier)

Tyrrel, a noble	Soldier
Lewis, a doctor	Lord Stanley
Queen Anne, wife of Richard	Duke Strange, son of Stanley
First messenger	Captain
Second messenger	Bray, servant of the Countess of Richmond
Third messenger	Dighton, a murderer (a big sloven)
Fourth messenger	
Fifth messenger	Mutes
Lord Lovel	The young King and his brother
Catesby	lying dead on a bed.
Henry, Earl of Richmond	The four daughters of King Edward.
Earl of Oxford	Soldiers, unarmed and armed.

ACT I. [Scene i.]

Brackenbury, a knight. Tyrrel.

[Brackenbury] [Alone]. O gracious ruler of the heavens and you who govern
the honor [here] on earth, spare Brackenbury. Mercifully end the
madness of [our] cruel Prince, and deliver [my] certain faith from
a harsh punishment. The thirst for power never ceases to shudder
with fright, nor is mad [lit. sick] ambition ever free from cares.
Cruel Richard rages in fear for [his] kingdom; he holds [his]
unjust sceptre in [his] trembling hand, and suspects new plots
against himself. When the King, with a great troop accompanying
[him], was visiting his native Gloucester [since he was] striving
for [popular] favor, and [while] thinking about the uncertain
jests of fate and of how easily unjust power falls under attack,
and fearing the extremely insecure status of [his] rule while [his]
nephew breathed in earthly air; he, [their] cruel uncle, desire[d]
that [his] two nephews [lit. twin nephew] [might] immediately give
up [their] breath to their own grief, and that the [two] boys
[might] quench [his] fear for [his] rule with their very own blood.
Recently John Green gave to me letters entrusted [to him] by the
King, intent upon [these] accursed [plans]. He ordered [me] to
effect the sad destruction of the princes, and to seize unmercifully
the princes whom I, the Constable of the Tower, hold in bondage.
Only Brackenbury can sacrifice your sons, Edward; only he [can]
kill your offspring. I shall willingly follow the orders of the
King; resolutely I shall serve you, Richard. But, oh, [my] piety
forbids [me] to kill the offspring of [your] brother. The wretched

[boys] lie within a dirty cell, and only a murderer will minister to [my] captives. O the horrible villainy of the Prince, [how] foul [and] cruel! [My] hesitating mind is turned about between fear and hope, and confusion scourges [my] divided mind. Now I am afraid of the King's threats. [My own] mind, sufficiently well known to me, [and] guilty of nothing, forbids me to fear. I shall follow wherever the fates prick [it]. What, Richard, will you prepare against your [loyal] subject? What will you cruelly breathe forth [against him]? What will you cruelly consider [doing]? I have been pious. I have never defiled my hands with the blood of kings. What will you accuse [me] of? I have kept [my] faith [to you]. Are you now ready to punish the immense good [I have done you]? I call to witness the majesty of the gods [that] I have been innocent, [that] I have been guiltless. Does [your] rule alone not fear a stain? Why do you, persevering virtue [lit. modesty], fly from the palace and seek the lowly cottage? Whoever will live piously will desert the palace. Splendor shining too brightly impedes the pious light of a happy fate, and [my] beaten mind is impinged upon [by the King]. But [even] if the fates keep me [from committing the crime], yet, Edward, I (wretchedly struck through at once by a sword) will come to you [as] a sad messenger of the slaughter of your children. But why does Tyrrel fly here from the King? Do we die or not? Alas, [my] heart quakes with fear. What, what harsh punishment has he prepared for my loyalty? I shall willingly accept whatever it is, even though I am ruined.

Tyrrel [To himself while approaching]. [O] listless mind, why do you hesitate
            to execute the orders of the King and [why] do you fashion foolish
            fears for yourself? He will not fear lightly who thinks sadly
            [about the plan to kill the princes]. Why Tyrrel, do you fear
            to gratify the Prince? The King commands [the murder]: It will
            be a guiltless necessity. You will free an anxious Richard from
            [his] great care, and the vast rewards of the King will bless you.
            The House of York will be happy with its own Prince [on the throne],
            and [hence] let the royal offspring cast out [their] inimical
            spirit[s]. Who will foolishly want to fight for dead [princes],
            or who will insanely consider defending the dead body of the princes?
            Whatever must be ventured will be [ventured]. Anxious modesty
            [i.e. scrupulousness] is a poor minister for a king [to have].
            [Aloud, to Brackenbury.] Will the honor of Brackenbury, a knight,
            continue loyal to [lit. live in the company of] the family of
            [their] parent, King [Edward]?

Brackenbury.   It will delay [i.e. continue loyal to Edward's children] until
            the last day of [my] life.

Tyrrel.   Do you not fear at all the dreadful ire of the Prince?

Brackenbury.   I shall willingly follow wherever the fates call me.

Tyrrel.   Is it fitting [or not] to execute the commands of the King?

Brackenbury.   It is never fitting for the King to command the worst of [all]
            evils.

Tyrrel.   Is it right that they live whom the Prince hates?

Brackenbury.   [It is] wrong to hate those whom all love.

Tyrrel.   Do you not consider it right that the Prince is distressed
            with fear for [his] authority?

Brackenbury.   I deem [it] a crime to heal a wound with a crime.

Tyrrel.   [Then] a kingdom can not be stable for those living.

Brackenbury.   It [i.e. a stable kingdom] will be hated by those dead.

Tyrrel.   The first precept of ruling is that you be able to endure hatred.

Brackenbury.   Disaster, which often passes by, will on some [future] occasion crush [us].

Tyrrel.   He does not wish to rule who fears to be hated.

Brackenbury.   Hated rulers are never kept for long.

Tyrrel.   Does it concern you [whether] the boy lives or dies?

Brackenbury.   Little, except that he is not killed by me as executioner.

Tyrrel.   Why does your hand fear the feeble boys?

Brackenbury.   I, who do not fear war [lit. camps], still dread crime.

Tyrrel.   [Why] will you, forgetful of the King, pay [him] this return [for his favors to you]?

Brackenbury.   Because I will pay no return by [lit. in] [committing] a crime.

Tyrrel.   Do you not fear at all the anger of a raging Prince?

Brackenbury.   A noble mind will never give in to terror.

Tyrrel.   But the savage King threatens you with many things. Lo, a late Phoebus [i.e. the evening sun] is joined to the deep sea and leaves a bare sky which must be illumined by [his] sister [Diana, the moon]; therefore, take to yourself the King's letters so that you may immediately entrust the keys of the jail to me so that I may on this night execute the King's commands.

[ACT I. Scene ii.]

Brackenbury. Tyrrel. John Dighton.

[Brackenbury] [Alone]. O blind desire for ruling, o too cruel villainy of a raging King, o infamous sceptre of the uncle which grows wet with the blood of his own [family]! Alas, o noble boys, the hands of

a close relative will destroy you. They [i.e. Dighton, Forest,

and Tyrrel] will crush [my] wards, and only your blood can afford

[you] an enemy. After the boy knew about [his] lost kingdom, and

that [his] uncle had taken the seized sceptre, bedewing [his]

cheeks with tears and drawing sighs from [his] inmost heart, the

unfortunate [boy] spoke thus: "I care nothing for the kingdom;

I pray for my life lest [my] uncle take this [from me]." Alas,

what Caucasian or hard-hearted Judas can spare [his] tears? Hereafter,

it will never please the wretched [Prince] to dress [lit. adorn]

himself [carefully]: [his] clothing will flow free of any knot

[lit. free with no limit].[97] The sad image of the lamenting

Prince will always wander before my eyes, nor will the lament of

the Prince [ever] cease to beat against [my] melancholy heart.

But Tyrrel returns [his] unhappy step to this place.

Tyrrel.   The rude Dighton and the murderer Forest are busy within with

their loyal office of murder. I shall wait [here] while they complete

the death of the princes.

Brackenbury.   Has each boy submitted to [his] hostile fate?

Tyrrel.   They are still living; but, [the murderers] are getting ready

to kill them [lit. are readying death for them].

Brackenbury.   Cannot the King's wrath be placated in [any] other way?

Tyrrel.   Fear, not anger, makes the King bloody.

---

[97] When the Prince learned that ". . . he should not reigne, but his vncle
should haue the croune. . . [he] beganne to sighe and sayd: Alas I would myne
vncle would let me haue my life although I lese my kyngedome. . . . After whiche
tyme, the prince neuer tyed his pointes, nor any thyng roughte of hym selfe. . ."
(Hall, p. 378). See also More, p. 450; and Hol., pp. 401-402.

Brackenbury.　Tell [me], what did the King say [lit. with what speech did
the King offer a response] when Green had brought back to him
such a message, [namely] that the princes would never be slain by
my sword?

Tyrrel.　　　When [lit. as] he first learned about these things, he was
at once plagued by a great stupor; blood deserted his lips, and
on the spot he was entirely pale, like the ashes of a dead man.
He breathed out sighs from the depths of [his] lungs, and, striking
the side nearest to [his] unsteady heart, he immediately left [his]
royal throne; furiously he paced [up and down] with steps violently
set in motion, shaking his head, and he harshly bellowed deep
within himself in [his] silent breast where [his] blood, as if poured
anew red hot from a furnace, parched [his] fervid cheeks;
and he turned totally red (just as if he had been immersed in a
reddish-purple sea or annointed with vermilion). [His] fiery eyes
glowed with a savage look; [his] hair bristled, with the hair
standing upright, just as if Orestes had been inflamed [again] by
these torments [lit. fire-brands]; for, like wraths aroused by
[lit. concerning] the slaughter of their own [kinsmen] pricked both
[men]. Yet they are different from one [another]: the one was
harassed by the shade of his dead mother, but the other by [his]
grave fear of [his] living nephews; and [hence his] violent anger
was cruelly kindled against you. On the night on which the King
learned of your answers, he groaned in the presence of [his] secret
page [lit. his servant of silent office], and broke forth mournfully
in these sounds: "Oh, what sane [man] will give any trust to anyone?
Where [is there] a grateful soul or where has devotion been banished?

It lies hidden, leaving the earth polluted with villainy. And

now it is not possible to confide in any men [at all]. Like a

parent, I nourished those sons whom I thought would be most loyal

to me if ever a sad necessity [should] burden [me]. These desert

me, [their] parent; they violate [their] faith, and they will

venture absolutely nothing at my commands." Immediately the page

standing by the King answered: "But, stretched out in a nearby

bed a man lies (now I dare to say this boldly): this man would

not refuse to undertake at any time that which might be extremely

difficult, provided that this [thing] be pleasing to you." Then,

when the King asked him who it was, he said [it was] I. Immediately

he hastened to [my] bed where he struck me and my brother who were

asleep [lit. given up to the bed]; then the King said jokingly:

"Does it please you to put yourselves in bed so early?" Then he

called me apart and made known [to me] the cruel plan of his

mind concerning the speedy and secret death of the princes. Considering

who advised [this], besides what I myself should become [by winning

the favor of the King], and not considering the lamentations of the

King [at all], I then willingly offered my aid to the King voluntarily.

Therefore, in the early morning, he gave me letters addressed to you

which I should deliver by my own hand, and he ordered that you

surrender to me the keys of [this] lofty Tower so that I might

quickly execute the mandate of the King, faithfully entrusted to me

in the night.

Dighton.   Each lifeless boy is suffocated.

Brackenbury.   Woe to me! A vague horror [i.e. a running shiver] runs through

        [my] limbs.

Tyrrel.   By what kind of death have the small boys been slain?

Dighton.　　　　When the wandering star [i.e. the moon] had brightened the

sad heavens, and the ever-watchful cock had announced the evening

shadows, lo, as soon as both nephew[s] were lying in bed, and

[as soon as] the two boys [lit. the twin boy] had received [their]

sweet sleep, we [i.e. Dighton and Forest] ourselves entered [their]

room with a secret step, and quickly covered the brothers in [their]

mattresses [and pillows]. We pressed down upon [them] rolled up

[in their mattresses] with very great force. Inasmuch as [their]

mouths were stopped up by the downy pillow[s], and the compressed

couches prevented [their] outcry, soon both, [their] breath having

been taken away, were suffocated because there was no way accessible

for [their] breathing. Lo, both slain [ones] lie prostrate on the

bed.

Brackenbury.　　Do I see the livid bodies of the Princes? Alas, their bed

is now defiled with their youthful slaughter. What harsh countenance

will refuse tears for [these] evils? Woe to me! They lie slain by

the fraud of [their] uncle. What [man] of Colchis, what nation

bordering the Caspian sea, what Scythian of [that] dark abode will

[even] dare these things? Busiris never stained your altars with

youthful blood, nor did Diomedes [ever] give small limbs to be

eaten by [his] flocks.[98]

Tyrrel.　　　　It is well [done]! Now, Richard, hold securely the throne of

[your] brother and take those things befitting a ruler [i.e. the

appurtenances of office]. Bury [them] beneath the bottom step of

_____

[98]Colchis and Scythia are located near the Caspian Sea, a region considered
particularly uncivilized and savage in ancient times. Both Busiris and Diomedes
fed the flesh of men to their horses.

the gloomy prison. Let a ditch sufficiently deep conceal the
brothers, and let them be buried at once, under a rocky mound.
Spread vague rumors, concerning the death here and there, [namely]
that [one] sister of the [fatal] three spontaneously destroyed
[their] natural terms of life. Fabricate that the princes died by
sudden death. These are the orders of the King. Attend to [them]
carefully. Now take your keys, stubborn Brackenbury!

Brackenbury.   O the cruel inhumanity of our age, o cruel heart of the King,
o barbarous mind, savagely uprooting the secure laws of nature, you
have, Procrustian monster, you have sacrificed the innocent
princes, the two guiltless boys! O earth, heaven and gloomy realm
of Tartar, will you look upon [such a] wicked crime? Will you,
Saturn, fear-inspiring with your three-pronged thunderbolt[s], endure
such great wickedness? Radiant Titan, immerse your gleaming head
entirely in Acheron's [waters], and let the day die to the world.
Who has [ever] been so dangerous an enemy to his own family that he
[would]make bloody [his] hand with youthful slaughter? Now, indeed,
Nero, wet with [the blood of] his maternal crime has become virtuous.
Submit impious Pelops: this crime [is] greater [than yours]: Only
Medea has sacrificed young children.[99] It has always been shameful
to slay a citizen [by cutting his throat] [and] exceedingly abhominable
to deprive a woman of light [i.e. to blind a woman], but [it is an
extremely horrible crime to deprive innocent, small infants (who
because of their age do not know what life is) of life. Why [should]

[99]Nero, having killed his mother Agrippina his brothers, his wife Octavia
is teacher Seneca, became a symbol for all tyrants after him. Pelops, with the
id of Myrtilus, killed the king of Elis in order to obtain his kingdom and the
and of his daugher Hippodamia. Medea, forsaken by Jason, slew their two children
n his sight.

he spare others, who [will] murder his own [family] and who [will] punish with a horrible death innocent boys, the highest charge of which beloved [boys] has been entrusted to him? Alas, alas, with what commotions will you, England, be disturbed? Depart, [my] piety, and let [my] loyalty [to Richard] seek [your] place.[100] Lo, a long thirst for blood is imminent to the realm.

[ACT I. Scene iii.][101]

Queen. Maid.

[Queen.]   Alas, my heart beats with a renewed fear; a cold tremor rushes through [my] lifeless limbs, [because] such nocturnal visions terrify wretched me, and [because such] cruel dreams disturb restless [me]. But you, Father, who turn the bright stars and who rule the fiery day-star with [its] roving fire, avert [this] wicked, deadly, [and] horrible omen. A sweet quiet had already covered all things everywhere, and sleep had readily come upon my weary eyes [when] I saw a wondrous boar, alas, on a swift course; and, gnashing with [his] savage teeth, he lacerated [my] sons and cruelly afflicted both Mighty ruler of the heavenly palaces, if the fates threaten anything harsh to [my] sons, may [their] wrath spring forth against [this, my] head, and may the thunderbolt of the [fates] now angered seek first the mother.

Servant [To herself]. When will there be any time free of disasters, and when will the sorrow of the terrified mother place a limit [on itself]? Will you foolishly remain silent about the sad message to the mother

---

[100]The interpretation of this line is based on Brackenbury's loyalty to Richard to the very end.

[101]Hall is the sole basis of this scene (pp. 379-380).

or does [her] mind perhaps rejoice to busy itself with all its
hardships and to shut within itself [its] long-enduring griefs?
[To the Queen.] O mighty Queen, once swollen with regal pride. . .

Queen.   Why are you struck dumb in the midst of your sad speech?
[Your] voice does not find the way to issue [its] charge, and [your]
unsightly [lit. shameful] cheeks are wet with diffuse tears.

Servant.   The boar, gnashing with [his] bloody teeth, has raged [again].

Queen.   Who still remains for [his] villainy?

Servant.   Ah, your sons!

Queen.   I wish to hear immediately of our [new] afflictions.

Servant.   Alas, both princes have been suffocated by a villain. Her
disquieted mind is overwhelmed. Rise up! Woe to me! Raise [your]
dejected spirits again, [o] wretched one! She is breathing; she
has revived; a slow death flies the miserable.

Queen.   Now, villainous uncle, you can rule. [Your] savage fury will
in no way fear [my] feeble boys. Brandish [your] evil sceptre!
There is still one thing lacking to your villainy: seek now our
blood. I will not be a miserable witness of your wrath. Whom
shall I unhappily weep for? [My] kinsmen? [my] children? or
myself? Why [lit. how] do the fates permit so much evil to abound?
I, a mother, killed my own [children] when I bared [your] sides,
Edward, of your retinue, and at the time [when] you, [my] sweet
boy, left the sanctuary. I, a mother bending lower than my knees,
beseech you, thundering Father, who brandish flaming avengers [i.e.
thunderbolts], let your weapons [of vengeance] be brandished against
this perjured [man]! Enraged one, despoil Olympus with your
thunderbolts, and let the falling down of heaven take vengeance on
the impious [King]!

Servant.   Rather, think calmly, and soothe [your] spirit, and quiet
[your] disturbed mind; relieve [your] cares!

Queen.   O abominable monstrosity of the uncle! Neither cruel Procrustes
nor savage Colchis knew of such. O false faith of an impious
Cardinal to whom I foolishly entrusted my son! O dearest sons, o
[my] children whom the bloody sword of the uncle has snatched away!
Nor is one crime sufficient for his villainy: he begrudges your
funeral to me [your] mother!

ACT II. [Scene i.]

Duke of Buckingham. Bishop of Ely.

[Buckingham.] O worthy Bishop of the island of Ely, put aside [your] grief!
[Be as] free [as you were] before, even though you remain in my
dwellings. For when the cruel King entrusted you to my safe-keeping,
I promised [you] that I would be [but] little severe [with you].
Preferably you will consider [me] a friend similar to yourself.
Now recall the condition of your earlier life, and consider [yourself]
not who you are [now], but what you were [before].

Ely.   O the joy to me (because I speak with your leave), because I
feel that I [am] free in this prison. But why do I not severely
reproach my misfortunes? What consideration of [your] generous
mind has been lacking [to me]? But the virtue of your mind is solace
[my] afflicted circumstances, which [virtue] does not care as much for
the power of the mighty as what the wish of the needy [may be].[102]

---

[102]The Bishop's early speeches in this scene must be read as being carefully calculated to draw out the Duke's concealed jealousy of King Richard:
". . . he [i.e. the Bishop of Ely] by the longe and often alternate proofe, as
well of prosperitee as   aduerse fortune, had gotten by greate experience
the very mother and mastres of wisedome, and depe insighte in pollitike and
worldly driftes, wherby perceiuying now the duke to common with hym, fed hym

Buckingham.   [My] consideration of your wish[es] is pleasing to me, however

adverse several things [may] seem to you. Since you pay [your]

respects to me, however unworthy, in so friendly a manner, I will

strive [hard] so that eventually you, [a man] of experience, may

affirm that these things which are [about to be] uttered by my

voice are true. Neither condemn [your] cruel misfortunes--rather

indeed approve of [them]--nor consider [it] so great an evil that

you are not free. How much happiness is there to enjoy in life

when a tyrant holds the harsh reins of government? Rather, consider

[it] a gain that you are not punished capitally. He has given [you]

your life. When has [his] rash anger not taken [life] away instead?

How often has he bloodied [his] violent hands with slaughters? How

often has [his] mind's madness decided in favor of destruction? I

cannot say [how often], nor are words sufficient to me. Grief

bids [me] to be silent. O villainy, believable in no age [past]

and which posterity will deny! The uncle has banished, alas, [his]

nephews from [their] father's kingdom. Did he deprive them of [their]

kingdom only? He killed [lit. gave death to] the wretched [boys].

[My] grief scarcely endures [its] restraints; it wants to take

vengeance.

---

with fayre woordes and many pleasaunte prayses, and perceiuynge by the grefe
of their communicacions the dukes pryde nowe and then to balke out a litle
brayde of enuy toward the glory of the kynge, and thereby felynge hym easye
to fall out yf the matter were well handeled, he craftely sought the wayes
to prycke him forward takynge alwayes the occasyon of his commyng, and also
kepynge hym selfe close within his bandes that he rather semed to folowe
hym then to leade hym" (Hall, p. 383). See also More, p. 454; and Hol.,
p. 404.

Ely.   [0] distinguished offspring of dukes, you recommend excellent

things. This was once well known in ancient countries: "Kingdoms

born of crime are immediately dissolved." Unless you effect a

cure for so much injury, a plague will seek out the hidden wounds

of the kingdom. Like honor it is, to kill a tyrant or an enemy.

Buckingham.   Yet I would rather that he (whose anger perhaps has harmed a

few) should reign safely than that [all] power be removed from the

regal throne. Nor is it so exceptional that he raged thus against

his own [kinsmen]: [His] wrath, which knows no moderation, was

driven by the [great] stimulus [of fear]. I know, however, that

his prudent mind [lit. head] will have regard for the interests

of the kingdom: a peace favorable to the citizens will flourish.

He, therefore, must be praised who is concerned with the care of

the kingdom [lit. whom the care of the kingdom holds], and to whom

the safety of his own citizens is dear.

Ely [Aside].   [His] haughty mind speaks with great despite, nor does it

contain itself; it mingles [his] secret hatred [of the King] in

with [his] praises. Now cautiously arouse in him a hatred of the

King in such a manner [as] you calculate that he will pursue [even]

further. [Aloud.] It is foolish to hide what you will at once

betray. I know, you will certainly put no trust in me if I should

wish for different things [than I do] only to please you. I call

God to witness, if my wishes had not been ineffectual, and [if]

the lasting title of the kingdom, which fell to Duke Edward,[102a] had

remained with [Prince] Henry, I would not have left your factions,

Henry. But when the vicissitudes of the fates decreed otherwise,

and they offered the sceptre to King Edward, which I preferred to

---

[102a]I.e. Edward Duke of York, who upon deposing Henry VI, became Edward IV.

have remained inviolate with Henry, I was not so foolishly aroused
to anger [at Edward's assuming the throne] that I would [allow
myself to] be mocked at [as being] the pious patron of a dead man.
Who enviously will dare to insult a victor? After prudently
accepting the authority of [Edward], the victor, I was immediately
received into [his] good grace[s], and thereupon, Edward, I never
falsified my loyalty to you while [you] were living, and I prayed
[thus] for your children: "May those born in the line of the King
wield the sceptre befitting royal authority, [and may they direct]
the long-enduring government of England." But what God has done
[lit. woven], it is not mine to undo [lit. unweave]. But he who
was only the Protector of the realm, and [who] now is distinguished
by the regal throne. . . [but], I will control myself. Sacred
things, rather, summon an old bishop [like myself] more: [my
sacred offices] do not befit [my] wishes for the kingdom, but
instead, since I am now sufficiently aware of my own wrongs, befit
only prayers [for my wrongs].

Buckingham [To himself]. Having spoken about King [Richard], he has become
silent. Willingly will I listen to what the wise [man] thinks
about the King. [Aloud.] Rather continue, Father, lest you restrain
the words [from your mouth], and safely expound upon the desires of
your mind. From me [lit. from here] not only is there no danger,
but advantage[s] more pleasing to you will immediately fall to your
desires. You will be an advisor to me in [all] the uncertain matters
which I was thinking about when I, by my entreaties, obtained from
the King your custody in my house. Perhaps another prison would
be more troublesome to you: here rather consider yourself free.

Ely.   I have gratitude [to you], illustrious Duke, equal to [your]
        good deeds [to me], but it is not pleasant to talk about [lit. to
        treat of] the deeds of princes. In this [i.e. in a matter of this
        kind], secret deceits often lies concealed under a gentle look [lit.
        mild forehead]. Those words spoken with good intent are often
        twisted with evil intent, and [this] fable of Aesop of Phrygia urges
        care [on my part]: A lion prince [once] gave to the wild beasts
        such a law [which], far and wide, dreadfully threatened [them with]
        the penalty of death unless [every] horned beast left the forest.
        A wild beast only swelling from [his] forehead, fearing the command
        of the king, wretchedly prepared [his] flight. By chance, a fox
        met him hastening away, and, full of wonder, asked the reason for
        [his] flight. "I flee the forest," he said. "I am afraid of the
        lion's orders." The fox laughed, [and] said to the wild beast:
        "Foolish one, you fear wrongly. The lion [said] nothing about you.
        Your forehead only swells: it bears no horn." And the harmless
        [little] beast said, "I know [lit. knew] this [well] enough, but
        if the bloody lion should say it is a horn, what then? Killed
        [by the lion], I will argue extremely well," he laughed, "[that]
        all things fall to a happy chance."

Buckingham.   Fear nothing! A roaring lion will in no way harm [you], nor
        will the Boar inflict a wound on you with [his] teeth. The Prince
        will hear nothing of those things which you secretly tell to me.

Ely.   By Hercules, if this speech [which I was about to speak] should
        [lit. may] strike his [i.e. King Richard's] ears, and he himself
        did not take it maliciously, I might then fear nothing; perhaps he
        would [even] offer [his] thanks. But if the bad [side to my speech]

were the mediator [with Richard] (as a guess [it would be]), rather
than the favorable side, and [its] truth were [lit. is] not pondered,
[my] words might produce great harm for us both.

Buckingham.   Whatever it is [you have to say], my zealous mind wants to hear
it. As you please, I will willingly make myself responsible. Fear
nothing; only comply with my wishes, Father.

Ely.   Since the Protector holds the sceptre, I will say nothing
about by what right the Prince claims this. I might [now] pray
(but yet humbly) [only] for what the safety of the country demands,
of which [country] he now controls the reins, and [of which] I
have [ever] been a faithful member. Would that merciful God had
added to those [his] natural gifts [for ruling] (granted that he
abounds in these, nor does he suffer want of our praise) what His
benevolent will has dispersed more freely unto your [eternal] honor.
The more he may abound in [your] natural endowments, the better he
may handle the reins of [his] royal authority. [But now] I will
restrain myself. It is more fitting that I remain silent about
these things.[103]

Buckingham. [To himself]. I wonder why he has stopped. Why did he become
silent in the middle of [his] speech? Yea, I shall speak seriously
with the tremulous father? O reverend Father, why do you restrain
[your] uncertain mind? [Your] speech, which started forth [from
your mouth], at once restrained itself, while you produced interrup-
tions [in your speech], concluding nothing, and you breathed quickly.

---

[103]More's History breaks off at this point (p. 455).

[Hence], I neither know with what loyalty you honor the King, nor what your affection toward [both of] us has been. Because you, a preacher, adorn our virtues (although I find in myself nothing worthy of [your] praises), that makes me now more uncertain of mind. But I suspect that your mind burns with hatred [for the King], or that moved by blind affection [for me] you conceive these things. A foolish fear hinders [you] so that you do not dare to [speak out]; a sense of shame, little befitting an old man, impedes [your speech]. Speak! I pledge [my] honor to your doubtful self that [this] retreat is safe: I will listen silently.

Ely [To himself]. How stands it? You perceive [his] promise. The Duke is exceedingly puffed up with pride. Greedily he devours [my] praises. He hates the Prince. Why do you fear to open your mind secretly to this man? You will either prepare the ruin of the King or [a need for] your flight when you kindle the torches of wrath in the Duke. [Aloud.] Since, by the judgement of the King, I have been your captive (it is possible with your leave to use this word although I feel nothing of a bothersome prison [here]), I have elevated [my] soul, terrified by the [recent] evils, by reading [lit. by books]. Opening a book, I found an excellent sentence, [namely,] that no one is born who shall live free only for himself, but [his] parents will claim part [of him], [his] kinsmen [will claim a] part, but [his] native land, the universal parent, ought particularly to attract [his] devotion. [Now,] when I turn over in my mind what is due to my native land, [and] when I consider, alas, its [present] condition (as much did the highest glory of [its] kings use to shine forth as now the tyrant oppresses [it] with [his] heavy yoke) it pleases [me] to fulfill what is due to my native

land. His sceptre promises the destruction of the kingdom. But

[one] great hope is not wanting to the wretched citizens when I

behold your excellent person, [your] honor, [your] mighty understanding,

[your] power in speaking equal [to your understanding], [your] very

great strength, and the rare virtue of a duke to whom the well-

being of [his] country is dear beyond [all] other things. I rejoice

for my tottering country upon which a nobleman has descended who

can cure [its]   great evils, [and] who may direct the reins of

government with an impartial hand, which [reins] the tyrant

Gloucester now holds (for that ancient name [of Gloucester] befits

him: the new name [of King] befits [him] little because he does

not hold the sceptre by right!). Nor would I dislike his rule if

the honor [of the title] had not at once made the pious habits

of the Duke unrestrained, and if he did not receive a new mentality

with [his] new name. O severe [are] the things the noble rule of

England has suffered! [But] more severe [are] the things about

to be suffered, if the tyrant [continues to] rule. Why should I

monstrously describe [his] crime at every point? I know what kind

of a road he has paved to the throne. Behold, he has defiled his

hand with the slaughter of noblemen whom he thought hindered his

depraved wishes. O accursed[104] thirst for rule, where do you draw

the minds of mortals? But [his] wicked fury continued, and as far

---

[104]Sacra is rendered here in its transferred sense of accursed, although
the chronicles support an ironical use of holy. See Hall: "Was not his firste
interprise to obtaine the crowne begonne and incepted by the murder of diuers
noble valiaunt trewe and vertuous personages: O a holy begynnyng to come to a
mischeuous endyng. . ." (p. 385). See also Hol., p. 407.

as he was pleased, he ventured. He placed no limit on [his] villainy

and he achieved an [even] greater crime by the trust [placed in him].

Will any age believe that an only son may condemn [his] mother of

infamous unchastity. Wickedly he branded [her] reputation with a

false crime, and falsely he called [his] two brothers[105] bastards,

and he marked [his] nephews with an impious stain, and condemned

[as] doubtful the birth of his own brother. Is this [man] to

destroy the noble honor of [his] family? But why do I ask? Was

this the end of [his] crime? This [was but] a step of [his] evil

in so far as crime does not stand still. Already possessing the

kingdom of his brother, he did not fear to venture greater [crimes].

The cruel uncle, alas, in killing the innocent [boys] filled [his]

hands with the destruction of his own kinsmen. Consequently, let

the flashing might of a thunderbolt burst forth [upon him]. Or perhaps

he who has sacrificed his own kinsmen will spare others? Who can

now madly hope for better things? Wicked crime [always] presages

greater monstrosities. Now, therefore, let the condition of the

times at length advise you. For the sake of the eternal will of

God, for the sake of English honor, if your family, proud in [its]

honors, [is] dear to you, help the miserable, break through the

delays of the fates, take the kingdom in hand, crush the tyrant

driven from [his] throne, avenge the honor of the kingdom which has

been taken away! Nor may a cause, extremely just, frighten [you

who are] uncertain. Defend the citizens! Let the safety of the

country be dear [to you]! Now a [great] comrade in [your] labor

---

[105]The chronicles make clear that the "two brothers" referred to here
are Richard's brothers, Edward and Clarence, and not the two princely brothers.
See Hall, p. 385; and Hol., p. 407.

can not be lacking [to you]. The entire populace is whispering
for want of a rebellion. [The people] would rather endure the
yoke of the barbarous Turks than that [this] evil King should
amuse himself with their blood. How much more would they now
trust in you, a prince, in whom an exalted birth shines forth?
Sleep on my wishes, and do not refuse the proffered throne of
England when you can be of [so] great advantage to many. And do
not let the labor [of ruling] deter you, if you are thinking about
what [labor] there is [in ruling]. But, however ardous [the
labor] may be, yet, for the sake of the public peace of the country,
by no means must [the labor] be abandoned. But if you stubbornly
refuse and will not let yourself be won over by [my] entreaties,
[then] I adjure you by the true God, by the faith of the greatest
of dukes, also by the faith once bound to St. George when you
were first admitted as a knight to the Order of the Garter, that
nothing will be advanced against our person through the fault of
this speech. I implore this [i.e. that you save the country] with
the public prayers of the citizens. But if you do not want the
sceptre which must be joined to another right hand, [then] return
the fallen House of Lancaster to [its] paternal throne, or join
the daughter of the father Edward to [some] powerful prince [lit.
to the distinguished marriage beds of a nobleman]. In this manner,
the tyrant will endure a sad ruin, and [this] weary nation will
put an end to [its] disasters. [Now] you have my opinion about
these affairs. [To himself.] Why is he so silent? I wonder.
I fear greatly for myself. He draws a deep breath. Will he deceive
[my] confidence [in him]?

Buckingham.   I see, Father, that [your] heart is torn with fear. I am

sorry that I, by remaining silent, have given [you] occasion for

grief. May good luck attend thee! I shall not deceive your

confidence. O great ruler of the heavens and judge of the world,

how very much the English nation has been bound to you, [o] merciful

God, who with [your] kindly strength has oftentimes protected

the wavering status of the kingdom! Now, at length, put an end to

[its] severe hardships! [O] Father, breathe forth the merciful

spirit of [your] mind so that we may seek under your auspices a

prince who will wield a just sceptre in [his] royal hand, and who

will at once bring aid to [our] weary affairs! Reverend Bishop

of the See of Ely, you have given to me a clear enough sample of

your mind, and I am a witness of [your] love for [your] country.

Our guilt [is] equal; therefore do not fear deceits. I shall

express entirely the thought of [my] mind about the King, [and]

why I, as an accomplice, joined my forces to him. After Edward,

the fourth of his name, could not restrain the whip-lashes of fate

[any longer], but [instead] the fates compelled [him] to die, I

was little benevolent toward his children because he had conferred

on [me] little advantage worthy of [my] merits and inimically had

not deemed [mine] the high titles of my ancestry. At that time,

[therefore] I little reverenced [his] children [when they were]

deprived of [their] inimical father. The old saying was being

openly spread abroad that a kingdom is easily destroyed whose reins

a boy king holds. Then, Richard, I, [your] comrade, supported

your beginnings; then I judged that [you] were a merciful man, and

now I see you [are] a savage [man]. He allured pious minds [so] very much by this fraud that he was proclaimed the Protector of

England, and of the King too, by public acclamation. His mind

was so influenced by [his] new title that when he took the second

position in the kingdom, immediately [the thought of] the sceptre

alone began to please him. He demanded for himself those things

befitting the royal authority until [lit. toward the time when]

[his] feeble nephew had completed his youthful years. After he

saw us hesitate [about his demand to be made an interim king],

and [that] we would not break [our] faith to the kingdom, then

[that] infamous uncle represented his nephews [as] bastards. At

length, we believed him, and at once we yielded [to him] the reins

of our kingdom. He had [already] condemned the heir of the Duke

of Clarence: the crime of [his] father had destroyed his rights

of ruling.[106] In this manner, Richard, you procured the throne

for yourself, and, at length, you rushed wherever your madness

drew [you]. It was permissible to rule as it pleased [you]. Now

it was propitious [for you] to fear no one; there was no fierce enemy

[of yours left]. Now no one could hinder your undertakings. But

who was the minister of so much destruction? You, you, a tyrant

born for the ruin of [our] country! You cruelly deprived a mother

of her own son; nor did you, cruel [one], abstain from the slaughter

of [your] blood relations. An unjust uncle, you murdered [your]

tender nephews, when the report of whose death had penetrated my

---

[106]"For well we knew that the duke of Clarence sonne, by reason of the attaynder of his father [Clarence, accused by the Queen's kinsmen of seeking the death of Edward by necromancy, was committed to the Tower, and executed in 1478] was disabled to inherite, and also the duke hym self was named to be a bastarde. . ." (Hall, p. 387). See Hol., p. 409.

ears, a general fear seized [my] trembling limbs, [my] deepest
blood deserted [my] gaping veins, [my] weakened limbs went limp
[lit. dissolved] with dread. We unknowingly promise health to
ourselves when the safety of our own home is uncertain. Many an
injury condemns [him as] unjust to me. In vain did I rightfully
demand the reward offered [to me by Richard], and I laid claim
to the name of High Constable. Bitterly calumniated [by him],
I received an ungrateful rejection. Will he who has never given
one's own [title to him] give new titles [to him]? But even if
he had given [me, my rightful title], he still would not have
given [it] graciously. For, by our help he possessed the honor
of the kingdom. I recognize [my] fault [now]. Yea, without my
aid, he never would have borne the sceptre of [his] brother in
his savage hand. The crime falls back upon my head, for I have
inflicted a wound on my country. I will [only] expiate this [crime]
if I effect a cure. Therefore, I will cure [it], and so I first
decided at the time when he harshly rejected [my] just complaint.
I shall contain myself no further. I shall relate in detail
whatever hidden thing lies in my silent mind. When I discovered
the mind of the King [to be] full of evil, [my] affection [for him]
turned into hatred. I prepared to take vengeance. I endured his
sight, which, however, I was annoyed [to do]; and I could not bear
[his] face. I left the royal palace: I sought [my] home. While
I undertook my journey, I mused that at that time the stolen
sceptre could readily be transferred to my right hand so that,
for a while, I was delighting myself with the uncertain title,
and I, coveting the throne of the kingdom, falsely considered
myself the rightful heir of the House of Lancaster. [While I was]

thinking about these things, the Countess of Richmond suddenly

meeting [me] along the way asked me [if] I would pray [to the King]

for the return of [her] exiled son. [She said that] if the King

should kindly assent [to his return], then she would betrothe her

son to the chaste marriage beds of the living daughter of King

Edward, [that] she cared nothing about a dowry, [that this] one

favor of the King would be [worth] two [dowries], nor would she,

the mother, demand more. From this cause, our [claims to the]

royal power died, [for] then it occurred to my mind that the first

right to the kingdom lies open to the mother and her son. The

throne was a dream, and I claimed the kingdom vainly. At first,

I scorned the devout wishes of the Countess; then, when my mind

considered further the entreaties of the mother, I thought that the

mother, inspired by the Holy Ghost, had perceived an immense good

for this kingdom of England. If [each] hostile house [i.e. of

Lancaster and York] which claims the uncertain sceptre as its

right should join in marriage [lit. join pious beds], [then] there

would be eternal tranquility for the citizens, and it would make

fast a solid and certain trust in the peace, and there would be

a certain heir for a doubtful England.

Ely.　　　　O assured [is] the hope, the safety, the solace of the country!

Merciful God has begun to look upon [his] afflicted [ones]. O the

sacred laws of legitimate marriages! I rejoice for you, [o] England!

Be thou happy! Comfort comes! To whom shall we now make safely

known such great secrets?

Buckingham.　　It is fitting to know the mind of the mother first.

Ely [Aside.]　　Now our undertakings will sufficiently follow [my] wishes.

　　[Aloud.] Behold, a faithful servant of the Countess approaches, and God, however slowly, will please us miserable ones. Bray,

servant of the mighty Countess, be a pleasing messenger of good

fortune to your mistress: "The boat that has been tossed about

has driven to a haven of peace. Soon [your] son, Henry, will bear

the sceptre in [his] hand if he will bind his faith by an oath

that he will join in marriage [lit. join by the conjugal torch]

with her who is [lit. was] the oldest [lit. older] daughter of

King Edward." May the mother, then, desire the happy thrones for

[her] son so that the impious King may be expelled from his throne.

Bray.   [As] a messenger, I shall bring so happy [news] to [my]

mistress; and I shall willingly execute any faithful charge for you.

Buckingham.   At last, I myself will rightly take vengeance on the King.

He will triumph [but] little over his badly divided kingdom. Now

the savage boar will discover a strong lion hostile to himself who

will make as much use of [his] claws as he [i.e. the boar] [does]

of his teeth. Now heap crime on crime! Savagely fill your deadly

hands with slaughter! Still hold back unfairly my rights! Rule

pompously! Hold up [your] lofty spirits! God, the avenger, pursues

the haughty from behind. Constrained [by me, Richard], you will

restore what you denied to me of [your] own free will. Recently

in York, swelling haughtily with pride, encircled with a crown,

[and] glittering in [his] bright vestments, he showed forth [his]

features to be gazed at by the dull citizens. At the same time,

he encircled the head of [his] wife with a diadem, and the fickle

mob celebrated [him] with divine honor.[107] His exalted spirit

portends [his] destruction!

---

[107]See Footnote 96.

Ely.   Cruelly, [o] savage one, you will pay for [your] tyranny with
[your] death. If I were free [Buckingham], stripped of your bonds,
and protected sufficiently by my whole isle [of Ely], I would not
fear at all the menaces of the raging King. Now, therefore, it is
fitting that I depart with your leave.

Buckingham.   A dispersed band weakly loses [its] strength: a united band
more strongly threatens [its] enemies. Delay a little while I
gather soldiers. [Then] an armed troop will protect [your] journey.

[ACT II. Scene ii.]

Lewis, a doctor.

The Countess mother [was] happy after she had received Bray's
messages concerning the marriage of her son, [namely,] that if the
Earl of Richmond would pledge the sacred vows of marriage to the
first daughter of King Edward, [then] he might hope for [his] lost
throne. [The Countess] has ordered [me] to go to the Queen with a
quick pace to attempt to influence [her] mind, as if of my own accord,
so that I, who am [lit. have been] skilled in the art of medicine,
might mix with my medical care [lit. medicines] the sacred oaths
and the promised bed [of marriage] of Earl Richmond. Now, then,
Lewis, it is fitting that your faithful commands be carried out.
Win over the mother lest she deny the conjugal couches of [her]
daughter to the Earl.

[ACT II. Scene iii.]

Bishop of Ely, fleeing.

Unwillingly I am compelled to desert the hospitality of the Duke. [His] disordered plans force [my] great fear. Now, therefore, I shall have regard for myself by my hasty flight. How much I now wretchedly fear the savage forces of [my] enemies, but I shall proceed cautiously; I shall seek [my] island [home], and soon I shall sail through the salt sea in a ship, and, as a foreigner, I will safely watch the battles from afar. You, you, [o] mighty judge of the world, I humbly beg, protect your servant from the cruel enemy.

[ACT II. Scene iv.]

Lewis. Queen.

[Lewis.]   Wretched Queen, who has served [lit. serving] the conjugal bed of your husband with a chaste faith, leave off [your] tears. I hope that there will be an end to your evils. For a short while receive [our] words affably in [your] ear, summoned by our entreaties I have learned the way by which the savage tyrant may pay the punishments due [him], and [by which] your grandchildren, the cruel King having been overthrown, may again wield the sceptre in [their] happy hand[s]. Richard has aroused the hatred of the nobles and of the people against himself: they wish to take [his] hated authority [from him]. Already the crowd has spread abroad by a wild murmuring that a more severe yoke has been placed on [them] than they can endure. May we expect a kind of rule of [such a] Prince, an uncle [who] has given over [his] infant nephew[s] to

death? Many a complaint of the citizens strikes Jove; they cannot
love whom they publicly curse. The populace would tear [its]
servile yoke from its neck if [another] heir to the kingdom were
known to it. Henry, the Earl of Richmond (now an exile), is the
certain heir of the Lancastrian family. If you bid him to marry
your daughter [lit. to join his marriage beds to your daughter],
no [future] heir will [ever have to] contest over [his] right to
rule.

Queen.   What joyous message has struck my ears? What do I hear? Is
not my wretched mind credulous?   Those less wretched [than I]
readily believe this [message] because they wish [it to be
true], but an obstinate Fortune will refuse what they wish. Belief
prone to rumor is always worse.[108] The tyrant [still] reigns.
Earl Henry [is] an exile. The two-headed crowd and the favor of
the people [are] doubtful. What easy way to the sceptre lies open
to my daughter?

Lewis.   A trembling fear will hinder [your] desire. Trust in [your]
cause: the well-being of the citizens will fight [for it]. Wise
mother, have regard for your family. Will you unmindful of the
recent slaughter of [your] children lie prostrate? Why will you
in this manner permit yourself [to be] unavenged? Let [your]
sorrow for the slaughter of your children and the shame of a chaste
wife incite you!

Queen.   [My] mind, leading [me] unwilling [to believe it], promises
[me] hope. I would like to endow my daughter Elizabeth with a

---

[108]The chronicles afford no basis for the interpretation given these
lines. In both Hall (p. 391) and Holinshed (p. 414), the Queen receives
Bray's message with great joy, and without the slightest hesitation or doubt.

marriage, but perhaps the mother of Henry will scorn her. Seek

her out! Investigate whether the ancient hatred of the House of

[her] exiled son can be turned from [its] evil [courses], so that

out of its wretched [state] it might become powerful [again].

Lewis.   Queen, I shall execute [your] commands.

Queen.   May God look after [us]! I will not proceed with [our] happy

plans hesitantly.

[ACT II. Scene v.]

Buckingham, to [his] soldiers.

Let that savage, common enemy, [my] soldiers, fall by [my]

avenging hand! At the same time, let whoever has been an ally of

the tyrant, and a comrade of [his] punishment[s] be overthrown!

Let their cruel grief express what [our] wrath can [do]! Would

that I could pour out in libation to God the blood of [the King's]

despicable head! No more splendid victim has [ever] been sacrificed

to Jove or has imbued [his] altars [with blood] than a wicked

king or an impious tyrant. No one holds a violent rule for a

long time. With so much crime [already], who can foolishly hope

for a secure kingdom or for certain faith [in him] for a long time?

I shall expose the deceit of [his] wicked mind to you. When he

saw war prepared for [by me], immediately he sent kind letters [to

me]; he promised [me] estates; he refused nothing. I have experience

[his] deceit [before]. I delayed. I begged [his] pardon [for not

going to see him]. Having endured [my] repulse painfully, he

immediately ordered [me] to come; I still refused. But yet I shall

come! I shall come at last, Richard, but [only] to your harm; and

I, the author of public peace for the wretched Britains, will hostilely be present to you as a bitter avenger. Having fled [his] sanctuary, the Marquis of Dorset has gathered a great force of soldiers in Yorkshire. The people of Devonshire will follow Courtney [as their] leader, and the holy person of the Bishop of Exeter has joined the forces of [his] brother [Courtney]. Guilford, a knight, with a hostile band, and many a troop of Kentish soldiers will seek out the impious King. Let the enemy be afflicted! [Our] wars demand [that] the cruel murderer of his own kinsmen pay for [his] impious punishment [of others]. Therefore, cut to pieces the tyrant, a plague of his own country, since [his] sacrifice will be pleasing to the citizens. Since our allies [lit. supports] are so great who desire to defend our factions and to give life to the country, I, as [your] leader, shall willingly endure all distresses so long as your enemy, and savage Nero, perishes. Why are we idle? Why are [our] pious arms idle? Do you very foolishly think that [your] perfidious enemies will be conquered by falling down and striking Jove with [your] prayers? Let [our] swords be brandished [instead]! [Your] savage enemy awaits you. Fight strongly! Let [each] man engage [lit. lay hands on] a man [of Richard's part]! Let [our] banners be raised on high! Let the trumpet sound the battle, and let [each] soldier be roused by the harsh sound of the trumpet!

ACT III. [Scene i.]

King Richard.[109]

O fate [is] always cruel [to me], when she cruelly exercises a

harsh destiny [on my son] and equally [cruel] when she withholds

an evil [destiny from the Earl of Richmond]. False Fortune scoffs

at human affairs too much, turning all things on [her] easily moved

wheel. These same ones whom she has placed on the topmost part

[of her wheel] at one time, at another time she pushes to the lowest

[part] and treads under [her] foot. Lo, who does not perceive that

[my] mighty house [has been] overturned suddenly by a whim of

wavering Fortune? First, alas, my only son, alas, died (O cruel

fate and too mournful a lot!), who might expect the illustrious

realms of [his] father [when he is] dead; just as that little

associate of a great herd, while scarcely covering his forehead

with [his] first horns, suddenly, high with [his] neck and lofty

with [his] head, leads [his] paternal flock and rules over the

herd. O sweet pledge [of my love], o honor of the royal house,

o wasted promise of your Britain, o vain hope, alas, of [your]

father, for whom I foolishly prayed for the warlike praises of

Achilles and the [long] years of Nestor, God has deprived [you]

of light! Never will you happily bear the sceptre with a mighty

hand, nor will you [ever] give laws to the British people, nor

will you [ever] put conquered nations under your yoke. You will

---

[109]The composition of this speech by Richard departs somewhat from Legge's
usual method of religiously following his source. The first twenty-six lines
(Richard's lament for his dead son Edward) and the last eighteen lines (Richard
plan to curb the growing enmity of the populace) are taken from one place in
Hall (p. 381), the middle section (11.27-56) from another (Hall, p. 393).
Furthermore, the mention of Edward's death and of Richard's plan is found in
a different context from the one used by Legge. None of this material appears
in Holinshed.

not subdue Frenchmen [lit. French backs turned in flight]; you will
not draw the rebellious Scots under your rule; wretchedly you will
lie without glory shut up in a deep mound of earth. Further, the
exile of the Earl of Richmond, remaining within the confines of
Brittainy is preparing for a bitter war, and he [who is] about to
seize my sceptre is gathering forces. Lo, at home, the populace
seeks our blood. A too obstinate rage influences [their] minds:
it arms ministers of evil toward our ruin. Some [of my] enemies
aim to aid the threatening Richmond with [their] forces, some to
place firm garrisons in [their] towers, some to serve those [already]
armed secretly at home, some to seek with entreaties [my] subjects
so that they will let fall their loyalty [to me]. I did not wish
to know about all [these] things; willingly I deceived [myself]
when I could perceive the dark beginnings, the plots, the deceits,
and the forces of soldiers being joined together. When I knew
that the Duke of Buckingham was the leader of this revolt and the
source of all the evil, I undertook either to put [him] off by open
war or to entice [him] piously with entreaties lest he alter his
loyalty [to me]. Also, I sent kind letters to the Duke [so that]
he might happily come to the palace. The Duke sensed [my] deceits.
He fabricated [lit. wove] causes for delay; he feigned that he was
oppressed by a pain in [his] stomach. [Then,] I ordered [him]
to break off all delay at once. He refused to come [lit. denied
that he would come] to the enemy of the country, and [now this]
worst of dukes, gathering his own soldiers, will madly produce
traitorous wars against me. What shall I do? The friend who was

nearest to me seeks to obtain the kingdom: he greatly hates [me] who greatly reverenced [me before]. O impious [is] the evil and the Duke, in consecrating [himself] to deepest hell [lit. Tartary]! Moreover, the populace, in an agitated mass like a storm [full] of winds, seeks [its] Prince for a cruel destruction. Richard alone is proclaimed the cause of evil. What [course of] action now remains, or whom shall I consult? No one can redeem [my] evil deeds. If the populace hates [me], I will perish. But the favor of the people may be courted: in that way the stain will be removed by which, alas, I have wickedly clothed my name so that if I will [now] become mild, humane, pious and liberal to my citizens, they will in no way condemn what evil has [already] burst forth upon the British people; and I will free [my] name from the impious villainy [connected with it]. The high walls [of the city] will raise on high hundreds of sacrifices [to the gods] so that [the people] freed from their cares will apply themselves [only] to pious prayers; and I will offer useful laws to my country. Perhaps, [then,] the populace, moved by [my] false piety, will rush forth to our support [lit. factions]. The fickle mob is [generally] led by mountains of gold and by sweet words.

[ACT III. Scene ii.]

Messenger. King Richard.

Messenger.   I bring news that the Duke of Buckingham has fled and that [his] mighty forces are now scattered.

King Richard. What was the cause of [their] sudden retreat [lit. of their turning their backs suddenly]?

Messenger.   As soon as the haughty [Duke] numbered a mighty force of

        Welshmen, he took the route along which the forest of Dean extends

        itself, and he hastened to cross over the noble river Sabrina [i.e.

        the Severn] with his army so that he might join forces with the

        army of Courtney. However, while the frightened Duke was raging at

        [his] impious army (but do not the gods look after the mortal race?),

        while the soldiers were looking at the nearby river (and up to that

        day it was not given to reaching its high banks) suddenly a severe

        rainstorm struck the earth, and a humid south-wind, full of rain,

        freed its liquids; and much water deeply covered [i.e. flooded]

        the fields [along the river]. Lo, fish were lifted into unknown

        abodes! Those [men] lying in [their] beds clung to trees in the

        fields, and marvelled at the roofs turned over everywhere in the

        middle of the streams of water. A boy in a cradle floated here

        and there through the fields; the wild beasts swam to the mountains.

        The waters covered the earth for ten days. [Every] soldier was

        stunned when the overflown river did not permit the army to join

        with the forces of Courtney. Moreover, the troop of Welshmen,

        unwillingly serving the Duke with no pay, also miserably destitute of

        food, immediately deserted him.[110] The Welsh force could be moved

        by no threats or by no prayers [of the Duke] so that it would

        remain together as [his] ally in war, nor would it proceed further.

---

[110]". . . Buckyngham. . . beynge a man of that courage and sharpe speche in maner agaynste their [i.e. of the Welsh army] willes had rather therto enforced and compelled by lordely and streite commaundemente then by liberall wayges and gentle reteynoure, which thinge was the verie occasion why they lefte hym desolate and cowardely forsoke hym" (Hall, p. 394). See also Hol., p. 417.

Left unprotected [lit. naked] to his enemies, the unfortunate prey
[i.e. the Duke] took flight.

Richard.   A happy message has come to our ears. Before [any] favorable
gods raise up the tottering [Buckingham], let a troop [of soldiers]
guard all ports everywhere lest the Duke break forth to foreign
countries. Whatever the Earl of Richmond is preparing, the [Duke
of Buckingham] will strive for also, whether the Earl will abandon
[his] undertakings or will menace [me] further. I, the Prince,
swear on [my] honor, whoever brings him back to me a captive will
receive a fitting reward. If he has been a bondsman, I will set
[him] free. But if free [already], I will give him a thousand
pounds. An armed fleet will sail the sea of Brittany so that the
traitorous Richmond will not touch England.[111] [One must] venture
evil lest evil increase. It is right to wrest with the sword what
entreaties cannot [command]. Whatever associate of [his] evil
comes into our hands will pay with [his] blood for the villainy
[already] begun.

[ACT III. Scene iii.]

Messenger. King Richard. [Stanley.]

Messenger.   The captive Buckingham is held in chains.

Richard.   O let us reverence with holy prayers the gods propitious to
me (but yet slow [to show me favor]) for [this] happy day! Explain,
[messenger,] by what strategems was the enemy taken!

Messenger.   When the Duke saw that [he] had been deserted by [his] Welsh
army, he was at once stunned; and smitten by so severe a fortune,
[and] in need of advice, he almost lost his mind, but still he had

---

[111]See Hall, pp. 394-395; and Hol., p. 418.

confidence in himself. Fearfully, he secretly fled to the home

of Banister to whom the Duke was inclined before with uncommon

love, and [whom] he had increased greatly in dignity.[112] He desired

to remain secretly in his dwellings until he might [either] restore

[his] army and [his] threats of war, or unarmed flee, [by] sailing

the sea of Brittany, and ally himself with the Earl of Richmond.

But [just as] if some one of the gods was bitterly hateful of the

Duke, he could not [possibly] escape the evil prepared [for him].

The servant Banister, whether fearing for his own life or moved by

your rewards, then betrayed the Duke to [John] Mitton, the sheriff

of Shropshire. [Mitton] proceeded [there] with an accompanying

band of soldiers; he took [the Duke] from the home of his own

servant not long after the time when he alone in the forest

contemplated [his] cruel fates; and [now] the faithful Mitton is

bringing the overpowered man to you.

Richard.   If consecrated loyalty will not keep me in power, I will try

to make firm my sceptre with blood, and I shall cruelly rule the

kingdom with a harsh rule. Now, therefore, let the Duke suffer

the severest of punishments! Let a cruel sword break through [his]

guilty head, and let the executioner grant no delay in [his]

punishment! Whoever fears hatred too much does not know how to

rule. Your loyalty, Stanley, has never been doubtful to me [up to

now]. [But] the Earl of Richmond thirsts for my titles. Your

son-in-law[113] has promised my sceptre to himself. Your wife, the

---

[112]"The duke thus abandoned. . . was. . . meruelousely dismayed. . . [and]
conueyghed him selfe into the house of Homfrey Banaster his servant beside
Shrewsburie, whome he had tendrely broughte vp, and whome he aboue all men
loued, fauoured and trusted. . ." (Hall, p. 394). See also Hol., p. 417.

[113]Stanley took as his second wife, Margaret Beaufort, the Countess of
Richmond, and mother, by a previous marriage, to Henry the Earl of Richmond.

Countess, wants to hand over to [her] son the sceptre taken by [his] victorious right hand. You will [now] fly with rapid steps to Lancaster. Shut her, [your wife], up in [her] most inmost chambers, and do not [even] let a way for the servants lie open to the woman. Let the mother send no letters to [her] son lest she foolishly prepare the sad ruin of the country, and lest the woman offer my sceptre to the rebels.[114] Moreover, you will leave your son, [Lord] Strange, distinguished in honor, with me as a pledge of your loyalty. The boy will testify to the constancy of [his] father. Nature has given to woman a mind disposed to guile, and furnished [her] breast with deceits: it denies [her] strength so that her great evil can be overcome [by man].

[ACT III. Scene iv.]

Duke of Buckingham.

O insecure [is] the grace of a flattering fortune! O exceedingly cruel [is] the chance of fearful battle! Alas, alas, human kind is mocked by the fates! Can anyone guarantee himself [a position] so secure that a day to be feared will not at once destroy [him]? Now, pale with fright, I whose name just recently shone bright among the English, am miserably pushed into ditches.[115] Why, alas, does it please [the fates] to cast down spirits whom the glitter of a deceitful palace, alas, has ruined? Alas, the gifts of Fortune [are] too enticing! The sea does not rage with [its] overflowing waters, nor does the Pontus Euxine, [116] stirred in its deepest waters, swell

---

[114]See Hall, p. 398; and Hol., p. 422.

[115]"Ditches' is undoubtedly meant to be taken figuratively; that is, Buckingham is "pushed into ditches" by the turn of Fortune's wheel.

[116]A strait now called the Black Sea.

in the manner that blind Fortune marks the fall, alas, of great
noblemen. Deadly and cruel [is] the favor of Richard! [But] why
do I miserably lament those times in which the grinding boar,
relying on my advice, prepared the snatched kingdom for himself
with [his] bloody teeth. Lo, now I am ruined by his savage blow.
[O my] native land, o the illustrious honor of England, what
fearful fates await you now after the cruel tyrant holds [you]
subdued to the yoke [of slavery]? Alas, alas, I am wretchedly
pressed down to the Stygian waters, and a bloody ax hangs over my
neck.

ACT IV. [Scene i.]

King Richard. Messenger. Lord Lovel. Catesby.

[Richard.]   Why have you mighty Fortune, having coaxed me with an extremely
false appearance, lifted [me] up so that I might fall more severely
from a high cliff? The end of one evil is the approach of future
[evil]. A cruel, rebellious army conspires against me. I am
miserably tormented with fear. I am disrupted by a raging sea of
troubles. That traitorous Earl of Richmond, to whom a hostile
band of citizens has sworn arms, in [his] camps across the sea
longs, alas, for the kingdom. Immediately, in [my] fear of his
great evil, I punished my own servants with bloody death.[117]

---

[117]"In the meane ceason, kynge Richard apprehended in dyuerse partes of
the realme certeyne gentylmen of the earle of Rychemondes faccion. . . [who]
were put to execucion at London. . . . Beside these persones, diuerse of his
household seruantes whome either he suspected or doubted, were by great crueltie
put to shamefull death" (Hall, p. 397). See also Hol., p. 421.

But a rumor troubles [my] agitated heart [even] more: the Queen
Mother wants to join the marriage beds of her daughter with the
Earl of Richmond so that the hostile House [of Lancaster] may return
into favor, and [so that] the English nation may unite its forces.
They promise themselves the sceptre snatched by the sword. O
wicked witchcraft! A powerful enemy would [lit. will] reign in
our palaces and would bind me over to the fates!

Messenger.   The Earl of Richmond lies [at anchor] on the sea.

Richard.   O fates to be lamented! Tell [me] what has been done!

Messenger.   When October had completed thrice four days [i.e. on October
12], [while] watching, in the morning, the deep sea with [our]
eyes, we saw roving ships come to the land. They sought the Port
of Dorchester, which men call the Pole. We, watching for a long
time in an uncertain crowd, waited there [along the shore]. Then,
in the admiral's ship, we recognized the cruel Earl of Richmond.
[Those on board] remained [there] for some time, perhaps expecting
other aid [to arrive],[118] and as soon as they saw us defending the
high banks, they at once called to shore. They asked whether we
were enemies, or a military force friendly to [their] leader. We
fashioned artful deceits on [our] face[s] [and said] that Buckingham
had stationed [his] soldiers there so that they might await the
arrival of the exiled Earl, and [so that] they might immediately
lead the uncertain [Earl] to the fortifications of the Duke. "Our

---

[118]Undoubtedly the Earl was expecting more ships to arrive, for he left
Brittany with a fleet of forty ships, but, after a tempest-tossed sailing,
only his ship and one other reached the coast of England. See Hall, pp. 395-
396; and Hol., p. 419.

combined armies," [we said,] "can readily overcome [the King]. The

King buried in [his] great fear will be overwhelmed." Suspecting

[our] tempting words, they entrusted [their] wide sails, filling

with wind, to the sea; and they fled to Brittany with sails extended.

King. Why do you, too fickle goddess, mock wretched [me]? Recently

you elevated me placed on the topmost part of [your] wheel, and you

promised [me] prosperous days in [your] gentle favor. [Then]

immediately you fixed [me] flat on [my] back to the sliding bottom

[of your wheel]. How changing! how malignant! how fickle [is]

the goddess [Fortune]!

Lovel. Why does heavy care trouble [your] enraged mind? Where [is

your] former strength? Let [your] lofty mind drive out [its]

cowardly fears. The strong [man] knows no fear. Noble excellence

wavers before no danger. Why do you fear the shades of the dead

Duke? Why the other rebels? Perhaps the dead will not lie in the

earth? Do you foolishly fear [their] dust? A promised marriage

and [your] faith given to the Scots will keep them loyal to [their]

obligation of peace.[119] Your ambassadors are [now] bringing your

messages to the Duke of Brittany. You have promised him the estates

of the rebels if he will aid your sceptre with [his] arms. Who

disposed [to rewards] will not rewards readily influence? Stop

fearing! What you fear is sufficiently secure.

Catesby. If the stubbornly moved Duke [of Brittany] is not won over

[lit. roused] by your rewards, another course [lit. enterprise]

---

[119]In order to keep the Scots at peace with England, King Richard arranged
for a treaty with Scotland (see Hall, pp. 398-401; and Hol., p. 425), and, to
confirm the treaty, for the marriage of his niece Anne to the King of Scotland's
son (see Hall, p. 401; and Hol., p. 425).

[yet] remains. Disengage from Richmond the promised marriage beds
of your niece. If the House of York would [lit. will] not offer
aid to the Lancasters (however much it roars savagely, it will
threaten in vain), break off the marriage of Richmond; and he will
not marry [lit. will not celebrate the conjugal torches of] Edward's
daughter, if you wish to enjoy [your own] desire.

King.   A drawn sword will be taken immediately and will end [this]
marriage. She will be married in hell [lit. Tartary] first!

Lovel.   But enormous is the crime of a violated sanctuary. Consider
better [plans]! This cure [lit. medicine] will not help your
disease. [More] guilt will not cure the guilty, nor must a crime
be purged with open crime. And recently the populace, which a
while ago you wanted to cultivate in several ways, has been attracted
to you. Struck by a monstrous crime, [the populace] will immediately
despise [you].

Catesby.   What can be accomplished by gentle entreaties must not be
esteemed equally with the severe threats, nor the cruel speech,
nor with the cold fear of a tyrant.

King.   Shall I foolishly permit marriages, opposed to me and to my
sceptre, to be contracted? It will never happen! Wicked impiety
will keep our throne firm. I will venture anything whatever.
Evil must be overcome by evil. It is readily permissible for the
one ruling to violate laws. Cultivate piety on every side in
other affairs! Let the sword be drawn! [Her] blood will preserve
the kingdom!

Lovel. The gentle Queen can be readily turned from every side by gentle words. Let ambassadors bring your biddings to her at once so that the mother may permit her daughters to be brought into the palace.

Catesby. If, by chance, the partner of your marriage bed dies, immediately win over [your] niece who must be led into marriage by you, and the hope of the Earl will be broken by that agreement.

King. What you say pleases [me]. Everything must be attempted rather than let the kingdom fall. However, [your] counsel [is] sad while [my] wife lives. [Hence,] it is fitting that she be given over to death.

Lovel. Oppressed by a long-lasting plague of worries, perhaps she will wither away, and [then] death may be more certain for her. Immediately suborn those who will secretly whisper that she will be disastrous for you because she is not fertile, [that] your sterile wife must be kept away from [your] marriage beds, [and that] it is fitting for a King to bless [his] palace with a happy descendant. [This] cruel plague of constant grief will bring a speedy fate to the faint-hearted woman.

King. Sooner would [lit. will] I afflict [her] with a deadly sword, [or] get rid of [her] with poison than that there should be a plague and destruction of my throne. And I honor you, [my] ever-ready friends, my faithful band of noblemen. Go to the cathedral! Then, greet the mother devoutly with my words, [namely,] that I ask [her] to respect [me] and that the sordid things in my life have been changed; [that] I [now] attack whatever destroys silence [i.e. peace]; [that] I cannot obtain the favor of the people before I

embrace hereafter the daughter of my brother whose two brothers
I have wretchedly given over to destruction, and [before] I treat
[her] son, the Marquis [of Dorset], with honor. Promise great
estates, and great wealth [to her son] if [that] beloved exile
will return immediately to England. [Lovel and Catesby depart.]
[King Richard, alone.] Dazed with fear, a tumult distracts [my]
mind. Fear for [my] kingdom seizes [it], nor can anything quiet
[it]. Now I can only cure the evil if, as a husband, I should
unite with [my] niece in marriage [lit. in a conjugal celebration].
But my wife obstructs [this marriage]. We have allowed crimes
before. Why do you delay in getting rid of [your] wife with poison?
Dare [it], [my] soul! Do you fear your sins? [Your] great share
in my villainy, [which] was performed before, shames [you] too
late. Why does it please [so] wretched [a one] to be pious after
such great villainies? You have done nothing [anyway]: we have
perpetrated [all] the villainies, nor do little [ones] please [us].
We will protect [my] kingdom! [Its] entire safety [is] in [my]
sword!

[ACT IV. Scene ii.]

Lovel. Queen Elizabeth. King Richard.

[Lovel.]   O illustrious woman, once the partner of the King in marriage,
the commands of the Prince have made us ambassadors to you so that
you, mighty mother, free from [your] sacred prison, might follow
[us] to [his] splendid palace. And do not be aroused at the formerly
great evil of the King who is so greatly sorry for [his] wicked life.
[His] mature age has convinced [him] to live conscientiously. [His]

mind, which has [often] fallen [into error] wants to put aside
its impure life, and has begun a long-lasting hatred of vice.
When you want to conquer, arms please [you] more. [But,] the
sword [once] drawn does not know how to put a limit on itself,
but a calm peace is more advantageous to the victor whom any tumult
of citizens frightens lest he lose again the glory obtained before.
The King has eagerly sought to be reverenced by the people. [But,]
the pious Prince does not know how to effect this [any] sooner
unless he may conscientiously honor you and your daughters, and
[unless] he may [lit. might] give in marriage those splendid [girls]
whose brothers, alas, he has shamefully murdered. Lo, consumed
with heavy grief he will perish. [His] cheeks are bedewed with
weeping by the avenger of crime[s]; and there has been wanting to
the correcting of [his] life only the honor of your daughters, and
[your] son, the noble Marquis of Dorset, a roving exile who wanders
about through unknown countries. If he should desert the arms of
Richmond, having returned home, [this] illustrious noble will at
once brilliantly flourish with a high command. Every gift of the
resplendent palace will lie open to him. He will seek nothing in
vain. Now, then, seek the brilliant light of the palace. [0]
Queen, return into favor with the Prince, and do not spurn the mind
of a King so favorable to you. But send to the palace [your]
daughters as a sweet pledge of your mind (and do not let [them] be
frightened still by [this] dark place!) whom the pious King loves
especially. Why are you silently gazing sadly at the ground? Why
do you turn your mind about with aimless uncertainty?

Queen.　　　　Because [his] hands [are] wet with the blood of [my] sons?
Did he not savagely kill the children of his brother, and sprinkle
our marriage beds with false ignominy?　But, [then, that] villainous
one could not spare [his own] mother:　he inflicted an infamous
wound on his own family!　Will the sword cease to rage cruelly
where madness reigns?　May anyone think that any manner of villainy
is lacking [in him]?　Cannot anyone be enraged [at him] with [good]
reason?　[Your] drawn sword, [Richard,] protects [only] what you
know will maintain you in your cruelties.　Whatever [your] villainy
has caused, a greater crime will defend the crime.　[That] palace
is in no way sweet which flows with my own blood.　What nuptials
should I expect for the blood of my children, or perhaps he will
solemnize the nuptials of my daughters before he gives a grave to
my sons?　I, [their] mother, demand first to bewail the obsequies
of my sons; and honor is due to [their] dead [brothers].

Lovel.　　　　Why do you renew [these] buried hatreds?　Will eternal wrath
press upon [your] wild heart?　Let it be possible [for the King] to
expiate the crime that has been done?　Why does it please [you] so
much to fill the sky with [your] groaning, or to pulsate the heavens
with [your] laments?　Why, alas, do you so often tear open the
wound, and [why] can you not permit the cure of the evil?　If
everyone sinned as often [as you], immediately an enraged Jupiter
would hurl forth [his] avenging thunderbolts, the foul earth would
lie desolate in a squalid situation, and Venus, [even though] begged
by all men, would never restore the　great devastation with her
progeny.　Does [Richard's] sword still frighten you?

Queen.　　　　I have been overthrown by its stroke.

Lovel.　　　　But striking better, it will heal [your] wound.

Queen.   Anger more often rushes to new weapons.

Lovel.   [His] mercy scorned will be more wrathful.

Queen.   But [his] ancient anger does not know mercy.

Lovel.   Why do you fear [his] arms when [his] ire is extinguished?

Queen.   You may not appease a thirst for blood unless you fill [it].

Lovel.   But, in respect to blood, what is necessary suffices.

Queen.   But whatever pleases a cruel madman [is] necessary.

Lovel.   But [your] foolish anger, without power, will be laughed at,
and soon will be extremely ashamed of [its] rash undertakings,
because if you, senseless with rage, [still] fear [his] heart and
[if] you are still frightened of the impious menaces of the King,
[then,] this [is your] only remaining hope: he must be fought by
prayer. You will in no way prevail against [his] contending forces;
for [lit. but] his mind, [when] strongly aroused, will seethe, and
will permit no power to resist it.

Queen [To herself]. Woe to me, a woman! Alas! Alas! What shall I unhappily
do? My reeling mind wavers; it fears everything. The lost throne
has bade [me] to hope again. Shall I surrender my daughters to the
King? Shall I deprive my [daughters] of honor? The palace is
proper for [my] daughters. But what are you doing? Whom do you
believe? He sacrificed your guiltless [sons], or perhaps [you think]
he will [now] spare [their] sister[s]? The right to the kingdom
[is] the same for both. To whose marriage bed, alas, does the
King, who has shamefully lied that these [girls] were born of an
adulterous mother, commend my daughters?

Lovel.   Why do you disquiet your troubled heart with uncertainty? If
the holy life of the King in no way persuades [you], but you still

foolishly imagine that his mind [is] savage, consider how much he, being enraged, may menace you if you will despise his kind wishes.

Queen.   Does he threaten anything more than [my] death?

Lovel.   Hating [your own] life, will you now destroy your daughters?

Queen.   O [my] dearest daughters! Alas! Alas! [My] daughters, the King prepares to endow you in happy marriages. Go where fortune bids you unhappy [ones], and suppliantly bow down at the knees of [your] uncle! Unhappy progeny of a Prince, forget [your] royal estate. Private persons will suit you more. Rule is harmful: it may delight in doing whatever necessity bids [it do]. All things [are] full of fear; yet nothing must be feared openly. The lion never scorns the prayers of timid wild animals, nor does he spurn suppliant voices. If a happy lot will bless [you], behold, your parent bids you go; but if a bloody fate should destroy [you], I myself will at once take vengeance on myself with the same death; and I, [your] mother will submit to penalties for my undertaking. [To a servant.] May you be a faithful sharer of my mind. Fly at once with a speedy pace to the shores of France, and urge a return to my son the Marquis. [Tell him that] he should not fear the uncertain issue of events, nor should he be afraid of the threats of the bloody Prince; [that] the King has repented [his] wicked villainy; [that] he mournfully weeps for the bloody corpses of [his] nephews, and [that] he has promised large rewards to him, and great honors and a life free from [all] evils. Therefore, let him quickly spread [his] propitious smile and bring himself back again to [his] dear country.

Richard [As his nieces approach]. I see two [120] sisters! O happy day! Compose

[your] countenance! I shall embrace them tightly. [To his nieces.]

[O] nieces who must be loved [by me], how willingly I kiss you. I

was grieved about [your] change of fortune which must be pitied,

and so I have taken [you], who have been wretchedly shut up, from

the holy prison, wherefore I shall change this [your] lamentable

cause for sorrow into joy; and I shall clothe [you] with excellent

clothing, and I shall arrange marriages with great noblemen for you.

[The girls go out, leaving Richard alone.] Now my mind rejoices.

I delight in the hoped for peace. [Only] the despised person of

[my] wife disturbs these nuptials. Anne brings [her] sad step here.

I shall conceal by [my] face the crimes conceived in [my] mind, and

I will soothe [her] sick mind with my pious words.

[ACT IV. Scene iii.]

Queen Anne. King Richard. Messenger.

[Queen Anne, to herself.] Alas, on how many waves of troubles do I toss?

What manner of terrifying evil does my mind presage? Shall I cause

[my] sighs to break forth into mournful sounds, and shall I smite

the glittering stars with [my] mournful lamentations? What shall

I, a miserable [one], do? Shall I bewail my fate? Lo, a rumor

has spread about that my life has already been taken away, and a

noisy report of my funeral has flown about. Therefore, a grave

will be sought for me [still] living; and [while still] alive I

---

[120]In Hall, the Queen delivered her five daughters to Richard (p. 406).
See also Hol., p. 429.

will honor our obsequies with [our] tears, and I will try to render
fitting funeral rites to myself. Why does my ungrateful [husband]
threaten death to me, and cruelly esteem our love not at all? The
Cardinal Bishop, a sincere father to me, announced [this] to me,
[while] bedewing his cheeks with weeping. "The King," he said,
"has for a long time now satisfied his love; neither will he give
[you] embraces, nor will he fix sweet kisses [on you in the future].
[He says] that you are sterile and [hence] not fit for the royal
bed. Royal marriages demand such a wife as can produce [that]
great ornament of the children who will bear the sceptre of his
father in [his] tender hand." My mind tosses about on many waves
of troubles. A rumor and an evil prophecy of my fate vexes [me].
What shall I, a miserable [one], do? Lo, they [i.e. rumor and
prophecy] seek [our] death, and to shut off the last days of our
life, and to snatch the broken threads of [our] life from the
[fatal] sisters. [To Richard.] Illustrious ornament of Britain,
mighty ruler, what have I, a miserable [one] deserved? Why am I
dragged toward death? Lo, talkative voices are noising about
[that I am] dead, and a mournful crowd summons [me] to the grave.
If [my] faith given to your marriage beds does not please [you],
or if foolishly I have enviously harmed your honor, yet let me die
[lit. may I die] modestly by your hands, and may your sword pierce
[my] wicked flesh, and do not let thousands of people [instead]
wound [me] with their voices; and [then] I, [your] queen, shall
[not] be slain by the sordid citizens.[121]

---

[121]See Hall, p. 407; and Hol., p. 430.

Richard.   Never would I cruelly prepare death for [my] beloved wife, and I would [never] wet [my] chaste hands with your blood. And do not let threats disturb you since the populace is customarily an instigator of futile deception. Nor has the talkative populace [ever] known how to spare [its own] Prince. Now leave off [your] tears, and take care of yourself more gently. Lo, the grave troubles of Britain weigh upon us [now], and rebellious citizens are stirring up wild commotions. It is fitting that the greatest leader curb these [commotions]. Afterwards, we will together delight in mutual embraces.

Messenger.   The Earl of Richmond has fled your hands.

Richard.   Tell me, why has he escaped a disgraceful imprisonment?

Messenger.   After [our] sails, smitten with a wind filling [their] slackened folds, had subdued the tossing waves, and [our] storm had touched the beach of Brittany, we immediately showed your commissions to the Duke of Brittany. [But,] pain was oppressing his weak limbs, nor was [his] sick mind sufficient for any business affairs. Hence, the concern for the affairs of the country was commanded by the Treasurer, [whom people] call Peter Landois. To him, we at once promised the estates of the rebels, or whatever a kind fortune has added [to them in the way of rents], if he would restore the exile Richmond and the other comrades in exile to their native land. [These] profuse promises overcame the Treasurer, and the approver of so great a reward delighted in the English because he could powerfully defend himself with the strength of the English, and because he might [now] smash the hatreds of [his]

envious enemy.[122] Immediately he quickly sought the Earl with
hasty step, but the Earl perceived his sly cunning first, and he
secretly withdrew himself to the Parisians. Then, those whom a
cruel Fortune had joined together as deserters [of their country]
followed [him to Paris]. And Landois grieved that [his] prey was
snatched away from him, but he grieved too late. Although he
wished to outstrip, with a speedy force, the escaped [Earl] [i.e.
he wanted to catch him before he got to the border], and [although]
horsemen brandishing pikes in their right hand[s], pounding the
ground with a quickly moving pace, rushed forth so that they could
stop [lit. hinder] the fleeing [Earl]; yet they immediately returned,
and such great labor ended in vain for them. For relying on the
French King, [he is now] safe enough. He is [now] begging the
[French King] for help against your sceptre. Nor is this the end
of evil. The Earl of Oxford, freed from prison, has fled from
Hammes Castle, and [one] suppliant Earl has joined the [other]
suppliant Earl.

King. O hostile message! O shining palaces about to endure a more
bitter end than Oedipus! O honor of a Prince shining with false
light! O cruel lot! O fates envious of rulers! But refrain from
injuring those gods whom you will foolishly incite in [your] wickedness! O dark realms of Pluto, and black Chaos, o [ye] lifeless

---

[122]"This Peter whiche was no lesse disdeyned then hated almost of all
the people of Britayne, thought that yf he dyd assent and satisfie kynge
Richardes petycion. . . , he shoulde be of powre. . . sufficiente to with-
stande. . . his enuious aduersaries" (Hall, p. 403). See also Hol., p. 424.

multitude [of hell] and whatever pushes away [from me] the will

of hidden Jove, spread now deceits hither [to me]! [My] villainy

will summon Richmond into your hands so that he may cast out [his]

evil spirits immediately, unless [my] griefs may long for [even]

harsher punishments [for him].

[ACT IV. Scene iv.]

Messenger. King.

[Messenger.]   Queen Anne, [still] in her prime, died just a little while

ago.

King.   O cruel fates! O too cruel will of the gods! The affairs

of mortals have nothing certain [in them]. Only sharer of [my]

life and beloved wife, farewell! Disclose [to me] the unmerciful

nature of [her] sad destruction!

Messenger.   After the melancholy one had remained gloomy for a long time,

she poured forth sighs often mingled, alas, with heavy tears;

often with false tears, she assailed [her] ungrateful husband

with [her] bitter laments. At length, a dazed madness seized the

troubled one, and she ran with a wandering step here and there as

if suffering a violent commotion within herself, and she immediately

asked in the speech of a broken voice: "What unmerciful power

disturbs my heart? Anne, it is [your] husband," she said. "Alas,

a faithful heart is an extremely inappropriate gift to a thankless

man." Afterwards, the hidden pupils [of her eyes] lay entirely

open, and the white of [her] eye, opening only slightly, shone.

Then she raised numerous vomitings, and fell often into a deep

eclipse of [her] mind. A cold sweat passed through her entire

body, and the bright color suddenly vanished from [her] lips; [her]

yellow forehead withered, [her] bluish temples burned, and every

hair of [her] eyebrows fell off. [Her] blue lips wasted away in

[their] shameful lack [of blood], and [her] tongue (horrible to

see!) in a lurid spectacle projected out of [her] mouth opening

larger than usual, and [her] bright finger-nails now shone no more,

but wasted away as if covered with poison. At length, the miserable

women, having struggled with the fates, fell dead.[123]

King.   Now I desire a happy marriage to [my] niece, and I shall

beguile the marriage beds of [my] niece promised in vain [to

Richmond]. But hither my niece comes with a hesitating step.

As a wooer, I shall begin to entice her marriage [to me].

[ACT IV. Scene v.]

King. Oldest daughter of Edward.

[King.]   O descendant from royal stock, and maiden worthy of the sceptre,

after (o the grief!) the fates have so cruelly seized [my] wife,

who may be better united with me in royal marriage than [one] who

is born of the high family of a king? Let us unite [our] souls;

promise [me your] faith in marriage: receive [me] as [your]

husband! Why are you silent, with a grim face?

Daughter of Edward. Shall I (o infamous villainy not to be propitiated by

any funeral piles!), shall I as [your] miserable wife stain my

hands with the red blood of [your] dead [victims]? Before Olympus

---

[123]The death of Anne, as described here, obviously intimates that she
was poisoned by Richard. The chronicles are not so definite; "But howsoever
that it [i.e. Anne's death] fortuned, either by inward thought and pensyuenes
of hearte, or by intoxicacion of poyson (which is affirmed to be most likely)
within a few daies after [Richard had comforted his wife with fair words],
the quene departed oute of this transitorie lyfe. . ." (Hall, p. 407). See
also Hol., pp. 430-431. In point of fact, Anne died of consumption, brought
on by her grief over the death of her only son.

will [not] fail his wife[124] and [before] the moon will govern the

day and the sun the night, flowing Etna will first emit cool waters,

and the wandering Nile will emit burning blades of iron. Shall I,

infamous uncle, wretchedly keep silent that the little nephews,

hateful to you, but dear brothers to me, were savagely killed by

your right hand? First Hesperian Tethys[125] will raise the bright

day from [her] deepest bay [lit. bosom]; first Lepus[126] will fly

from the hateful dog. Jupiter [always] punishes infamous villainy,

however hidden, and never permits crafty deceits. Sliding rocks

weigh upon [lit. weighed upon] the shoulders of Sisyphus, and

cruel Procrustes pays a severe penalty because, [while] living,

they killed their own guests.[127] You cruelly killed, not [your]

guests, but, alas, your own nephews, [who only] recently had left

behind [their] swaddling clothes.

---

[124]From Olympus, the dwelling place of Zeus and the gods, the name
"Olympius" was often applied to Zeus, the father of the gods, who was noted
for his many wives and love affairs. Context would seem to require [not].

[125]The wife of Neptune and goddess of the sea.

[126]The constellation Lepus, or the hare.

[127]Classical authorities attribute various crimes to Sisyphus as the
reason for his punishment (he had to roll uphill a huge marble block, which
as soon as it reached the top rolled down again). The one probably alluded
to in this passage is his attacking of travellers, whom he killed with a
huge block of stone.

Procrustes cruelly killed his guests either by stretching them or
by lopping them to make them fit his beds.

Richard.   Come now, maiden, banish your harsh words lest both [our]

persons waste away on account of a single crime! I confess that

my throne was acquired by the blood and death of the guiltless

[boys]. It pleased the fates [to do] so. Have your brothers been

slain? I am sorry; the deed grieves [me]. Are they dead? [My]

former deed cannot be colored. Shall I weep for the dead? Tears

avail nothing. What do you wish that I do? perhaps I may repay

the twin destruction of [your] brothers with [my] blood poured

forth by this [my] right hand? I will do [it]: I will offer [my]

breast to readied swords, and if it is more pleasing [to you], I

shall die by your arms [i.e. at your hands]. I shall seek out

fires, floods, earth or the menacing Caucasus; I shall hasten to

the infernal regions of the shady grove of black Stygian pool if

I should [thereby] be pleasing to you, royal heroine.[128]

Daughter of Edward. It may be love, it may be hate, it may be anger, or it

may be faith; I do not care. It pleases [me] to hate whatever

you intend [to do]. Sooner your sword will penetrate [my] breasts

than that the lust of [one] related [to me] will defile [my] body.

O Jupiter, expert with [your] fierce thunderbolt [of vengeance],

why does the earth not burn [with] your three-pronged torch? Why

does the gaping earth not swallow [him] up on the spot? Monstrous

[is] the depravity of [this] savage Prince, surpassing the race of

Gorgons[129] in fear.

---

[128]Although the chronicles provide a basis for this scene as a whole
(see Hall, p. 407; Hol., p. 431), they provide none for this speech by Richard.
Richard's wooing of Elizabeth here (especially his offering his breast to her
sword) is comparable to his wooing of Anne in Shakespeare's Richard III.

[129]The Gorgons (Stethno, Euryale, Medusa) were monsters with snakes for
hair, whose look turned persons to stone.

Richard.　　　Most wicked one, be silent! Will [your] belief be silent

only under arms? Does [my] love avail nothing? Does not a royal

marriage move [you] at all, and do not [my] bitter tears avail

[anything]? There is a double way of ruling for a prince: love

and fear. It is advantageous for kings to try both.

Daughter of Edward. If you force [me] to die, I willing yield.

King.　　　[Then,] die!

Daughter of Edward. Death will be more pleasing to me, and it is better

[for me], oppressed with hardships, to die at once than [for me],

encompassed with cares, to enjoy light for a long while.

King.　　　[Then,] die, foolish one!

Daughter.　　Do you threaten nothing further? I prefer to die a virgin

than to live incestuously with a tyrannical man, hateful to the

gods and men.

Richard.　　Alas, unfortunately what you are doing will contemn your

marriage beds. Be my living queen! Be silent about [your] miserable

brothers.

Daughter.　　He is not miserable who knows how to die.

King.　　　You are not willing [then]? Lo, there is no fear in [my]

sword, and [my] sword [once] drawn does not ever know how to spare

[anyone].

Daughter.　　Rise up ye shades of Nero, and ye grim furies of Cleopatra;

give a similar fate to these nuptials as the house of Oedipus

endured. Is it not sufficient [that you, Richard] have killed [my]

princely brothers and have defiled [your] hand with noble slaughter?

Why, then, do you as [my] husband wish to defile a chaste virgin?

O the manners! O the wicked times! But sooner let a hawk assail

my flesh, sooner send your army cruelly against me or whatever cruel

monstrosity you nourish, than that I, a chaste virgin, [should]
yield to [your] adulterous marriage beds!

Richard.   She has departed, and has foolishly fled from our marriage
proposals [lit. marriage beds]. The foolish maiden refuses [our]
royal affections. [For] now I shall put off these things: perhaps
the threats of the raving girl will die while I look after the
interests of the country.

[ACT IV. Scene vi.][130]

Messenger. King.

[Messenger.]   Recently, haughty Richmond bore high spirits. Haughtily he
was puffed up in his lofty head, but at last he has fallen miserably.
[Just] lately, his enterprise has shamed [him], and his menaces
have been broken.

King.   O pleasing day which strengthens my sceptre! Now, certainly,
a firm assurance of peace will emerge, but tell [me] everything,
for hope nourishes the miserable.

Messenger.   The King of France still in the first flower of his youth is
scarcely active, nor has [his] first beard outlined [lit. painted]
[his] cheeks, nor does [his] youthful hand maintain the sceptre
sufficiently [well]. Rather, [his] tender age, which must be cared
for, is entrusted to [his] guardians until after [his] vigor learns
about ruling with strength. The Earl [of Richmond] often troubled
these [guardians] with [his] hostile desires and ardently implored
aid for [his] weakened circumstances. Neither did he cease to

---

[130]See Hall, p. 408; and Hol., p. 432.

spend in vain [his] entreaties, while he anxiously wearied many

men with much labor, nor could [his] exhausted spirit endure the

delays, and [hence] he has often taken it ill that his complaints

have been disappointed. While the manifold favor of [his] nobles

urges [him] to endure [his] tedious rejection [by the French],

his mind despairs. The exile longs to live better and is ashamed

of [his] empty-handed labor.

King.   Now it is fitting that [we] fortunate ones celebrate [this]

hallow day. O day excellent to me with [your] white stone,[131]

now a more gentle fortune flows to [my] happy affairs! How often

the Earl has recently stirred up storms in vain, and how little

has [his] grave results threatened [us] recently! Yea, rather,

the crime will turn back upon its perpetrator. Now [our] fleet

lies upon the calm sea in vain; now it wrongly keeps watch for

Richmond's return. Therefore, forbid [our] ships to cleave now

to the sea, and let [every] soldier who guards a hostile harbor

put aside [his] arms. This will be the end of evils! It is possible

[now] to rule safely. Now fear will end unless you may still fear

that which must not be feared.

ACT V. [Scene i.]

Messenger. [One] wife. [Another] wife. An old woman.

[Messenger.]   What swift whirlwind carries me through the air? Fly, fly,

citizen! the Earl hangs fast upon [my] rear! Richmond's wrath

menaces [us] dreadfully. While we thought that the Earl's flame

---

[131]In ancient times white stones were used to mark lucky days, and black
stones to mark unlucky ones.

of war had been extinguished, and the Duke of Richmond's hope for
war had been broken, he touched Milford Haven [in Wales] with an
enormous infantry; and now treads upon a Wales entirely delivered
over to him. The raging Earl threatens all England!

[One] wife.   Wherefore, wherefore, husband, do you fly [your] beloved wife?
And how many prayers of [your] wife will you permit to be spent
in vain? Behold, [my] cheeks flow with much weeping. Have pity!
But if it pleases [you] to fly [our] pleasant hearths, let your
wife go too, a small burden on a journey.

Another wife. I beseech you by the will of the gods and by the promised
faith of [our] marriage bed, [and] by the tender years of [our]
sons that you will not forsake your sad home, alas, to cruel
[soldiers].

Old woman.   O son, the comfort of your mother, stay! But if, a deserter,
you leave [your] home to the enemy, let [your] sword seek out the
breasts formerly well known [to you, my] son. I, [your] mother,
will die by your wound.

[ACT V. Scene ii.]

Earl Henry. Rice ap Thomas, a Welshman.

[Henry, alone.] At last, I perceive the hoped for dwellings of my native
land, and [at last] I realize the greatest happiness of [all]
miserable exiles. O be secure, but be secure for a long time, [o]
beloved country, torn by the impious teeth of the raging boar!
Grant [me, my] country, [your] indulgence if I should wage pious
battles: grant [your] indulgence, I beg! Your cause arouses [me],
and the dire evil of the Prince calls for war. [Your] King has
died! A Nero [now] occupies [his] kingdom. The little boy died

with his brother, the King. The sacred altars [lit. temples]
alone protect the Queen. I have come as a pious avenger of the
blood of kings. Richard will be punished by Henry ([indeed] he
has been punished [already]) if merciful God will grant our
wishes. I see Rice ap Thomas, [descended] from Welsh stock
[approaching].

Rice.   O famous Prince, born of regal stock, noble Earl of Richmond,
excellent in honor, the only hope of the British nation, you, the
[one] longed for by your English citizens, have come after many
prayers and [after] long delays of time!

Henry.   I have always held fast in my mind [my] native land. Vigorously
I shall remove the servile yoke from [its] neck.

Rice.   Now you, the comfort and true head of the country, you alone
offer hope for our afflicted affairs; and England, happy with so
great a king, rejoices.

Henry.   Citizens always reverence in their inmost heart him whom they
[yet] will not confess with their lip[s] [to be their] prince.

Rice.   May God, who shakes the skies with his three-pronged flame
and [who] thrusts the unfaithful down into the deep caves of
Proserpine, bury [lit. cover] me alive with black earth, if I
shall deceive [my] faith promised to you. If you bid [me] to set
up your standards on the fields of Wales, as an impious reaper,
I shall rush forth into the Welsh field[s]. Whichever walls you
may want cast down, a battering ram, driven by this hand, will
quickly disperse [their] stones. And there will not be any soldier
in my camp who will not follow you.

Henry.   Rice, your loyalty is pleasing to me. If the will of God makes

prosperous my undertakings, I promise that you will be the future

ruler of all Wales.[132]

[ACT V. Scene iii.]

Burchier. Hungerford. Soldiers.

[Hungerford.] Renowned Burchier, resplendent with the rank of knight,

luckily I have escaped the wicked hands of the enemy, and I have

sadly removed [my] willing band away from Captain Brackenbury's

army through the thick shadows of the night.[133]

Burchier.   How often, Hungerford, have we, having turned [our] backs on

our leader, [Brackenbury,] slipped [and slid] through recesses

up to this point! But o you peaceful time of the sweet night,

protect [us] still! Titan, delay the day, until, safe from the

arms of the tyrant, we have reached the tents of the famous Earl

Henry. [They depart.]

Soldier. [Alone.] Fortunately, black night, I flee through your shadows.

Let him who will hinder me be afflicted by [my] sword! [He departs,

flying.]

---

[132]See Hall, p. 411; and Hol., p. 435.

[133]"For they [i.e. Hungerford, Burchier and others] beynge aduertised
that kynge Richarde had theim in suspicion and gealosye. . . forsooke preuely
their Capteyne Robert Brackenbury, and by nocturnall wandryng, and in maner
by vnknowen pathes and vncertaine waies searchyng, at the last came to the earle
Henry" (Hall, p. 413). See also Hol., p. 437.

Henry. [Alone and lost.][134] What place is this, what region, what district

of the kingdom? Where am I? The night rushes away. Alas, where

[are] my allies? Everything is hostile. What place is free from

deceit? Shall I ask anyone? Take care [that his] loyalty is

certain! The native warmth [of my body] has left [my] internal

joints; [my] limbs are stiff with rigidity. I can scarcely speak

for fear. I tremble all over. Worry abides in [my] mind. My

step-father Stanley has given me these causes for sorrow. What slow

delay keeps him? While I was considering the various jests of

fate, and while I was only thinking about the dubious loyalty of

the citizens, I ordered [my] army to advance. Then I began to

condemn the slow delays of my step-father. Afterwards fear and

hope [began to] besiege [my] doubtful heart, and while I was

considering too deeply [lit. enough] in [my] mind what obstructs

[my chances for success], I, having wandered [lit. slipped] into

the dense shadows, have fled the sight [of my army]. Deprived of

its leader, the army [now] wanders aimlessly. As a deserter, I

have been left unarmed to the enemy.

Earl of Oxford [Coming upon Henry]. A great concern, illustrious Earl,

weighed on [our] uneasy minds, [and] a grave fear disturbed [us]

violently because you, [our] absent leader, abandoned [your]

---

[134]"Whyle he [i.e. the Earl] thus pensyue dragged behynde his hoost
. . . he for the depe darcknes coulde not perceaue the steppes of theim
[i.e. his soldiers] that passed on before, and had wandred hether and thether,
sekynge after his compaignie and. . . he dyuerted to a very lytle village beynge
aboute. iii. myles from his armye, takynge great thought and muche fearynge
least he should be espied,. . .not once auenturynge to aske or demaunde a question
of any creature. . ." (Hall, p. 413). See also Hol., p. 437.

soldiers when the highest ridges of the mountains were subdued by
the black night; nor did any private person issue orders [to them].
Soon a heavy grief invaded [my] sad breast. Sometimes the army
called for [its] leader in vain; sometimes we feared the uncertain
loyalty of the citizens; and [now], late in the evening, we happily
delight in [your] sight, however much [our] mind is still disturbed
by the fear which has shaken [it].

Henry.   Why do you fear? Let [your] cowardly fear be expelled! It
often pleases [me] to reflect upon secret affairs alone.

Hungerford [Coming upon Henry]. Wretchedly having escaped from the treacheries
of the cruel tyrant, I humbly wish to live under your command,
Earl, and to follow [your] banners, illustrious leader.

Henry.   Famous descendant and noble offspring of knights, worthwhile
glory will now readily follow after you [and your son]. The
gracious will of the citizens delights me, and happily I embrace
your   great loyalty. But tell [me]: what troops does the
tyrant lead?

Hungerford.   Few soldiers willingly follow [his] standards, and fear [alone]
forces [them] to join the arms of Richard. [His] dubious army
fears him more than [you]. [Every] soldier [of his] dares to
trust nothing to his arms.

Henry.   Transport [your] soldiers to their camp [sites]!

[ACT V. Scene iv.]135

Earl Henry. Lord Stanley.

[Henry.]   Unless my wishes deceive [me], my step-father, Stanley, the
distinguished ornament of his family, approaches. Do I not see

---

135See Hall, pp. 411-412; and Hol., pp. 435-436.

[your] real person, or am I mistaken, deceived by your ghost?
[My] spirit takes strength. [My] mind rejoices, and my heart is
free from its fear.

Stanley.   And sweet joy invigorates our limbs. It is pleasing to see
my son-in-law. Give me [your] long awaited embraces! May God,
who has given you favor, in turn, favor your undertakings, [and]
accomplish [them]!

Henry.   He will favor [them] if it is possible to enjoy your help.

Stanley.   Would that what I wish [to do] were possible!

Henry.   Why can't you? Why is it not possible?

Stanley.   Often what you wish [to do] cannot be accomplished, however,
without great harm.

Henry.   Why will you fear when you may be of service to your country?

Stanley.   Because the life of my son is dear to me.

Henry.   Does Richard keep [him] as a pledge of your loyalty?

Stanley.   So that I might not aid you, he holds [him] given in pledge.

Henry.   O cunning crime! O barbarous tyrant! [His] bloody fear wrests
the loyalty of those whom he believes [to be] little loyal through
[their] love [of him].

Stanley.   Restrain your anger and control your noble heart! If I cannot
aid [you] openly, yet secretly our assistance will never be lacking
to you.

Henry.   He has departed. Alas, the apathetic loyalty of [my] step-
father disturbs me. How much the help of this man has been counted
on [lit. has shone on] by me? But, [my] anxious heart is disquieted
with complaints in vain. Is it pleasing to fill the shy with vain
complaints? Yea, rather, it is fitting to cast away [my] gloomy
deliberations.

[ACT V. Scene v.]

Duke of Norfolk. King Richard.

[Duke of Norfolk alone.] [My] armed force awaits its leader. Money will
summon [any soldier] to battle, nor will it permit delays. Hither
comes Prince Richard with a hesitant step. Alone he is considering
secret matters, and cares weigh upon [him]. What sudden chance
[lit. motive] has troubled your looks? Why are [your] lips white?
Why are you dazed with a wavering mind?

Richard.   Beloved personage of Norfolk, noble Duke, whose loyalty to
me has always been distinguished, I shall, [as though] faithless
[in you], hide nothing [from you] by a false brow. [Our] horrible
dreams of last night terrified [us]. After the buried night had
urged rest [for me], and [after] a deep sleep had stolen upon [our]
soft eyelids, suddenly a grim troop of furies pressed upon [us]
and tore to pieces [our] trembling body in [their] savage attack,
and I was [made] the horrible prey for [these] raging demons; and,
at length, a great trembling disturbed [our] slumbers, and a horrid
fear struck our limbs. Alas, why do the violent shades of the
infernal regions menace [us]?[136]

Norfolk.   Why do you fear [your] dreams and the foolish menaces of
night? And why do the false jests of [your] mind terrify you?
My drawn sword now announces the best [kind of] prophecy. Dare
enough, and do not fear your plans! So many rebellious citizens
will afford booty to you, and [their] fettered hands will confess
the victory.

_____

[136]See Hall, p. 414; and Hol., p. 438.

Richard.   Not any fear at all has crushed [my] tremulous breast, nor

has the revolt shaken [my] inactive body. We have learned to dare

before. Our enemies have already reached places nearby with

[their] arms. They summon [us] to battle. Our army will stand

against the adverse arms.

Norfolk [Alone]. What do we do [now]? Alas, what are the blind fates

contemplating? What is the suspected loyalty of the citizens

preparing? Such recently discovered words warn me as follows:

"Renowned Norfolk, you have undertaken nothing more rash, for the

King has been sold out for money; Lord Richard has been betrayed."

But [yet] no stain will [ever] condemn our loyalty [to Richard].

[While] alive I shall never abandon the standards of Richard.[137]

[ACT V. Scene vi.]

Richard's Oration to [his] soldiers.

Loyal comrades, soldiers and subjects, although I once perpetrated

bloody deed[s] and dire evil[s], I have sufficiently atoned for

[my] guilt with pious tears, and I have suffered punishments for

[my] crime[s]. I have sufficiently avenged [my] crime by [my]

sorrow [lit. by its sorrow]. Therefore, let so great a repentance

move you! It is better to defend what has [already] been obtained

---

[137]". . . the nyghte before he shoulde set forwarde towarde the kynge,
one wrote on his gate.
  Iack of Norffolke be not to bolde.
  For Dykon thy maister is bought and solde.
Yet all this notwithstandynge he regarded more his othe his honour and promyse
made to king Richard. . ." (Hall, p. 419). See also Hol., p. 444.

than to strive for [it in the first place].[138] Fight courageously!

Desire strongly to defend the kingdom obtained by [your] influence!

There is no need for much bloodshed: A Welsh enemy attacks [us].

He impudently claims the kingdom. [A few] disloyal bands of

Englishmen, wicked murderers, and an extravagant race [of men],[139]

and the French race, in hatred of your country, follow him. But

God has entrusted me to the hands of [you] citizens whose loyalty

has always been cultivated [lit. striven after] by me, [and] by

whose influence I obtained the glory of ruling. And, unless I,

as an interpreter of [your] countenances, am beguiled, [your]

savage looks demand that the victory must be given to me. Your

eyes threaten destruction to the cruel enemy. You have won, I say;

the army of Englishmen has won! I [already] see the field flowing

with their blood! Soon my horrible massacre will destroy not only

the conquered French, but also the trifling Welsh. But why do I

delay [their] fates? Why do I keep you with these words [of mine]

from rushing upon [them]? Grant my pardon (as much as a merciful

God will now voluntarily grant) if that one [i.e. Richmond] should

conquer [us]. [For if he does] horrible crosses await you; the

sword, chains and a harsh yoke for [your] neck; and the sword of

the enemy will seek out our limbs. I care nothing for myself, [but]

may your safety be assured! Have regard for the interests of

---

[138]"For if wyse men say trew, there is some pollycie in gettyng, but much more in kepyng" (Hall, p. 415). See also Hol., p. 439.

[139]". . . the earle of Richmond Captaine of this rebellion. . . is a Welsh mylkesoppe. . . . Secondarely feare not and put a way all doubtes, for when the traitors and runagates of our realme, shall see vs with banner displaied come against them. . .will either shamefully flye, or humbly submitt themselfes to our grace and marcie" (Hall, p. 415). See also Hol., p. 446.

yourselves, of [your] children [and] of [your] wives! Look out

for [your] country! This [above all] needs your help! Be courageous!

May [our] clean manner of living kill the enemy, and may no one

fear the uncertain outcome of the battle! The greatest omens of

victory have been given to us. It is not unknown to you that the

safety of [you] soldiers will rest upon the very great prudence of

[your] leader. Behold, he considers of no importance the scornful

looks of Henry. In vain, you fear the threats and the unconquered

strength of the leader, Richmond. Wherefore, let [our] standards

in hostile array shine forth on the fields [of battle]. Let

[every] soldier in hostile array rush forth in a hasty march, and

let savage enemy wound savage enemy! Victory awaits you, you,

noble comrades, for I shall pierce with this right hand the soul

of him who was the cause of [these] civil wars. Either I shall

die today, or I shall obtain glory.

[ACT V. Scene vii.]

Messenger. King Richard. Duke of Norfolk.

[Messenger.] High-minded Prince, I have accomplished your orders. Stanley

answered in extremely harsh speech [that] if you afflict his son,

he has more [sons].[140]

Richard. Then, [this] ungrateful enemy and wicked traitor has refused

[to obey] my orders. I will kill [his] son. I will pay you at

once, father [Stanley], for your worthy vows! Why does the son of

[this] wicked father live for so long [a time]? O [my] wrath [is]

---

[140]"The lorde Stanley aunswered the pursiuaunt that yf the kynge dyd so
[i.e. killed his son], he had more sonnes a lyue, and as to come to hym he
was not then so determined. . ." (Hall, p. 420). See also Hol., p. 446.

too patient, [too] slow after so great a crime. [To the Messenger.]
Carry out my commands! Send quickly to me the [one] who may
deliver the head cut off of his slain [son]!

Norfolk.   Control [your] mind, and do not let the impious father annoy
[you]. The battles now demand [our presence]: they demand another
time [for his execution]. Banners shine nearby with the emblems
of the enemy.

Richard.   Shall I, unavenged, spare the son of wicked father?

Norfolk.   The son will atone for the crime of [his] father after the battl

Richard.   [To his guards]. Now, then, lead the hated offspring of the wicked
father into the camp! When the battle has ended, immediately he
will be capitally punished [lit. he will pay the penalty with his
head] for [his] father's crime.

[ACT V. Scene viii.]

Henry's Oration to [his] soldiers.

O avenger of evil, [o] you British nation who follow my standards,
do not imagine [any] foolish fears, for if a just Jupiter pays
heed to any battles [at all], he will help us (who will rejoice to
see the country free) to remove the yoke of the King [lit. will
favor the yoke of the King removed by us]. Lo, we rightfully demand
the sceptre taken by fraud. What better cause for war can be
offered [us] than the enemy of [our] country, [and] the destruction
of [its] royal family? Therefore, let the tyrant fall in bloody
death! Richard surpasses the impious Scythians in [his] evil. He
has surpassed you, infamous Nero, in the slaughter of [your] mother.
[For,] he has afflicted his own nephews with [his] impious sword.

[Nor] did the son refrain from the disgracing of [his own] mother.

The illicit desire of the uncle has [even] ventured to defile [his]

niece. Will you, [my army,] grant the titles of [his] brother to

[his] hands? Let [your] fear cease, and assail the enemy in hostile

array. Fear not the [enemies']   great arms: they, whose fear

[of the King] compels [them] to follow [him], will desert [their]

leader in the midst of the battle. [Our] enemies will little

defend their leader. But [even if] they are loyal, and do not

spurn [their] leader, [even if] they do fight bitterly and rush

forth by the many thousands, still it [is] not the number of

troops, but the virtue of the leader that obtains victory, and

brings honor.[141] Will you fear the arms of him who fears no

crime, [who] has subdued his own nephews with death? [Is there

any] piety, sanctity, shame, [or] faith in this man? Sanctuaries

have been broken into, a brother has been bastardized [lit. beaten

down],[142] a niece has been tempted with pollution [by him] whose

faith, in short, has been false. What has [this] plague on his

country not perpetrated? Gird your bodies [lit. body] with a

sword against the enemy. Rush forth into battle and vigorously

---

[141]"Remember that victorie is not gotten with the multitude of men, but with the courages of hartes and valiauntnes of myndes" (Hall, p. 418). See also Hol., p. 443.

[142]The "brother" referred to here is taken to mean Edward, although one or both of the princes may be meant since *occisus* means "slain" also. See Hall: "Yea a tyraunt more then Nero, for he hath not only murdered his nephewe beyng his kynge and souereigne lord, bastarded his noble brethern and defamed the wombe of his. . . mother, but also compased. . . how to stuprate and carnally know his awne nece. . ." (p. 417). See also Hol., p. 442.

rend [his] army! Let [our] banners be raised on high! Let whoever

is faithful kill in the battle [those who are] disloyal; [let] the

pious [kill] the impious! You [who are] peaceful will assail the

tyrant; you [who are] gentle [will assail] the unmerciful [man]!

For if it were possible, without injuring the honor of a prince,

I would bow down, humbly seeking at your knees that Henry, the

true heir of the English throne, might conquer Richard who holds

the sceptre by fraud. But if that man conquers, your wandering

Henry will be banished from the country, or will suffer grave

punishments; and it will shame you to offer [your] necks to the

victor. Let [him] be assailed on the other side while he now

readies [his] forces! Either let him kill [me] or he will die!

This [much] is certain to me.

Upon [Henry's] return [to the field of battle], let guns go off, and trumpets sound. Let soldiers outside the hall stir [with great commotion] until Lord Stanley is on the stage ready to speak as follows:

Stanley to [his] soldiers.

Hasten! Free the country from tyranny! Carry forth [our] standards

in hostile array when the battle grows hot so that the true heir

may hold the kingdom of England! Pious virtue will fight against

evil. Fight only, [and] the victory [will] now [be] yours! If

you conquer, the country [will be] free of tyranny. Rush forth

into the midst of the enemy with a quickened step.

Let [battle] noises be made as soon as Lord Stanley has finished speaking and has departed for the [battle] field with his army. Then, let Lord Northumberland come from the [battle] field with his men. Let the noise cease as he speaks.

[Oration] of the Earl of Northumberland to [his] soldiers.

Do not, [my] army, condemn [our] illustrious race of Northumbrians,

nor consider our moon [on our battle standards] cowardly because, flying the weapons of the enemy, I have turned [our] backs. At

[long] last, I curse the monstrous villainy of the King. I am

horrified at [his] hands wet with the blood of his own family.

An ancient prophecy [lit. a prophetic antiquity] has counselled

that the victory would be to the King if he should gather his

forces before the moon has changed. We are the moon. Therefore,

we, soldiers, have changed the moon so that the tyrant may at

once pay penalties worthy of [his] villainy.[143]

Let [battle] noises be heard again. Then let a captain run after a few
soldiers, driving them back to the [battle] field, while speaking as follows:

Captain.

Cowardly soldier, where are you fleeing? Unless you return, you

will die by my sword.

After [more battle] noises, let soldiers run from the field over the stage,
one after another, flinging away their arms. Then, let some come in halting
and wounded. After this, let Henry, Earl of Richmond come in triumphing,
with the body of King Richard dead on a horse. Catesby, Ratcliff, and others
[are] bound.

[Messenger.] The contention has been settled. Mars has granted [his]

judgment. Richard lies dead, but yet, like a Duke, he lies.

After the fierce armies saw themselves together, and the trumpet

had sounded the battle signal to arms, [each] fierce army rushed

into the readied battle. At length, with [his] army fleeing,

Richard, seeing the Earl, rushed forth against him on [his]

galloping horse, just as the ferocious Nemean lion, [when its]

young has been seized, flies, savagely roaring, here and there

through the fields. Brandon stoutly bore the standards of the

Earl. [Richard] made his spear warm with his [i.e. Brandon's]

blood. Then, Cheney, strong with arms, challenged [lit. offered

[143]The chronicles offer no basis for this prophecy, although they do note
Northumberland's last minute desertion of Richard. See Hall, p. 419; and Hcl.,
p. 445.

himself to] Richard. This man only fell [to the ground] before
the strength of Richard. He had come to [his] enemy whom alone
he sought mightily. Fiercely he delayed on the Earl alone. On
the other hand, the Earl defended himself with great skill. For
a long time, the Earl was engaged in an indecisive battle until
so many enemies to that man [i.e. Richard] came together [there]
that he, gouged with many wounds, fell dead. O [you would have
been] a leader truly famous in warlike glory if France had felt
your fierce arms, or if you had perfidiously deceived the faith
promised to the Scots.[144] But the avenger of evil, the mighty
father of heaven, has taken vengeance on your life, but yet late
enough.

Oration of Earl Henry.[145]

Mighty ruler of Olympus, the glory of the stars, you who are the
shepherd of faithful earth-bound men, and [you] who have dominion
over the souls of princes, you [who] have erected happy monuments
to kings, [you who] have encircled the head[s] of kings with
glittering crown[s], [who] alone [have] overcome the false majesty
of the gods, and [who] have afflicted enemies hateful to their
own nation, great honor and thanks are due to you who have granted
us [this] splendid triumph! [Even] an armed force will yield to
your commands. If anyone should be very angry at the massacre of

---

[144]See Footnote 18.

[145]See Hall, p. 420; and Hol., pp. 445-446.

Asytages, or [if] Pelops, the son of Tantalus [should be angry] at

the Phrygian king, the former will dread Cyrus, and [the latter] will

quake at [his] avenger.[146]   [Hence], a Henry will dare to drive

out a Richard. But you, o governor of the shining heavens, [you]

whom the earth and the vast creation of world honors, as long as

[my] body uses air and the fatal sisters have not closed the last

day of [my] life, as long as a gentle breath [of air] nourishes

[our] youthful limbs, let us sing of you in constant praise; let

us, [o] mighty God, offer the gratitude owing to you. [For] you

mercifully have permitted the monster [Richard], a plague, alas,

to his own citizens, to be subdued by my forces. But [now], you

soldiers who have endured grave sorrows, tend at once to the wounds

inflicted on [your] bodies so that [your] bloody sore[s] will not

grow worse [lit. increase further]. The rest of you [will] mercifully

give graves to the dead, for [lit. and] worthy honor is due to the

dead.

[ACT V. Scene ix.]

Lord Strange, a boy. Earl Henry. Lord Stanley.

[Strange.]   The sea does not always swell with violent waves, nor does

Jupiter always strike the sea with a storm. Aeolus does not always

---

[146]I.e., if anyone complains to God about the crime of anyone else, God
will surely provide vengeance. In the case of Astyages' merciless treatment
of his son Cyrus, Cyrus himself was sent as the avenger. In the case of
Tantalus' inhumanity to his son Pelops, the gods themselves took vengeance.

raise up sharp winds, nor does blind fate always tread upon lowly men. Sometimes, the flood of the raging sea is calmed, and [all] at once Titan's gleaming head shines forth, and a propitious fate will at length lift up downtrodden men. Behold, the mighty victor, once living in obscurity on French shores and [now] King of the British, is master of his own kingdom! O [my] beloved King, live and reside happily with your subjects for many years, and mercifully receive these captives into [your] faithful protection.[147]

Henry.   O offspring of the Stanleys dear to me, o Lord Strange, behold, I look upon you [at last] with [great] pleasure, [and] I will give back to you the captives which you have delivered to me.

Stanley.   O my son, my happy spirit rejoices that [my] dear son has returned safe to [his] father and that he has escaped the right hand of the bloody tyrant, [and] because you have returned safe [to me] after so many dire dangers.

Henry.   I am joyous for the kingdom and for myself: for the kingdom because it is free from a severe tyranny; [and] equally for myself because I shall wield the regal sceptre of my kingdom. Therefore, let us suppliantly sing praises with a pious voice to the supreme God who gave [us] our realms.

---

[147]". . . the Lorde [Strange] was deliuered to the kepers of the kynges tentes to be kept as a prisoner, whyche when the felde was done and their master slayne. . . they submitted them selfes as prysoners to the Lord Straunge, and he gently receyued them and brought them to the newe proclamed king, where of him and of his Father he was receyued with greate ioye and gladnes" (Hall, pp. 420-421). See also Hol., p. 448.

Epilogue.

You have seen the dead bodies of the [little] princes, [and] the frightening
obsequies of raging noblemen. You have seen the deadly battles of powerful
persons and the fitting rewards which the tyrant has received. Illustrious
Henry, the Earl of Richmond [first] pacified [all] disturbances with the
blood of Richard. [Then] inspired by the happy advice [and] by the wise
heart of the Bishop of Ely, and by the warlike spirit of the famous Buckingham,
then by influence of his mother, Margaret (who founded at her own expense
this our famous College consecrated to Christ),[148] [King Henry VII] left to
all ages many signs, once famous, of [his] royal power [and] of his [great]
mental ability which has never been praised sufficiently. This offspring from
the royal stock of Lancaster took a wife born of the blood of York. Thus
the contentions of the two Houses ended with [this] eternal compact. Thereupon,
from this [marriage there was made] a haven of peace for wretched Englishmen,
and there was an end of deadly discord. From this [marriage], that noble
offspring and certain heir Henry [VIII], the son of [his] father Henry [VII],
proceeded, who in governing the chief circumstances of the British realm,
has, already ruled in his own right. Then, [Henry VIII], who [was] a true
patron of [his] afflicted country, left one by far more excellent than [his]
several other benefits, however many, when he begot the   mighty Princess
Elizabeth, a daughter worthy of [her] father, and a maiden withstanding old
age, who has happily ruled in peace the united English realms for so many
completed courses of Phoebus, whom may the right hand of the supreme thunderer
[always] defend, and may he protect her life by shielding [her].

----

[148]"This our college" is probably a reference to St. John's College because
the play is known to have been enacted there, and because all colleges at that
time were formally "consecrated" to Christ. The phrase, however, may refer to
Christ's College since dicatum may mean "dedicated" as well as "consecrated,"
and since Lady Margaret is credited with being a founder of both colleges in
question.

The end. [αune.] of January.

        Anthony Cade

End of the three-part tragedy,

acted on three nights at St. John's

College, Cambridge, and written

by Thomas Legg, Doctor of Civil Law

and Rector of Gonville and Caius

College.

        1583

APPENDIX A

COLLATION OF MANUSCRIPTS

The following list contains all the textual variants (with the exception of punctuation variants) occurring in Part I, and in the first one
hundred lines of Act III, Part II, and in the first one hundred lines of
Act III, Part III, in the nine manuscripts studied. Each entry consists
of a lemma (which is always the reading of the text as presented) enclosed
by a single square bracket. Outside the bracket, each reading that varies
with the lemma is noted, together with the manuscript in which the variant
is found. The lemma is generally the reading of MS. C, the copy-text, but
in those cases in which a reading from another manuscript is substituted in
the text for the C reading, the C reading is given the first place outside
the square bracket; other variants (as is the case when C is the lemma)
follow in alphabetical order. All manuscripts not listed with variant
readings are to be understood to agree with the lemma.

Following the direction of W. W. Greg that "punctuation need only be
'taken down' when it is itself in question,"* I have presented punctuation
variants only when they, depending on which punctuation is chosen, substan-
tively affect the meaning of a passage.

Manuscript abbreviations have been expanded without notation when there
is not doubt as to what letters are to be supplied; e.g. magnū is silently
expanded to magnum. When there is doubt, the portion of the word in doubt
is put in pointed brackets (See Part I, III, iii, 16: profudit] < > fundit

---

*W. W. Greg, The Calculus of Variants (Oxford, 1927), p. 16.

A); or, where one of two readings must be correct, both readings are given

(See Part I, III, i, 38: perditur] perditur or proditur A;   proditur BDI).

The abbreviations used in this list are few. The symbol ">" means

"becomes" and is used to indicate a revision found in a manuscript. The

pointed brackets "< >" are used to indicate a doubtful reading either of a

letter(s), word(s), or line(s). The abbreviation "ed." placed immediately

outside the square bracket enclosing the lemma is used to note an emendation

by the editor.

Part I

Argument

```
 1  Edwardus]  Edouardus F
 2  quorum]  quorum omitted D
 3  major natu]  natu maior G
 6  vitae annum]  annum vitae G
 7  defuncti] defunct A
    Edwardi]  Edouardi F
 9  teneram adhuc]  adhuc teneram FGI
    viderat]  videret DGI
10  sibi aditum]  aditum sibi DFGI
11  primum]  primo E;    primum omitted I
12  amicos]  per amicos H
    Edwardi iter]  Edwardus quintus iter DGI;    Edouardus quintus iter F
13  milite]  millite E
15  ipse clam cum amicis]  ipse cum amicis clam D;    clam ipse cum amicis G
16  inde]  idem I
    periculum sibi]  sibi periculum I
17  tenelli]  tenella F
    tutela]  tutela omitted F;    tutelam I
18  propinquis]  propinquit D;    propinquens > propinqui<s> E
    demandaretur]  commendaretur I
20  abuti]  ire G
21  nobilem regis]  et regis F
22  uterinum]  uterin< > > uterinum F
    ipso]  ipo E
    avulsum]  avulsu > avulsos E
23  conjecit]  conjicit D
24  Pontefracti]  Pontifracti G
    plectuntur]  plectantur E
25  suam]  suam omitted G
    accipit]  accepit EG
```

26 confugerat] perfugerat G
27 ducem] Edwardum ducem G
28 tum] dum I
30 nobilem virum] virum nobilem A
            virum] vir< > > virum E
32 afficit] affecit EF
35 morte] morti DFI
36 infami] infamiae ADEF
    pena] poenae > poena E

Act I. Scene i.

1 laetis] laetus D
2 confidit] confidet B
3 quaerit is] quaeritis A
4 magnum...genus] et quanquam nihil magnum generosum genus G
5 jubebat] promisit G
   Edwardi] Eduardi D;   Edwardu< > > Edwardi E;   Edouardi F
   tamen regis] regis tamen H
6 postquam] post quam D
   tuos] suos > tuos A
7 Graie] Gray D
8 dulci] dulce E
   veneno] venen< > > veneno A
   gestiebam] gustiebam D
9 altis] altus H
   inclytus titulis] titulis inclytus > inclylus titulis E
   honos] honor DFG;   honorum E
10 spernebat] spernebam I
11 cognatus] cognat<i/u>s A
   heros regis] regis heros > heros regis (in margin) G
12 Inimicus] Inimicis CE;   Inimicis > amicis (in margin in different
            hand) A;   Inimicis > Inimicus B
13 his...traditur] his cura majoris fillii quod traditur A;
                    his cura major, filii quod traditur BD;
                    his cura major filii quod traditur EH;
                    his cura filii major quod traditur F;
                    his cura quod commissa major filii GI
14 regium] regem H
   nepotem] nepotum D
   avunculus] avunlculus H
16 animis] annis > animis (in margin) C;   animis > annis A;   annis DFGHI
   altius] altior G
   primis] primis A;   primus DFI
17 tenera] tenero ABCEFHI
18 hac] haec D
   peste] peste omitted H
19 est] est omitted H
20 maritus] mariti > maritus (in margin) E
21 fata] facta G
   regis impia] impia regis F
22 saevae] saeva D

25 versat] versit D; verset F
26 domus tantum] tantum domum E; tant<a/u>m domum F
27 ruinas] ruina A
28 ditata] ditat< > > ditata D
   sum] sim G
   domun] domum > domus A
31 huc] hinc F
   properat] properabat CE; pr< >p< >rabat A; properabat > properat B
32 comitatur] comitatus > comitatur C; commitatum D
33 regale] regali I
34 filii] fillii A
35 at] et G
36 audet] adet > audet (in margin) E
   adeptum] ademptum A
38 multisque] multis A
   urit] <corit> G
39 filiis] filliis A
   nihil] nihil minetur I
40 minetur] minetur omitted I
   infidum] insidum > insid< > E
   sibi] sibi regnum I
41 regnum] regnum omitted I
   Lancastriae] Lancastria DFI
   Edwardo] Eduardo D; Edouardo F
   invidet] incidet D; invidit E
42 nec] nec > et B; et D
   victrici] victrice H
43 potest] < > A
44 majisque] ma< >que A; majusque D
46 laceram] laceratam E; lacera< > G
49 lusit] lucet > lusit E
50 Regina] Reginae EG
   Elizabethae] Elizabetha ABDFI
52 publicum] publico I
53 turbidae] turbida F
   ludibria] lugubria F
55 filii] fillii A
   caput corona] caput praestans corona A
56 Sacrum...cardinis] O emicans honore Cardinio pater GI
   cardinis] Cardinalis A; Cardines F; Cardinio G; Cardineo I
57 Insignis archipresul] Insignis Archipraesul Eboracensium G
          archipresul] Archipraesull E
58 miserias] miseriat F
   miserum] miseram > miserum H
59 vnquam] uniq< > > unquam A
   lachrymis] lacrimis AH
60 Edwardi] Eduardi D; Edouardi F
   gemo] gen< > > geno E
   diram] duram D
61 odiumve...heroum] nec triste procerum plango demens odium G; nec
                      triste procerum plango demens nunc odium I

   odiumve] odium ne D; odiumque H; odium GI

```
62   Walliam]  Galliam F
63   stipatus]  stipato > stipatus C;     stipato D
     armato]  armatus > armato C;      armatus D
65   Edwardus]  Edward< > A;    Eduardus D;    Edouardus F
66   monere]  monere > movere H
     desinit]  <desinit> > desinet A;     desin <i/e>t E
67   sepiat]  saeviat > forsan sepiat (in margin) C;   muniat F
68   committeret]  comiteret A
69   clauderet]  clauderat E
71   cum]  tum DFGI
     mali]  male G
     nihil princeps]  princeps nihil B
72   armari]  armati > armari E;  armati F
73   putabunt]  putabant E;  putabant > putabunt F
77   illico]  ilico F
78   Belli]  bell<i> > bella<a> A
     furore]  furori E
     inundabit]  inundabunt A;    inundavit DE
79   terrendum]  terend< >m > terenda E;    horrendum G
80   insana]  insanam E
81   amoris faedus ictum]  faedus amoris ictum F;    amoris ictum foedus H;
                           amoris faedus istum I
82   authorem]  autorem C;    auctorem E
84   gelidus]  gellidus DE
85   suis]  istis EH
     animo]  animmo E;  annuo G
86   literis]  litteris DEGH
     edico]  edico or dico A;    ed< > D;    et edico E
87   filii cingant]  fillii cingant A;    cingant filii DF;    filii tegant >
                     filii cingant H
     latus]  latus omitted I
89   secretos]  secreta D
     sagax]  saga< > H
     repeto]  repet<a/o> D
91   ne]  nec D
     praeda]  praedae D
     nudis]  nudus DFGI;    nudis > nudus EH
     offeratur]  < >fferatur D;  afferatur F;    auferatur G
94   filii]  fillii A
96   parcet]  parcit E
     patrui]  potui D;    pat< > >patrui E
97   infaelix]  infaelicis DF;    infaelis > infaelix H
98   falsa]  falso H
     mentiri]  mentir<e> > mentiri D
99   aestimator]  aexistimator F
100  terrere]  timere E;    timere > terrere H
101  timor]  tremor G
102  semper]  semperque DFGI
     sibi]  sibi omitted F
104  sepultis]  sepulto GI
     regis]  reges F;    principis I
     litibus]  odio GI
105  nec]  ne I
```

106 Britannia] Brittania <u>DI</u>;   Britania <u>E</u>
    sanata] pacata <u>GI</u>
107 odia] odea <u>E</u>
    movebit] monebit <u>HI</u>
108 sospes] sospes <u>omitted H</u>
109 Quae] Que <u>A</u>
109-111] <u>These lines are omitted in H.</u>
110 Bis...dies] Bis caelo stellifero excidit sera dies <u>G</u>
    sera] serae <u>I</u>
    caelo dies] Phaebus caelo <u>E</u>
    dies]] dies <u>omitted AC (in C, a metrical notation for two syllables</u>
        <u>appears in the space where dies should be. In the margin is</u>
        <u>the notation syllaba deest.)</u>
111 Northamptonem...tangerent] Cum fessa Nòrthampton viderat corpora <u>G</u>;
                         Cum fessa Northampton viderant corpora <u>I</u>
    Northamptonem] Northamptoneam <u>A</u>;   Northamptonum <u>D</u>
    [cum]] cum <u>omitted AC (in C, a blank space is left for the missing</u>
        <u>word. Apparently the notation syllabla deest in margin at</u>
        <u>1. 110 is meant to refer to this blank also.)</u>

112 Et] at <u>G</u>
    claudit] claudat <u>E</u>
    latus] corpus <u>A</u>
113 Walliae] Wallia <u>D</u>
    accelerans] accellerans <u>ADE</u>
114 frequens...principem] Rex plurimo stipatus est satellite <u>G</u>;
                  Rex plurimo stipatus fest satellite <u>I</u>
    sepiebat] seniebat <u>C</u>;   sa<m>ebat > sanebat <u>E</u>
115 illique...labor] illique multos junxit assiduus labor > assiduus labor
                illique multos junxit <u>H</u>
    assiduus] assideus <u>I</u>
116 Riverius [heros] literas] Riveriaras litteras <u>C</u>;   Riveriarias literas
                      <u>A</u>;   Riverius literas <u>DF</u>;   Riverias litteras
                      > Riverius litteras <u>E</u>;   Riverius litteras <u>H</u>
117 milite] millite <u>E</u>
    principis] princepis <u>E</u>
118 Nudavit] nudabit <u>A</u>;   nudabat <u>DF</u>
    Riverius] Reverius <u>A</u>
119 suo] suoque <u>BDFGI</u>;   et suo <u>E</u>
    junctus] <u>In C, in margin after this line is the notation</u>:   pro junctus
           pone
120 regi] Rege > Regi <u>E</u>
121 literis] litteris <u>EH</u>
122 aeternum] aeternam <u>E</u>
123 multaque...beat] multisque precibus gaudium onerat publicum <u>GI</u>
    multaque] multaque > multumque <u>E</u>;   multisque <u>GI</u>
    prece] praese <u>E</u>;   precibus <u>GI</u>
    commune] comune <u>A</u>
124 Buckinghamiae] Buckingamiae <u>AEH</u>
126 comites] commites <u>D</u>
127 Scribit] scribet <u>A</u>
128 Graium] Graum <u>D</u>
    literis] litteris <u>AEH</u>

```
130  simul]  <t>uos G;  tuos I
131  Regina]  Regina omitted I
     Postquam...vexerit]  Postquam flatu secundo vererit > Postquam secundo
                              flatu vexerit A
     vexerit]  vixerit > vexerit E
133  jactat]  jactum A
134  prosperae]  prospae A;    pros erae > prosperae E
     laetari]  laetar< > > laetori D
135  nec]  <inde> or <mec> A
137  Cardinal]  Nuntius I
     sinistris credit]  credit sinistris A
138  parum]  pacum I
139  credunt]  credent F
     quod]  qui DFGI
140  cavet]  cavit E
     minus]  nimis F
141  Sperare...desinit]  Sperare nunquam magna virtus desinit > virtus
                              desinit magna numquam sperare F
     nunquam magna]  nunquam magna > magna nunquam B;    magna nunquam DFGI;
                              nunquam magnam H
142  turbaris]  turbasis I
143  odia]  mala DF
145  Sancivit]  sanxivit E
     icta]  ista DF
146  Cum]  tum D
     quaerunt]  quaerant E
147  Privata...salus]  Publica quies privata vincit odia G;  line omitted,
                              but then squeezed in in right margin E
154  miseram]  miserum ABC
155  excelsus]  excelsas > excelsus E
158  ventisque]  ventis G
159  summo]  summ<a/o> A
     nutant]  mutant > nutant CE;    muntant D
```

Act II. Scene i.

```
 3  cruentae]  cruentiae D
 5  Talis]  Talem G
 6  suae]  sue A
6a-6b]  These lines are omitted in DF.
6b  restitutam]  restitutam > restitutum E
 7  tuam]  tam DFI
 8  hic toti labor]  hic tibi labor DF;  hic totae labor E;    hic totus
                              labor I
     Britanniae]  Britaniae E
 9  persolvimus]  pervolvimus > persolvimus E;    prosolvimus F
10  Wallicae]  Walliae E
12  Wallia]  Wallica F
     carebat]  carebit F
13  ac]  at or ac D;    at G
     suum]  sum A;    suam H
     reparat]  reperat B;    reperat or reparat E
```

15 principis] principes F
   et] et omitted EH
16 qua] qui F
   recta] recta omitted E
   Stonistratfordiam] Stonistratfordanum E
17 die] dic or die FI
   celeri] ceteri I
18 quod] quando G
23 bello] bella E
24 nequeunt] nequiunt E;   nequeant H
25 patebant] patebunt F
26 jure multum] multum jure A;   jure vobis multum H
27 languidos] languidus G
28 juvat] jubet EH
29 placidam...proximae] Placida frui quite vobis nuntio G
   placidam] placidum E;   placida G
30 et] est D
   Buckinghamiae] Buckingmiae AE;   Bukinghamia F
31 cervus] servus AD;   servus > cervus G
32 stemmate] stemate EI
33 en] cum E
34 jubas] juvas D
35 vacuumque] vacuum que D
   perlustrat] perlustrant E
   viris] vires E
36 imperans] imparans E
37 vagum] vagnina A
39 secretas] secretus ABEGH
40 Annon] At non E
   miser] miseram E;   misera H
   status] cohors H
41 Diuque] denique E
   ut] ut omitted GI
   virtus jacet] jacet virtus I
42 sanguine] sanguini E
43 titulis genus] genus titulis F
45 vetantque] vitante > vetantus E
   nepote] nepate E
46 matris cedit] sedet matria or credit matris E;   cedit matris H
   cedit] sedet or cedit E;   redit G;   crevit I
47 succumbit] succumbat E
49 honor] honos A
50 omnino] somnino A;   animo EG
   suae] sua A
52 honore quando tamen] quando honore tamen DF;   quando tamen honore I
   haud] hand omitted I
   cedimus] credimus C;   credimus > cedimus AE;   cedimus omitted I
53 nepotem] nepot<a>m B
55 regni] Regn< > > Regis E
   thoros] thores A
   amor nisi quod impulit] placeret hoc regi nisi GI
56 suos] sibi > suos E;   suo H
57 minusque...circundare] et comite stipare nobili minus GI

```
     nobili]   nobile F
     comite]   commite D
58   Parum]   paruum F
     decorum]   decori ACEH
     aut]   at E;     et GI
     nobis]   vobis ACE
59   comes...tuebitur] magis tuetur regulum potentior B;     magis tuetur
                    regulum comes potentior GI
60   quod...male]   comes.  Malum quod nos manet, si qui male B
61   precantur]   minantur GI
     regiumque]   regium (que probably blotted out) E
     claudant]   claudunt EF
62   praeveniant]   praeveniunt ACEG;   praeveniempt D;     perveniant F;
                    praevenient HI
     amores]   amoris > amores E
63   ut]   et DFGI
64   quocunque]   quorum D
     tenella]   tutela E
     flectitur]   flectetur D
66   animis]   annis DFGHI
     respuunt]   respiunt A
67]  This line is omitted in I.
     in]   in omitted H
69   Edwardus]   Eduardus DF
71   serae]   sacrae E;   fere G
     noverca]   novercae E;     novarca I
     disciplinae]   disciplina DE
     suaserat]   suaserit A;   evasserat D;     evaserat F
72   heu]   hem DFI
     damnavit]   dammavit G
73   nec]   non GI
     resarsit]   resursit > resarsit A;   resuesit D;     resarcit G
     tardior]   tardior sensus I
74   sensus]   sensus omitted I
     Clarentius]   Clarentus ACG
75   ille illo]   ille A
76   quam]   quum G;   quam > quum H
     cessit]     cesserit GI
     olim]   tam G;     tum I
77   nimis...mala]     Nimis heu nimis tum fatentur nostra perspecuum mala>
                    Nimis fatentur nostra perspecuum mala B;   Nimis
                    fatentur nostra perspicuum mala G;   Nimis fatentur
                    nostra prespicuum mala I
     suadebant]     suadebat E
78   maritus]   maritum G
     quem]   quam > quod E;     quam F
     colit]   colat AE
79   quam...res diu]  Quam dura semper fata res nostras premunt GI
     quam]   quod D
     premebat]   permebat A;   praememat F;   premunt GI
80   quantam]   quantum ADI
     tum]     tum omitted A
     luem]   tuam > luem A;   luem omitted I
```

81 perfida...averterit] perfida malum prudentia nisi averterat G̲;
                         perfida malum prudentia nisi averterit I̲
   perfida] perfidam F̲
   mens nisi] nisi mens B̲
   averterit] adverteret A̲E̲;   auertit D̲;   averterat G̲
83 durisque] suisque B̲G̲I̲;   dirisque D̲F̲;   ducisque > <durisque> H̲
   vindicat] vendicat H̲
84 potenti] POTENTI C̲
   liberavit] liberarit G̲
85 heu] hem E̲I̲
   quot] quos A̲
   concitus] percitus F̲
86 morte] morti I̲
   damnatos] dammnatos F̲;   damnatus I̲
88 suo] suo omitted F̲
   ira] illi or ille H̲
89 stragi] stragique I̲
   heu] HEU C̲;   una B̲D̲F̲G̲I̲
90 plangimus] plangemus E̲
91 solus] sola F̲
   haeret] haereat E̲H̲
92 stipabit] stipabat E̲
   thronum] thronum omitted I̲
94 luet] luent A̲; lucet D̲;   luet > sciet E̲
95 sacrato] sacrato or sacratae D̲
97 Gloucester continues to speak] Hastings begins to speak here and ends
                                   with l. 104.
   vetet] vetat F̲
99 Edwardus] Eduardus D̲F̲
   medetur] medet F̲
100 dexteras] dextram A̲;   dextras E̲G̲H̲
    nos] mox G̲;   <nec> inserted after nos above line H̲
101 pignora] foedera B̲I̲
102-103] These lines are omitted in I̲.
    regis tum] tum regis H̲
103 quam]   quam > quum G̲
    ficta] facta E̲
    dubia] dubia omitted E̲
105 Gloucester still speaking] Gloucester resumes speaking B̲
    quemquam ne] quenquam vel E̲;   quenquam I̲
108 mensis] anni (in margin is this note: mensis, potius, nam sic versus
             non constat.) C̲; animi B̲D̲F̲G̲H̲I̲; animi > animum E̲
109 lustris] miseris > luseris F̲
110 mutare] muturare B̲D̲F̲G̲H̲I̲
111 fieri solet] solet fieri H̲
112 robustius] rubustius B̲D̲
    viresque] vires D̲
    colligit] colligit <enudo> E̲
114 stirpe] sterpe D̲E̲
    princeps] principis A̲
115 Visa...Anglia] Ardere Britannia visa tumultu sit > Ardere Britannia
                    tumultu visa sit G̲
    ardere rursus] rursus ardere F̲

116 et...civilia] et bella bacchari simul civilia G̲
117 tuae] tue A̲
    ut] ut omitted G̲
    secreto] secreti A̲
119 tua] tuu A̲
    signa] signum A̲
    Buckinghamium] Buckinghamium > Buckingamiam C̲;   Buckingamium >
                    Buckingamii A̲;   Buckingamium E̲;   Buckingamum H̲;
                    Buckingham< > I̲
    ducem] ducis > ducem A̲
120 miscere] misceri AC̲;   misceri > miscere E̲
121 quaerebam...simul] cupiebam ut haec patam loqui tecum queam G̲;
                        quaerebam ut haec simul loqui tecum queam I̲
    haec] hec A̲
    possem loqui] loqui passem BDFGI̲
123 statim] statui F̲
    premi] brevi F̲;   primum G̲
    decet] docet G̲
    majus] magis > majus E̲
124 natum malum] multum malum A̲;   motum malum DF̲
    nescit] crescit > nescit E̲
125 sanare] servare E̲
    regni luem tantam] regni luem tantum A̲;   regni tandem luem E̲;   luem
                        tantam regni F̲;   regni tantam luem GH̲
126 ferent] fierent E̲;   feret GH̲
127 Buckingham continues speaking to l. 128] Buckingham ends speech here F̲
128] This line is omitted in F.
    gnatumque] natumque H̲
129 dux] dux > ducem F̲
    ergo] go F̲
130 scelere] selere D̲
    labantis] labentis E̲
131 jura] nostra E̲
    praecipitis] praeceptis F̲;   praecipis H̲
    regis] regibus EH̲
132 coruscum] corruscum D̲
134 medela] medicina GI̲
    confert] confer A̲
135 abest] adest F̲
136 jam] iam crossed out G̲
137 rege] lege A̲
    cunctas] cunctos ACEHI̲
    labes] labem CEH̲;   lubem A̲
138 quin] quam E̲
139 intraque...decet] Expedit et intra tecta claudere hospitem G̲
    hospitem] hostem F̲
140 tum conscium] conscium tum E̲
    tum] tum omitted I̲
141 mox famule] mox famulae ADEF̲;   moxa famulo H̲
    petas claves] claves petas F̲
    claves] clames A̲;   clames or claves H̲
142 abdidat] addidat H̲
143 abnuantur] abnuant A̲;   abnuat DF̲

144 nec...foras] Nullusque claustris servus irrumpat latens G̲;   Nullisque
      claustris servus <e>rumpat latens I̲
145] This line is omitted in GI̲.
   sed...singuli] sed singuli cladantur intus sedulo F̲
146 nostrisque] nostrasque A̲
   admone clam] admone iam clam A̲C̲;   advove clam D̲;   admone E̲
148 nostrum] nostram B̲;   nostram or nostrum G̲
   sepiant] sepiunt G̲
149 adibimus] adivimus F̲;   invisimus GI̲
151 captos] captas A̲
   claudis] cladis F̲
   audax] adhuc H̲
152 illico...mobilis] En mobilis populi tumultum concitas G̲;   En nobilis
      populi tumultum concitas I̲
   tumultum] tum multum F̲
   plebs] plebis > plebs E̲
   ciebit] ciebat > ciebit H̲
153 dum] si GI̲
155 Et] en DFGI̲
   dignitatem] dignitatem > dignitatis H̲
   sui] suae H̲
157 lacerare quaerunt] lacerareque ruunt G̲;   lacerare que runt H̲;
      lacerare quaerunt I̲
157a sancti...patrum] sancti senatus quamvis et jussa A̲;   sancti senatus
      quamvis et jussu B̲G̲I̲;   sancti senatus quamvis jussa
      patruum E̲;   line is omitted in DF̲
158] This line is omitted in I̲.
   longa] longu > longa A̲
   Britonum] Britonnum B̲;   Brittonum E̲
161 profundere] perfundere C̲
   principum] princip< >m > principum A̲;   principem E̲
162 At] a A̲
   premi] primi F̲
163 is] hic F̲
164 Edwardum] Eduardum D̲
   Britannia] Britania A̲E̲
165 trahet] trahit E̲
166 ardore...omnia] Belli tumultu regna vesano flagrant G̲
167 nostraque...scelus] Nostramque pacem strage cives expi<a>nt G̲;
      Nostraque pacem strage cives expiant I̲
   populus] populos A̲
168 munit] <iminuit> E̲
   assiduus] assidus A̲;   assiduis D̲
169 perrumpat] perunpat A̲;   Irrumpat D̲F̲;   perrumpant E̲;   prorumpat I̲
   hinc] huic F̲;   hic G̲;   <huic> H̲;   hinc or huic I̲
170 nostrumque...praeverteret] Nostrumque prius iter queat praevertere GI̲;
      Nostrumque iter ad regen prius praeverteret
      H̲
172 nitidaque] nudamque D̲;   niveamque F̲;   nitidamque GI̲
   jubebit] jusserit B̲;   videbit F̲;   jubebat H̲
174 principi] principis H̲
   fides sic] sic fides E̲H̲

180 orco] arco A
    natabunt] nubunt A
181 saevis] saevus DH
182 fidem] fides or fidem H
183 animus] animis A;   <animus> or <animis> H
    animus triste presagit] animus mihi praesagit triste I
    praesagit] presagat D
184 cor pavet] torpent F
185 demiror] dimiror E
    hi] h< > A;   heu F
    claves] claves omitted with blank space left I
187 onerabant] onerabunt F;   onerab< >nt > onerabant H
    dape] dapes DFI
188 an jam] <annuam> H
    retentum] retentae F;   retent< >m > retentam H
    mulctant] mulctabunt A;   mulctent I
189 amat] amant > amat C;   amet D;   amant I
190 haeret] horret BI
    haud] non E
191 fugio] fugis F
    nullus] nulla E
192 conscius demens] demens conscius G
193] This line is missing in F.
    ullos] nullos I
194 certum] rectum A
    eveniet] evenit D;   eveniat I
195 duces adibo] adibo duces > duces adibo (in margin) G
201 infandum] nefandum DEFI
202 nil] nil > nihil E;   nihil I
203 nostra] nostram I
204 Tale] Tace BDFGI
    scelestum] sceleste G
205 nostrum] <nostra> E
206 perdes] prodes BI;   perdis E
    Britonum] Britannum B;   Brittonum E
207 Atro] < > A;   atro omitted H
    mulctate] multate A;   mulctare E
208 cingant] jungant G
209 Quo] quos A
    trahitis] trahetis BG
210 nunc me] me nunc G
211 morte] forte ACE;   forte > morte H
    mulctent] mulctet DFGI
    damnent] damnet DFGI
212 num] nam DFHI
    This line ends Scene i of Act II in all manuscripts except G which adds
    three lines which appear as lines 6-8 of Scene ii of Act II.

                    Act II. Scene ii.

1-8] These lines are omitted in G. Lines 6-8 appear at the end of Scene i.
  1 praeceps] preceps E

2 muto] muta > muto E
   sedes] fides > sedes E
4 properare Glocestrium] properare nunc Glocestrium BDFI
5 capit] capiat F
6 Cinctus] cunctus > cinctus E;   cunct< >s > cunctis H
   Edwardus] Eduardus DF
   confert] profert G
   gradum] gradium A
7 stemmata] stemate E;   stemata I
8 plebei] plebeii BGH
9 Britannis] Britannus D;   Brittanis E
10 Gnatus] Gratus FGH
   est] uste > est E
   mi] in > mi E
11 barbaras] barbaricas F
12 tantis] vestris G
   votis] vobis BDFI
13 deus] < >eus > beus B;   decus > deus D
14 tuam] tum D
17 regale] regalem G
18 commune] communem E
   persuadet] persuadit E
20 sulcabit] sulcabit G
21 quercus] quaerens G
   oblitum] oblitam > oblitum E
22 corrumpat] corrumpit I
   fides] fide F
23 ponam libens] libens ponam F
25 Grai] graie > Grai C;   Graie BDEFGHI
26 Riverium] Reverium A
   ferum] patruum DF
27a] This line is omitted in D.
   scindere] cingere H
28 Anglos] Angliam EH
30 Marchio] Marquio G
31 irrupit] errupit A;   erupit H
   Belini] Bellini A;   belini > belina E;   Beleni F
32] This line is missing in E.
   regis] Reges G
33 longam oneravit ingenti] longum ingenti oneravit H
   salum] solum AC;   satum I
34 uterinus] ulterius ABC;   ulterias > ulterius E;   Dorsettus I
37 Imo...doli] Imo tuas latent aures tanti doli F
   Imo] Immo AD
   latent] latant D
39 perduellionis] perduelionis AI
   esse aio] aio esse F
   reum] rerum AE
40 Grai] Graie > Grai C;   Graie BDGHI;   Graii AE
   teque] te F
41 Vaghanne] Vahame CHI;   Vahanne ADE;   Vahanme F;   Vaghame G
42 Hawt] Haut A;   Haute DFH;   Hawte E;   Hawt omitted GI (blank space
        left in I)
   squallenti] squalenti DEG;   squallente F

3 statim] statim omitted H
   luant] luent A;   luent > luant H
4 Puerum] Puerum > Puer A;   Puer EH
   misellum] misellum > misellus A;   misellus > misell< > E;   misellus
              H
   lachrymis] macrimis AH
   genas] genus F
5 vincula] vinculum E;   vincla G;   vincul<u>m I
   correptum] abreptum E
   fratrem] frenum F
6] This line is omitted in I.
7 volumus] vollumus D
8 principi] principis > principi H
   astabis] stabis D;   ad stabis E
9 regique] Regisque ABDEFI

                    Act II. Scene iii.

2 suisque] quisque ACE;   tuisque H
3 hostes] hostis AE
   impie] IMPIE C;   intimos DFGI
6 ambitio] ambitioque > ambitio D
   regni parva] parva Regni H
   suspecti] suspecta F
7 sinit] sinet EG
   anxium] axium H
8 soli] solii > soli C;   solii ABDGHI;   soli > solii E;   socii F
   manet] staret (with note in margin: forsan manet) C;   staret BEGHI;
           stares DF
9 tutior] tutor F
2 globos] globus > globum > globu< > E
3 Britanniae] Britaniae E
4 verus] longus G
5 huc] hic AG
   minister] injuste ACE
   celeri] sceleri E
8 Ducine] duri ne C;   duci ne DE;   dur< >e > durne H
   illi] ille CE
9 Claudiano] Claudian< > A;   Claudiona D
   astabam] ad stabam EH
1 Glocestrium] Glocestrium > Glocestrii A
2 ducis] duci H
   lauta] tanta ACEH;   tanta > lauta G
4 selectos] scelestos F
5 ferre jussit aequo] jussit aequo ferre D;   jussit ferre aequo F
6 illius] illius omitted B
   formidabile] formidabilia I
8 longus] < > > longus A
   usus] < >osus C
9 dura] cura DF
   intonat] in tonat A

30 vitae] vita I
    afflictae] afflictus I
    minus] minas EG
31 refudit] refundit > refudit C;   refundit ADFGHI
32 Deferre] diferri G
    lauta] tanta CEHI
    lauta jussit] jussit lauta F
    fercula] fircula E
34 didicit] dedicit D
35 verba confirment] confirment verba F
    confirment] conferment EH
37 at] et I
    exequi] exiqui F;   exit is written after exequi in G.
39 imperitis] imperitus CH;   imperitus > imperitis E
    vulnera] vulneri F
41 metu] metus G

Act III. Scene i.

1   sceleris] faces DFH
2   mitisque] mitis H
3   domus] domas I
4   heu heu] heu heu heu E
    quam diu] quamdiu DEFGI
5   vitam] victa D
    luctibus] luctubus ABHI
6   Alecto] [ALECTO] C;   Erinnis DFGI
    regiam] reginam E
7   Megaera crudelis] Megaera crudel<e/i>s C;   Megaera crudeles A;
                       Megara crudelis DFI;   crudeles Megera E;   Medaca
                       crudelis G;   crudelis megaera H
10 devehet] detrahit I
12 lugubres] lugubris E
13 Non dum] Nondum C
14 nec] ne A
    vices] vires G
15 caelo] caelum AC
16 umbris] umbras EH
17 celere] celare F;   colere I
19 placare] praeclara > pa< >are A;   placere EH;   pacare GI
    matris] matri H
20] This line is omitted in A.
    sed] si > sin (in margin) C
    regiae] Regia D;   Reginae E
21 tanti nocte stepitus] nocte strepitus tanti B;   tanti n<o>ctis
                           strepitus F;   tanti nocte quid stepitus H
22 Splendens... Eboracensium] Antistes excellens honore Cardinis G
    Eboracensium] Eboracensum E;   Eboracensis F
23 renovare me] me renovare A
24 postquam soporem Luna] post qua Luna D
    Increpuit] increbuit > increpuit C;   increvit A;   increbuit BDFGI
27 duris] diris E
    praemi] primum F

28 principem] principum H
capiat] cupiat G
29-31] These lines are omitted in EH.
29 tanta] tantae F
31 labante] labente I
32 colligit] collegit F
34 quid] quod D
volvitis] voluitis ABDFGI; vol<u/v>itis EH
35 spiratis] spiraris C
36 jaculare] jugulare AF
faces] faces omitted I
37 innocens] inocens DE
puer] puer omitted I
38 parvus quid] quid parvus E; purus quid G
perditur] perditur or proditur A; proditur BDI
39 totam] totum AE
40 labante] labente E
41 imbre] imbrae E
perfusae] profusae ABDFI
42 magnis] magis E
43 regias] regiasque A; regiae BDFGI
vestes] vestis BDFGI
44 rubores] ruboris A
muricis] maricis F; myricis G
49 gemit] gemuit FG
50 seram] feram I
sentiens] sensiunt AC; sentiunt DEFGHI
51 reclamat anxia] [RECLAMAT ANXIA] C; reclamat anxia omitted DFGI
53 capere] rapere ABDFGI
suppelectilem] supellectilem DFGI; supelectilem E; suppellectilem H
54 regia] regina F
excelsas] excesas H
55 leves] lenes EH
morae] more H
vehentibus] vehementibus ACE; vehementibus > veheentibus H
56 hinc] huic F
via] via omitted A
57 perforare] perforari DFGI
58 qua] quam D; quia F
asylo] < > A; asyla B; asylum DF
palatium] pallatium A; patium D
59 filium] filii or filium E; fili<a/u>m I
60 filias vocans] vocans filias F
61 tremens] tumens F
63 pascitur] poscitur DFI
64 Eboracensis...pater] Honore praestans summe Cardineo pater G
65 quid malis] malid quid F
67 timemus jam] iam timemus F
timere] videre BDFGI
68 magnae] magnae > magna E
parvae] parva A; patriae E; parvv<a/ae>F
sumus] sumu G

70 durum] duram H
   parant] praeparant I
71 tenet] ten< > I
72 an non] annon ABGHI
   Perimus] periimus G
73 anxias] anxeas G
74 istud omne] illud omne E;   omne istud G
75 quicquid] quidquidne A;   quicquamne BDFGI
   laevat] laenas A
76 mitius] intus G
   cogita] cogitat > cogita A
77 suadet] suadit E
80 moras duces] moras dulces CH;   dulces moras A;   mores dulces > moras
                 dulces E
81 subditis] subditus F
   stipatus] stipatis > stipatus E
82 nihil quisquam timore] mihi quisquam timore D;   timore nihil quisquam
                 F
83 sorte foelici] sorte falice A;   faelici sorte G
   cadent] cad< >nt I
86 deos supplex] supplex deos G
87 obruant] obruat ACEH
89 prudens] pradens > prudens E
   graves] gravet > graves A
90 numen] nument > numen A
91 torquet] torquent BDEFGHI
   manu] metu G
92 coronant] coronat E;   coronent G
93 huic] hinc E;   huic or hinc H;   hui<e> I
   fratri] fratre > fratri (in margin) E
   regni] < > > regni A;   regina > regni E
94 tibi] sibi E
96 tuo] tuam > tuo E;   tuum H
   quem] quo H
   filio] filiu > filio E;   filium H
98 sana] serna E;   serna or serva H
99 ut] et G
   manu] viam > manu (in margin) C
100 regnum] regni I
    cadat] cadet DI
101 fingant] fingunt D;   fingat EH
    novam] novum H
    Lancastriae] Lancastria ACH;   Lancastriae > Lancastria E
102 litabit] litabat DGI
103 capit] captat A
104 cuiquam ne] cuiquam A
    sigillum] sigillam I
    tradere] traddere F;   tradere omitted I
105 quin] o quin A;   quae E;   cui F
107 magna] magni F;   magni > magna G
    temere] timere CH;   timore E
    proditur] perditur G

10 ergo] ego DF
    sigillum] sagillum F
    petet] petat ABDF; petant I
11 duces] duces omitted I
    damnent] damnant > damnent C; damnant A

Act III. Scene ii.

2 Thamesim] Thamesin BEGH; Temesim I
3 perrumpat] perumumpat D; prorumpat GHI
   ad Asylum] ad sylum E
   profugus] profuga DFGI
4 fugam] fidem DF
5 surripiunt] surripiant AH
6 hic] his A
7 insanos] insanus A
9 en...abdita] Mecum sarcinas arripito quisquis es fidelis principi G
   abdita] abditu H
10] This line is missing in G.
    parant] parat B
11 tantus tumultus] tumultus tantus H
    quodnam] Qodnam I
12 Tamesis] Thamasis E; Thamesis GH
13 simul malta] multa simul BDFI; simul multa > multa simul (in margin)
                  G
14 quidnam] quodnam G
15 servent] feriant D; ferrent FGI; ferunt H
    si] sis > si C
    minentur] minantur EH;
    vehant] veham I
16 vindicent] vendicent H
17 muniat] muneat E
19 [metus]] metus omitted ACEH
20 Spargens] spergens I
    vel] an I
21 agnitum] agnitus H
23 praeceps] princeps E
    moras Tumultus] tumultus moras H
26 clauduntur] claudunt F
    heroes] Herois I
27 fides] fidei A
28 imbellis] imbecillis DF
    aetas regis] regis aetas DF
    admittit] admittet A; addmittit F
29 facile...licet] facile scelusque concitat [MAGNAM > QUISQUIS] licet C;
                     Scelusque facile concitat timidum licet DFI; facile
                     scelusque concitat timidum licet > scelusque facile
                     concitat timidum licet G
30 clam rege at expidere] [CLAM REGE AT] expedire C; clam regi at
                            expidere B; sanu statim expidere DFGI
    decet] dicet A

31 errat] erret F;   err<e/a>t G;   erat H
    hic] qui D
    patet] patat D;   pateat H
32] This line is omitted in H.
    advolat mihi] advolat [MIHI] C;   huc advolet mihi A;   heros advolat
                DFG;   advolat (mihi omitted) I
    huc] his > huc G
33 chara] clara I
    civium] procerum I
34 complexus est] complexus (est omitted) A;   est amplexus DF;   est
                complexus EH;   amplexus est I
35 et] ut CEFGHI
    colere] colorem E
    chara] cara H
36 benigna] benigni BDFGHI
    tanti] tanta BDFGHI
38 nulla] nullum CGH;   multum > multo E
39 futili] futuli AD
40 varioque] vanoque G
    turbari] turbare ACEF
    Britannos] Britonas G
41 video] vidio D
42 tota] tuta GI
    raptores] raptori AC;   raptare DFI;   raptori > raptores E;
                raptari GH
    volantes] volentes I
43 vexare] vexari E;   novare F
    vana] vano BDEFGI
44 quicquid] quidquid E
    mentiuntur] mentiantur E
45 perspecta...fuit] Perspecta mihi satis fides Glocestria G
    Glocestriae] Glocestri<a/ae> C;   Glocestria BDEFGI;   Glocestrii H
48 qui] ed.;   quos ABCDEFGHI
    premit proceres] proceres premit B;   premunt proceres G
49 probris] probis A;   propriis I
    perfidi] perfidi or profidi AC;   profidi D
50 frigent] figent CEH;   fingunt A
51 litem] vitem I
52 patres] patre F
53 vestra] nostra DF;   vestra > vestram E;   vestram > vestra G
    posteram] postera ACEH
    praeverteret] perverteret BDE;   praeverterit I
54 funeri] funere DF
55 vos] nos D
56 suaderi] suadere DF
57 causa semper] semper causa I
58 claudunt] claudant ABD
59 dum] sed G
    adventat] adventet F
60 pacata] sperata E;   placata F;   parata G;   grata H

Act III. Scene iii.

2 sospes] sopes A;   hospes H
patrios] patruos F
lares] lares > laures D
4 majus] magis F;   magīs > magius G
5 salve] salva G
6 post...nunquam] post tot ruinas < > Asiae Argolicus H
tot] te > tot E
nunquam] erant BGI
7 Argolicas] Argolicos A;   Argivas H
opes] se<d>es H
8 primi] primi omitted E;   primus H
viserent] viserunt A;   viscerent > visere< > E;   viseret H
10 redditum] red< >itum A;   reditum EGH
11 ereptus] erreptus F
esset] esses ACDEFGHI
Cephalerim] Cephalenum AB;   Cephaberum D;   Cephalerim > cepha< > E;
            Cephalerum FI;   Cephalenum virum G
parant] parat B
12 quam] quia ACEH
crescit] cressit D
amissae] admissae > amissa< > E;   admissae GHI
13-14] These lines are squeezed on a single line in G.
13 diu postquam] postquam diu F
carebam] carebas ACDEFGHI
14 negavit] negant DF
longum iter] longam iter D;   iter longum G
mihi] sibi H
15 rex] rexque A
16 profudit] < >fudit A
18 sol nostro ut alter] Nostro alter ut sol G
20 civis] cives D
21 Praetor continues speaking to end of Act] Praetor ends speech with
            l. 20. Glocester begins speech at l. 21 and continues to end
            of the Act. DE
noster] vester BDFGI;   vester omitted H
mei] <mihi> mei D
22 en] et F
23 chari] chare BDFI
Britanni] Britannis DF;   Britanne I
videte] ed.; vides ABCDEFGHI
tuum] tuam H
24 subdite] abdite DF

Act IV. Scene i.

1 Regina] Reginae I
aedibus] sedibus G
squalens] squallens ABGHI
sedet] sedens E
3 declaratus] declaratur E

4 suffragiis] sufragii F
5 praesuli] praesuli omitted G
Eboracensi] Eborum DEFI; Cardinali G
6 hunc...vulnerat] Hunc Claudianus jure potens vulnerat DFI; Hunc voce
multum Claudianus verberat H; Hinc Claudianus jure
probris vulnerat G
7 levi] levae AC
8 cuncta] juncta or cuncta G
9 Pontefracti] Pontefacti A; Pontifracti GI
manent] manet A
10 fata] fato D
luant] luent > luant D; luent G

Act IV. Scene ii.

2 nihil] nihill A; nil DFGI
4 infamiam...potest] infamem generosus animus sustulit G
5 tam diu] tand<e/i>m E
latebit] latebet F
6 gnatum] quantum G
7 ut] et F
querulo] quer< > A
8 Britanniae] Britannos G
9 concita] concito ACDFHI; cancito E
10 sit] fuit GI
11 Eborum] Eburum CH
13 solum] solum > solium (in margin) E
tuetur] tenetur D
14 moderata] moderatum F
15 deliciis] dilitiis F
16 colludit] colludet DFH; colludat G; colludet seni I
immixtus] immistus BDFI
19 dedecus] dedicus D
20 damnet] damnat EG
fidem labes] fidem labes > labes fidem B; labes fidem H
21 dum] si GI
profuga] perfuga BCI; profuga or perfuga AE; perfida H
25 assensu] assensa D; consensu G
26 dubia] dubio A
27 cognita] nota BGI
28 ut...carcere] ut...carcere fatri suo ACDH; ut...carcere fratri suo
(last two words underlined to denote words are to be
omitted here) E; ut...carcere fratri suo (last word
crossed out) F; fratri suo remittat GI
29 fratri...fidem] At te neminem tantum petit negotium magis, tua GI
fratri suo restituat. at] restituat EBORACENSIS at C; restituat
Eboracensis at AH; fratri restituant suo
E; suo restituat, at F
31 honore...inclyte] si sanctitas honore praestans Cardinis GI
inclyte] inclytae A

32 praestare...sanctitas] praestare gravetur si non tua sanctitas F;
                           Illustris Archipraesul haud gravabitur GI
   tua] tuu< > H
33 hoc] id BGI
35 detinet] detenet H
   gnatum] gratum > gnatum E;   natum GH
36 gerat] gerit BDFGI
37 premant] premat B
38 odium protervia] protervia odium G
39 vestrae] nostrae BDF
40 audio] audi DF
   fovente...deo] favente...deo D;   namque fovente spiritum deo H;   dei
                   namque spirante spiritu G;   dei spirante namque
                   spiritu I
43 Quem...commovet] Quem solitudo regis aut patriae salus G
44 procerumque...patriae] Non commovet procerumque deflectens honor G
   honos] honor BDFGI
45 salus...sacris] Dum mater insontem sacris claustris premit G
   jactata] jactatae A;   jactata omitted G
46 gnatum...dedecus] Vesana nequitur Britannis consulit G
   gnatum] natum H
   dedecus] dedicus D
47 ingens...principi] Et dedecus erit neque tutum principi G
48 nec...parvulo] et futili plebs percrebrescrit murmure G
   tutum] tantum A
   carcere fratre] fratre carere H
   parvulo] parvulus F
49-50] These lines are missing in G.
49 lacerat] lacessit BDEFI
51 solum] sola G
   mater ortum] ortum mater I
52 tantum] tantam C;   tant<a/u>m E
   stulta] stullitia F
   delitiis] diliciis F
   putet] putat FGHI
53 regni] regna > regni D
   patriam] sese G
54 dulcis matris] matris dulcis H
55 quod] quo H
   haec] hic E
   suadere] persuadere G
   sanctus] Cardinis DF;   Cardineus EG;   cardinius I
56 excellens] exellens F;   Eborum G
   assentior] assentior > assensior C;   assensio F
57 sin] sui F;   sui or sin H
58 vi] ut I
59 haereret parvulus] haereret ulnis parvulus BDEFGI
60 fratri] fratris ACH
   aut] aut omitted H
61 tremit] tremet ACE;   timet GH
62 at] et G
   hic] haec F
   sepiet] muniet G;   sapiet I

63 hic] sic G
64 regemque] Regisque DFGI
   subditi] sibi F
65 tum] nunc GI
   vocat] vocet A
66 si] sin BDFGI
   recusat] recuset EFGH
67 [Cardineus]] Cardineus omitted ACH: Cardinus DF
   avehat] auferat GI; avehat cito H
68 aula] aulam G
   fratrem] frater BDFI; fratris G
   oblectet] deflectet F
69 aut] ut A
   gratus] gnatis A
   Angliae] Angli A
70] This line is missing in A.
   meis] meisque D
71 sin] sui F; sin or sui H
   aede] aede omitted (domo in margin) E
72 suum] suus F
   impetrat] impetret FH
74 decet] deset > decet D; licet I
   quod] quem BDEFGI
75 ferunt] <ferint> > <fernat > A
   mox] non F
   firmavit] firmarit G
76 pepigit] p< >egit A; pepegit FGH
   bonis] bonis > bonos E
77 multis] multos ACE
   constitit] constetit F
78 Isther] Asther B; blank space in I
   Alanis] Alanus A; Allonis F
79 violare] violare > violar C
80 perenni] perimi C; perinni A; < > > per aeque (in margin) E;
                perrenni F; perinni H
   sparsa] ed.; sparsus ABCDEFGH; spersus I
81 sacrilegus] sacrilega ACEGH
84 vacet] vacat H
86 damnibitur] culpabitur GI
87 impedient [caecus] amor] impediet amor ACEH
   solusque] solisque F
88 Quin...protervia] Quin matris hoc faciet magis protervia G
   Quin] Quum AC
   matris impediet] matris impediet amor impediet A
89 pignori] pignore I
90 putet] putat H
92 optarem] optabam F
   muliebrem] muliebre CEI
93 perturbet] perturbat D; perturbent E
   Angliam] Anglia A
   minus] simul I

94 quibus...scelus] quibus odium tantum (blank) peperit scelus C; quibus
    odium tantum peperit scelus AH; quibus odium peperit
    scelus tantum suum DEF
96 aut] at EF
97 propinqui] propinque A
98 cui] enim D
101 nobis] nolis D
102 suspecta...fuit] suspecta cui proceres relinquent filium E
    cui] enim D
    fides procerum] procerum fides F
103 relinquent] relinquam I
104 sibi...manserit] utr<ii> si loco decoro manserit G; utrisque si loco
    decoro manserit I
    loco mater] mater loco FH
    decoro manserit] decoro (manserit omitted) DF
106 sit] est ABD
108 frigidae] fridigae E
    sin] suic G
105 Dux Gloc. begins to speak here.] Buckingham continues to speak to
    1. 169. DEFGHI
    ergo] ego I
    nobis] vobis D
    deneget] < > > de< >eget A; deniget D
111 furtum] furt< >m I
    gnatum] gnat<u/a> I
114 dedicus] dedicus D
    quam] quia F
115 pulchrum] pulcrum D
116 cadentem] cadentis F
117 possumus] possimus AGI
    matri] matrem A
118 vi] vi omitted G
    decebit] dicebit A; decepit I
119 ludibrio] ludibria > ludibrio D; ludibriam > ludibria G
120 ego] ergo G
    laederem] luderem A
121 tribuit] [TRIBUIT] C; struxit DEFGI
    plurimum] plurimum omitted I
122 suum] sum E
123 dedissem] dedisse I
    avisve] avis<que> G
    paciscerer] paciferer BD; patescerer E
125 saeviat] saeviet DI
    vincula] vincla B; vincla > vincula G
    minetur] minatur AH
    horridus] horidus E
126 adversa] adusa E; ad versa H
127 oppressit] oprressit G
    aut] aut omitted GI
    alienum] alieno BDEFGI
    prodigo] prodigum > prodigo C; prodigum BDFGI; prodigio E
    prodigo alienum] alieno prodigum I

128 tueatur:] tueatur ABDE; tueatur, F; tuentur, H
ereptum] areptum A
129 sane.] sane ADF; sane: E; sane, G
130 metus] metu F
131 annon] an non DEF; anno I
132 pacta] parta A
jura] juro I
135] This line is omitted in AC.
136 nunquid] nunquam BG
patronus] patronis A
137 Petrus ista] ista Petrus F
pepegit] pepigit ABDE
138 prodigos] prodigus AC; prodigas B; prodigas > prodigos G
139 monet] jussit BGI; movet AD
sibique] sibi H
furt<a/o> H
140 desirit uxor] uxor evadit BGI; desirit conjux DEF
142 hinc] huic AGI; huic or hinc H
hinc caedi] caedi hinc F
144 ergo] erga F
145 nec] puer AC; <purum> H
jus] jura F; vis > jus E
violat] violet D
147 ve] ne DHI
148 quod] quae GI
149 nunquam] non nunquam E
150 servemus] serviemus A
151 ducem tamen] tamen ducem H
152 jus] vis E; jus or vis H
153 moramur] moremur F
154 contraque...satis] est quisquis contra vim locus tutus satis BI
et quisquis contra vim locus tutus satis G
155 legis] leges BDFI; Regis G
impediant] impediunt BDFGHI
minas] BDFI
156 si...necessitas] Necessitas si dura quam poenam lenit G
157 tristis ducem] ducem tristis F; tristis (omitted) ducem H
158 regium] regnum C
159 nescia] nescio A
160 innocens] <   > H
162 pacta] pact<is> A; peracta F
impetrat] impetret G
163 imploret] implorat H
165 ferret aetas] aetas ferret F
166 horreret] horret A
167 si] sit ACH; sin or sui I
advolat] advolet G
168 sed] si BD
169 Last line of Buckingham's speech] First line of Ely's speech DFGI
haec] hoc E
nequit] nequis A

170-179]   G compresses these 10 lines into 5 lines:

>Divina sundent jura Pontificum quibus
>Decreta suffragantur ut corpus sacra
>servent, labore forte quid par<i/e>t suo.
>Aliena caedant aera creditoribus,
>Erepta furto bona vacent dominis suis.

170 jura]   iuera ACH;   iuera > iura E
172 quos]   quas C
173˙ indulgent]   indigent C
174 sacram]   sacra BDG
175 cedant]   cedent DFGI
177 damnum]   dammnum F;   dominum I
     reparet]   reperet D;   repararet I
178 excussis]   excussus CH;   excassus A
179 saeviret]   sevieret A
180 Probatur]   probabitur DFI
     haec]   hoc E
     sane mihi]   mihi sane F
     sententia]   sentantia H
181 uxor...fugit]   Uxor maritum adultera aris si fugit G
     fugit]   fugeret DFI
184 haeret]   herit E
     num]   nunc DE
     paedagogus]   pedigogus D
185 tremit]   tremet BDFI
     timebat]   timebit F
     hic   is F
186 novi]   novem I
     sacra]   sacris A
     viris]   vires BD
187 consciis]   consiliis D
188 huic]   hinc AFI;   huic or hinc EH
189 ingenium]   ignavum CH;   ignavit A
191 princeps egere]   egere princips H
192 Is]   ibi G
     possit]   posset G
193 Stanley begins to speak here.]   Buckingham continues to speak in H.
195 haerere...potest]   iam certa dubiae mentis est opinio GI
     non]   non omitted A;   nunquam H
197 forte]   sorte C
198 detinet]   detenet F
199 deneget]   denegat H
201 restituat]   restituet ABCDEFHI
     restituat]   restituet ACH;   restituet manus BDFI;   resituet cohors E;
                  restituat manus G
202 Howard begins to speak here.]   Buck. continues to speak H
203 aetasque]   aetas I
     deliciis]   dilitiis F
204 nunc]   nun I
     poscit]   possit C

205 moror] moror e quidem H̲
207 sacro] sacra D̲
liberabunt] līberabant G̲
210 Buckinghamiae] Buckingamiae H̲
211 Howarde] Howard H̲
stemmate] stematē I̲
212 haud] hunc F̲
ponit] ponāt F̲
214 eximent] erimēnt D̲
robusti asylo] Asȳlo robusti G̲
215 planget] plangit I̲
ereptum] ereptum > ereptam A̲;   ereptam D̲F̲G̲I̲;   erept<a/u>m H̲
215a infausta...nimis] [INFAUSTA MATER FILIO ET PETULANS NIMIS] C̲;   line
                 omitted D̲E̲F̲G̲I̲
217 proximi] proximis I̲

Act IV. Scene iii.

1 Regina] Rigina C̲;   Reginae E̲G̲H̲
2 quamvis verba] verba quamvis G̲
3 nostra] nostra omitted A̲
5 suadente natura] natura suadente F̲
6 haereret] haereat G̲
7 aetasque] aetas A̲
promptius] promptior H̲
10 denique...ruit] et pax suis turbata sedibus ruit G̲
denique] denuo D̲F̲I̲
11 Britanniae] Britannia B̲D̲H̲;   Britaniae E̲;   Britannia F̲
metu pavida] pavida metu G̲
12 squalens] squallens A̲B̲C̲E̲H̲
si] sic G̲
13 unus] ed.;   una A̲B̲C̲D̲E̲F̲G̲H̲I̲
15 odium...illico] Plebs nide fratrum suspicatur odium G̲
16 Sacras] sacratus I̲
metu] metus > metu (in margin) E̲
17 reddas] redas A̲;   reddes D̲F̲I̲
18 e] et G̲
liberas] liberos F̲
19 et] ut A̲C̲H̲
21 Regina] Elizabeth G̲
Summo...pater] O emicans honore Cardineo pater G̲I̲
23 repugno] recuso F̲
tutius] tutius > suae (in margin) E̲
27 infestus] on festus E̲
diu] di< > > diu (in margin) E̲
29 tantum] tanto A̲C̲H̲
30 recidiva] recidiva omitted;   recidiva > residiva G̲;   rescidiva I̲
31 oppressa] repressa A̲
vel] nec D̲F̲
34 decet magis] magis decet F̲
35 gnatum] gratum > gnatum > gnatum (in margins) E̲;   natum H̲
cum] tum A̲

37   illum] ullum A
     quisquam] quispiam BD;   quisq< > H
     potest] potest omitted A
39   ah] ah omitted F
     negare] negaret > negare F
41   nunc] nam G
42   inclyta optaret] optaret inclita H
44   sin] sin omitted A
     matura] natura DE
45   pie] piae BDEFI
     preci] p< > G
48   carcere pium] in carcere tum H
49   ulnis matris] matris ulnis BDFI
50   usque] usquam G
51   aleret] alat ACDEFGHI
     saeva] saeva or saevam I
52   barbaros] barbaras A;   barbarus F
     filius] filios G
53   contenta] contentas > contenta A
54   tamen] tamen omitted H
56   tum] tunc ABDEFGI
57   multo] mult<et> A
     lassa] classa > lassa (in margin) E
     morbo] labore H
     desident] dissident > dissuunt A;   decidunt B;   decidunt > decident
          G
58   et] e DF
     labantes] labantis DFG
     tollunt] ed.;   tollit BCDEFGHI;   totli A
61   fila] filiam A
     chara] cara H
     amputent] amputant G
62   ducem] ducem omitted G
63   arguet] arguit E
64   putat] putet DG
66   nulli unquam fuit] nulli fuit D;   nulli unquam fides asyli fuit H
67   sinat] sinant > sinat C;   sinant DEFG;   sinent I
69   meis] iis G
     timere] timore F
70   poenas...malim] poenas asilo quos dedisse vestris dextram A
     malim] mall< > I
71] This line is omitted in A.
72   aliquid ergo] ergo aliquid H
73   quicquam] quenquam G
74   premant] premunt G
75   colorem] colorem colorem A
     morantur] mirantur > morantur D
76   hi] hi omitted H;   hii I
     [non]] ed.;   non omitted ABCDEFGHI
     negligant] negligunt G
77   Movetur] movetur or monetur I
     [dice]] ed.;   dice omitted ABCDEFGHI
     posthac] poshac I

80 Imo] Immo EH
   pias] pius DF
81 innocens] inocens D
   meos] meas D; meus FI; me< > G
82 sum] sim DFGI
83 causa quae] causa qui F; causaque G
84 matrive] matri ne EG; matri > matra ne F
   regi clara] Regi chara DF; clara lege G
85] This line is missing in ABC.
   propinquum] propinquos I
   laudat] laudat > ludit (in margin) E
86 hic] huc A
   avunculus] avunculis A
90 flagitent] flagitant GHI
92 gelidus] gelidos I
   corde] corda ABD
93 ad...filium] ad exteros gnatum jubeat mittere G; ad exteros jubeat
                gnatum mittere I
94 juvet] jubet A; juret F; juvat I
95 manus...exprimet] Dolor tibi violantus illum exprimet GI
   violenta posthac]
97 muniunt] muniunt omitted A; muni<u/e>nt E
98 didicit] dedicit D
   imbellis] rebellis I
99 nil] nihil I
100 promissam asylo] asylo promissam F; promissam sacris G
101 sacris] sacro I
   solutum liberent] solutum liberant DF; solutum carcere liberent I
102 invitae] vitae DF
103 est] et H
   amor] amor omitted F
   erga] ergo A
104 tremesceret] tremisceret CGHI; tremesce< >ret > tremesceret A;
                 trem<i/e>sceret E
106 nil] nihil GH
107 evadat] evolet G; evadas I
108 nepos fugam] nepos in fugam G
109 longa] longum I
   discessum] descessum A; dissessum I
110 aut] at G
   filium] filii A
   magis] magis potest A
111 potest] potest omitted A
112 aut] at > aut (in margin) E
   violavit] violabit AB
   Thracia] Thrasia ACEI; Tharsia H
113 mereri] merere DFGI
115 cavum] carum D; canum G
116 nequaquam] nequicquam G
118 cujus] cuivis B; cuique G
119 metuque] metumque D
120 faxit] faxint > faxit (in margin) E
121 ut] et G

122 turpiter] turpitur H
    gnatum] natum H
    putat] putet G
125 frater una fratris ut] frater ut una fratris F
    ludat] ludet AC; laedet F
126 lucisse] lusisse C
    iam] iam omitted F
129 dentur] denter C
130 juncti] junctus ABCDEFI; junxit G
    sanguine] sanguini F
131 quorum] quocum G
    ea] en > ea (in margin) E
    ea esse] esse ea H
    esse aetas] aetas esse G
134 ludit] laedit > ludit D
135 fingeret] fugit G
137 Suumque] tuumque B; binumque D
138 pati] pasti D
140 quam...cito] Quam fatre cognatus puer, ludos facit GI
    quam] quum > quam E
    fratre] frater D
    quorum cito] et statim > QUORUM CITO; et statim DEF
140a] GI add this line after l. 140: Extraneos quisque libenter, et statim
    cognato] ed.; cognatus ABCDEFGHI
142 deliciae] dilitiae F
    queant] possunt D
143 inscius] nescius DFI
144 quis...prodidit] quis iste nuncius secreta prodidit A; quis ista
                 nuncius secreta prodidit BH; Quis ista sibi secreta
                 dixit nuntius DEF; Quis ista nuncius secreta
                 pandidit G; Quid ista nuncius secreta paubidit I
145 Claudianus] Claudiantis A
    audiet] audiat FG
146 at...parvulum] At finge non rogasse sive parvulum BH; At non rogasse
               fingae finge parvulum A; At non negasse finge: sine
               parvalum DFI; At non rogasse finge, sine parvulum E;
               At non rogasse fin<e/ae> sive parvulum G
147 sane] <sane> A; sine BG; sine DFI; sine or sive E
    ardere] ardore DF
150 sacrilega] sacriliga F; sacrilege G; sacrilegia I
151 securus latere] latere securus BDEFGI
152 quin] qui A; cum F
152 quin] qui A; cum F
153 Britanna] Britannia ACEH; Britania D; Britanniae FI
    nulli] nulla H
154 jura sui matri sinum] jura matri suum ABDFI; jura sui matri EG;
                        jura in matris H
    sinum] suum ABDFHI
155 vis] vis omitted G
156 auferet] aufert F; auferent G
157 matre] <marte> E; Marte G
    victus] virtus D
    hostiles] hostibes A; hostiles DF; hostibes > hostium (in margin) E

158 Edwardus] Eduardus D̲F̲H̲
159 extorta] extortu A̲;   extort<a/u> I̲
    sacras] sacras om̲it̲ted I̲
160 fugi] fugi > fug̲it̲ C̲;   fugit A̲;   sacras fugi I̲
    gravida] gravidae A̲
    ubi] ibi B̲D̲E̲F̲I̲;   ⁻illi G̲
161 nactus] mac̲tu̲s > nactus (in̲ mar̲gin̲) E̲
162 fuit] erat E̲
163 dubiamque] ⁻dubiam F̲
164 sedem] fidem > sed̲em̲ C̲;   fidem A̲;   sidem > fidem I̲
165 gnatum] natum G̲H̲
166 templum] templ̲a̲ F̲G̲
167 tam] tum F̲
    regiae] regi G̲
169 manebit aedib̲us̲] aedibus manebit F̲
172 invideo] invidio D̲I̲
    duris] duras F̲
173 agimus] agim̲us̲ > agemus E̲
174 purg̲it̲] pingat G̲
175 nec] non A̲B̲D̲I̲
    flectitur] ⁻in̲ flectitur E̲
    prece] preci D̲;   prece om̲itted F̲
176 juvat] jussos I̲
177 defero] difer̲o̲ B̲;   differo D̲
    times] times > t̲imet E̲
179 acriter] acrit̲ur̲ A̲
180 patruo] parvulo C̲;   patrue A̲;   avunculo H̲
182 suos] suo C̲F̲I̲;   ⁻hoc A̲
183 tibi vitam m̲ih̲i] mihi v̲itam tibi B̲D̲F̲G̲I̲;   tibi vitam meam H̲
184 pignori] pignore E̲
185 tuum mater] mater tuum G̲
187 deferes] deseres A̲B̲D̲F̲G̲I̲;   deseres or̲ deferes H̲
188 tremiscit] Tremescit A̲D̲F̲H̲I̲;   Tremi̲scet G̲
    cogitat num] cogitat n̲on̲ A̲;   cogitationum̲ D̲F̲
    vicimus] Vincimus B̲G̲I̲;   ⁻Vincinus D̲
189 nostros horridus] ⁻horridus nostros B̲G̲I̲
    timor] tremor I̲
192 hinc] hic A̲
    natus] nat̲i̲ H̲;   gnatus I̲
    urget sortis] ⁻sor< >s urg̲et H̲
    illinc] illic B̲D̲F̲G̲H̲I̲
    fortis] sortis C̲;   fortius B̲D̲F̲;   sor< >s H̲
193 atque] et G̲
194 beatum] beat̲u̲ > beatum A̲
195 Edwarde] Eduarde D̲;   ⁻Eduardo F̲
    nato] gnato A̲I̲
196 sceptra] septra F̲
198 regisque] Regis A̲
    genus] decus F̲
199 prodis] perdi̲s̲ G̲
200 neci mater] mat̲er̲ neci G̲
201 annon] an non D̲
    injusta] injuss̲a̲ D̲

202 protector] potentor > protector A
203 priorem principis] prioris principis ACH;   priori principis > priorem
                       principis E;   priorem prioris F
204 contentus...sinat] contentus illo sit: non poscit istu patria D
204a solatium...patria] This line is omitted in D.
205 unum] unus A
    utrunque] utrumque EFHI
    unum utrunque] utrunque unum G
206 cui] cui > vero E
207 horrescis] horescis ABD
208 tantam] tantum ABDI;   tantam > tantas E
    feres] feris D
210 properare] properaret E;   properato F;   properate I
    Cardineus] Cardinis DF
211 quaerelae] quae< > D;   quaerelae > quaerelas E;   querelis G
    nec] nec > ac E
    parvas] parvas > parvi E;   parvuas F
213 tegunt] teg<a/u>nt
214 nunquam] nunc G
    miles viam] viam miles BH
215 hostis occupat] occupat hostis D
216 aut] at G
    amotum] amatum A
    sedes] domus H
217 Queen continues to speak.] Howard begins to speak. B
218 semperque] semper ACH
    sancta] sancti ABCDEGI; sacratae H
220 videre filium] filium videre H
221] This line is omitted in H.
    patrisque] paterisque EF
    ultimum] ultinum A;   <ultinam> D
223 maneat] manet G
224 utresque] intresque A
    gnatum] gnatos G;   natum H
225 ferre] ferr<et> A
    nec] ne A
226 tuam] tuum AC
227 armatur] armatus F
228 charam] char<u/a>m C;   charum EFGH
230 immerito] merito DFI
234 regni] regum A
236 Tam...fui] tam stulta aut inops mentis nunquam fui F
237 vos] nos F
    rear] reor DE
239 ego] ega B;   ergo DEFGI
241 ruet] ruit E
    patriae] patria D
242 naturae moratur] moratur natura H
244 caedem] caede BDEFGI;   caedam I
245 veterum] neutrum F
246 fraterno] fraterna I
247 sin] sin omitted A
    regna] regni H

fratri] fratri omitted H
parcere] parcere haud DEF
252 tutum] tantum G
253 iisdem] eisdem EI
254 mercedes] ed.; merces ABCDEFGHI
singulas] singulos AC; singulos > singulas E
256 minari] mirari CH; mirare A; marari D; in mari G
turbines] <turbines> > turbides A
257 conscia] consciae DG; conscia > consciae E
258 sancto] sanctum C
259 dura] dira G
260 patruus] patruis A; patrus D
261 vestris] vestrum E
263 ego] ego omitted A
264 mater illum] mater de illum H
denuo] domo G
caro] charo I
265 quando] at quando A
summi] suum A; sumi F; summi (at end of line) G
summi ante] ante summi H
267 splendeacit] splendescat A; splendescit fides DF
268 dexterae] dextera A; dextrae GI
potentia] potenti<a/ae> G
271 vestra] vestra omitted A; vesta E
272 relinquite] relinquere AC
273 Edwardi] Eduardi DF
thori] throni DF
castam] castamque A
274 quantoque] quanto F; quantumque G; quantumcumque I
nimis] minas H
275 tanto] tantum DFGI
minus decet] decet minus F
276 pignus] pign<a/u> I
277 vana] una GHI
278 precabor] precabar BDFI
longos] longas DF
281 maestae matris] justa matris A; maest<a/ae> matris G; matris
maestae F
284 denuo] deneo G
285 nostra labris] labris nostra I
imprimentur] imprementur AG
286 timebis] timetis H
id] iam F
dedit] dedi CH
tuum] tuae A
287 sentis] statis D
288 mutare] imitare BDFGHI; immitare E
lachrymas] lacrimas AB
289 animus] animis A
291 sume] sunne > sume E
e] e omitted G
292 quicquid (2nd one)] quisquam AC; quicqui<s> E; quicquam GH

293 Edwardi] Eduardi DF
294 Edwardus] Eduardus DF
295 gnatus] natus GH
     Edwardi] Eduardi DF
297 utero] utere I
298 sustulit] suffulcit BFGI;   suffulsit DE
299 morte] mortis G
300 fratrem] fratrum H
301 avulsit] avulsum F
302 en] < > > en E
303 una] uno F
305 exitus tristis] tristis exitas A
306 fluctibus] luctibus G
     vita] una F
307 quaerant] quaerunt ADFGI
309 oculos] oculos omitted B;   occulos D
     ut] ad D
     mea] me > mea E
310 pereas] pereat F
314 talis e sinu] talis sinu DFI
315 avulsit] evulsit ACEG
316 perfusa] profusa DF;   offusa H
     lachrymis] lacrimis FH
317 implicat] implicet DF
318 spargens] spergens I
319 miseram] [MISERAM] C;   anhelans DEFGI
320 rupta] rapta BDH
     egredi] egridi F
321 reperit] repperit AF
322 chara] charae F
323 relinquit] reliquit ACEFHI;   reliquit reliquit G
325 colludes] colludis E
326a-326d] The four lines are omitted in D.
326a prolos C
     chara] clara H
     Edwardi] Eduardi F
     implico] implica B
326b meis lubens] lubens meis F
326c en] in E
326d beatum] beato F

                    Act V. Scene i.

  1 teneri] tenere D
  3 cecidet] ce< >idit > cecidit E
     tuto] tuta D
  7 qualis] quales I
     sentiens] sen<t/s>iens I
  8-10] G gives four lines instead of three:
                  sagax canis postquam diu presso vias
                Scrutatur ore cum vicinam praedam percipit

                    Cervice tota pugnat et gemitu vocat
                    Dominum morantem talis omnibus modis
 8 canis]   cavis A
    vicinam]   vicina A
 9 cervice]   cervici F
11 aptare]   optare D
    dimicat]   dimicat omitted A;   demicat F
12 prope]   proposito G
    inhiat]   inhiat omitted A
14 reginae]   Regina H
15 poscet]   poscit BDEFGHI
16 dum]   de H
    lite]   litae A
    pugnant]   pugnent F
    anxii]   anxia A
17 dux]   dum D
    obstrepant]   ostrepunt A;   obstrepunt G;   obstre<b/p>ant I
18 Buckingamiae]   Buckingamie BDEFGI
20] This line is omitted in A.
21] This line is omitted in G.
23 fraudes]   frades > fraudes E
24 infensus]   insensus ABDEFH
26 hi]   hii EI
27 Catesbei]   Catesbeie BG;   Catisbie I
    parare]   parere D
28 huc]   hunc G
29 tumet]   temet A
    huic]   ego F
31 maximum]   magnum ACH
32 alis]   alas H
33 accipit]   <exci>pit H
36 mulcetur]   mulceret G
37 potens]   natus BI
38 immunis]   imunis A;   immanis F
    deae]   deae omitted G
    suum]   suam CGH;   suae DFI;   suam > suum E
39 fragili]   fragile CH;   fragulae > fraguli E
40 excelsus]   exelsus G
    Buckingamus]   Buckingamius FGH
41 ambiguus]   ambiguo F
42 ore]   ore omitted AF
    nigri]   nigro F
    licto]   lecto D;   lecta E
43 caput frustra]   frustra capit G
    ruit]   ruet > ruit C;   ruet AH
44 omni]   omnis F
    arbitrio]   arbitro AC
    vacet]   tacet D
    Locus]   at locus A
45 Buckingham speaks this line.]   Catesby continues speaking to 1. 63 in A
    Nudate]   nudat A
    vestra]   vestrum F

46 Catesby begins speech here.] Catesby omitted B;   Catesby still
                                          speaking A
    nihil] nil D
    generosa] generosi H
    magnanimi] animi H
50 manus] manus omitted F
51 inultas] multas ABDGI;   inultas F
52 dura] duris AC
    fratris] frater AC
54 vindictam] vindictum A
    genu] genibus G
55 propinquis] propinquus BDH;   propinqu<a>s > propinquis E
    fieri] feri A
56 ista tecum] tecum ista F
57 pepercit] perpersit DI;   peperrit E;   perercerit G;   peperceret H
58 traxerunt] traxerint BEG
    spiritum] spiritu F
58a] This line is omitted in DF.
    affine] affines H
59] This line is omitted in BI.
    tuas] tuis A
60 timori] timore CEH;   timere A
61 extinguant] extinguat AC
62 Cates. still speaking] Buck. speaks
    regem] reg< >m > regum E
    vincet] vivet G;   vincit H
    scelere] celere G
63 Cates. ends speech with this line.] Buck. begins a two-line speech F
    fremat] fremant H
64 Buck. begins a speech.]   Cates. is speaking A;   Buck. ends his two-
                                     line speech E
    brevis pueri] brevis est pueri H
    restinguitur] restingentur G;   resternigitur G
65 Cates. speaks.] Buck. speaks A
    ira] odium G
    est] est omitted G
    pueri] ira H
66 Buck. speaks.] Cates. speaks to l. 68 A
    Minuet] minuit A
    ruet] ruit BE
67 sinet] sinit BD
    parentis] parentes A
    immensus] immensis A
69 Criminis (appears as first word of Buck. speech)] Criminis (appears
                        as last word of Cates. speech) A
70 istius] illius F
74 semper timebit] semper timebet A;   timebit semper I
75 quenquam] quanquam F
76] This entire line is in the margin in E.
    nos] non E
    tueri] tuere A
77 vestram necem] necem vestram D;   vestro necem F
79 mortuus] mortuis AI
    gnatus] natus H

81 scelere novo] novo scelere H
84 quasi] cuasi F
85 nutu] n<a/u>tu D;   jussu H
87 ducem] duum A;   ducere G
88 secretus] secretos D
    excubitor] exccibito I
    tuos] tuos omitted I
89 falsum] falsam D
90] G adds five lines after l. 90:
                ut scrutatur vias presso canis
                Face< >o pererrat quemlibet rostro locum
                feram sagax odore dum reperit
                loco retentus dum propior illi fuit
                Dominum labrante provocat suum sono.
    forte si] si forte B
91 timendum] timenda E;   time dum G
93 inimica] inimice A;   inimic< > E
    solet] soles H
94 fingit] finget BD
95 mistum] minstum A
97 cur] quid BFG
    quodve] quodne DEFHI;   quidve G
    diu omitted] diu (at end of line) BDFGI
98 datos] datos A;   datus E
99 inertis] meritis C;   meritus A;   meritis > inertis H
    viri] viri or vici I
100 huic] huuc F
    ira regis] regis ita BD;   regis ira FGI
101 premunt] premint A
103 cujus] cuivis CH;   quivis A
    tremunt] trement ACEH
104 salutem] saltem A
    huic] hinc ABDFHI
    eris] eris omitted A;   ergo F
105 summis] summus H
106 Properata] properate I
108 tu] in or tu I
    jactatae] jactata A
    columna] columni A;   columnia D;   colun< > I
110 vitam munies] vitam munies munies A
112 minas] minis ACH
113 tuam] suam DF
    parva] prarva C;   parta G
114 possis] posses D
    decent] decet H
115 invidae] invidiae H
116 regis] regia ACH
    in necem] IN NECEM C;   in necem omitted EFGI
117 solum] in necem solum EGI;   in nece solum F

Act. V. Scene ii.

```
 1  [O]]  O omitted ACH
 2  una]  vinca BI
    nec]  et B
 3  parat necem]  necem parat G
 4  Edwardo]  Eduardo DFG;    Edowardo I
    satus]  satis E;    salus I
 6  opaci]  chari G
 7  aut]  an D
 8  sua] ed.;    suae ABCDEFGHI
    litabit]  libabit I
    deas]  deus A;    deos D
11  salubre]  salubrae A
    jubet]  decet DGHI
13  fieri...mora]  brevisque consiliis mora fieri solet F
    mora]  mora datur BD
14  datur. Buck. medela]  Buck. datur medela A;    Buck. medela BD
15  paratur]  paretur G
16  semper]  semperque D
    ira]  ara E
17  acerrime]  acerime D
18  summumque]  simulque G
    caelorum]  colerem A
19  consulas]  consules G
    sequar]  sequor BCDEHI
20  Tremulos]  tremulus > tremulos (in margin) C;    tremulus EI
21]  This line is omitted in I.
    juvenile]  juvenili A
    regis]  ragis C;    principis H
23  patimur]  patiamur DF
    nobis parat]  parat nobis BDFGI
24]  This line is omitted in A.
27  aemuli]  aemulam F
28  consulere]  studere BGI
    propriae]  propria A;    proprie DF
    decet]  juvat BDEFGI
31  vestraeque]  vestreque H
    fautores]  salubres H
    fautores salutis]  salutis fautores I
32  tuam si]  si tuam F
    si]  si omitted G
33  tenent]  tenant DF
    tenent coelum]  caelum tenent G
    supremos]  supremo HI
35  vxorem ducet]  ducet uxorem H
36a-36e]  These five lines are omitted in D.
36a  supellex]  suppellex A;    supelex F
36b  succumbent]  succumbunt ACE;    subibunt F
36c  eosdem]  deasque G
36d  ovibus]  o vibus BG
    lupus]  lupis F
37  aquis]  aqua F
    Tamesis]  Thamesis BDFG;    Tamasis E
38  priusquam]  prius quam BD
```

40 regulos] regulum A
    transferas] transferens A
42 autumas] aestimas G; aestimmas I
44 lares] lai A
46] This line is missing in ACFH.
47 Angliae] Anglie E
48 caederent] cederent EF; redderent G; caderent or caederent H
49 cingi] cingit G
50 dimissi] demissi CH
    monebunt] movebunt A; decebunt EDFI; decebant G
    nuntii] inimici A
52 Britanniae] Angliae F
53 suum] sunt ACH; suum > sunt E
    capiunt] rapiunt G
54 urbe] urbi F
    nudati] nudata G
57 erepta] ereptra A
    posside] possede A
58 haud] non BDEFGI
    fallet] fallit FGI
    dolus] dolos BD
59 quique] quoque ADFGI
    considet] confidet ABDI
60 intelligent] intelligit G
63 coire] c<a/oi>ere E; coiere G
65 comes consilii] consilii comes B
67 possessa] posessa D; possessu > possessa E
68 nostro] nosto D; nostrae G
    authoritas] aucthoritas F
    voto] voci G; volo I
69 praemis] pecuniis G
71 ut] < >t H
    possunt] queant BDFGI
72 coget] cogit G
    metus] timor D
73 difficile] deficilae A; defficile H
74 anxius] anxie ACH
75 sollicitus] solicitus D
    usque] cusque G
79 defert] differt D
80 multum] mutum I
81 juvare...decet] juvare partes vel mori prius decet G
    sceptra hunc vel] sceptra vel BDEFI
82 Edwardo] Eduardo DF
83 nunquam] <   >am G
    convelli] canvelli H
84 tentare] <   >ntare G
85 reluctantem] reluctante FH
87 Catesbei] Catesbeie BDEGI; Catsbee F; Catsbe<i/ii> H
    quin] quid G
88 advoca] advotae CH; ad vota A; avoca D; ad voca E; revoca G
    animae] animi BDFI
    dolos] doles A; doles > dolos E
    fraudes] fraudis > fraudes E

89 totumque] totum <u>DFG</u>
90 procuret Hastingus] Hastingus procuret <u>H</u>
92 spiritum] spiritam <u>BI</u>
   inimicum] inimicus > inimicum <u>G</u>
   expuat] expernat <u>A</u>;   exprimat <u>D</u>
93 pertinax] partinax <u>F</u>
   amor] amor <u>omitted</u> <u>F</u>
   nimis] minis <u>AB</u>;   minus <u>DF</u>
94 solus tu] tu solus <u>BI</u>
   Lecestriae] Lancastriae <u>ABCH</u>;   Leicestriae <u>FI</u>
95 duces] ducis <u>H</u>
96 pereat] pareat <u>A</u>
   nostra crescat] crescat nostra <u>F</u>
99 nec] ne< > <u>A</u>
   ulla] nulla <u>A</u>
   possit] posset <u>DEF</u>;   posse <u>I</u>

Act <u>V</u>. <u>Scene iii</u>.

1 dubioque] undique <u>B</u>
   perculsum] per<v>ulsum <u>A</u>
2 huc] hec huc <u>A</u>
   rotat] rotatur > rotat <u>C</u>;   rotatur <u>BDFGI</u>;   rotatatur <u>E</u>
3 evolvere] e<x>olvere <u>I</u>
   ominatur] animatur <u>G</u>
   mens] maius <u>G</u>
5 alia praetorio] alia in praetorio <u>GH</u>
6 deliberat] diliberat <u>D</u>
   pater ille] ille pater <u>G</u>
7 versat] versus <u>A</u>
   callida] callide <u>DEFGI</u>
8 per nos] pueros <u>ACH</u>;   Nervos <u>DF</u>
10 metuo] metuo <u>omitted</u> <u>F</u>
   Ponas] pone <u>G</u>
11 Stanlei] Stanleii <u>BCE</u>;   Stanleie <u>I</u>
12 mentem] metum <u>CH</u>;   metu <u>A</u>
   vana] nova <u>BI</u>
13 patrare] putrare > patrare <u>E</u>
   quamdiu] quando in <u>A</u>
14 Catsbeius] Catesbeus <u>I</u>
   inde] inde <u>omitted</u> <u>F</u>
16 fides at adultera] fides et adultera <u>A</u>;   fides et adultera <u>D</u>;   fides
                      adultera <u>F</u>
17 tecta] <fepta> <u>or</u> <septa> <u>I</u>
19 exprimunt] expriment <u>H</u>
   exprimunt pauci] pauci exprimunt <u>I</u>
20 constitit] constabit <u>B</u>;   constabit > constitit <u>F</u>
21 jusso] jussu <u>BDFGI</u>;   jusso > jussu <u>E</u>
   Lecestrii] Lecestri <u>D</u>;   Leicestre <u>F</u>;   Leicestriae <u>G</u>
   summe] summum <u>G</u>
   colunt] colit <u>G</u>
22 multumque] multum <u>H</u>
   potens] petens <u>G</u>

Northamptoniis] Northamptonus F;   Norhamptonus H
23 colloco] collico H
24 malis] mal G
25 regni caeca] caeca regni G
   vim timet] vim regni (regni appears twice in this line) timet A;
       < > timet G
28 sceleris] scelus C; scelus > sceleris H
29 et] in BD
30 at] ad > at E
31 ubi] tibi F
   sepiant] sepiat D; sepiam I
   clientes] clientibus A
32 metuet] metuit E
34 benignis] benignius G
   blandi] bland H; blandi omitted I
36 ipsa] ipse BDEFGI
37 communicavi] communico G
38 torquebat] torquebit D
40 celavit] caelavit C; celant G
   aeque] aegre H
   fero] feror I
41 fugere] fugare D
   fuga] fugae F
42 atque] at H
   ira] irae H
   perderet] prodere G
43 innocens] inocens AD
44 maneret] manet H
45 damnaret] damnavit E; damna G
46 crede nulla] nulla crede G
47 rude] unde G
48 salum] solum A; satum F
49 fallat] fallit AC; fallet H
   astrictam] astrinctam D
   Catsbeius] Catisbeius A
50] This line is omitted in G.
   Mox] Mors ACH
   fidem] finem ACH

Act V. Scene iv.

3 oculos] occulos D
4 semperque] et usque DEF
6 tantum] tan< >m > tantum E
   placent] placet C
7 summum] summam AH; summa E
8 multum] multa F; multorum G
   exagitat] excogitat F
   fides] sedes ACH
9 consilia] concilia AI
10 loco] in G
13 regnum] iam regnum G

15 timet] timent E
    excitat] exitat DF
16 imperio] imperia B
17 et] at I
    regali] reguli E
18 ignavus] ignavis A
19 si] si omitted G
20 tuetur] < >tur G
    invitum] invitus F
    tenes] tenet H
21 aperire] aperive CH;   < >ire G
    ferro] ferre I
22 obstabit] ostabit BI;   ostabat D
23 Pontefracti] Pontifracti GI;   Pontefractes H
26 ultro] ultra A
    vocat] dabit G
27 ferro] serro F
    infestum] infaustum G;   inimicum H;   infectum I
    expuant] expiant AC;   exprimant D;   expirant FI
28 firmas] firmes A;   firmes BD;   firmus G;   firmas or firmus H;
            firmes or firmos I
    amicos] amicus G;   amicos or amicus H
    labant] lab< >nt G
29 perire praesentes] praesentes perire A;   praeire praesentes G
30 sagax] fugax F
31 ut] et D
    unus] minus A
    occupet pariter] pariter occupet FH
32 resistit mens] mens resistit I
    levi] leni DEF
33 prement] premet G
    mox dura] mors dura G;   dura mox I
34 Catsb.] Gloc. A
    tuum] num A;   unum F
36 profundet] profundit ABEI;   profundat D
    artus] Arctus DF;   arctos G
    Ithacum] Ithicum BDGI
37 consistet] consistit AEI
    maris] maris > macis F
38 noxque] nox G
    splendorem] spendorem E
39 abominatur] abhominator I
    quassans] quas<sans> A
40 se] si A;   et BD
    Edwardi] Eduardi DFG;   Edowardi I
42 possunt] possint BGI
    regis irati] irati regis F
44 discant parere] discant parere > parere discant B;   discat parere G
    principis] principi D
45 mactabo] mutctabo F
46 Conjugis...Shori] Captus Shori vesanus ardet conjuge G
47 flammas...continet] Amoris et sui faces non continet G
    nec] non FG

48 veneficiis] veneficus D
49 suae] suae omitted I
50 furore] favore G
51 patronus] patronus A
    tuetur infoelix] infaelix intuetur F
52 nefandi] nephandi F;   infandi G
    suspiceris] suspicionis G
53 incusa] incussa F
    suae] suae > suum F
55 Proceres] plures GI
    confluent] confluunt DEFGI
56 favere quos] favere certo quos H
57 ...opprimam...arguam] ...arguam...opprimam I
    reumque] rerumque > reumque E
58 mox] moxque A
59 sentiet] sensiet C
61 novus] novusque ACE
62 Howardi] Howarde DFI;   Lovelli G
    invisa] ed.;   invise ABCDEFGHI
65 Solumne] solumque AG
    poscis dirae] dirae poscis BI; poscis dirae > poscis diram E;   dirae
                                                           possis I
    neci] necem E
66 pater] < > G
67 vinculis] vinc< > G
68 animum...specus] animum fidelem sapiens domet spec< > G;
                       animum ut fidelem latens domet specus I
    domet] donet D
69 animo pertinax] pertinax animo BDFGI
    abnuat] abnuet ACEH
70 movet] novit C;   movit A;   monet DI
    tristis] tristes BD
71 ferrum] serrum F
    noxium] moxium A
73 est] et or est A;   et D
    modus] metus A

Act V. Scene v.

Lovellus omitted from list of characters] Lovellus added to list of
                                            characters G

 1 huc meus jam] huc [MEUS JAM] C;   huc eunti BDEFG;   huc (meus jam
                        omitted) I
 2 omen] omne G
    avertat] avertet D
 4 dira] dura ADH
    tremebat] premebat G
 8 gestit] gessit A
 9 casu] causa A
10 invida] invidia A
11 Howard] Lovell G

```
   Hastinge]  Hastingi ACEH
12 ades]  adest G
   sacrate]  sacratae A
13 secretas]  secretus BI;     secretas > secretus G
   commoda paululum]  commoda pululum C;    commoda paulum B;    paululum
                                      accomoda F
14 Howard]  Lovell G
15 nil]  nihil BI;    non G
   opus]  op< >a > opus E
16 nil]  nihil BDFGI
   videt]  providet H
17 quam]  cum F;    quam > quum G;    quum H
   sibi damnate sacerdote]  sacerdote sibi B;    sibi sacerdote damnate
                                   BFGI
   dannato]  dammato G
18 Hastinge]  Lovell continues to speak in G
   nunquam]  nunquid CE;    nunquid AGH
   excidit]  excidet H
   menti]  ment< > A
19 nefanda]  nefandi A;    infanda E;    nephanda F
   tristis]  tristes D
20 sub]  scis G
   moenibus]  membris I
   totus]  tot<i>s G
21 ultimo]  ultimus G
22 tui]  tibi BD
24 excidit]  accidit BI;    excidet G
25 nec iis]  necis D;    aut iis G
26 Imo]  timeo F
28 cognosceres]  cognosces D
29 ah]  oh BDEG;    o I
   sciam]  sciem D
30 fui]  sin A
31 temporum]  tempora A
32 Pontefracti]  Pontifracti I
33 nostrum]  <    > G
   suo]  suam > suo G
   sanciunt]  sanctiunt A;    sanxiunt F
34 nunquam]  <    >quam G
36 jactata...deus]  Nec tanta nullis fluctibus vita: Ha:  Call:  Id deus
                                    G
   jactata]  jacta A
   vita]  vita<ae> A;    diu H
37 satis scio]  scio satis D;    satis (scio probably in binding, not
                         filmed) E
38 Howard]  Lovell G
   rumpis]  rumpas DFI
   nobilis]  nobiles E
39 nam]  tam B;    iam GI
   expectat]  exspectat I
40 consulat]  ed.;    consulant ABCDEFGI
41 discessit]  discesit B;    descesit D
   tibi]  tibi luem ACGH
```

42 luem parari] parari ACGH
43 Catsbei] Catsbeii BGI

Act V. Scene vi.

1 magna] magni I
   regni cura] cura regni H
   tutorem] tutarem D
2 patres] patris A
5 seligit] seligit BCE
6 consulat] consultant D
7 ut tot] et tot ACGH;   et ut DFI
   procuret] percurrat G
8 comitia] commitia F
   regis anxius] anxius regis F
10 esse] esses A
13 potentis imperii] imperii potentis F
14 exitum] exitium A
15 nae] ne AHI;   nec D
   somniator] somnitor A
   fui] sui A
18] This line is omitted in A.
21a] This line is omitted in DF.
22 Nil] nihil BG
   hortus] mortus I
23 esset] essem > esset G
   vellem] velim H
25 poscat] poscit B;   poscat omitted H
26 patres] patris A
28 ne] nec DEFGI
   forte] fortasse F
   precor] precor omitted G
29 Operam navare maximam] optimam navare operam H
   navare] naturae A
   patres decet] patr<   > G
30 ut dum] ne dum H
   manu] <   > G
31 pellamus] pellimus A
   discordiam] discor< > G
32 dira] dire BEFGI;   diu D
   exercuit] exerarvit I
33 secura] sacrata B;   sacra I
34 claraque] clarique AEFGH
   poscit] possit I
35 sacramento] sacramenta A
   data] dato I
37 satellitium] satellitum A
   ergo] erga G
38 consentiant] consentiunt A
39 sin] sed I
   dissentiant] dissentiunt A

40   purgare]   purgate D
     patriae]   patriam BDEFGI;   patria A
     maculam]   macula BDEFGI
42   dux]   dum F
44   labellum]   lavellum I
45   tegit]   premit B
46   destinatis]   dis > destinatis (at end of line) C;   destinatis (at end
                       of line) A;   distinatis D
     his]   hic G;   hiis I
     patres]   patras D;   patros I
47   exitum]   exitium BGI
48   regius]   regis BDEFGHI
51   honorem altum nec]   honorem altium nec A;   honorem nec BDFI;   honore
                          altum nec G;
     excuso]   excuset G
     decus]   genus H
53   Verbes]   ed.;   verbis ABCEFGHI;   virbis D
     demittunt]   dimittunt BDI
54]   This line is omitted in H.
     justas]   justat BI
     luat]   luet F
55   haec]   has G;   hae I
57   erant]   erat A
58   hi]   hii I
     Pontefracti]   Pontofracti FGI
60   venefica]   veneficiis G
     prodidit]   perdidit BG;   prodidit or perdidit EI
61   fluit]   luit G
     tabo]   tabe G
     corpus]   corcus > copus E
     oculi]   occuli D
     somnum]   somnium A
62   invidet]   invidit BGHI;   inviddet > invi<dent> E
     cibi]   sibi ACG;   tibi D;   cibi > sibi H
63   venas]   veanas D
64   brachium]   braclium D
     exaruit]   exarcuit A;   exurit F
65   palpitat]   palputat A
     tremulum]   tremulus > tremulum C;   tremulus E
66   pulcra]   pulchra AEFGHI
     destinatur heu morti]   destinatur HEU morti C;   destinatur morti
                          BDEGI;   destinantur morte F
     mea]   MEA C;   pallaca DEGI;   pellaca F
67   conjugis]   regis I
68   nunquam consuleret]   consuleret nunquam F
69   alloquar]   alloquor C
70   fecerint]   fuerint A
     poenas]   poena I
     luent]   luant ABDEFGI
72   quin]   quum DG;   quid F
73   proditio proditio]   proditi proditio B;   proditi proditi D
74   esse]   esse omitted F
75   esse aio]   aio esse I

74a] This line is omitted in D.
75 heu] hic D
    Stanleium] Stanleum DH
76 genas] genus A
77 Vos] < > G
    perduellem] perduellam A;   < >uell< >m G
    neci] mihi F;   mei I
78 sacra] <   > G
    morituro] moli[turo A;   < >orituro G
    finiet] finiat G;   timet I
80 mihi quam] quam mihi DFI
    pendat] pendeat HI
82 Dominumque] dominum BDFGI
    Stanleius] Stanleum F;   Standleium GH
83 scelerisque] sceleris DFI
85 nostra] nostre A
86 miser voces] voces miser F
87 Aedon] Adon F
88 dire] diri BDEFGHI
89 prodidit] perdidit GH;   perdidit or prodidit I
92 morte] nocte AC
    potens erit] potens quid erit G;   potens erat H
    versutia] versutiae G
93 suumque] suum F
94 lachrymis] lacrimis H
95 heu] hea A
    numen] nunc G
    voce] voco ABDEFI;   voc< > G
96 defugistis] diffugitis H
    inferi] miseri A;   tu feri F
97 innocens] inocens E
99 didicit] dedicit D
    vivere] videre A
    meam] mea ABDEFGH;   me I
101 commovet] comovet A;   concitat B
102 lachrymae] lachryme A
    queant] queat A;   queunt E
103] This line is omitted in F.
    huic] huic? EFGI;   hunc? D
    impio] impio > impiam E
    caput?] caput DEFGI
104 auferte,] auferte AEG;   auferte. DFI
106 solus] solis A
    vestras] vestros G
    colos] caelos A
107 impetrant] impetrat BDEGI
    genus] genas AC
108 caeca] Seca A
    praemonstrant] praemonstrabunt F
109 perterritus] perteritus D
110 somno] somnio I
    Stanleius] Stanleus DE
    commovet] commovit G

112 longus] longos A
    diffluit] deffluit B; difluit D; defluit F
113 insignia] insigna A; in signum F
    dederunt] dederant A
114 insidenti] in<s/f>identi C; infidenti A
115 nefandum] nephandum F
116 sibi quaerunt] sibi quaerunt > quaerunt sibi B; quaerunt sibi G
117 inanes] inanes or manes AH
118 demetere] <demere> E; demere > demetere G
119 salutis nulla] nulla salutis G
120 jus] vis > vires E
121 lachrimis] lachrimas ACEH
    manus] munus F
123] This line is omitted in H.
    perditum] perditum or proditum CE; proditum D
    reparans] rep< >us B; raparans D
124 cohorte] cohortae F
125 jam] <me> H
    obruet] obruit AG

Act V. Scene vii.

1 peroptati] peroptate BGI; properate D
    adestis] adestis, AE
2 nobis] vobis A
3 sui] sui sceleris DFG
    impiique] impii C; imperii A; impiisque F
4 sceleris peremissent] peremissent DFG
    peremissent] perimissent ACF
5 idque] id BI
    licet diu] diu licet F
    celaverint] sceleraverint A; c< >laverint B
6 astu] astum B
    istius] ipsius F
9 miseri] miser E
    induimus] induimur G
    ipsique] ipseque ABDEFGI; ipse H
    opprimuntur] oppremuntur F
11 magis...pessimos] majus doli authores mali ac in pessimos GI
    doli] dolis F
    hujus] huis F
    principes] principis ACDFGI
12 ac sceleris autores] in authores sceleris F
    ac] ac omitted GI
    authores] machinatores GI
    redundabit] redundavit BG
15 ut] et B
    innotesceret] inotesceret D; innotescerent E
16 Cives] Gloc AC
16] This line is omitted in G.
17 cedem tegens] tegens caedem F; (caedem omitted) tegens H
18] This line is omitted in H.

19 saevi] sui A
20 nobilem virum] virum nobilem H
21 plerunque] plerumque F
    authorem] authores A
    redit] ruit G
22 Last line of Cives speech] Start of Nuntius speech G
    crudelis] crudele E
26 tollit clarus heros] tollit [CLARUS] heros C;   tollit heros DEFGI
27 casto] castit A
    concipit] concepit FG
28 o] o omitted FI
30 utinam] ut F
32 ense] ensem F
    obicem] ob rem A
33 Extinxit] exstinxit C;   extinguit DEFGI
34 animusque]   animuque > animusque E;   animus H
    credulus] crudelus A
36 auctore] authore BDFGHI
37-38] These lines are omitted in I.
37-79] These lines are omitted in G.
37 huc] hic D
    serviens] saeviens D
39 nefandis] nephandis F
41 turba] turbo A
42 tectos] testes F;   terhuas H
    principis] principes AC;   principis > principi I
    Glocestrii] Glocestriae FH
43] This line is omitted in AC.
    Buckinghamii] Buckinghamiae F
45 Angliae] Angliae E
46 culmina] calmina A
48 inepti] <incaepti> I
    ruentis maxima] ruentis qui maxima F
49 regni] regna F
    Britanni] Britanni > Britannae E
50 principis] parvuli I
51 traxisse...regium] traxisse secum: dissoluta principis I
52 nescit...moribus] vita nimis m<o/e>ntemque sedis regium I
53 splendore...pristino] fecisse pollutum notis opprobrii I
    pristino] pristrino E
53a] I adds this line here: regnumque deturbasso de summo gradu
54 dictis...virum] dictis suis, factis suis clarrissimum I
    virum] virum? DEF
55 nescit? nescit DFHI;   nescit, E
56 quot] quos > quot D
    virginum] verginum A;   virgine > virginum E
57 rupit] rapit H
    conjugalis] conjugatis I
58 infamis] infames BDFGI
    pellices] pellices > pellicis F
59 nota] nata A
61 hunc] hanc I
    suprema] supremo A;   suprem<a/e> E

63 pendat] pondet H̲
　　maximas] iam gra̅ves I̲
64 turpem...polluit] vivendo qui rectam reliquit semitam I̲
　　qui] qui o̲m̲i̲t̲t̲e̲d̲ H̲
66 suum] suam D̲
67 turba] turbo̅ A̲
68 fallet] falli̅t A̲H̲I̲;　　fall<a/e>t F̲
　　singulos] singuli̅s D̲
69 jurantum] juvantem A̅;　　<iurautum> B̲;　　in tantum D̲;　　jurantem >
　　　　　　　　jura< > E̅;　　in cantum F̲;　　in cantum o̲r̲ iurantum I̲
70 Praeceps] preces D̲F̲
71 caecum] Saecum A̲;　　serum D̲
73 nam] Man D̲
　　tantulo qui̅ tanta] tanta qui tantulo F̲;　　qui possint tanta H̲
　　possunt] possent B̲D̲E̲I̲;　　possint H̲
75 pulchrae] pulcrae D̲
76 pulchreque] pulchrae̅que A̲;　　pulcreque D̲;　　pulchr<e> H̲
　　chartula] cartula H̲
77 pulchra] pulcra D̲
　　postremo] postrem<a/o> C̲;　　postrema A̲
78 mirum]　　vincum I̲
　　mirum videtur] vi̅detur mirum F̲
79 parari] parare A̲C̲
80 Shora] Shori A̲C̲
　　tremulum] tremula H̲
81 linteo] luteo A̲
　　luit] luat G̲
82 meretrix] me̅ritrix D̲F̲
　　truci] duci D̲F̲
83 descende] discende A̲F̲;　　de< >nde G̲
84 grata] grat D̲;　　gnata G̲
　　rape] cape G̲
85 Laedem] laeden F̲
　　Europam puta,] E̅uropam, puta B̲D̲;　　Europam puta: E̲;　　Europam puta F̲H̲;
　　　　　　　　Europam puto>G̲;　　Europam puto I̲
　　desere] deserere D̲;　　decere F̲;　　desere > deserere H̲
87 proba] probra H̲
89 spoliare] < >T̅iare G̲
　　fama] forma D̲F̲;　　fa< > G̲
90 supplices] su̅ppices E̲
91 adultera] adulteri A̲
92 conjugum] conjuge A̲
93 lectumque] lectum D̲F̲
　　probro] proba A̲
94 privatos thoros] pri< >　< > G̲
95 laedat venus] <　> >　> G̲
96 Quemcunque...poenitet] Quem<　>　<　>　<　> G̲
　　poenitet] penetet E̲
93-99] T̲h̲e̲s̲e̲ l̲i̲n̲e̲s̲ a̲r̲e̲ m̲i̲s̲s̲i̲n̲g̲ i̲n̲ G̲, p̲r̲o̲b̲a̲b̲l̲y̲ o̲b̲l̲i̲t̲e̲r̲a̲t̲e̲d̲ b̲y̲ w̲a̲t̲e̲r̲.
98 sanent] fanent F̲
　　posteros] poteras H̲
99 foedet] faedet A̲C̲F̲H̲

100 admovit] admov<e/i>t C;   admovet A
101 regnandi] regendi A
102 afflictam] afflictum A
103 scandat] scandant A;   secundat F
    culmina] calumna A
105 diffunditur] defunditur D
106 faveret] faverat D
107 Regno] Rege A;   Regi B
108 Vaghanus] ed.;   Vahamus CFH;   Vahannis AE;   Vahanus BDI;   Vaghamus G
109 laethali] laetali F

Part II
Act III. (first 100 lines)

1 veneranda] venerande I
4 quilibet] quaelibet ACH
7 regiam] regiam > regnum E;   reg<ium> H
8 mone] monere A
9 illico] ilico F
13 consulunt] consulant F
14 onus] omnis I
    allicit] allicit > allicet H
15 furor] favor D
16 vexabit] vexabat B
    aeternis] aeternus AB
    minis] male I
17 eligunt] elegunt H
    fraude domos] fraude domus F;   domos fraude I
18 cingunt] cingant HI
19 tantumque...premit] tantumque vulgus calcat infestum tuam B;
                        cautumque vulgus calcat infestum tuam I
    tantumque] cautumque DEFI
22 ducem] illum D
23 illum] illum omitted BI
    metuo deterreat] metuo ne deterreat BI
26 semotus] remotus H
27 negat] negat > neget E
    Protector] Potector H
28 suspicatur] suspicatur > suspicabitur E
31 nuncia] nuncia > nunciat E
34 sollicita mandabit] mandavit sollicitum H
35 rogamus] rogemus B
    numani] inani ACH;   numani omitted DF;   immani > unanimi (in margin)
        E
37 cinctus] canctus A;   septus BI
    ecce] esse D
40 pugnans] pugnas D
    pervicax] perjurax D
41 ludit] ludet AD
44 profusa flagitat cohors] profusa flageta cohors A;   profusa turba
                            flagitat BI;   profusa flagitat chohors E

45 excelse] et excelse H
   re] te AC;   de H
46 praestantiam] praesentiam D
   alloqui] aloqui A
48 audet] audes F
   eloqui] elloqui H
   pios] pias H
49 testaris] firmabis BI
50 Quaecunque] quecunque AE; quicunque D
51 decreta] secreta H
53 laetatur] laetur D
54 solveret] solveres I
55 vitaeque] vitaque DE
   suae] sua DF
   securitas] severitas F
61 Injusta] injustae F
   quam] quem H
   Venus suae] sua Venus H
65 regnum] regium E
   et] ut AH
   debitum] debitam AC;   debita I
66 cives finxerint] cives sanxerint BDEF;   sanxerint cives I
67 ...manes veneror olim mei] ...vereror manes mortui H
70 thronum quod] quod thronum I
72 dolis] dolus E
73 scelestus] scelustus I
74 tollam] colla F
75 potius...malis] tutus latebo magis ab invidae malis I
   tutus] tutos A
76 pulsat] pusat H
78 Vos...piget] vos at tamen mihi dixisse non piget DE;   vos at mihi
                 dixisse non piget tament F
   at] et I
80 nec...obsecro] Nec vos minus nepotem ametis obsecro BI;   Nec vos
                 nepotem obsecro colatis nunc minus DEF
   nepotem] nepotes H
82 parum] par A
83 laboribus...tamen] meis adjutus is tamen laboribus BI
86 traditur] traditus F
87 veterata] vetera A
88 bonoque...odia] Proterva languent odia consilio bono BI
   consilio] consilia H
89 maximi nutu magis] nutu magis maximi H
90 nil] vos BI
   damnate] ed.;   damnes ACDEFH;   ferte BI
   optimi viri] o cives mei BI;   o cives probe DEF
91 subditi] suditi A
92 o] o omitted BFI
93 sinant] sinunt BHI
96 Sin...pertinax] sin intueri te negabis principem I
   non vis] (NON VIS) C;   renuis B;   spernas DEF
97 sperant] speravit A;   speruunt F

99 hisce] his B̲I̲
    statuas] studens A̲
    audiant] audeant D̲

Part III
Act III. (first 100 lines)

2   parcit] parat H̲
    malam] malum H̲
3   nimis] minus H̲
6   calcat pede] pedibus premit B̲I̲
9   heu...meus] Primo unigenitus filius periit mens B̲I̲.
    gnatus] gratis A̲
    primo] prima A̲
    vnicus] unictus > victus E̲;   vinctu⸱ H̲
11 speret] tractet B̲I̲;   sperat D̲H̲
12 ut] at H̲
    magni parvus] parvis magni F̲
13 primisque] primis H̲
    tegens] gerens D̲
14 arduus] Cardines I̲
18 o patris heu spes vana] genitoris o spes vana B̲;   genitoris o spes
                                                    unica I̲
19 Achillis] Achilles D̲
    nestoris] nostris A̲
20 praecabar] praecatur > praeceres E̲
    luce privavit deus] vita destituit deus I̲
21 gestabis] gestebas A̲C̲;   gestabas > gestabis D̲A̲
23 gentes] gentis H̲
    mittes] mittas A̲C̲
24 Franca] Franca > Franciae E̲
    Scotos] Scotus A̲
    trahes] trahis H̲
25 gloria] nomine B̲I̲
26 clausus] humatus B̲I̲
27 exul] exuit I̲
    haerens] haeres I̲
28 dirum] diram A̲
30 populus] populos A̲
32 ministera] ministra A̲;   ministres B̲D̲E̲F̲H̲I̲
33 quidam] quidnam C̲H̲;   quidem   quidam E̲
    minantem] exulantem B̲;   exultantem I̲
34 quidam] quidnam C̲H̲
35 quidam] quidnam C̲H̲
    domi] demi I̲
36 quidam] quidnam C̲H̲
37 rogare precibus] precibus rogari I̲
    infensi] infensis H̲
38 volui] velim D̲
    lubens] labens A̲
39 consilia] concilia D̲
40 militumque vires] militumque validas vires I̲

```
     vires]  vire A
     jungere]  jugere A;    cogere BI
41   furoris]  furoris omitted I
42   scirem]  sciam A
43   precibus]  precibus omitted I
     pie]  piae A
44   caepi]  volui H
     ne]  non F;    vel I
     mutet]  mutaet A;    mutat D
45   addi]  misi BI;    dedi DEF
     item]  [ITEM] C;    mox BE;    magis DF;    item omitted I
     litteras]  literas ABCDI
46   aulam]  aulam ut E
     celeri]  ceteri A
46a  This line does not appear in ACDEFH]  Viridi latere suspicatus viperam
                                                                          BI
47   Sentit...morae]  Statim sub herbe texuit causas morae BI
     dolos]  dulos F
48   stomachique...compremi]  stomachique se dolore [FINGIT COM]premi C;
                              stomachique dixit se premi morbo gravi BI;
                              stomachique se dolore rudit premi DF;
                              stomachique se dolore respondet premi E
49   omnem...rumpere]  cunctas moras illico jubebam rumpere BI
50   patriae sese negat]  sese patriae statim negat I
51   cogens]  gogens A
     dux]  dari F
52   commovet]  suscipit BI;    commovit DF
56   devovende]  devovendo F;    d< >ovende H
57   plebs]  plebis I
     ventis]  mentis A
58   neci petit]  cuncti potunt I
60   aut quem consulam]  aut quid consilii est I
62   pereo]  pareo F
     sed]  si BI
65   erumpat]  irrumpat I
66   damnent]  damnet I
     nihil]  nihil > illud E
     humanus pius]  humanas p< >a I
68   et]  a BEI
69   sacrificiis]  sacrificis E;    sacrificii F
     surgent]  surgunt A
71   feram meae]  meae feram BI
72   nostras populus]  populus nostras F
     ruet]  ruit H;    ruat I
74   ducitur]  vincitur I
75   Adfero]  affero FH
76   magnaeque...copiae]  eiusque magnae dissipantur copiae BI
     quod]  quid D
     dissipantur]  discipantur D
78   Wallicorum]  Wolictiorum I
79   danica]  damna I
80   Sabrinam]  Sabrinum FH
```

81 superare] superat A
    flumen] fulmen A
82 courtneorum] Courtnieorum BI
    at] et BI
83 agmine] agmine > agmini E
84 annon] at non D;   anno I
    curant] <   > I
    numina] numina omitted I
85 flumina] fulmina A
87 ruina caeli] cepti ruina H
88 divesque] dives H
90 piscis] pisces I
    auras] aulas BI
91a] This line is omitted in D.
    vadis] undas E
93 passim] passi<s> I
95 stupet miles] miles stupet B
    Courtneorum] Courtneiorum BDI;   Cournaorum F
96 fluctus] fluctibus A;   fluvius BDEF;   fluminia I
    sinet] sinit BDEFI
97 at] et I
    nullo] sine B;   sinisti I
    premio] premis A;   stipendus B;   pendem > pendes I
98 duci carens simul] duci et <malico> simul I
99 misera...deserunt] absque comeatu desertunt illum statim I
    deserunt] deferent A;   deserant D
100 nullis] nullus D
    Cambra] Cambrica B;   Cambria DF

APPENDIX B

Chart I.
(Totals of all variants in the 215 lines of Part I, II, i.)

MS.A		Subst. Var.		MS.B		Subst. Var.
Total Variants:	293	82		Total Variants:	267	86
Total Unique Var:	43	11		Total Unique Var:	7	2
A=B	37	12		B=A	37	12
A=C	50(2)	19(1)		B=C	45	17
A=E	47(4)	15		B=E	39	13
A=F	20	2		B=F	24	4
A=G	33	8		B=G	39(1)	12
A=H	40	12		B=H	43	15
A=I	23	3		B=I	33(4)	11(3)
A=D*	46(1)	22(1)		B=D*	62(1)	27

MS.C		Subst. Var.		MS.E		Subst. Var.
Total Variants:	285	95		Total Variants:	317	99
Total Unique Var:	1	1		Total Unique Var:	50	20
C=A	50(2)	19(1)		E=A	47(4)	15
C=B	45	17		E=B	39	13
C=E	50	19		E=C	50	19
C=F	23	4		E=F	21(1)	2
C=G	39	11		E=G	34(1)	8(1)
C=H	48	17		E=H	49(5)	15(2)
C=I	29	7		E=I	27(2)	7(1)
C=D*	53	22		E=D*	32(1)	18

*MS.D is set apart as a special case. Since D is the control manuscript and so cannot vary from itself, only its unique readings could have been recorded if certain conditions were not permitted. D has no variants (except unique variants) but will be treated as having variants in this tabulation when at least two manuscipts vary from it, in which case the manuscripts agreeing with D will be counted as varying with D. E.g. in line 71 (serae] sacrae E; fere G), D is considered a variant of E and G, agreeing with ABCFHI.

MS.F

	Subst.	Var.
Total Variants:	207	37
Total Unique Var:	50	14
F=A	20	2
F=B	24	4
F=C	23	4
F=E	21(1)	2
F=G	23	3
F=H	24	4
F=I	22	4
F=D*	84(13)	44(8)

MS.G

	Subst.	Var.
Total Variants:	283	94
Total Unique Var:	32	20
G=A	33	8
G=B	39(1)	12
G=C	39	11
G=E	34(1)	8(1)
G=F	23	3
G=H	38(2)	10
G=I	45(17)	22(15)
G=D*	45	16

MS.H

	Subst.	Var.
Total Variants:	294	87
Total Unique Var:	24	7
H=A	40	12
H=B	43	15
H=C	48	17
H=E	49(5)	15(2)
H=F	24	4
H=G	38(2)	10
H=I	28	7
H=D*	48(1)	27

MS.I

	Subst.	Var.
Total Variants:	242	80
Total Unique Var:	35	19
I=A	23	3
I=B	33(4)	11(3)
I=C	29	7
I=E	27(2)	7(1)
I=F	22	4
I=G	45(17)	22(15)
I=H	28	7
I=D*	49	18

MS.D*

	Subst.	Var.
Total Variants:	438	170
Total Unique Var:	17	6
D=A	46(1)	22(1)
D=B	62(1)	27
D=C	53	22
D=E	32(1)	18
D=F	84(13)	44(8)
D=G	45	16
D=H	48(1)	27
D=I	49	18

<u>Chart</u> II.

(Significant Groups of Variants from Part I, Act II, Scene I.)

6a] <u>Line omitted DF</u>
6b] <u>Line omitted DF</u>
15 et] et <u>omitted EH</u>
28 juvat] jubet <u>EH</u>
41 ut] ut <u>omitted GI</u>
52 honore quando tamen] quando honore tamen <u>DF</u>;   quando tamen honore <u>I</u>
52 haud cedimus] haud cedimus <u>omitted GI</u>
55 amor nisi quod impulit] placeret hoc regi nisi <u>GI</u>
57] <u>GI have a line completely different from the rest</u>
58 decorum] decori <u>ACEH</u>
58 nobis] vobis <u>ACE</u>
58 aut] at <u>E</u>; et <u>GI</u>
59 comes magis potentior tuebitur] magis tuebitur regulum potentior <u>B</u>;
                                    magis tuebitur regulum comes potentior <u>GI</u>
61 precantur] minantur <u>GI</u>
66 annis] animis <u>ABCE</u>
69 Edwardus] Eduardus <u>DF</u>
71 suaserit] suaserit <u>A</u>;   evasserat <u>D</u>;   evaserat <u>F</u>
73 nec] non <u>GI</u>
76 cessit] cesserit <u>GI</u>
76 olim] tam <u>G</u>;   tum <u>I</u>
77 nimis heu nimis tum nostra suadebant mala] Nimis ~~heu nimis tum~~ fatentur nostra
                     perspicuum mala <u>B</u>;   nimis fatentur nostra perspicuum
                     mala <u>G</u>;   nimis fatentur nostra prespicuum mala <u>I</u>
79] <u>GI have a line completely different from the rest</u>
81 mens nisi sagax] prudentia nisi <u>GI</u>
83 durisque] suisque <u>BGI</u>;   dirisque <u>DF</u>
89 una] heu <u>ACEH</u>
101 pignora] foedera <u>BGI</u>
110 maturare] mutare <u>ACE</u>
120 miscere] misceri <u>AC</u>;   misceri > miscere <u>E</u>
121 loqui possem] possem loqui <u>ACEH</u>
124 motum malum] multum malum <u>A</u>;   natum malum <u>DF</u>
131 regis] regibus <u>EH</u>
134 medela] medicina <u>GI</u>
143 abnuantur] abnuant <u>A</u>;   abnuatur <u>I</u>;   abnuat <u>DF</u>
144] <u>GI have a line completely different from the rest</u>
145] <u>Line omitted GI</u>
146] <u>iam added before clam AC</u>
149 adibimus] adivimus <u>F</u>;   invisimus <u>GI</u>
152] <u>GI have a line completely different from the rest</u>
153 dum] si <u>GI</u>
157a] <u>Line omitted DF</u>
157a jussu] jussa <u>ACEH</u>;   jussu <u>omitted DF</u>
166] <u>GI have a line completely different from the rest</u>
167] <u>GI have a line completely different from the rest</u>
169 perrumpat] perumpat <u>A</u>;   perrumpant <u>E</u>;   prorumpat <u>I</u>;   irrumpat <u>DF</u>
170] <u>GI have a line completely different from the rest</u>

174 fides sic] sic fides <u>EH</u>
190 haeret] horret <u>BI</u>
204 tace] tale <u>ACEH</u>
206 perdes] perdis <u>E</u>;   prodes <u>BI</u>
211 morte] forte <u>ACE</u>;   forte > morte <u>H</u>
211 mulctet] mulctent <u>ABCEH</u>
211 damnet] damnent <u>ABCEH</u>

CHART III.
(Totals of all variants in Part II, III. 1-100, and Part III, III. 1-100)

MS.A		Subst. Var.		MS.B		Subst. Var.
Total Variants:	189	25		Total Variants:	176	39
Total Unique Var:	31	7		Total Unique Var:	8	4
A=B	21(1)	0		B=A	21(1)	0
A=C	39(4)	9(1)		B=C	23	0
A=E	22	0		B=E	21	2(1)
A=F	19	0		B=F	21	1
A=H	35(2)	9(1)		B=H	24	0
A=I	19	0		B=I	58(33)	32(30)
A=D*	38(1)	27		B=D*	20	6

MS.C		Subst. Var.		MS.E		Subst. Var.
Total Variants:	169	18		Total Variants:	137	5
Total Unique Var:	1	0		Total Unique Var:	8	2
C=A	39(4)	9(1)		E=A	22	0
C=B	23	0		E=B	21(1)	2(1)
C=E	23	0		E=C	23	0
C=F	22	0		E=F	21	0
C=H	39(2)	9(1)		E=H	23	0
C=I	22	0		E=I	19	1
C=D*	42	24		E=D*	56(2)	29

MS.F		Subst. Var.		MS.H		Subst. Var.
Total Variants:	148	7		Total Variants:	206	31
Total Unique Var:	21	5		Total Unique Var:	37	13
F=A	19	0		H=A	35(2)	9(1)
F=B	21	1		H=B	24	0
F=C	22	0		H=C	39(2)	9(1)
F=E	21	0		H=E	23	0
F=H	24(2)	0		H=F	24(2)	0
F=I	20	1		H=I	24(1)	0
F=D*	57(5)	32		H=D*	39(1)	22

	MS.I			MS.D*	
		Subst. Var.			Subst. Var.
Total Variants:	207	61	Total Variants:	287	184
Total Unique Var:	45	27	Total Unique Var:	19	8
I=A	19	0	D=A	38(1)	27
I=B	58(33)	32(30)	D=B	20	6
I=C	22	0	D=C	42	32
I=E	19	1	D=E	56(2)	37
I=F	20	1	D=F	57(5)	40(3)
I=H	24(1)	0	D=H	39(1)	30
I=D*	16	4	D=I	16	4

*The tabulations for D have been set apart due to the special nature of its "variants." (See Note in Chart I)

Chart IV.

(Groups of Substantive Variants in the first 100 lines of Act III, Part II,
and the first 100 lines of Act III, Part III)

Part II. Act III.

 4 quilibet] quaelibet ACH
19 cautumque licet at sermo popularis premit] tantumque licet at sermo
               popularis premit ACH;   tantumque vulgus calcat infestum
               tamen B;   cautumque vulgus calcat infestum tamen I
23 illum] illum omitted BI
23 metuo deterreat] metuo ne deterreat BI
37 cinctus] canctus A;   septus BI
44 profusa flagitat cohors] profusa flagitat cohors A;   profusa turba
                              flagitat BI;   profusa flagitat cohohors E
45 re] te AC;   de H
49 testaris] firmabis BI
66 sanxeriat] finxerint ACH
80 nec vos nepotem obsecro colatis nunc minus] nec vos colatis nepotem
               nunc minus obsecro AC;   nec vos colatis nepotes nunc minus
               obsecro H;   nec vos minus nepotem ametis obsecro BI
83 laboribus meis adjutus is tamen] meis adjutus is tamen laboribus BI
88] BI have a line completely different from the rest.
90 nil] vos BI
90 damnes] ferte BI
90 o cives probe] o cives mei BI;   optimi viri ACH
96 spernas] (non vis) ACH;   renuis B;   [   ] I
99 hisce] his BI

Part III. Act III.

18 o patris heu spes vana] genitoris o spes vana B;   genitoris o spes
                            unica I
25 gloria] nomine BI
26 clausus] humatus BI
40 jungere] jugere A;   cogere BI
45 dedi] addi ACH;   misi BI
45 magis] item ACH;   mox BE;   [   ] I
46a] This line is added in BI.
47] BI have a line completely different from the rest.
48 stomachique se dolore rudit premi] stomachique se dolore [fingit
               com]premi ACH;   stomachique se dolore respondet premi E;
               stomachique dixit se premi morbo gravi BI
49] BI have a line completely different from the rest.
52 commovet] commovit DF;   suscipit BI
62 sed] si BI
71 feram meae] meae ferum BI
76] BI have a line completely different from the rest.
90 auras] aulas BI

Chart V

(A list of significant variants found in Part I, and in 100 lines of Part II,
Act III, and in 100 lines of Part III, Act III)

Part I

Act I. Scene i.

```
 18  peste]   peste omitted H
 19  est]   est omitted H
 40  minetur]   minetur omitted I
 41  regnum]   regnum omitted I
 42  nec]   nec > et B;     et D
 63  stipatus]   stipato DF;     stipato > stipatus C
 71  tum]   cum ABCEH
 85  suis]   istis EH
 87  latus]   latus omitted I
 91  nudus]   nudis ABC;   nudis >   nudus EH
102  semper]   semperque DFGI
102  sibi]   sibi omitted F
108  sospes]   sospes omitted H
107  movebit]   monebit HI
108  sospes]   sospes omitted H
109-111]   These three lines are missing in H.
139  quod]   qui DFGI
143  odia]   mala DF
145  icta]   ista DF
```

Act II. Scene i.

```
 6a]   Line omitted DF
 6b]   Line omitted DF
  7  tuam]   tam DFI
 15  et]   et omitted EH
 16  recta]   recta omitted E
 28  juvat]   jubet EH
 41  ut]   ut omitted GI
 55  amor nisi quod impulit]   placeret hoc regi nisi GI
 52  honore quando tamen]   quando honore tamen DF:     quando tamen honore I
 57  GI have a line completely different from the rest
 58  decorum]   decori ACEH
 58  nobis]   vobis ACE
 58  aut]   at E;   et GI
 59  comes...tuebitur]   magis tuebitur   regulum potentior B;     magis tuebitur
       regulum comes potentior GI
 61  precantur]   minantur GI
 63  ut]   et DFGI
 66  annis]   animis ABCE
 67]   Line   omitted I
 72  heu]   hem DFI
```

```
73  nec]  non GI
76  cessit]  cesserit GI
76  olim]  tam G;  tum I
79]  GI have a line completely different from the rest.
80  luem omitted I
81  mens nisi sagax]  prudentia nisi GI
83  durisque]suisque BGI;     dirisque DF
88  suo]   suo omitted F
89  una]   HEU ACEH
92  thronum ]  thronum omitted I
101 pignora]  foedera BI
102-103]  These lines omitted I
103 dubia]  dubia omitted E
110 maturare]  mutare ACE
117 ut]  ut omitted G.
120 miscere]  misceri AC;  misceri > miscere E
121 loqui possem]  possem loqui ACEH
124 motum malum]  multum malum A;    natum malum DF
128]  Line omitted F
131 regis]  regibus EH
134 medela]  medicina GI
140 tum]  tum ommitted I
144]  GI have a line completely different from the rest.
145]  Line omitted GI
146 clam]  iam added before clam AC
149 adibimus]  adivimus F; invisimus GI
152 GI have a line completely different from the rest.
153 dum]  si GI
157a patrum]  patrum omitted A
     jussu]  jussa ACEH;    jussu ommitted DF
157a]  Line ommitted DF
158]  Line omitted I.
166, 167, 170]  GI have completely different lines from the rest.
169 perrumpat]  perumpat A;    perrumpant E;    prorumpat I;    irrumpat DF
174 fides sic]  sic fides EH
185 claves]  claves omitted I
190 haeret]  horret BI
193]  Line ommitted F
204 tace]  tale ACEH
206 perdes]  perdis E;  prodes BI
207 atro]  atro omitted H
211 mulctet]  mulctent ABCEH
211 damnet]  damnent ABCEH
```

Act II. Scene ii.

```
1-5]  These lines are omitted in G.
  4  nunc]  nunc omitted ACEH
27a]  Line omitted  D
 28  Anglos]  Angliam EH
32]  Line omitted  E
 39  reum]  rerum AE
 43  statim]  statim omitted H
```

46] Line omitted I

Act II. Scene iii.

```
 2  suisque]   quisque ACE;      tuisque H
 3  intimos]   impie ABCEH
15  huc]  hic AG
15  minister]   injuste ACE
19  astabam]   ad stabam EH
22  lauta]   tanta ACEH
26  illius]   illius omitted B
29  dura]   cura DF
30  minus]   minas EG
32  lauta]   tanta CEHI
```

Act III. Scene i.

```
  1  sceleris]   faces DFH
  6  Alecto]   Erinnis DFGI
  7  Megara crudelis]   crudelis (Megera) E;      crudelis megaera H
 20]  Line omitted A
 29-31]  These lines are omitted EH
 36  faces]   faces omitted I
 37  puer]   puer omitted I
 51  reclamat anxia]   reclamat anxia omitted DFGI
 53  capere]   rapere ABDFGI
 56  via]   via omitted A
 67  timere]   videre BDFGI
111  duces]   duces omitted I
```

Act III. Scene ii.

```
 4  fugam]   fidem DF
10]  Line omitted G
19  metus]   metus omitted ACEH
28  imbellis]   imbecillis DF
28  aetas regis]   regis aetas DF
29  facile scelusque concitat quisquis licet]   scelusque facile concitat
                                               timidum licet DFGI
30  clam...expidere]   clam regi at sanu statim expidere DFGI
32]  Line omitted H
42  tota]   tuta GI
53  vestra]   nostra DF;      vestram E
55  vos]   nos D
```

Act III. Scene iii.

```
6  nunquam]   erant BGI
8  primi]   primi omitted E;      primus H
```

11 esses] esset B
12 quam] quia ACEH
13 carebas] carebam B
14 negavit] negant DE
21 vester] vester omitted H;   noster ACE
24 subdite] abdite DF

Act IV. Scene i.

5 praesuli] praesuli omitted G
5 Eboracensi] Eborum DEFI;   Cardinali G

Act IV. Scene ii.

 2 nihil] nil DFGI
10 sit] fuit GI
13 tuetur] tenetur D
21 dum] si GI
27 cognita] nota BGI
29, 31, 32] These lines in GI are completely different from the rest.
33 hoc] id BGI
39 vestrae] nostrae BDF
40 audio] audi DF
45 jactata] jactata omitted G
49-50] These lines are omitted in G.
60 aut] aut omitted H
65 tum] nunc GI
66 si] sin BDFGI
67] cito added H
70] Line omitted A
71 aede] aede omitted E
86 damnibitur] culpabitur GI
88 Quin] Quum AC
96 aut] at EF
98 cui] enim D
101 nobis] nolis D
104 manserit] manserit omitted DF
118 vi] vi omitted G
121 struxit] tribuit ABCH
121 plurimum] plurimum omitted I
127 aut] aut omitted GI
135] Line omitted AC
136 nunquid] nunquam BG
139 monet] jussit BGI;   movet AD
140 deserit conjux] uxor evadit BGI;   deserit uxor ACH
147 ve] ne DHI
148 quod] quae GI
157 tristis] tristis omitted H
180 Probatur] Probabitur DFI
181 fugit] fugeret DFI
195 non] non omitted A

201 manus] cohors E;   manus omitted ACH
215a] Line omitted DEFGI

Act IV. Scene iii.

  3 nostra] nostra omitted A
 19 et] ut ACH
 31 vel] nec DF
 37 potest] potest omitted A
 39 ah] ah omitted F
 44 sin] sin omitted A
 51 alat] aleret B
 54 tamen] tamen omitted H
 58 et] o DF
 62 ducem] ducem omitted G
 71] Line omitted A
 76 hi] hi omitted H
 85] Line omitted ABC
102 invitae] vitae DF
103 amor] amor omitted F
111 potest] potest omitted A
126 iam] iam omitted F
138 pati] posti D
147 ardere] ardore DF
155 vis] vis omitted G
159 sacras] sacras omitted I
160 ubi] ibi BDEFI;   illi G
175 preci] preci omitted F
175 nec] non ABDI
189 nostros horridus] horridus nostros BGI
204] D has obviously combined lines 204-205.
221] Line omitted H
247 haud] haud omitted ABCGHI
263 ego] ego omitted A
271 vestra] vestra omitted A;   vesta E
272 relinquite] relinquere AC
273 thori] throni DF
277 vana] una GHI
291 e] e omitted G
309 occulos] occulos omitted B
314 e] e omitted DFI
319 anhelans] miseram ABH;   [MISERAM] C
326a-326d] These lines are omitted in D

Act V. Scene i.

 20] Line omitted A
 21] Line omitted G
 31 maximum] magnum ACH
 37 potens] natus BI

```
42   ore]  ore omitted AF
58a]  Line omitted DF
59]  Line omitted BI
88   tuos]  tuos omitted I
90   forte si]  si forte B
90a-90e]  These lines are added in G
97   diu]  diu omitted ACEH
97   cur]  quid BFG
100  ira regis]  regis ita BD;    regis ira FGI
113  tuam]  suam DF
116  in necem]  in necem omitted EFGI
```

Act V.   Scene ii.

```
1    o]  o omitted ACH
2    una]  vinca BI
2    nec]  et B
11   jubet]  decet DGHI
13   mora]  mora datur DGHI
21]  Line omitted I
23   nobis parat]  parat nobis BDFGI
24]  Line omitted A
28   consulere]  studere BGI
28   juvat]  decet ACH
32   si]  si omitted G
36a-36e]  These lines are omitted in D.
46]  This line is omitted in ACFH.      58 haud]  non BDEFGI.
71   possunt]  queant BDFGI
81   hunc]  hunc omitted BDEFI
94   solus tu]  tu solus BI
```

Act V.   Scene iii.

```
1    dubioque]  undique B
5    in added GH
12   vana]  nova BI
29   et]  in BD
50]  Line omitted G
50   Mox]  Mors ACH
50   fidem]  finem ACH
```

Act V.   Scene iv.

```
4    semperque]  et usque DEF
8    fides]  sedes ACH
31   occupet paritur]  paritur occupet FH
32   levi]  leni DEF
40   se]  si A;    et BD
55   Proceres]  plures GI
```

Act V. Scene v.

17 sibi sacerdote damnato] sibi damnato sacerdote ACEH;   sacerdote sibi
damnato B
22 tui] tibi BD
24 excidit] accidit BI;   excidet G
29 ah] oh BDEG;   o I
39 nam] tam B;   iam GI

Act V. Scene vi.

7 ut tot] et tot ACGH;   et ut DFI
18] Line omitted A
21a] Line omitted in DF
25 poscat] poscat omitted H
22 Nil] nihil BGI
32 dire] dira ACH;   diu D
54] Line omitted H
66 destinatur morti] destinatur heu morti ACH
74 esse] esse omitted F
74 aio] aio omitted I
74a] Line omitted D
92 morte] nocte AC
103] Line omitted F
123] Line omitted H

Act V. Scene vii.

3 sceleris added DFG
4 sceleris omitted DFG
5 idque] id BI
12 ac] ac omitted GI
12 authores] machinatores GI
16] Line omitted G
16 Cives] Gloc AC
17 caedem] caedem omitted H
18] Line omitted H
26 tollit heros] tollit clarus heros ABCH
28 o] o omitted FI
33 extinguit] extinxit ABCH
37-79] These lines are omitted in G
37-38] These lines are omitted in I
43] Line omitted AC
64 qui] qui omitted H
70 Praeceps] preces DF
82 truci] duci DF
89 fama] forma DF

Part II

Act III.

23 illum] illum omitted BI
23 metuo dereat] metuo ne deterreat BI
37 cinctus] canctus A;   septus BI
44 profusa flagitat cohors] profusa flagitat cohohors E;   profusa turba
                              flagitat BI
49 testaris] firmabis BI
66 sanxerint] finxerint ACH
80 nec...minus] nec vos colatis nepotem nunc minus obsecro ACH (nepotes);
                  nec vos minus nepotem ametis obsecro BI
83 laboribus...tamen] meis adjutus is tamen laboribus BI
88 BI have a line completely different from the rest.
90 nil] vos BI
90 damnes] ferte BI
90 o cives probe] o cives mei BI;   optimi viri ACH
96 spernas] (non vis) ACH;   reunis B;   [   ] I

Part III

Act III.

25 gloria] nomine BI
26 clausus] humatus BI
40 jungere] jugere A;   cogere BI
45 dedi] addi ACH;   misi BI
45 magis] item ACH;   mox BE;   [   ] I
46a] This line has been added BI
47] BI have a line completely different from the rest.
48 stomachique...premi] stomachique se dolore [fingit com] premi ACH;
                          stomachique se dolore respondet premi E;
                          stomachique dixit se premi morbo gravi BI
49] BI have a line completely different from the rest.
52 commovet] commovit DF;   suscipit BI
62 sed] si BI
71 feram meae] meae feram BI
76] BI have a line completely different from the rest.
90 auras] aulas BI

APPENDIX C

1. The Stage Directions

The following is a list of all the stage directions together with sigla denoting the manuscripts in which they appear. In this list are distinguished two types of stage directions: marginal and non-marginal. With certain qualifications for those listed for MS.E, all stage directions not preceded by a single asterisk are marginal; that is, each appears in the margin beside the passage to which it applies (the line reference is keyed to the manuscript first cited). Non-marginal stage directions, marked in the list by a single asterisk, appear within the text of the play; that is, each comes between two Latin speeches.

The stage directions listed for MS.E require special mention inasmuch as most of its stage directions are listed separately at the end of the manuscript. Although not marginal in the strictest sense, they were obviously intended to be marginal, and hence have not been marked with an asterisk. E also has three stage directions that appear, not in the list at the end, but in the margins beside the lines to which they apply. These have been marked with a double asterisk. Finally, on one occasion, E has the same stage direction (Part I: III.iii.21) in two places, once in the margin where it belongs and again in the list at the end.

Stage directions with only minor differences (i.e. accidental as opposed to substantive differences) are treated as identical in this list.

Part I

III.i.   (beside the list of characters)

Deducta scena appareat Regina (velut in Asylo) cum 5 filiabus et

ancillis, sar< >, viscis et insidentes. G

III.i.16

Let his servants be about him with swordes B, D, F, G

III.i.20

Let them be knocking in the palace as removinge B, D, F, G

III.i.64

The queene sitting on the ground with fardells about hir B, D, F, G

III.i.64

A curtaine being drawne let the queene appeare in the sanctuary,

her 5 daughters and maydes about her sittinge on packs, fardells,

chests, cofers. D, E, F, G

III.ii.6.

Certaine come in with harnesse and other carriage like porters B, D, G, H

III.ii.11

Some of these are armed some unarmed or half armed B, D, G, H

III.iii.21

The kinge now is going about the stage with these wordes B, D, E, G, H

IV.ii.216

After they come downe from theyr seate B, D, E, F, G, H, I

V.vi.73

Let the protector give a blow on the counsel table and let one of them

of his gard break in therat with his halbeard strike the lord Stanley

on the head. D, E, F, G, H

Part II

II.ii.158.

The mayor and others going to the duke D, E, F, H

II.ii.177

Rounding the mayor in the eare D, E, F, H

II.ii.186.

These words are spoken by a few of the dukes servantes. I

II.ii.197.

Weepinge behinde the duke turninge his face to the wall B, D, E, F, I

III.i. (at the start of the scene)

Let the mayor come first accompanied with citizens, then the duke
with other nobles they assemble at Bernhardes Castle. D, E, F, H

III.i.8.

He sendeth his man into the palace B, I

III.i.27.

His servant returninge and to him secretlye reportinge. To his
servant whome he sendeth again. B, D, E, F, H, I

III.ii.76.

The duke and noblemen go into the kinges palaice the maior and citizens
departe away. B, D, E, F, H, I

V.i. (immediately after last line of Part II)

After they have thus declared what everything signifieth let the
singers singe < > being placed on the toppe of some of the houses

in the mean season let such ceremonyes be used for the coronation
as the chronicle declareth and after let them departe in this order
folowinge B, I

Part III

V.i.14.

Heare let divers mutes run over the stage from divers places for
fear. D, E, F

V.iii.12.

Let here divers mutes armed souldiers run over the stage one after
an other to the Earle of Richmond B, D, E, F, H

V.v.i.

Speaking to his < >. E

V.vi.i.

Lett them put on the head peacis and exhort one another E

V.viii.43.

Here the battell is joyned D, E, F

V.viii.(after 1.43)

*Upon his Returne let Guns goe of and trumpetts sound with all stirre
of souldiers: without the Hall: untill such tyme as the Lord
Stanley be on the stage ready to speake as followeth: A, B, C, D, E,
F, H, I

V.viii.46.

The Battell A, C, D, E, F

V.viii.(after l.51)

*Let here the like noyse be made us before, assoone as the Lord
Stanley hath spoken, who followeth the rest to the feild, After a
little space, let the Lord Northumberland come with his Bande from
the field, at whose speech lett the noyse cease. A, B, C, D, E, F, H, I

V.viii.54.

The Battell A, C, D, F

V.viii.(after l.60)

*Let here be the like noyse, as before, and after a while let a
Captayne run after a Souldier, or two, with sword drawne, drivinge
them againe to the field and say as followeth. A, B, C, D, E, F, H, I

V.viii.(after l.62)

*After the like noise againe, let souldiers run from the field over
the stage, one after another flinginge of their harnesse and at
length some come haltinge and wounded. After this let Henry Earle
of Richmond come triumphinge havinge the body of Kinge Richard dead
on a horse: Catsbey: Ratclyfe, and others bounde. A, B, C, D, E, F, H, I

In margin, at the start of the Epilogue.

Let a noble man put the Crowne upon kinge He: head at the end of
this action] A, C; Let...oration B, I
*Let a noble man put on the crowne upon kinge Henries head att the
end of his oration, and the songe sunge which is in the end of the
booke. After an Epilogue is to be made, wher in lett bee declared
the happy uniteinge of both houses, of whome the Queenes majestie
came, and is undoubted heyre, wishinge her a prosperous raigne. D

*Let a noble man put on the crowne uppon kinge Henryes head at the
end of his oration. And the songe sunge which is in the end of the
booke E, F, H

2. The Song

The words of the song reproduced here appear in all manuscripts at the end
of Part I (see the Text and Translation); the words and music of the song,
as reproduced here, only appear near the end of MS.E.

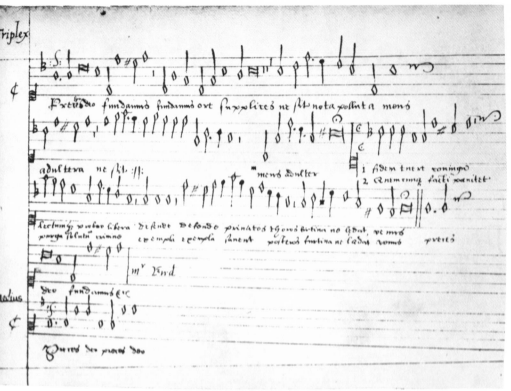

A Garland Series

RENAISSANCE DRAMA

A COLLECTION OF
CRITICAL EDITIONS

edited by
STEPHEN ORGEL
The Johns Hopkins University

Thomas Legge's
RICHARDUS TERTIUS

*A Critical Edition
with a Translation*

ROBERT J. LORDI

GARLAND PUBLISHING, INC.
NEW YORK & LONDON • 1979

All volumes in this series are printed on
acid-free, 250-year-life paper.

Library of Congress Cataloging in Publication Data

Legge, Thomas, 1535–1607.
  Thomas Legge's Richardus Tertius.

  (Renaissance drama)
  English and Latin.
    1. Richard III, King of England, 1452–1485—Drama.
  I. Lordi, Robert Joseph, 1923–   II. Title.
  III. Title: Richardus Tertius.   IV. Series.
  PA8540.L64R513   1979   822'.2   78-66843
  ISBN 0-8240-9741-6